Dr. Daniel G. Amen, board-certified in child, adolescent, and adult psychiatry and licensed in nuclear brain imaging, has discovered that there are seven types of attention deficit disorder, each with its own distinctive brain dysfunctions and treatments

Type 1—*Classic ADD*—Inattentive, distractible, disorganized, hyperactive, restless, and impulsive.

Type 2—*Inattentive ADD*—Easily distracted with low attention span, but not hyperactive. Instead, often appears sluggish or apathetic.

Type 3—*Overfocused ADD*—Excessive worrying, argumentative, and compulsive; often gets locked in a spiral of negative thoughts.

Type 4—*Temporal Lobe ADD*—Quick temper and rage, periods of panic and fear, mildly paranoid.

Type 5—*Limbic ADD*—Moodiness, low energy. Socially isolated, chronic low-grade depression, frequent feelings of hopelessness.

Type 6—*Ring of Fire ADD*—Angry, aggressive, sensitive to noise, light, clothes, and touch; often inflexible, experiencing periods of mean, unpredictable behavior and grandiose thinking.

Type 7—*Anxious ADD*—Anxious, tense, nervous, predicts the worst, gets anxious with timed tests, social anxiety, and often has physical stress symptoms, such as headaches and gastrointestinal symptoms, conflict avoidant.

"Daniel Amen's work in SPECT brain imaging, the first major breakthrough in psychiatry and psychology in the last fifty years, brings these fields out of the dark ages and into partnership with other medical disciplines. He takes complex matters of brain function and helps the layperson and professional work together as a healing team."

—EARL A. HENSLIN, PSY.D., BCETS, AMERICAN ACADEMY OF
EXPERTS IN TRAUMATIC STRESS

continued . . .

"*Thanks to the cutting-edge work of Dr. Amen, I have at long last been properly diagnosed with adult ADD. I am on the appropriate medication, am working with an ADD coach, and seeing each day of my life come more and more into focus. What an unexpected joy! I recommend this book to anyone who has concerns with ADD or even the slightest interest in human behavior.*" —JOAN BAEZ

"*For patients, parents, and doctors alike, Dr. Amen's new book provides a wealth of material on ADD, backed up by illuminating and helpful brain imaging. Clear and readable, and a must for understanding this disorder.*"
—WILLIAM R. COLLIE, M.D., SAFE HARBOR
CLINIC FOR BEHAVIORAL MEDICINE

"*Dr. Amen's* Healing ADD *contains a wealth of startling new insights about ADD. A must-read for every professional in the juvenile justice system. A breakthrough work on diagnosing and treating ADD, it is certain to be a classic.*"
—THOMAS C. EDWARDS, JUDGE, SUPERIOR COURT,
STATE OF CALIFORNIA

"Healing ADD *should be required reading for all clinicians and educators. Dr. Amen's work should abolish the notion that ADD is merely a myth. His elegant SPECT brain studies make ADD understandable to a three-year-old and have brought psychiatry from 'witchcraft' to neuroscience.*"
—CLAIRE FRIEND, M.D., CHILD AND ADULT PSYCHIATRIST

"*Nearly a third of my practice is filled with adult ADD. Dr. Amen is a courageous pioneer, a conscientious scientist, and a caring physician—a spectacular combination.*"
—FRANK L. ANNIS, M.D., DIPLOMAT,
AMERICAN BOARD OF PSYCHIATRY AND NEUROLOGY

"Healing ADD *provides details on multiple treatment options, including pharmacological, educational, behavioral, and herbal. It is essential reading for those who treat ADD and those who are directly or indirectly affected by ADD.*"
—J. KIRK CLOPTON, M.D., PH.D., DIRECTOR,
GOLDEN HILLS PSYCHIATRY

"Dr. Amen's groundbreaking discoveries make the complexities of ADD easy to understand. His pioneering use of SPECT imaging confirms what other expert clinicians could only suspect. ADD is not a weakness of the human spirit. Readers of his book will understand how to help themselves, family members, or fellow human beings."

—DENNIS ALTERS, M.D., CHILD, ADOLESCENT, AND ADULT PSYCHIATRIST AND AUTHOR OF *WIZARD'S WAY*

"With the tremendous research done by Dr. Amen, we can now measure the physiology that has gone wrong and enable patients to take charge of their lives."

—RENÉ ESPY, D.C., N.D., ZONE HEALTH ASSOCIATES

"Once again challenging older concepts about attention deficit disorder, Dr. Amen writes with a clarity, simplicity, and passion I have come to admire. Healing ADD is a worthy extension of Change Your Brain, Change Your Life."

—TERENCE F. MCGUIRE, M.D., PSYCHIATRIST

"Dr. Amen has taken a unique and useful approach in Healing ADD. Providing good direction for designing an effective treatment program, this will be a tremendous aid in understanding and managing the complex needs of those with ADD. An excellent book for clinicians, patients, and their families."

—RICHARD GILBERT, M.D., PSYCHIATRIST

Healing ADD

ADD

The Breakthrough Program
that Allows You to See
and Heal the Seven Types of
Attention Deficit Disorder

Daniel G. Amen, M.D.

BERKLEY BOOKS, NEW YORK

THE BERKLEY PUBLISHING GROUP
Published by the Penguin Group
Penguin Group (USA) LLC
375 Hudson Street, New York, New York 10014

USA • Canada • UK • Ireland • Australia • New Zealand • India • South Africa • China

penguin.com

A Penguin Random House Company

Library of Congress Cataloging-in-Publication Data

Amen, Daniel G., author.
{Healing ADD}
Healing ADD from the inside out : the breakthrough program that allows you to see and heal the seven
types of attention deficit disorder / Daniel G. Amen, M.D.—Revised edition.
pages cm
Revision of: Healing ADD. ©2001.
Includes bibliographical references and index.
ISBN 978-0-425-26997-8 (pbk.)
1. Attention-deficit hyperactivity disorder—Treatment.   2. Attention-deficit disorder in adults—Treatment.
I. Title.
RC394.A85A445 2013
616.85'89—dc23   2013033615

PUBLISHING HISTORY
G. P. Putnam's Sons hardcover edition / February 2001
Berkley trade paperback edition / June 2002
Revised Berkley trade paperback edition / December 2013

PRINTED IN THE UNITED STATES OF AMERICA

10   9

Cover design by Jason Gill.

To Antony, Breanne, Kaitlyn, Chloe,
Angelina, Julian, Eli, Emmy, and Liam,
my eternal source of inspiration.

Contents

Healing ADD Starter Report

I f you have attention deficit disorder (ADD), also known as attention deficit hyperactivity disorder (ADHD), I know you are not likely to read this entire book. I have been working with people who have ADD for over thirty years. You have many strengths, but a long attention span is usually not one of them. So, to honor the fact that many people with ADD have a short attention span, get distracted easily, and have poor follow-through, I developed a starter report to help you quickly get on your way to Healing ADD. In the rest of the book you will find the logic and research behind these strategies, along with many other life-enhancing strategies and stories.

STEP ONE: DO YOU OR A LOVED ONE REALLY HAVE ADD?

The first step is to discover if you or a loved one really has it. ADD is called a developmental disorder, because people have it early in life. It is not something that shows up in middle age. If you have ADD symptoms, but never had them as a child, it is likely due to something else, such as depression, chronic stress, hormonal changes, a head injury, or some form of toxic exposure.

There Are Five Hallmark Symptoms of ADD

1. **Short attention span**, for regular, routine, everyday tasks. People with ADD have a difficult time with boring tasks and need stimulation or excitement in order to stay engaged. Many people with ADD can pay attention just fine for things that are new, novel, interesting, highly stimulating, or frightening.

2. **Distractibility.** People with ADD tend to notice more in their environment than others, which makes them easily distracted by outside stimuli, such as light, sounds, smells, certain tastes, or even the clothes they wear. Their keen sensitivity causes them to get easily off task.

3. **Disorganization.** Most people with ADD tend to struggle with organization of time and space. They tend to be late and have trouble completing tasks on time. Many things get done at the last moment or even later. They also tend to struggle keeping their spaces tidy, especially their rooms, book bags, filing cabinets, drawers, closets, and paperwork.

4. **Procrastination.** Tasks and duties get put off until the last moment. Things tend not to get done until there are deadlines or someone else is mad at them for not doing it.

5. **Poor internal supervision.** Many people with ADD have issues with judgment and impulse control, and struggle not to say or do things without fully thinking them through. They also have a harder time learning from their mistakes.

STEP TWO: KNOW YOUR TYPE OF ADD

Once you know if you or a loved one has ADD, it is critical to know which type you have. ADD is not one thing. In this book I present seven distinct types of ADD. One treatment does not fit everyone. It is also possible to have more than one type. You can take the Amen Clinics ADD Type Test online at amenclinics.com/HealingADDtypetest.com to find out which type or types you or a loved one may have.

Summary of the Seven Types of ADD

Type 1. Classic ADD (ADHD)—inattentive, distractible, disorganized, hyperactive, restless, and impulsive.

Type 2. Inattentive ADD—inattentive, easily distracted, disorganized, and often described as space cadets, daydreamers, and couch potatoes. Not hyperactive!

Type 3. Overfocused ADD—inattentive, trouble shifting attention, frequently get stuck in loops of negative thoughts or behaviors, obsessive, excessive worrying, inflexible, frequent oppositional and argumentative behavior. May or may not be hyperactive.

Type 4. Temporal Lobe ADD—inattentive, easily distracted, disorganized, irritable, short fuse, dark thoughts, mood instability, and may struggle with learning disabilities. May or may not be hyperactive.

Type 5. Limbic ADD—inattentive, easily distracted, disorganized, chronic low-grade sadness or negativity, "glass half empty syndrome," low energy, tends to be more isolated socially, and frequent feelings of hopelessness and worthlessness. May or may not be hyperactive.

Type 6. Ring of Fire ADD—inattentive, easily distracted, irritable, overly sensitive, cyclic moodiness, and oppositional. May or may not be hyperactive.

Type 7. Anxious ADD—inattentive, easily distracted, disorganized, anxious, tense, nervous, predicts the worst, gets anxious with timed tests, social anxiety, and often has physical stress symptoms, such as headaches and gastrointestinal symptoms. May or may not be hyperactive.

Knowing your type is essential to getting the right help for yourself.

STEP THREE: USE THE AMEN CLINICS METHOD FOR EVALUATING ADD NO MATTER WHERE YOU ARE

At the Amen Clinics we have a very specific method for evaluating and treating our patients that has yielded very successful outcomes. You can use it no matter where you are. It involves four processes:

1. **Four Circle Assessments**: Know your **biology** (the physical process that makes you who you are—genetic or family history, nutritional status, exercise, health, sleep), know your **psychology** (your developmental history and the quality of your thoughts), know your **social** circle (your current stresses in life and the health of those with whom you spend the most time), and know your **spiritual** circle (why you care about life, what is your sense of meaning and purpose).

2. **Evaluate the physical functioning of your brain.** At the Amen Clinics we use **brain SPECT imaging**, a sophisticated brain imaging tool, and quantitative EEG, that help us understand the underlying biology of individual patients. For those who cannot get their brain function evaluated directly, we have developed **online questionnaires** to help predict what we might learn from a scan. In addition, we test brain function through **computerized neuropsychological tests** that measure: mood, anxiety, stress, social skills, attention, memory, executive function, information processing efficiency, response speed, impulsivity, and negativity bias. These are also available online.

3. **Know your important numbers.** It is also critical to know some important numbers, such as your height, weight, waist size, blood pressure, and specific lab tests, such as your CBC, blood sugar, thyroid levels, etc. If your thyroid or other lab values are off you will never be your best. A detailed list of these numbers can be found in Chapter 3.

   Understanding these first three processes leads us to a targeted plan to optimize your specific brain and situation, rather than treating a general diagnostic category like ADD, anxiety, or depression. The best treatments use a combination of all four circles: biological (diet, exercise, supplements, meds, and neurofeedback), psychological (learning how to heal past hurts and thinking honestly and clearly), social (managing stress and improving your relationships), and spiritual (getting in touch with a deep sense of meaning and purpose).

4. **Boost your brain's reserve.** The last part of our method is to help boost the brain's reserve, or the extra brain function you have to deal with whatever stresses come your way in the future, such as losses, hormonal swings, and aging. Boost your brain's reserve with three strategies:

1. Brain envy—you have to care about the health of your brain.
2. Avoid bad—avoid anything that hurts it, such as drugs, alcohol, brain injuries, environmental toxins, poor nutrition, etc.
3. Do good—engage in regular brain-healthy habits, such as exercise, a great diet, targeted supplements, new learning, and stress management techniques.

STEP FOUR: COMMON TREATMENTS FOR ALL TYPES

Things to do today! There are many treatments common to all people with ADD. Here are the most important ones to start with today.

1. Take a 100-percent multivitamin and mineral supplement every day. Studies have reported that they help people with learning and help prevent chronic illness.
2. Adults, take about 2,000 to 6,000 mg of high-quality fish oil a day (1,000 to 2,000 mg for children). Research suggests that fish oil higher in the EPA form of omega-3s may be the most helpful, but it depends on your type (see Chapter 20).
3. Eliminate caffeine and nicotine. Both interfere with sleep and several of the treatment recommendations in the program.
4. Exercise daily for 30 to 45 minutes. For kids, if you cannot find a safe exercise (no brain injuries please from football, hockey, or soccer headers), take them on long, fast walks. Table tennis is my favorite brain game.
5. Limit television, video games, and device time to no more than 30 minutes a day. This may be hard for kids and teens, but it can make a huge difference.
6. Food is a drug. Most people with ADD do best with a higher protein, lower simple carbohydrate diet, but this isn't true for all types of ADD. See Chapter 19 for more information on diet.
7. In dealing with kids, employees, and spouses with ADD—NO YELLING! Many people with ADD have low activity in the front part of their brains, due to lower levels of the neurotransmitter dopamine. As a way to feel more alert they often find themselves seeking conflict or

excitement. They can be masterful at making other people mad or angry at them. Do not lose your temper with them, because it often makes things worse. If they get you to explode, their unconscious, low-energy frontal cortex turns on and unconsciously they come to crave it. Never let your anger be their medication. They can get addicted to it.

8. Test ADD kids and adults for learning disabilities. They occur in up to 60 percent of people with ADD. These are more common in Type 4: Temporal Lobe ADD. The local schools are often set up to do this testing for school-age children. See the Amen Clinics Learning Disability Screening Questionnaire online at amenclinics.com/learningquestionnaire.com.

9. Never give up seeking help.

STEP FIVE: NATURAL TREATMENTS FOR EACH TYPE

Just because you or a loved one has ADD does not mean that medication is the first intervention to try. Many people, in my experience, respond to natural treatments and they are at least something to seriously consider before medication. See below for a summary of the supplements for each type of ADD. But, just because something is natural does not mean it is without risk or side effects. See Chapter 19 for more information.

STEP SIX: WHEN YOU MAY NEED MEDICATION

Medication is an important issue to consider. People who have mild to even moderate ADD may be able to treat the disorder through natural means. People with more severe forms of ADD often need medication. It is usually not the first thing to do, but when necessary and if prescribed properly it can make a huge positive difference. See below for a summary of the medications for each type of ADD.

STEP SEVEN: NEVER FORGET THE ADD STRENGTHS

I like to start any lecture about ADD by talking about its many strengths. People with ADD are often highly intelligent, competent, and successful.

BIOLOGICAL ADD TREATMENT SUMMARY

Here Is a Summary of the Major Treatments for Each Type.

ADD Type	Diet	Natural Supplements	Medications
Type 1. Classic ADD	higher protein, lower carb	Rhodiola, green tea, ginseng, L-tyrosine, zinc, grape seed or pine bark (abbreviated stimulating supplements)	Stimulants such as Adderall, Vyvanse, Ritalin, or Concerta Stimulants or Provigil, Nuvigil
Type 2. Inattentive ADD	higher protein, lower carb	stimulating supplements	Stimulants or Provigil, Nuvigil
Type 3. Overfocused ADD	lower protein, higher smart carb	5-HTP PLUS stimulating supplements	Serotonin and norepinephrine enhancing meds such as Effexor or Cymbalata; or a serotonin enhancing med, such as Zoloft, Paxil, Prozac, Celexa, or Lexapro, PLUS a stimulant
Type 4. Temporal Lobe ADD	higher protein, lower carb, maybe "ketogenic diet"	GABA, gingko, vinpoce-tine, huperzine A, ALC, PS, NAC, and ALA PLUS stimulating supplements	If mood instability, consider anticonvulsants such as Neurontin, Lamictal, Trileptal or Depakote, PLUS a stimulant
Type 5. Limbic ADD	higher protein, lower carb	SAMe PLUS stimulating supplements	Stimulants such as Adderall, Vyvanse, Ritalin, or Concerta
Type 6. Ring of Fire ADD	higher protein, lower carb	GABA, 5HTP PLUS stimu-lating supplements	Anticonvulsants together with a serotonin enhancing med and then if needed a stimulant. Guanfacine or clonidine can also be used.
Type 7. Anxious ADD	higher protein, lower carb	L-theanine, Relora, Mag-nesium, Holy Basil, PLUS stimulating supplements	Strattera, desipramine, imipramine

It is well known that many CEOs have ADD and they tend to thrive when they hire people to keep them on track and organized. People with ADD often make wonderful writers, artists, and salespeople. There is a high incidence of people with ADD among certain professions, such as ER physicians and trauma nurses. They tend to be people who run toward fires, as opposed to people like me who tend to run away from dangerous situations. In wartime, ADD people tend to be our heroes because they are better able to throw caution to the wind, but in peacetime that same trait can get them into trouble. Never let the idea that you have ADD hold you back from reaching for your dreams or be an excuse on why you cannot get there.

A Brief Introduction to Your Brain and Brain SPECT Imaging

ADD is a brain-based disorder. As such, it is important to learn about your brain and how we look at it. The human brain typically weighs about three pounds and it has the consistency of soft butter. It is housed in a very hard skull that has many sharp boney ridges and was never meant to hit a soccer ball or be in the ring with a 300-pound mixed martial arts fighter who wants to literally smash your head repeatedly against the canvas.

The most noticeable structure in human brains is the cerebral cortex, the wrinkly mass that sits atop and covers the rest of the brain. The cortex has four main areas or lobes: frontal, temporal, parietal, and occipital.

The frontal lobes consist of the motor cortex, which is in charge of movement; the premotor cortex, which plans movement; and the prefrontal cortex (PFC), which is considered the executive part of the brain. The PFC is the most evolved part of the human brain: the center of focus, forethought, judgment, organization, planning, impulse control, empathy, and learning from the mistakes you make. It makes up 30 percent of the human brain. Compare that to our closest cousin, the chimpanzee, whose PFC is only 11 percent; a dog, whose PFC is just 7 percent; or a cat, whose PFC is only 3.5 percent. It's a good thing a cat has nine lives, because their PFC isn't going to do much to keep them out of trouble.

Outside View of the Brain

left side view of brain

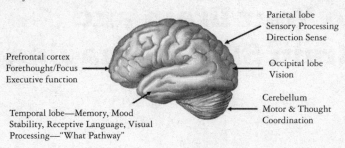

Parietal lobe
Sensory Processing
Direction Sense

Prefrontal cortex
Forethought/Focus
Executive function

Occipital lobe
Vision

Cerebellum
Motor & Thought
Coordination

Temporal lobe—Memory, Mood
Stability, Receptive Language, Visual
Processing—"What Pathway"

Inside View of the Brain

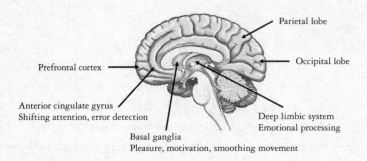

Parietal lobe

Prefrontal cortex

Occipital lobe

Anterior cingulate gyrus
Shifting attention, error detection

Deep limbic system
Emotional processing

Basal ganglia
Pleasure, motivation, smoothing movement

The temporal lobes, underneath your temples and behind your eyes, are the seat of auditory processing, naming things, getting memories into long-term storage, and emotional reactions. They are called the "What Pathway" in the brain as they name what things are. The parietal lobes, to the top side and back of the brain, are the centers for sensory processing and direction sense. They are called the "Where Pathway" because they help us know where things are. And the occipital lobes, at the back of the cortex, are concerned primarily with vision. Information from the world enters the back part of the brain (temporal and parietal lobes), is processed, and then passes to the front part of the brain for decision making. The cerebellum at the back bottom part of the brain is involved with motor and thought coordination. It is essential for processing complex information.

Sitting beneath the cortex is the deep limbic or emotional system. This is the part of the brain that colors our emotions and is involved with bonding, nesting, and emotions. Also, beneath the cortex are two large structures called the basal ganglia, involved with motivation, pleasure, and smoothing motor movements. Deep in your frontal lobes is the anterior cingulate gyrus, involved with error detection and sifting attention.

The cortex is divided into two hemispheres, left and right. While the two sides overlap in function, the left side in right-handed people is generally the seat of language, and tends to be the analytical, logical, detail-oriented part of the brain; while the right hemisphere sees the big picture and is responsible for hunches and intuition. The opposite is often, but not always, true in left-handed people.

BRAIN SPECT IMAGING

Over the last twenty-three years the Amen Clinics have used a variety of tools to look at and evaluate brain function. The most common of which is a study called brain SPECT imaging. SPECT (single photon emission computed tomography) is a nuclear medicine study that evaluates blood flow and activity patterns in the brain. It looks at how the brain works. It is different than CAT scans and MRIs, which are anatomy studies that look at the structure of the brain. SPECT looks at function and, in my opinion, is much more helpful in psychiatric illnesses like ADD.

SPECT scans basically show us three pieces of information about activity and blood flow in the brain:

- healthy activity
- too little activity
- too much activity

It also helps us see if the brain has been hurt from a physical trauma, or if it has had some sort of toxic exposure. At the clinics we read each scan with a high level of detail. For illustration purposes in this book I will show you two types of scans: surface and active. Surface scans look at the outside surface of the brain, and show areas of low activity. Active scans show areas of high or increased activity.

Throughout the book you will see many brain SPECT images. Here is an example of two "surface" SPECT scans. A healthy scan shows full,

Healthy vs Toxic Outside Surface SPECT Studies

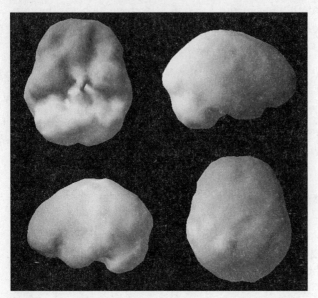

Healthy

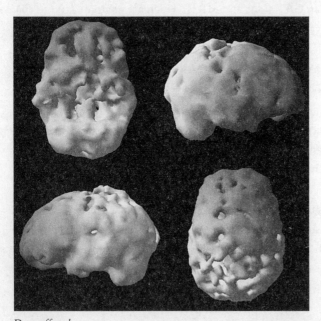

Drug affected

Healthy vs Hyperactive Active SPECT Studies

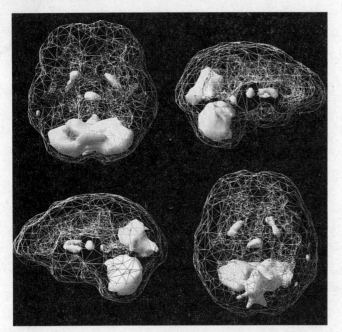

Healthy

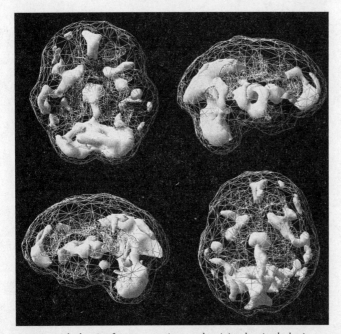

Anxiety with obsessive features, note increased activity deep in the brain

even, symmetrical activity. The top left image is looking underneath the brain. The bottom right image is looking down from the top, the other images look at the brain from the side. The surface scans look at the top 45 percent of brain activity. Anything below that shows up as a hole or a dent. So, the scan images with "holes" throughout the book are typically not missing activity, they are low in activity. The image next to the healthy one is of a person who was affected by toxicity from drug and alcohol exposure.

Here is an example of a set of "Active" SPECT scans. The grey background is average activity. The white areas represent the top 15 percent of brain activity, which in adults is mostly in the back, bottom part of the brain, the cerebellum. Overall, children have much more activity than adults. Again, the top left image is looking underneath the brain. The bottom right image is looking down from the top, the other images look at the brain from the side.

For more information on brain SPECT imaging and the research behind it, visit amenclinics.com/the-science/brain-spect-abstracts.

Preface to the Revised Edition of Healing ADD

A lot has happened in the world of ADD/ADHD over the last thirteen years since I first wrote *Healing ADD*. It is now being diagnosed much more frequently. Statistics from the Centers for Disease Control report that nearly one in five high school–age boys and 11 percent of school-age children overall have received a medical diagnosis of ADD. The figures showed that an estimated 6.4 million children between the ages of 6 to 17 had received an ADD diagnosis at some point in their lives, a 16 percent increase since 2007 and a 41 percent increase in the past decade.

The frenetic pace of the world is seemingly making it even more common. Children and adults are not just obsessed with smart phones, tablets, and video games, they are often using two or three of these devices at the same time! There are new medications and non-medication options to help ameliorate the symptoms of ADD. The long-term outcome of having untreated ADD is becoming clearer, and it is not good news. Untreated ADD increases the risk of depression, drug abuse, obesity, smoking, Type 2 diabetes, and Alzheimer's disease. We are also learning more about how diet and exercise can impact ADD. In a replicated study from Europe, 70 percent of ADD children showed greater than a 50 percent reduction of symptoms on an elimination diet, which means that food intake can make ADD symptoms better or worse. In another study, exercise significantly enhanced executive function in ADD children. Taking PE out of schools to save money may actually be costing our society much more in the long run in terms of lost learning and productivity.

In addition, our brain SPECT imaging database has grown from about 10,000 scans in 2001 to over 85,000 scans at the end of 2013, making our experience with both ADD and SPECT much more robust. Looking at the brains of tens of thousands of ADD individuals has taught us many valuable lessons, especially on the variability of ADD in the brain and in clinical practice. Subtyping ADD into six types was the major breakthrough I discussed in *Healing ADD*. In this version I have added a new type based on our brain imaging work and clinical experience: Anxious ADD. I have also included more information on the impact of toxic exposure as one of the potential causes of ADD. Additionally, we have discovered that the cerebellum at the back bottom part of the brain is more involved in ADD than anyone knew. The cerebellum is involved with coordination, potentially explaining why physical exercise can be helpful in lessening the symptoms of ADD.

In our clinical practice at Amen Clinics, using natural treatments has become much more common as a first line therapy. We are definitely not opposed to medication and there are many examples throughout the book where medication has been helpful, even lifesaving. But we are opposed to the indiscriminate use of medication, which we are seeing even more commonly in the new patients who come to our clinics. One child who came to our Reston, Virginia, office was on seventeen medications! I will discuss new natural treatment options for each of the ADD types.

In addition, our own method for evaluating and treating psychiatric illnesses in general and ADD in particular has evolved. The traditional way most psychiatrists make diagnoses and decide on treatment is based on symptom clusters found in the American Psychiatric Association's Diagnostic and Statistical Manual (DSM). If you have six out of nine of these symptoms without any clear medical issues, then you are given a specific diagnosis, such as ADD or ADHD. Symptom clusters drive diagnosis and subsequent treatment.

CURRENT APPROACH OF MOST PSYCHIATRISTS

Symptom Clusters = Diagnosis and Treatment Recommendations and Discouraging Outcomes

However, it is becoming clearer that this method of symptom-based diagnosis has outcomes that are not very impressive. According to Tom Insel, Director of the National Institutes for Mental Health, "For the antidepressants . . . the rate of response continues to be slow and low. In the largest effectiveness study to date, with more than four thousand patients with major depressive disorder in primary care and community settings, only 31 percent were in remission after 14 weeks of optimal treatment. In most double-blind trials of antidepressants, the placebo response rate hovers around 30 percent . . . The unfortunate reality is that current medications help too few people to get better and very few people to get well."

In the 1990s the largest, longest, and most expensive treatment study on ADHD was undertaken at six sites in the United States, involving many of America's most prominent ADHD researchers. It was called the Multimodal Treatment of Attention Deficit Hyperactivity Disorder (MTA) Study. The trial included 579 ADHD children who were given fourteen months of intensive medication management (MM), behavior therapy (BT), combined MM/BT, or a referral to a local physician (community care—CC) in which the families may or may not have actually followed through and received any treatment. Follow-up assessments were then conducted at approximately two, three, six, and eight years. For the children in the active treatment group the researchers took a "spare-no-expense" approach to ensure that the children received optimal versions of MM or BT. A conservative cost estimate for the fourteen months of MM was $4,150, $11,430 for BT, and $16,980 for the combined MM/BT. Despite the best care:

- BT failed to result in any significant reduction in core ADHD symptoms beyond those children who had simply been referred to their primary care doctor.
- Combined MM/BT was no better than MM alone at the end of fourteen months and all follow-up assessments.
- While both MM and MM/BT did better than BT alone and CC on the primary ADHD outcomes at the end of fourteen months, the effect of this benefit was dramatically reduced at two years and disappeared entirely at three, six, and eight years.
- The researchers reported that "although the study provided strong support for the immediate reduction of symptoms with intensive medication management, the long-term follow-up data fail to provide support for continued medication treatment beyond two years for the majority of children."
- In the eight year study period, 10.4 percent of the "optimally-treated" children required one or more psychiatric hospitalizations; the BT group without medication had an even higher incidence of hospitalization, 12.3 percent, compared to only 8.3 percent of those who had simply been referred to community care and may or may not have actually received any treatment.

Given the findings from this study, the evidence is clear that the gold-standard, commonly recognized, "evidence-based" treatments fail to result in sustained benefit for the vast majority of ADHD children who receive them. In fact, new brain imaging research suggests that using stimulants alone may actually be making the situation worse for many. Gene-Jack Wang and colleagues at the Brookhaven National Laboratory found that treatment with Ritalin over a year increased the dopamine transporters (proteins that help clear dopamine, the neurotransmitter that helps us focus) out of the brain's synapses, meaning that there is less dopamine to do its work. Taking the stimulant seems to increase the need for it.

AMEN CLINICS METHOD
(DISCUSSED IN DETAIL IN CHAPTER 3)

Symptom Clusters + Four Circle Assessments + Imaging and Lab Studies = More Targeted Diagnosis and Treatment and High Levels of Success

Our treatment outcomes at six months show high levels of improvement at 75 percent for very complicated patients, and an increased quality of life in 85 percent. Mental health treatment clearly needs a makeover. In this version of *Healing ADD* I will clearly outline the method we use at the Amen Clinics for evaluating and treating patients and give you many tools you can use in your own life to effectively manage and even thrive with ADD.

Introduction

An estimated seventeen million people in the United States have attention deficit disorder (ADD), which was later renamed as attention deficit hyperactivity disorder (ADHD). I prefer the name ADD, as ADHD highlights the hyperactive component of the disorder (H) and discards half the people who have it, particularly girls, who are typically not hyperactive. According to the CDC, 13.2 percent of boys at one time have been diagnosed with ADD, 5.6 percent of girls.

ADD is the most common learning and behavior problem in children. But the issue doesn't end there: It is also one of the most common problems in adults, and has been associated with job failures, relationship breakups, loneliness, a tremendous sense of underachievement, drug abuse, Alzheimer's disease, obesity, and Type 2 diabetes. Despite its prevalence, many myths and misconceptions about ADD abound in our society. Here are just a few of them:

MYTHS

- ADD is a flavor-of-the-month illness, a fad diagnosis. It's just an excuse for bad behavior.
- ADD is overdiagnosed. Every child who acts up a bit, or adult who is lazy, gets placed on Ritalin or Adderall.
- ADD is only a disorder of hyperactive boys.

- ADD is only a minor problem. People make too much of a fuss over it.
- ADD is an American invention, made up by a society seeking simple solutions to complex social problems.
- Bad parents or bad teachers cause ADD. If only our society had old-fashioned values, there wouldn't be these problems.
- People with ADD should just try harder. Everybody gives them excuses and coddles them.
- Everyone outgrows ADD by the age of twelve or thirteen.
- Medication alone is the best treatment for ADD, and has few side effects for most people.

FACTS

- ADD has been described in the medical literature for about one hundred years. In 1902, pediatrician George Still described a group of children who were hyperactive, impulsive, and inattentive. Unfortunately, he didn't understand that ADD is a medical disorder and labeled these children as "morally defective."
- Less than half of those with ADD are being treated.
- Arkansas and Alabama had the highest percentage of children treated, while California had the lowest. An article in the Journal of the American Medical Association concluded that there was no evidence that ADD is overdiagnosed in our society.
- Many people with ADD are never hyperactive. The non-hyperactive or "inattentive" ADD folks are often ignored because they do not bring enough negative attention to themselves. Many of these children, teenagers, or adults earn the unjust labels "willful," "lazy," "unmotivated," or "not that smart." Females, in our experience, tend to have inattentive ADD, and it often devastates their lives.
- Left untreated or ineffectively treated ADD is a very serious societal problem!

  33 percent never finish high school compared to the national average of 8.7 percent (25 percent repeat at least one grade).

  52 percent of untreated teens and adults abuse drugs or alcohol.

19 percent smoke cigarettes (compared to 10 percent of the general population).

46 percent of untreated hyperactive boys will be arrested for a felony by age sixteen, compared to 11 percent for controls and 21 percent of ADD adults versus 1 percent for controls.

21 to 25 percent of inmates in a number of studies have been found to have ADD.

75 percent have interpersonal problems; untreated ADD sufferers have a higher percentage of motor vehicle accidents, speeding tickets, citations for driving without a license, and suspended or revoked licenses.

People with ADD also have many more medical visits and emergency-room visits and get injured up to five times more than others.

Parents of ADD children divorce three times more often than the general population.

ADD is found in every country where it has been studied. I once had a patient from Ethiopia who had been expelled from his tribe for being so easily distracted and impulsive.

Ineffective parents or teachers can certainly make ADD symptoms worse, but they are generally not the sole cause. ADD behaviors often make even the most skilled parents and teachers appear stressed and inept.

- The harder many people with ADD try, the worse things get for them. Brain-imaging studies show that when people with ADD try to concentrate, the parts of their brains involved with concentration, focus, and follow-through (prefrontal cortex and cerebellum) actually shut down—just when they need them to turn on.

- Many people never outgrow ADD and have symptoms that interfere with their whole lives. Thirty to sixty-five percent of children diagnosed with ADD will have disabling symptoms into adulthood.

- Treatment can be very effective when properly targeted, especially when using a comprehensive approach, including education, support, exercise, nutrition, and personalized supplements or medications. Unfortunately, when children or adults do get treatment for ADD, shotgun medications are usually the only treatment given.

Why are there so many myths and negative reactions about ADD when physicians know so much about it? The answer is simple. Until now, you couldn't see ADD. On the outside, ADD children, teens, and adults look like everyone else. Sure, they may be more distractible, more impulsive, and more restless. And after all, it's a lot easier just to chalk up someone's problem as bad behavior or a child as "someone who doesn't try hard enough," rather than to go deeper and understand why. But unless you know the story of an ADD person's life, you can't see that he or she has ADD. Until now!

THE GOOD NEWS

ADD is real. We can see it in the brain. Brain imaging research conducted at my clinic and at other centers around the world have uncovered the ADD brain. Based on our research with tens of thousands of ADD patients using brain SPECT imaging we have been able to see areas of vulnerability in the ADD brain, and why it has such a negative impact on learning, behavior, and emotions. Humans have an innate distrust of the intangible, but seeing the ADD brain can cause the destructive myths and prejudices to fade away.

As you'll see in the pages that follow, ADD affects many areas of the brain, primarily the prefrontal cortex and cerebellum (the brain's controllers of concentration, attention span, judgment, organization, planning, and impulse control), the anterior cingulate gyrus (the brain's gear shifter and place of error detection), the temporal lobes (involved in memory, learning, and emotional reactions), the basal ganglia (which produce the neurotransmitter dopamine that drives the prefrontal cortex), and the deep limbic system (involved with setting emotional tone and bonding). But the good news is that with targeted treatment, people with ADD often get much better. Before-and-after imaging shows that, with effective treatment, brain function can dramatically improve and give sufferers more access to their own abilities.

Effective treatment does not make ADD sufferers different people: It removes the barriers hindering them from being the people they already are. I think of effective treatment for ADD like glasses for people who have trouble seeing. The glasses do not change people, they just make their vision more effective.

This book will give you a completely new perspective on ADD. You'll see actual ADD brain images (many before and after treatment) and identify the seven types of ADD that we have described (based on a combination of our work with many others in the field). You can also take a comprehensive questionnaire that will allow you to identify ADD (and which type) within yourself or others. That's right, seven types of ADD—not the simple types currently catalogued in the Diagnostic and Statistical Manual, Version V (DSM-V). Most importantly, this book offers promising new solutions. Understanding the nuanced complexities of ADD allows us to treat most people more effectively.

Type 1: Classic ADD—sufferers are inattentive, easily distracted, disorganized, hyperactive, restless, and impulsive.

Type 2: Inattentive ADD—sufferers are inattentive, easily distracted, disorganized, and often described as space cadets, daydreamers, or couch potatoes.

Type 3: Overfocused ADD—sufferers tend to have trouble shifting attention, which makes them look like they cannot pay attention; they frequently get stuck in loops of negative thoughts or behaviors; can be obsessive, worried, and inflexible; and are frequently oppositional, argumentative, and fault finding. Opposed to most ADD types, their organization is often fine or in some cases they are obsessively organized.

Type 4: Temporal Lobe ADD—sufferers are inattentive, easily distracted, disorganized, and struggle with mood instability, irritability, memory problems. This type is often associated with learning problems.

Type 5: Limbic ADD—sufferers are inattentive, easily distracted, disorganized, and struggle with low-grade sadness, negativity (e.g., "glass half empty syndrome"), low energy, and social withdrawal.

Type 6: Ring of Fire ADD—sufferers are inattentive, extremely distracted (too many thoughts), irritable, overly sensitive to the environment, hyperverbal, oppositional, and experience cyclic moodiness.

Type 7: Anxious ADD—sufferers are inattentive, easily distracted, disorganized, anxious, tense, nervous, predict the worst, struggle with timed tests, social anxiety, and often have physical stress symptoms, such as headaches and gastrointestinal symptoms.

Knowing which ADD type you or your child or loved one has is critical to developing an effective treatment program. Treating five of the seven types of ADD with stimulant medication alone often makes things worse. You'll learn that specifically tailored interventions, on the other hand, often lead to quick, dramatic, and lasting improvement.

A STEP-BY-STEP PROGRAM FOR HEALING EACH TYPE OF ADD

After helping you properly identify if ADD is an issue for you (or someone else you know) and which type, this book will give you a plan on how to treat it, the same plans we give our patients at Amen Clinics, including the same clear step-by-step brain enhancement program for optimizing brain function and overcoming ADD barriers. This program is effective, powerful, and easy to understand. While much of the program can be done outside of the doctor's office, for the medication and psychotherapeutic components you'll need to consult a healthcare professional. We currently have six clinics across the United States and hundreds of affiliated centers. A list of Amen Affiliated Education Centers can be found at www.amenclinics.com.

For all types, I'll give you suggestions for:

- education
- emotional and social support
- physical exercise
- mental exercise
- school and work strategies
- social skill strategies
- thinking skills

- coaching
- self-regulation exercises

For the individual types, you will also get:

- supplement options
- medication options
- neurofeedback strategies

This book will give you an effective program for enhancing brain function and overcoming the ADD traits that sabotage chances for success in all aspects of living—in relationships, at work or school, and within yourself. ADD affects whole families, not just individuals. Therefore, the following pages will also have extensive material on the dynamics of living in an ADD household (for parents, spouses, and siblings), along with many practical suggestions for effective cohabitation.

A NOTE TO OTHER HELPERS

A note for teachers, school counselors, principals, social workers, policemen, parole officers, marital therapists, psychologists, physicians, attorneys, and even IRS agents:

Many people with ADD have societal problems and this program can teach you how to work with them. Here are some common examples of the societal challenges people with ADD face:

- difficulties in school and spending excessive time in principal's office
- frequent speeding tickets and accidents
- getting in trouble with the law (Many teens with ADD tend to find trouble. For example, an ADD kid is with a group of teenagers and a police officer walks up to them. The teen with ADD is the one who will likely say something disrespectful and get himself hauled off to jail.)

- problems with parole officers (The incidence of ADD in prison is very high and parole officers frequently bust their clients with ADD for not following through on their programs.)

- relationship problems (Marital therapists often unknowingly spend excessive time with ADD clients because of their difficulties in relationships. When this dynamic is ignored, the ADD person or couple may stay in therapy unnecessarily for many years.)

- legal difficulties (People with ADD are overrepresented as clients in attorneys' offices. Lawyers frequently see ADD clients in domestic disputes, divorces, civil suits, and criminal cases.)

- tax problems (IRS agents frequently encounter people with ADD. Procrastination is a common problem in ADD and many put off filing or paying their taxes until the last possible minute and beyond. In my experience, IRS agents don't care if you have ADD. So it is better to get your ADD treated.)

Healing ADD

PART 1

ADD

Uncovered

CHAPTER 1

Why I Care

Plus ADD Throughout the Life Cycle

I often tell people I know more about ADD than I want to. I have not only studied ADD from the perspective of a clinician and researcher, I have lived with it at home. My first wife, Robbin, and my current wife, Tana, both have ADD. What can I say, I love exciting women. Also, several of my own children have ADD as well. For years I lived with the guilt that is often associated with having a family member who has this disorder. I thought that I was a terrible husband and a terrible father. These feelings were compounded by the fact that I was a psychiatrist and that I "should" have a perfect marriage and I "should" have well-behaved children. Things "should" have been better than they were. My son, Antony, used to joke that our family was like the cartoon Simpson family poster that read, "Okay, everybody, let's pretend that we're a nice, normal family" as they were getting ready to take a family picture. It was not until my children were diagnosed and treated properly that the clouds of guilt began to give way to understanding. I know this disorder from the inside out. I know what it is like:

- to have trouble holding a small child because she is in nonstop motion
- to chase a child through the store
- to chase a four-year-old child who is darting across a busy parking lot, all the while imaging her being struck by a car, which gratefully

3

never happened, but I have the emotional scars from the visual images

- to watch a child take four hours to do twenty minutes of homework
- to watch a child stare at a writing assignment for hours, unable to get thoughts from his brain to the paper
- to go to teachers' conferences where my child has been described as bright, spacey, and underachieving
- to have to repeat myself thirty-two times to get a child up in the morning
- to be asked for help at 11:00 P.M. the night before a term paper was due when the child knew about it for four weeks!
- to be angry every school morning for years because a child is continually ten minutes late
- to be amazed that a child's room can become so messy in such a short period of time
- to be always on alert in a store or at a friend's house so that my child won't touch or break something
- to be frustrated by trying to teach a child something, only to have him or her continually be distracted by something irrelevant
- to feel guilty about the negative feelings I have toward a child after I've told him or her not to do something for the umpteenth time
- to be embarrassed to the point of madness by a child's behavior in a restaurant (and wonder why I'm spending money to suffer)
- to be interrupted without mercy while I'm on the telephone
- to live through angry outbursts that have little or no provocation

My adopted son Antony was diagnosed with ADD when he was twelve years old. His biological father, Jim, was described as someone who never sat still, was impulsive, and had to be chained to his chair to get his homework done. It was only through the patience and diligence of Jim's mother, that Jim even finished high school. Like many ADD adults, Jim thrived in the military, as a Marine military police officer. The structure seemed to be very helpful for him. But after the service Jim struggled in all areas of his life. He had several marriages, many jobs, trouble with alcohol, and in his thirties, he shot and killed himself.

I was able to adopt Antony when he was three years old. I married his mother, Robbin, who had once been married to Jim. I could adopt Antony even though Jim was alive at the time because Jim never paid child support. In Oklahoma, where I was in medical school, there was a law that if a parent did not live up to their obligation, the stepparent could adopt the child.

I adored Antony, but his room used to follow the second law of physics, meaning that things went from order to disorder. I used to ask him if he planned to have his room that messy. His handwriting was a mess and a half an hour of homework used to take him three hours to do, with his mother yelling at him to sit down and get it done. Antony's school performance alternated from being excellent if he loved his teacher, to mediocre, despite having a high IQ. As part of a study I was doing on ADD with an electrical brain imaging study called quantitative EEG, I scanned Antony's brain. His scan pattern was clearly consistent with ADD. He had an excessive amount of slow brain wave activity in the front part of his brain. When I saw the results it made perfect sense to me.

On the surface, Breanne, my oldest daughter, was the perfect child. She was always easy, always sweet, her room was always clean and her homework always done. If I only had Breanne I would have been a terrible child psychiatrist. I would have thought Breanne was so wonderful because I was such a good dad. If I saw your child acting up in the grocery store, I would have thought to myself "give me your child for a week and I will straighten him out and then teach you how to be a good parent." Well God knew I was like that, so God gave me Kaitlyn.

Hyperactive from before birth, we thought Kaitlyn was going to be a boy, because the lore is that the more active babies are inside their mother's womb the more likely they are to be boys. Well she wasn't. Trying to hold Kaitlyn when she was a year old was like trying to hold a live salmon. I had a spiritual crisis because of this child. Many Catholic churches have the tradition of young children sitting with their parents at mass. It was no fun with Kaitlyn, because she was the worst-behaved child at church, which was not only embarrassing, it was bad for business. I treated half the children in the congregation and if my child was the worst one, people would lose confidence in me. So after a while I stopped going to church.

Have you ever seen children on little yellow leashes in the mall? After having Kaitlyn I believed in little yellow leashes because she was always trying to get away. But my problem was that I wrote a column in the *Daily Republic*, a local newspaper where I lived, and whenever I went to the mall people recognized me and said things like, "Hey, you're Dr. Amen! I loved your column." I just could not deal with, "Hey, you're Dr. Amen! Why is your child on a leash?" So what I used to do with Kaitlyn was put her in her stroller and tie her shoelaces together so she couldn't get out. Now, I am not proud of that but when you have a hyperactive child you do things just to survive.

When Katie was three years old I went back to church, but left her at home. I went to pray for a healing. I believe in healings. At the time I knew that 30 percent of three-year-olds look hyperactive, while only 5 to 10 percent of four-year-olds are hyperactive. So the first time you can really diagnose ADD with confidence is about four years old. I lit candles at church, and even put an extra fifty dollars in the offering, trying to bribe God. I wrote to the Pope and asked him to send a blessed picture that I could put by her bed. But he must have had a secretary with ADD because no one wrote me back. At the age of four years old I brought Katie to a colleague who diagnosed her with ADD.

During Kaitlyn's evaluation the psychologist looked at Robbin, and then at me and basically asked us who had it. As we will see, ADD usually runs in families. Obviously, it couldn't be me, I thought, except I do have an older brother who was hyperactive as a child and did not do well in school. But those issues were never mine. I tended to be anxious, on time, and focused. The answer came when our doctor asked Robbin how she studied. At the time Robbin was slowly finishing her bachelor's degree. Robbin said she could never study at home; there were too many distractions. She would get into her car and park underneath a streetlamp, where there were no kids, no noise, nothing, then she could study. When Robbin was diagnosed with ADD, a new world of hope and understanding happened between us. The treatment for ADD significantly helped Kaitlyn too.

Even though Breanne was the perfect child, the truth is I never thought she was very smart. It hurts me to say that, but that was how I felt. I had to teach her simple things over and over and she did not learn her times tables until she was in fifth grade. I had her tested by a psychologist in the third grade who basically told me the same thing: she wasn't that smart. She didn't say it that way, but I could read between the lines. But the psychologist said Breanne would be okay because she worked so hard. In fact, in eighth grade Breanne won a presidential scholar award, not for academics but for effort. In tenth grade, however, things started to fall apart. She was in a college prep school and stayed up every night until one or two o'clock in the morning to get her homework done. Then one night, while studying genetics in biology, she came to me confused and in tears and said she thought she could never be as smart as her friends. It broke my heart. The next day I pulled up her brain scan that I had done when she was eight years old. When I first started to do brain SPECT scans in 1991 I scanned everyone I knew. I had scanned my three kids, my mother, even myself. At the time I only had the experience of someone who had seen fifty scans. Now, seven years later, I had seen thousands of scans. With experienced eyes I was horrified by what I saw. Breanne had low overall activity, especially in the front part of her brain.

I came home that night and told Breanne what I saw and told her I wanted to get a new set of scans. Because of the injection of a radiopharmaceutical that is necessary for the SPECT scan, she protested, "I don't want a scan, Dad. All you think about are scans." But I am a child psychiatrist. I know how to get my way with kids. I felt this was very important and so I asked her what it would take to get her to agree to a scan. She told me she wanted a telephone line in her room. I started to think that maybe she was smarter than I thought. Well, her new SPECT studies were virtually identical to the ones seven years earlier. I cried when I saw them.

I put her on a low dose of medication, and the next night I rescanned her. Her brain normalized. Breanne's learning struggles had nothing to do with her intelligence. The low activity in her brain was limiting the access she had to her own brain. I had her continue with the low dose of medicine along with some supplements. A week later Breanne and I went

Breanne's Concentration SPECT Study Before and After Treatment (Underside Surface View)

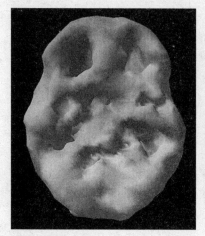 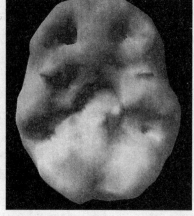

Overall low activity   *Improved activity*

to dinner together. She said learning was much easier for her. In fact, she said, "I think I am going to be a geneticist. I can see the DNA molecule rotate in my head. Don't you think it's the future, Dad?" I was floored. Three months later, Breanne brought home straight A's. These were the first A's of her life. Over spring break that year I was invited to Israel to speak to an International ADD Conference. I took Breanne with me. On the plane I saw Breanne do schoolwork for eight straight hours. I leaned over to her and asked, "So what do you think the difference is, being treated for ADD?" What she said was so telling.

"I used to hate school, Dad, because I had trouble learning. A one hour class seemed like it went on all day long. It was painful. Now, I can pay attention, and that same class seems like it goes by in twenty minutes and I love it because I can do it." That statement is critical. Many kids and adults hate school and learning because it is hard, and no one likes feeling incompetent.

Breanne went on to say, "I used to be very religious in school."

"What does that mean?" I asked.

"After ten minutes I was so lost in class that I would pray to God that the teacher would not call on me, because I had no idea what was going on. Now, I can track things and learning is much easier." She said she now understood concepts of biology for the first time. Usually a shy child in class, she started raising her hand and even participated in debates. At dinner one night she winked at me and said, "I kicked butt in a debate today, Dad." This was not the same child I knew. She had a completely different perception of herself—one that fit the reality of her being smart, competent, and able to look forward to a bright future.

Even though I had heard these stories from my patients for many years, it was something else to hear it from my own daughter. Through the rest of high school and college, Breanne got straight A's, and was accepted to one of the best veterinarian schools in the world at the University of Edinburgh. Even though Breanne decided not to go, because she had just given birth to her first child, she knew she was good enough to be accepted, which made all the difference in how she thought about herself.

Whenever I tell Breanne's story at lectures many women come up to me afterwards with tears in their eyes and tell me that they can relate to her. If only they knew, how life would have been different for them. My comment to them is, "You cannot change the past, but you can certainly start where you are now and work hard to change the future." I want your future to be the best it can be, no matter where you start from.

As we will see, ADD has deep genetic roots. When Kaitlyn had my grandson Liam, he so reminded me of her. Trying to hold him was like holding a live salmon. He is sweet, but very busy. And the ADD activity and beat go on.

I have used the principles in this book to guide the treatment of my patients and to help my own family. I know this information will help you.

ADD THROUGHOUT THE LIFE CYCLE

One of the best ways to diagnose ADD is to understand a detailed history of a person's life. Here's a look at ADD throughout the life cycle. It is important to note that ADD does not just appear in the teenage years or in adulthood. When you know what to look for, you can see that ADD symptoms have been present for most of a person's life.

Many hyperactive ADD children (Classic ADD) are noted to be

overly active in the womb. One mother told me that her unborn child kicked her so hard during the eighth month of pregnancy that he broke her ninth rib! Many are also difficult from birth: A significant number are colicky, fussy eaters, have a difficult time being comforted, are sensitive to noise and touch, and have eating and sleeping difficulties. As toddlers, they're often excessively active, mischievous, demanding, difficult to toilet train, and noncompliant with parental requests (like the terrible twos on overdrive).

Most ADD children are not recognized as such until they go to school: In kindergarten or in first or second grade, schoolteachers often notice the difference between these children and others. Teachers have a large database of expected behavior, while most parents do not. By the time they have entered school, hyperactive boys' problems with aggression, defiance, and oppositional behavior have often emerged. These problems often lead to social isolation and poor self-esteem.

Many ADD kids have varying degrees of poor school performance related to failure to finish assigned tasks, disruptive behavior during class, and poor peer relations. The time that these problems become apparent often relates to intelligence and the school setting. Often, the brighter the child, the later he or she is diagnosed. Up until that time, the child is likely to be labeled as an underachiever, willful, defiant, or oppositional.

At one time, it was believed that ADD symptoms disappeared by puberty. However, current studies indicate that only 25 to 50 percent of ADD kids fully outgrow their symptoms by puberty. Many do not outgrow their symptoms and they have difficulty with their family, school, and/or the community. This misperception occurred in part because most ADD children outgrow *the hyperactive component* before or at puberty. The problems with inattention and impulsivity remain, and many teenagers are taken off their medication just at a time when their defiant behavior is at its peak. I have seen that many teens experience serious school and social failure after the pediatrician or family doctor prematurely takes them off their medication.

There is a high incidence of conflicts in ADD families, especially during the teenage years. These conflicts often center around failure to do schoolwork, problems completing routine chores, and difficulty being trusted to obey the rules. I have seen many teenagers sent away from home (to a residential treatment setting, boarding school, or relative's house) as a way for the family to survive the turmoil.

Many adults with ADD live lives of chronic frustration. Psychiatrists Henry Mann and Stanley Greenspan wrote the first article on ADD in adults in 1977, yet the medical community was very slow to recognize ADD in adults. It has only been since the late 1980s that professionals began talking about ADD beyond the adolescent years. Still, even now many professionals do not understand ADD in adults and often describe these people as having character problems, anxiety, depression, or even manic-depressive disorder. Their childhood ADD symptoms are assumed to have just melted away. Adults with ADD often come to our clinic with the following concerns:

- Concerns about a child with ADD. Most adults with ADD are only diagnosed after they bring one of their children in for evaluation. During a thorough history, the child psychiatrists ask about family history. Through these questions the light goes on for many people.
- Poor school/work performance caused by the following symptoms: poor sustained attention span to reading, paperwork, etc.; high susceptibility to boredom by tedious material; poor organization and planning; procrastination until deadlines are imminent; restlessness, trouble staying in a confined space (not a phobia); impulsive decision making; inability to work well independently; failure to listen carefully to directions; frequent impulsive job changes; poor academic grades for ability; frequent lateness for work/appointments; or a tendency to misplace things frequently.
- Symptoms of trouble thinking clearly, generally poor self-discipline, moodiness, chronic anxiety, restlessness, substance abuse, uncontrolled anger, marital problems, sleep problems, financial problems, or impulsiveness.

ADD IN THE ELDERLY

There is also no question in my mind that ADD exists in the elderly and that it seriously handicaps many of them. I have diagnosed many elderly people with ADD, mostly after I have seen their children, grandchildren, or great-grandchildren. My oldest patient, Betty, was ninety-four when she came to see me. I had seen three generations of people in her family: her son, grandson, and great-granddaughter. When I asked her why she wanted to be evaluated, she said that she wanted to be able to finish reading the paper in the morning. ADD symptoms in the elderly cause social isolation, difficult behavior, and a higher incidence of cognitive problems. For decades geriatric psychiatrists have used medications like Ritalin to help sharpen cognitive skills. Perhaps they were, in part, treating the very high incidence of ADD in the elderly.

Watch for the Wall

Many bright children with ADD, especially Type 2 (Inattentive ADD), are not diagnosed until later in their development, if at all. They do fine for a while and then slam into failure: The Wall! Depending on intelligence, class size, and knowledge level of the parents, they may not have problems until third grade, sixth grade, ninth grade, or even college. I've treated some college professors who received good grades in graduate school but still had the majority of symptoms of the disorder. They state, however, that it took them four or five times the amount of time and effort to do as well as their peers.

My son, whose greatest difficulties were in the ninth grade, actually got straight A's in the sixth grade. He said, "In sixth grade, I knew everything that the teacher was talking about. It was easy. In ninth grade, I did not know as much and I couldn't bring myself to focus on all the material I needed to learn."

The Wall is different for each person with ADD.

ADD STORIES THROUGH THE LIFE CYCLE

ADD may not make someone look different on the outside, but you can see it plainly when you know what to look for. The following case histories demonstrate how ADD impacts people throughout the life cycle. The names and details have been altered, as they have been throughout this book, to protect the confidentiality of my patients.

Children

ALFIE

Alfie, age ten, had trouble from the time he was very young. In preschool the teachers complained about his lack of attention, hyperactivity, and disruptive, impulsive behavior. Alfie's work was sloppy, he frequently forgot or lost assignments, and his desk at school and his room at home were usually a mess! Alfie constantly challenged his parents, seemed to thrive on chaos and conflict, and frequently hurt himself by doing stupid things, such as jumping out of trees. He had already broken three bones. Homework was always a struggle. Work that typically took their other kids thirty minutes to finish took Alfie three or four hours to complete, with his parents having to provide constant supervision. While doing his homework, he was up every five minutes looking for food or bothering his older sister. In second grade, Alfie started to hate school and thought he was stupid, even though he tested above average. Alfie typically blamed others for his problems.

His parents were at their wits' end and constantly talked about the problems. They alternated between blaming Alfie, blaming the "lousy" school, and blaming themselves. When Alfie was five years old, his mother took him to his family doctor because of his high activity level and difficult nature. While she was talking to the physician Alfie sat perfectly still and was polite and attentive. The doctor told Alfie's mother, in no uncertain terms, that there was nothing the matter with the boy and that she needed parenting classes. The mother left the doctor's office in tears because he had confirmed her worst fear: she was a defective parent who caused her son's problems. Despite the parenting classes, the problems continued.

When he was in fifth grade, Alfie came to the Amen Clinics for an evaluation. It was clear from watching him that he had difficulty concentrating, was distractible, active, and impulsive. He scored poorly on the Conner's Continuous Performance Test (C-CPT), a fifteen-minute test of attention. Alfie's diet was erratic and filled with lots of sugar and artificial dyes and he got little exercise. His lab tests, including thyroid studies, zinc, and blood chemistries were all normal. Alfie had Classic ADD: He was inattentive, distractible, disorganized, hyperactive, and impulsive. I changed his diet, increased his exercise, gave him EPA omega-3 fatty acids and a brain-directed multiple vitamin, talked with the school on effective classroom management techniques, and had his parents attend a parenting group designed specifically for dealing with ADD children. We also taught Alfie some specialized biofeedback techniques. Six months into his treatment, Alfie was a different child. He was less impulsive, his attention span had increased, and he was calmer. His grades improved dramatically. Six years later he likes himself, is effective at school, and has healthy relationships at home and with friends.

ANGELICA

Angelica, age four, was very busy. Ever since she could walk, she ran. Her parents had to keep their eyes on her at all times. She ran off as soon as her mother, Jill's, back was turned. She was her own "little wrecking crew" when she went shopping with her mom or dad. Her parents brought her to see me after she ran into the street and was almost hit by an oncoming car.

Angelica was also moody, irritable, oppositional, very talkative, and able to throw epic tantrums. Jill could not take Angelica anywhere without a commotion, which made the mother feel isolated and alone, which is not uncommon for mothers of ADD children. In restaurants she wiggled, yelled out, and screamed if she didn't get her way. Other adults would stare at Angelica's parents with disapproving looks that said, "Why don't you beat that bratty child to behave better!" The parents often felt humiliated. Spanking, in fact, seemed to backfire. The more they spanked Angelica, the more she would act up—as if she wanted more punishment. Angelica had a very short attention span, never playing with anything for longer than a few minutes. She could tear her room apart in a moment.

Angelica tore up my office too. She messed up the papers on my desk, tossed books off my bookcase, and slapped her mother when she tried to get her to sit still. The parents were at their wits' end. Angelica had the type of ADD we call the Ring of Fire. Likely, it had genetic roots. Jill's father was an alcoholic and she had a brother who had been diagnosed with both ADD and bipolar disorder. Angelica's father had a mother who had been hospitalized for suicidal thoughts. Angelica had already seen two child psychiatrists who had tried her on Ritalin and Adderall; both of these medications made her worse. She didn't sleep or eat and was markedly more irritable. With an atypical response to medication, I ordered a brain SPECT study, which showed multiple areas of overactivity in her brain, which is why it is called the Ring of Fire (more on this pattern coming soon). As we will see, this pattern can have a number of causes, from food allergies, inflammation, or an early bipolar pattern. The goal of treatment was to eliminate anything that could be trouble for her and calm her brain. I put her on an elimination diet to see if she was sensitive to food, and placed her on a group of supplements to calm her brain, including omega-3 fatty acids, GABA, 5HTP, l-tyrosine, and brain-directed multiple vitamins. Within several weeks she became more settled, more cooperative, more playful, more attentive, and much more relaxed. Her mother was amazed at how little she was yelling at Angelica now. The parents also took a parenting class, which helped them gain the skills necessary to deal with a very challenging child.

Teenagers

KRYSTLE

Krystle's mother came to one of my lectures. When I described ADD, she started to cry, knowing that the symptoms I had listed fit her daughter's life. Shortly thereafter, she brought Krystle to our office. Krystle had a short attention span, was easily distracted, disorganized, and often did not finish her assignments. Even when she did them, she often forgot to turn them in. Krystle had low energy and struggled with motivation. She wanted to be a teacher, but believed she was not smart enough. She sat in my office, already demoralized at age fifteen.

Krystle had Inattentive ADD, a common but frequently undiagnosed condition in females. I started her on an omega-3 fatty acid supplement, a brain-directed multiple vitamin, and a low dose of a stimulant medication. In addition, I had her increase her exercise and protein intake, and worked with her on self-esteem and school strategies. Within two weeks of starting treatment, Krystle dramatically improved. I remember her coming into my office so tickled that she could finally get her work done. In the semester after she started treatment, her grade point average went from a 2.1 to a 3.2. She was thrilled that she could keep up with her friends at school and no longer thought of herself as "stupid." The demoralized girl I had first met was developing into a hopeful and forward-looking woman.

GREGG

When Gregg first came to see me at the age of fourteen, he was a wreck. He had just been expelled from his third school for fighting and breaking the rules. He told off teachers for fun and picked fights with other kids on the school grounds. He also never did his homework and he talked about dropping out of school, saying he didn't need an education to take care of himself. At home he was defiant, restless, messy, and disobedient. He teased his younger brother and sister without mercy. Anytime his parents would speak to him, he'd get defensive and challenging. His parents were at their wits' end, and their next step was a residential treatment center.

When I first saw him he was a "turned-off" teenager with averted eyes and nothing much to say. He told me that he didn't want to be sent away but that he wasn't able to get along with his family. He found school very hard and thought he was stupid. When I did a test of verbal intelligence on him, however, his demeanor started to change. He liked the test and seemed challenged by it. His verbal IQ score was 142, in the superior range and far from stupid. Looking back in Gregg's history, it was clear he had had symptoms of ADD his whole life. He was a fidgety kid with awful handwriting and a messy desk. He had trouble waiting his turn in school, and endured being called stupid because he had trouble learning.

Due to the severity of his problems, and the potential departure of Gregg from the family, I ordered a brain SPECT study to evaluate the functioning of his brain. The study showed that he had two problems. When Gregg tried to concentrate, the front part of his brain, which should increase in activity, actually decreased. This is the part of the brain that controls attention span, judgment, impulse control, and critical thinking. His brain study also showed decreased activity in his left temporal lobe, which, when abnormal, often causes problems with learning, and sometimes violent or aggressive behavior. I diagnosed Gregg with Temporal Lobe ADD.

As I explained these findings to Gregg, he became visibly relieved. "You mean," he said, "the harder I try to concentrate, the worse it gets for me." He responded very nicely to a combination of medication to balance the trouble in his frontal and temporal lobes (a stimulant and anticonvulsant), in addition to a brain-directed multiple vitamin, omega-3 fatty acid supplement, neurofeedback over his left temporal lobe, an improved diet, and exercise. He was able to remain at home, finish high school, and start college—a far cry from the stupid troublemaker he and everyone else thought he was.

Adults

BRETT

Brett, twenty-seven, had just been fired from his fourth job in a year. He blamed his bosses for expecting too much of him, but it was the same old story. Brett had trouble with details, he was often late to work, he seemed disorganized, and he would miss important deadlines. The end came when he impulsively told off a difficult customer who complained about his attitude.

All his life Brett had similar problems, and his mother was tired of bailing him out. He dropped out of school in the eleventh grade, despite having been found to have a high IQ. He was restless, fidgety, impulsive, and had a fleeting attention span. When he was in school, small amounts of homework would take him several hours to complete, even with much nagging and yelling from his mother. Brett had mastered the art of getting people angry at him, and it seemed to others that he intentionally stirred things up.

Brett had had lifelong symptoms of Classic ADD that had gone unnoticed, even though Brett had been tested on three separate occasions. With appropriate treatment at last, his life made a dramatic turn-around. He returned to school, finished a technical degree in fire-inspection technology, and got a job. He has kept that job for eight years now and feels that he is happier, more focused, and more positive than ever before.

LARRY

Larry, sixty-two, came into therapy because his wife threatened to start divorce proceedings against him if he didn't get help. She complained that he never talked to her, he was unreliable, he never finished projects that he started, and he was very negative. He tended to be moody, tired, and disinterested in sex. As a child, he had mediocre to poor grades in school, and as an adult he went from job to job, complaining of boredom.

Larry was referred to me by his marital therapist, and rightly so: Larry had Limbic ADD, with problems that looked like a combination of ADD and mild, chronic depression.

Larry's SPECT study showed decreased prefrontal cortex activity and increased activity in the deep limbic system of his brain. Seeing his scan convinced him of the need for treatment. He started on an intense aerobic exercise program, changed his diet, and took an omega-3 fatty acid supplement, a brain-directed multiple vitamin, and SAMe, a dietary supplement that has been shown to support mood and, in my experience, help with attention. Within a month his mood was better and he felt more focused. As Larry improved, the couple progressed quickly in marital therapy and have been happier than when they were first married.

SARAH

Sarah, forty-two, was anxious and frustrated when she first came to see me. She also complained of being irritable and short with her children and husband. Furthermore, she had trouble getting to sleep, which was new, and couldn't get out of bed in the morning. In school, growing up, she was easily distracted, and homework took her forever to do. She often froze during tests and scored very poorly on timed tests. In addition, she would never speak up in class. In college, she purposefully took classes where there were no oral assignments. She told me if she had to give a presentation in class, she just didn't show up. She would rather get an F than speak in front of the class.

Sarah's grandmother, father, and sister had problems with anxiety. She also had two nephews who had been diagnosed with ADD. As I listened to her story, it was clear that Sarah had Anxious ADD, where her internal anxiety was constantly distracting her. Her lab tests were all fine, except she had a low progesterone level, which is common for many women in their early forties. When progesterone goes low, anxiety often increases, and can cause issues with sleep and anxiety. Sarah responded nicely to relaxation exercises, diet and exercise changes, and a combination of supplements to boost the neurotransmitter GABA and dopamine, omega-3 fatty acids, along with progesterone cream.

CHAPTER 2

ADD: Core Symptoms and Why It Is Increasing in the Population

Despite what it may seem from the constant media reports, ADD is not new. As early as the seventeenth century, the philosopher John Locke described a perplexing group of young students who, "try as they might, they cannot keep their minds from straying." History is full of references to people fitting the symptom pattern of inattention, restlessness, hyperactivity, and impulsivity. Abraham Lincoln's third son, Tad, fit the picture. He was described as hyperactive, impulsive (bursting into the Oval Office while chasing his brother), and inattentive. He had learning problems. His mother hired tutor after tutor to come into the White House to help Tad, but they all quit, saying that he was not teachable. One wonders if Mary Todd Lincoln didn't have ADD herself. She too struggled with impulsivity. On a number of occasions she overspent the White House budget, causing political embarrassment and ridicule for the president. One time when President Lincoln was reviewing the troops, a young captain's wife caught his eye. Mrs. Lincoln noticed her husband looking at the young woman and started screaming at her husband in front of the whole crowd.

ADD is not even new in the medical literature. George Still, a pediatrician at the turn of the last century, described children who were hyperactive, inattentive, and impulsive. Unfortunately, he labeled them "morally defective." During the great flu epidemic of 1918, many chil-

Diagnostic and Statistical Manual	
of the American Psychiatric Association (DSM)	

DSM Version	Name for ADD
1	Hyperactivity of Childhood
2	Hyperkinetic Reaction of Childhood
3	Attention Deficit Disorder with or without hyperactivity
3R	Attention Deficit Hyperactivity Disorder
4	Attention Deficit/Hyperactivity Disorder
5	Attention Deficit/Hyperactivity Disorder

dren also contracted viral encephalitis and meningitis. Of those who survived the brain infections, many were described with symptoms now considered classic for ADD. By the 1930s, the label "minimal brain damage" was coined to describe these children. The label was changed in the 1960s to "minimal brain dysfunction" because no anatomical abnormality could be found in the children. Whatever its name, ADD has been part of the psychiatric terminology since the inception of the Diagnostic and Statistical Manual (DSM) in 1952. (The DSM is the diagnostic bible listing clinical criteria for various psychiatric disorders). Every version of the DSM has described the core symptoms of ADD, albeit by a different name every time.

ADD CORE SYMPTOMS

There is a group of core symptoms common to those who have ADD. These include short attention span for routine, everyday tasks, distractibility, organizational problems (for spaces and time), difficulty with follow-through, and poor internal supervision or judgment. These symptoms exist over a prolonged period of time and are present from an early age, although they may not be evident until a child is pushed to concentrate or to organize his or her life.

SHORT ATTENTION SPAN FOR REGULAR, ROUTINE TASKS

A short attention span is the hallmark symptom of this disorder. People with ADD have trouble sustaining attention and effort over prolonged periods of time, unless they are intensely interested. Their minds tend to wander and they frequently get off task, thinking about or doing other things than the task at hand. Yet, one of the things that often fools inexperienced clinicians assessing this disorder is that people with ADD do not have a short attention span for everything. Often, people with ADD can pay attention perfectly well to things that are new, novel, highly stimulating, interesting, or frightening. These things provide enough of their own intrinsic stimulation, which activates the brain functions that help people with ADD focus and concentrate. When asked about attention span, most people with ADD say that they can pay attention "just fine." But they often spontaneously add the phrase ". . . if I'm interested." That is the most important part of the answer: People with ADD need outside stimulation in order to focus. This is one of the reasons they often like scary movies, excitement-filled activities, such as driving fast, or a good argument.

In one study, researchers found a deficiency of adrenaline (the hormone frequently associated with stress or excitement) in the urine samples of ADD children.

I often think of ADD as "adrenaline deficit disorder," because people with ADD can focus with excitement and interest, but not without it. My son who has ADD without hyperactivity (Type 2), for example, used to take four hours to do a half hour of homework, frequently getting off task. Yet, if you gave him a car stereo magazine, he would quickly read it from cover to cover and remember every little detail in it.

People with ADD have problems paying attention to regular, routine, everyday matters such as homework, schoolwork, chores, or paperwork—problems that have plagued them their whole lives. The mundane is terrible for them and not by choice. As we will see later on, they need excitement or interest to stimulate an underactive brain.

Attention patterns are crucial to a diagnosis of ADD. A person's tendency to deny that they have attentional problems (because they can concentrate with intense interest) is often a roadblock to accepting the diagnosis or getting proper treatment. I make sure that I ask about attention span for regular, routine, everyday tasks. I also ask about attention span from others who know the person well. Other people may be better observers than the person being evaluated. Parents, siblings, spouses, and friends are often quick to complain about attention and focusing abilities, even when the person has completely denied any trouble concentrating.

In addition to clinical history (from family and friends as well as the person being evaluated), our office also uses the Conner's Continuous Performance Task (C-CPT), to measure attention span and impulse control to aid in making the diagnosis of ADD. The Conner's CPT is a computer-based fifteen-minute test of attention, response time, and impulse control. On the screen, letters flash at one-second, two-second, and four-second intervals. Every time you see a letter, you hit the space bar, except when you see the letter X. Whenever you see the letter X you just let it go and do not hit the space bar. People with ADD often have erratic response times (good when the letters come fast at one second intervals, but slower when the letters come at two- or four-second intervals) and more impulsive responses, hitting an excessive number of X's. This test frustrates many people with ADD. We also use a sophisticated computerized neuropsychological test, called WebNeuro, that gives us scores on attention, impulsivity, memory, information processing speed, and executive function.

DISTRACTIBILITY

Distractibility differs from a short attention span. The issue here is not an inability to sustain attention, but rather a hypersensitivity to the environment. Most of us can block out unnecessary environmental stimuli: traffic sounds, the sound of the air conditioner or heater turning on, the smell of food from the cafeteria, birds flying by the classroom window, even the feel of our own clothing against our skin. People with ADD, however, are often hypersensitive to their senses, and they have trouble suppressing the sounds, sights, smells, and feel of the environment—the sensory noise that surrounds us. The distractibility is likely due to the underlying mechanism of ADD, underactivity in the prefrontal cortex of the brain.

The prefrontal cortex has many inhibitory tracks that signal other areas of the brain to settle down. It sends these inhibitory signals to the thalamus (a structure deep in the brain that gates incoming information) and the parietal lobes (our sensory cortex) so that we do not become overwhelmed or sense too much of the environment. However, when the prefrontal cortex is underactive, the thalamus and parietal lobes can bombard us with too much environmental information. The prefrontal cortex also sends inhibitory signals to the brain's emotional centers. When this input is not strong enough, people get distracted by their internal thoughts and feelings.

Here are some examples: Many of my patients tell me that they frequently feel irritated by their own clothing. Most people never feel their own clothing unless their attention is directed to it. When directed to think about the shoes on your feet, you can easily feel them, but since you don't need to pay attention to the feeling of your shoes, your brain blocks out the unnecessary sensation. People with ADD have trouble here. One of my daughters with Type 3 (Overfocused) ADD used to repetitively take off her socks if the seam was not perfectly aligned.

ADD patients also routinely cut the tags out of their clothing. I remember the weekend my ex-wife (who was later diagnosed with ADD) moved into my apartment after our wedding. Unbeknownst to me, she cut the tags out of all of my shirts. When I asked her why, she said she thought I would appreciate it. She hated how tags felt and always removed them from her clothing. I had never felt a tag in my life, and asked her if she wouldn't mind asking me first next time before she took scissors to my clothes.

The hypersensitivity to touch can also cause sexual problems, because many people with ADD do not like to be touched, or they react negatively if touched the "wrong" way. The distractibility also makes it harder to have an orgasm. In lectures, I often ask, "What does an orgasm require, besides a reasonable lover?" The answer is focus. You have to pay attention to the feeling long enough in order to make it happen. Many people, especially women, with ADD struggle to have orgasms, and with the right treatment they feel so much better.

In a similar way, sight sensitivity is a frequent problem. While it may not seem like much of an issue, seeing too much can cause problems in many situations. When driving, for example, it is important to focus on the road. Many people with ADD, however, see everything around them, becoming bombarded with visual stimuli. Reading a book also requires you to block out extraneous visual stimuli. Unfortunately, many people with ADD are unable to do this and they are frequently distracted by the movements around them. Later in the book, I will write about the Irlen Syndrome, a visual processing problem, commonly associated with ADD. Many people with ADD also complain of being excessively bothered by sounds, especially the chewing sounds of others. I have several young patients who will not go to school because they are so bothered by the sounds that other students make. I once evaluated an inmate who told me that he got murderous thoughts when other inmates would drag chess pieces across the chess board while playing the game. The noise, he said, would make him crazy. Other patients have told me that they need white noise (such as that of fans) to block out the other sounds in the environment. My ex-wife used to sleep with a fan on in our room in order not to hear all of the other sounds in the house—whether it is seventy degrees out or twenty degrees out. I often hid under the covers to avoid the noise and the cold breeze from the fan.

Sensitivity to taste is another common problem. Many people with ADD will eat only foods with a certain taste or texture. Parents frequently complain that they have trouble finding foods their children will eat. One of my patients went through a two-year period where he would only eat burritos with peanut butter and bananas.

Organizational Problems (Space and Time)

Organizational struggles are also very common in ADD, specifically disorganization for space, time, projects, and long-term goals. A common ADD trait, space disorganization is often seen early in the lives of ADD children. When you look at their rooms, closets, dresser drawers, desks, or book bags, you frequently see a disaster. Things are left half done, half

put away, or dropped wherever. I used to tell my son that his room followed the second law of physics, entropy, in which things degrade from
order to disorder. His room showed hyper-entropy. I remember helping
him clean his room on Sunday afternoons, but by Sunday evening it often
looked a mess. Once, when he was in the third grade, I went to an open
house at his school. All of the desks were in neat rows . . . except one. It
was out of place with papers hanging out of it. My heart sank. I knew it
was Antony's desk, and when I opened the desk's lid I saw his name.

Other people often complain bitterly about the disorganization, such
as bosses, teachers, children, and spouses. I have received letters from
wives writing about their ADD husbands. "He'll tell you he's organized,"
they write, "but I am enclosing a picture of his office [filing cabinet,
closet, or garage]. What do you think?" The pictures show spaces that
are incredibly overstuffed and disorganized.

People with Type 3 Overfocused ADD often appear very organized on
the outside. They are often perfectly dressed, and parts of their living
spaces may be very neat. For example, they may insist on perfect living
rooms, but if you go into their drawers or their closets, you'll find a disaster.

Similarly, time organization plagues people with ADD. They tend
to be late and have trouble predicting how long things will take them to

do. Often they will agree to do too many things at once, not realizing the time commitment involved. The chronic tardiness lands many ADD people in deep trouble. For example, they get fired from jobs for being late to work, not once, but on a chronic basis. Many of my patients' spouses have told me that they have to lie in order to be on time for appointments or engagements. "If I tell her we have to leave at noon, invariably she won't be ready until 12:30 or 1:00 P.M. It makes me so mad! So in order for me not to feel so stressed out I tell her we have to leave at 11:00. She hasn't caught on yet."

ADD people often take a haphazard or disorganized approach to projects or chores, dramatically increasing the time it takes to complete them. For example, one of my patients planned to clean out the garage over the weekend. On Friday night he put half of the garage contents into the driveway, but then he started organizing the boxes that were inside the garage. Three weeks later the neighbors started to complain about the mess in the driveway. One of the college students I treat complained about spending excessive time on projects. When I asked him to explain the process of doing a project, it was clear that it had no beginning, middle, or end: he was working on multiple ideas that did not have any structure to them.

In addition, many people with ADD take a disorganized approach to their own lives. They frequently lack long-term goals and tend to live from crisis to crisis or problem to problem.

DIFFICULTY WITH FOLLOW-THROUGH

People with ADD frequently suffer from poor follow-through, lacking the staying power to see projects through to the end. They will do something so long as there is intense interest. In addition, they put things off until the very last minute—until the looming deadline generates enough stress to entice them to get it done. For example, if there is a term paper due in a month, they will put it off, put it off, and put it off until they are pushed to the wall of the deadline, working feverishly to finish, even if they have told themselves that this time they will get to their project early.

Often people with ADD have so many different interests, they will only do a project as long as it holds their curiosity. I once saw a college professor for evaluation. His wife sat in on the initial session. I asked him how many projects he started last year. He said, "I think about three hundred." His wife added in an irritated tone, "He only finished three, and none of them were for me."

Many people with ADD will complete 50 to 80 percent of their task and then go off to another project. They frequently get distracted by other things and fail to follow through with the task at hand. Many people with ADD pay late fees on bills, even though they had the money to pay the bill on time.

Poor follow-through affects many areas of life. Here are some examples:

- schoolwork—fails to turn in assigned work
- chores at home—things often put off until the very last minute or not done at all
- work—reports or paperwork not turned in on time
- finances—late charges paid, even when the money is there because bills were not paid on time
- friendships—promises go unfulfilled
- health—fail to follow through on diets, taking supplements or medication, or getting their lab work done when asked.

POOR INTERNAL SUPERVISION

Many people with ADD have poor internal supervision. The prefrontal cortex (PFC) is the brain's chief executive officer because it is so heavily involved with forethought, planning, impulse control, and decision making. North Carolina neuropsychiatrist Thomas Gualtieri, M.D., succinctly summarized the human functions of the PFC: "the capacity to formulate goals, to make plans for their execution, to carry them out in an effective way, and to change course and improvise in the face of obstacles or failure, and to do so successfully, in the absence of external direction or structure. The capacity of the individual to generate goals and to achieve them is considered to be an essential aspect of a mature and effective personality. It is not a social convention or an artifact of culture. It is hard wired in the construction of the prefrontal cortex and its connections."

When there are problems in the prefrontal cortex, as is typical in ADD patients, forethought is a constant struggle. The PFC helps you think about what you say or do before you say or do it. The PFC helps you, in accordance with your experience, select among alternatives in social and work situations. For example, a person with good PFC function is more likely to have a tempered, reasonable disagreement with a spouse. A person with poor PFC function is more likely to do or say something that will make the situation worse. Likewise, if you're a check-out clerk with good PFC function and a difficult, complaining person (who has poor PFC function) comes through your line, you are more likely to keep quiet or give a thoughtful response that helps the situation. If you have poor PFC function, you are more likely to do or say something that will inflame the situation. The PFC helps you problem-solve, see ahead of a situation, and, by learning through experience, pick between the most helpful alternatives.

The PFC is also the part of the brain that helps you learn from your mistakes. Good PFC function doesn't mean you won't make mistakes; everyone does. Rather, you won't make the same mistake over and over. You are able to learn from the past and apply its lessons. A student with good PFC function can learn that if he or she starts a long-term project early, there is more time for research and less anxiety over getting it done. A student with decreased PFC function doesn't learn from past frustrations and may tend to put everything off until the last minute. In general, poor PFC function leads people to make repetitive mistakes. Their actions are not based on experience, or forethought, but rather on the moment.

The moment is what matters. This phrase comes up over and over with my ADD patients. For many people with ADD, forethought is a struggle. It is natural for them to act out what is important to them at the immediate moment, not two moments from now or five moments from now, but now! A person with ADD may be ready for work a few minutes early, but rather than leave the house and be on time or a few minutes early, she may do another couple of things that make her late. Likewise, a person with ADD may be sexually attracted to someone he just met, and even though he is married and his personal goal is to stay married, he may have a sexual encounter that puts his marriage at risk. The moment was what mattered.

In the same vein, many people with ADD take what I call a crisis management approach to their lives. Rather than having clearly defined goals and acting in a manner consistent to reach them, they ricochet from crisis to crisis. In school, people with ADD have difficulty with long-term planning. Instead of keeping up as the semester goes along, they focus on the crisis in front of them at the moment—the next test or term paper. At work they are under continual stress. Deadlines loom and tasks go uncompleted. It seems as though there is a need for constant stress in order to get consistent work done. The constant stress, however, takes a physical toll on everyone involved (the person, his or her family, coworkers, employers, friends, etc.).

ADD IS INCREASING IN THE POPULATION

ADD is increasing in the population, a fact that frightens me, and it should frighten you as well. When you look at the fallout from untreated ADD, our society may be in for a lot more problems, especially considering that ADD remains underdiagnosed and undertreated. Thirty years ago, teachers would typically have one or two Classic ADD kids in their classrooms. Now I hear them say they have three, four, or five of these kids. What is happening? Are we just better at recognizing ADD? Are societal influences causing more ADD symptoms? One answer comes from David Comings, M.D., a geneticist from the City of Hope Hospital in Los Angeles. In his book *The Gene Bomb* he postulates that as our society becomes more technologically advanced, we require students to stay in school longer to get the best jobs. The students who drop out of the educational system first are those with ADD and learning disabilities. (Remember, 33 percent of untreated people with ADD never finish high school.) If you drop out of school first, what behavior are you likely to engage in first? You guessed it: sex. I see a much higher percentage of teenage pregnancies in ADD girls. They do not think through the consequences of their behavior. Also, according to Dr. Comings, ADD women have their first baby on average at the age of twenty. Non-ADD women have their first baby on average at the age of twenty-six. ADD women tend to have more children. Non-ADD women tend to have fewer children.

There is a historical example of how this childbearing dynamic can change a population. I am of Lebanese heritage. Lebanon was first made a country in 1943, but had long-standing roots in the Phoenician culture. At the time, in 1943, the country's population was approximately half Christian and half Muslim. The Lebanese parliament was set up as half Christian and half Muslim to reflect the population. At the time, however, the Christians were better educated than their Muslim counterparts. They tended to stay in school longer. They also tended to have fewer children. Thirty-two years later—in 1975, when civil war broke out in Lebanon—the country was only one-third Christian and two-thirds Muslim. Part of the reason for the civil war was the change in population dynamics. In thirty-two years, a generation and a half, the population showed a dramatic shift.

Let's bring this example closer to home. In 1972, renowned psychologist Thomas Auchenbauch performed a study to determine the incidence of learning and behavioral problems in children among the general population. At the time, using standardized instruments that he developed, he reported that 10 percent of the childhood population had learning or behavioral problems. A generation later, in 1992, he repeated the study using the same psychological instruments on basically the same population. He found a staggering difference: Eighteen percent of the childhood population now met the criteria for learning or behavioral problems. The incidence of problems had nearly doubled in a generation. Why? One reason is that ADD parents are having more ADD children.

SOCIETAL CONTRIBUTIONS TO ADD

There are other factors contributing to the rise of ADD and related problems in our society: an increase in processed foods and lower fat in the diet, excessive television and computer (phone, tablet) time, video games, and decreased exercise. Moreover, we are also better at diagnosing ADD. In addition to having improved psychological assessment tools, ADD has received repeated national exposure over the past twenty years. It has been on the cover of *Time*, *Newsweek*, and *U.S. News & World Report*. Almost all of the talk shows have done repeated programs on ADD, and there have been several national best-selling books. ADD has become part of movies, TV shows, courtroom dramas, and national legislation. We are at least better at thinking about it and talking about it. Over the last twenty years we have seen strong interest in the medical and mental-health community to learn more about ADD and get beyond the myths and the hype of ADD.

As far as excess television is concerned, the research is compelling: Kids who watch the most TV do the worst in school. TV is a "no brain" activity. Everything is provided to the brain (sounds, sights, plots, outcome, entertainment), so it doesn't have to work to learn or make new connections. Like a muscle, the more you use your brain, the stronger it becomes and the more it can do. The opposite is also true: The less you work it, the weaker it becomes. Repeatedly engaging in "no brain" activities, such as TV, decreases a person's ability to focus. In addition, the pacing of TV has changed over the past thirty years. Thirty years ago a thirty-second commercial had ten three-second scenes. The same commercial in 2000 has thirty one-second scenes. We are being programmed to need more stimulation in order to pay attention.

Video games are often another serious problem. I have seen that many ADD children literally become addicted to playing video games. They will play for hours at a time, to the detriment of their responsibilities, and go through tantrums and withdrawal symptoms when forced to stop. A study on brain-imaging and video games was published in the journal *Nature*. In the study, PET scans were taken while a group of people played action video games. The researchers were trying to see where video games worked in the brain. They discovered that the basal ganglia (where the "attention" neurotransmitter dopamine works in the brain) were much more active when the video games were being played than at rest. Both cocaine and Ritalin work in the basal ganglia. Side note: the reason cocaine is highly addictive and prescription stimulants like Ritalin tend not to be is related to how each drug is metabolized. Cocaine has a powerful, immediate effect that stimulates an enormous release of the neurotransmitter dopamine. The pleasure this brings rapidly fades, leaving the desire for more. Ritalin, and other stimulants like Adderall, on the other hand, work more slowly, inducing no high or pleasure in most people and the effects stay around for a longer time. Similarly, video games bring pleasure and focus by increasing dopamine release. The problem with them is that the more dopamine is released, the less neurotransmitter is available later on to do schoolwork, homework, chores, and so on.

Many parents have told me that the more a child or teen plays video games, the worse he does in school and the more irritable he tends to be when asked to stop playing. In a 2011 study, teens who reported five hours or more of video games/Internet daily use had a significantly higher risk for sadness, suicidal thoughts, and planning.

In another study from the Centers for Disease Control it was found that female video-game players reported greater depression and poorer overall health than nonplayers. Male video-game players reported a higher body mass index and more Internet use time overall than male nonplayers.

Another study from Norway found that as computer game playing increased there was a higher prevalence of sleeping problems, depression, suicide ideations, anxiety, obsessions/compulsions, and alcohol/substance abuse. And, in a study published in the journal *Pediatrics*, a two-year study of elementary and high school children in Singapore found that the prevalence of pathological gaming was about 9 percent, similar to other countries. Lower social competence and greater impulsivity seemed to act as risk factors for becoming pathological gamers, whereas depression, anxiety, social phobias, and lower school performance seemed to act as the consequences of excessive gaming.

I saw the negative effects of video games in my own house. Nintendo came into our home when my son was ten years old. Initially, I thought that it was very cool. I never had exciting games like these when I was a child. I was outside playing basketball, baseball, or riding my bike with friends. But over the next few years I saw Antony spending more and more time with the video games and less time on his homework. Moreover, he would become argumentative when he was told to stop playing. I decided that Nintendo had to go. We were all better off without it.

One cannot overlook other aspects of the Internet as a potential source of serious problems for children and ourselves. The Internet is such a valuable source of information, but it is also filled with danger and time wasters. Because of the impulsivity and excitement-seeking nature of many people with ADD, they frequently visit sexually explicit sites, engage in racy conversations with others, and find creative ways to get into trouble. One of my teenage patients thought she fell in love on a dating site. She was seventeen when the story unfolded. She met a man from Louisiana in a chat room. They talked for hours, sent scanned photos, started talking over the telephone, and decided to marry after two months, even though they had never met in person. When I found out about it in therapy, I called a meeting with her parents. When she tried to break it off with this man, he threatened to kill her. We discovered that he had recently gotten out of prison for violent behavior. It's essential that parents supervise time children spend on the Internet and that they put limits over the kinds of sites available. Recent studies have shown that the kids who spend the most time on the Internet have the poorest social skills. Balance and supervision are the biggest keys.

I have become more concerned recently about a child's exposure to how computer and TV screens flash (or refresh themselves). If you look at some computer monitors or television screens through a video camera, you will see black lines quickly roll across the screen. TV and computer screens flash at different speeds, up to thirty flashes or cycles per second. Interestingly, this speed of flashing is similar to a concentration brain state. Your brain gravitates to that rhythm, and you tune in to whatever is drawing your attention—forced focus, so to speak. "Entrainment" is the technical term of this phenomenon: Your brain picks up the rhythm in the environment. So if a light (or TV) flashes at a slow rate, one's brain picks up the slow rate and that person feels sleepy. If it flashes at a fast rate, you may feel energized or anxious. If your brain picks up a concentration flashing rate, you will focus on the TV or computer screen, even though you may not be at all interested in what's on it. Have you ever had the experience of watching TV even though you didn't want to—the feeling of being mesmerized or compelled to watch, even though you were bored with what was on? I have. One example of mass entrainment occurred in late 1997 in Japan. Tens of thousands of Japanese children were watching the top-rated Nintendo cartoon *Pokémon*. During one scene there was an explosion in which red, white, and yellow lights flashed at approximately 4.5 cycles (or flashes) per second for several seconds. All of a sudden kids started to have seizures. Seven hundred and thirty Japanese children went to emergency rooms that night, reporting seizures. Most of the children had never had a seizure before. The 4.5 cycles per second happened to be a seizure frequency. That was a dramatic example, but I wonder what all of this exposure to computer flashing is doing to our children. As far as I know, no one is studying it, and we should be.

Video games and television have led to another major contributor in the rise of ADD in our society: the lack of exercise. Exercise increases blood flow to all parts of the body, including the brain. As kids watch more TV and spend more time exercising only their thumbs with video games, they are becoming more sluggish and less attentive. Through the years I have seen a direct relationship between the level of exercise a person gets and the severity of their symptoms. I have seen a number of ADD professionals (such as physicians and attorneys) get through school by exercising two to four hours a day. I have also noted that when my ADD patients are playing sports, such as basketball, where there is intense aerobic exercise, they do better in school, without any change in their medication. Exercise is important on many levels, and we'll talk more about it later on.

CHAPTER 3

The Amen Clinics Method for Assessing ADD and More

Our largest referral network at the Amen Clinics is from our own patients and their families. Over the last twenty-four years we have seen tens of thousands of patients from all fifty states and ninety-three countries. The reason people come from all over the world for our help is that our process is very different from our colleagues' in mental health. We believe it is essential to thoroughly evaluate a person's life and their brain before developing a treatment plan. "How do you know unless you look?" is a mantra we've been saying for more than two decades.

Our outcomes demonstrate the effectiveness of our method. Beginning in December 2010, we started to study every new patient who walked through our doors. We did our usual thorough assessment, but in addition, gave our patients standard assessment tools we could use in an outcome study, including the Quality of Life Inventory (QOLI), Brief Symptom Inventory (BSI), which measures nine different domains of psychological functioning, and the Beck Depression Inventory-II (BDI-II). We then called our patients at six weeks, three months, and six months after their assessment. At six months, our outcome research director, Melissa Jourdain, re-administered the QOLI, BSI, BDI-II, and asked our patients if they were better (better, same, worse) and how compliant they were (very, somewhat, not at all). We see complex patients. Of the first five hundred patients, on average they had 4.2 different diagnoses, such as ADD, depression, anxiety, and addictions, and they had seen 3.3 mental health or medical providers, and had tried six different medications. This was not an easy group to treat. After six months, 75 percent of our patients had improvements across all measures. Eight-five percent had an improved quality of life. You can read the whole study in the peer reviewed medical journal, *Advances in Mind Body Medicine*.

Here, I am going to give you an outline of our four-step method and help you also apply it to your life if you cannot come to one of our clinics.

Step One: We use our "Amen Clinics Four Circles" approach to get an in-depth understanding of your biological, psychological, social, and spiritual well-being through a detailed clinical history. Understanding the four circles helps us understand each individual we evaluate and it gives us important directions for treatment, which should also be within these four circles.

Step Two: We gather information on how your brain actually functions, through our work with brain SPECT imaging. We generally do two SPECT studies, including one at rest and one when performing a concentration task, typically the Conner's CPT, a fifteen-minute test of attention and impulse control. For those who cannot get scanned we also use the Amen Clinics Brain Type Questionnaire to help predict what the SPECT study might look like. In addition, we have our patients take a computerized neuropsychological assessment to test different aspects of brain function, such as memory, mood, reaction time, and processing speed and efficiency.

Step Three: We measure your important health numbers, such as body mass index, height to waist ratio, and certain lab tests to make sure your body is functioning at its best (your brain and body are totally interconnected). All of this information, taken together, leads to a targeted plan to optimize your brain and your life.

Step Four: We also help you boost your brain's reserve to be able to deal with whatever stresses may come your way in the future.

STEP ONE: AMEN CLINICS FOUR CIRCLES ASSESSMENT: BIOLOGICAL, PSYCHOLOGICAL, SOCIAL, AND SPIRITUAL

When I was a first-year medical student at Oral Roberts University (ORU) in Tulsa, Oklahoma, our dean, Dr. Sid Garrett, gave us one of our first lectures on how to help people of any age for any problem. That

DETAILED CLINICAL ASSESSMENTS

BIOLOGICAL

- Brain health
- Physical health
- Nutrition
- Exercise
- Sleep
- Hydration
- Hormones
- Blood sugar level
- Supplements
- Genetics (family history)
- Trauma/injuries
- Allergies
- Toxins (environment mold, drugs, excessive caffeine, alchohol, smoking)
- Infections
- Physical illness
- Medication

PSYCHOLOGICAL

- Self talk
- Self concept
- Body image
- Upbringing
- Development
- Past emotional trauma
- Generational histories and issues (i.e., immigrants, survivors of trauma, children or grandchildren of alcoholics)
- Past successes
- Past failures
- Grief/loss
- Hope
- Sense of worth
- Sense of power or control

SOCIAL

- Quality of current environment
- Sense of connection to family, friends, and community
- Health habits of friends and family
- Relationships
- Stresses
- Health
- Finances
- Work, school
- Current successes or failures
- Information

SPIRITUAL

- Sense of meaning and purpose
- Why does my life matter?
- Connection to higher power?
- Who am I accountable to?
- Connection to past generations
- Connections to future generations
- Connection to planet
- Morality
- Values

lecture has stayed with me for the last thirty-five years. Dr. Garrett told us, "Always think of people as whole beings, never just as their symptoms." He insisted that whenever we evaluated anyone, we should take into consideration the four circles:

- Biology: how the physical body functions (body)
- Psychology: developmental issues and thought patterns (mind)
- Social: social support and current life situation (connections)
- Spiritual: what life means

At the Amen Clinics we use these four circles to take a balanced, comprehensive approach to assessment and healing. These principles have impacted my own life and career, and once you understand them, they can help you heal in the most balanced way possible.

Biological Factors

The first circle to evaluate is your biology: the physical aspects of your brain and body and how they function together. In order for your biology to operate at peak efficiency, its machinery (cells, connections, chemicals, energy, blood flow, and waste processing) needs to work right. The brain is like a supercomputer, with both hardware and software. Think of your biology as your hardware. Within the biology circle are factors such as your genetics, overall physical health, nutrition, exercise, sleep, and hormones, as well as environmental issues, such as toxins. When the brain's biology is healthy, all of these factors work together in a positive way to maximize your success. When trauma, toxins, illness, or deficiencies affect your biology, you feel disrupted or out of synch and you are more likely to suffer with ADD symptoms.

For example, when you don't get enough sleep, you have overall decreased blood flow to your brain, which disrupts thinking, memory, and concentration. Likewise, a brain injury hurts the machinery of the brain, causing you to struggle with depression, memory issues, and temper problems. When you eat a high sugar or simple carbohydrate diet, your blood sugar often becomes dysregulated, causing you to feel sluggish and foggy-headed.

DETAILED CLINICAL ASSESSMENTS

BIOLOGICAL

- Brain health
- Physical health
- Nutrition
- Exercise
- Sleep
- Hydration
- Hormones
- Blood sugar level
- Supplements
- Genetics (family history)

- Toxins (environment mold, drugs, excessive caffeine, alcohol smoking)
- Infections
- Physical illness
- Medication
- Trauma/injuries
- Allergies

GENETICS

Since ADD tends to run in families, it is important to get a good look at the family, starting with the grandparents, or even farther back if possible, from each side and learning as much as possible about the primary family members.

In the last two decades scientists have made progress in understanding the genetics of ADD. The pioneering works of David Comings, Florence Levy, and others have demonstrated a genetic component to this disorder. Specific gene sites implicated in ADD include the dopamine transporter gene on chromosome 5, and the D4 receptor gene on chromosome 11. Child psychiatrist Florence Levy from Australia found that 81 percent of identical twins (who share identical genetic material) had ADD, while fraternal twins (who have sibling genetic material) share ADD only 29 percent of the time.

Based on both my clinical experience and the medical literature, it is safe to conclude that a very high percentage of ADD is passed down genetically. In my experience, if one parent has ADD, then 60 percent of the offspring will have it as well. If both parents have ADD then 85 to 90 percent of the children will have it. Anyone who does this work over time has no doubt it is a genetic family disorder and that contributes to the high incidence of family dysfunction in ADD households. There are often multiple challenging people in an ADD family, not just one challenging child.

HEAD INJURY

I have also seen other factors involved in causing ADD. One of the most common is unrecognized head injury, especially to the front part of the brain. In my experience, many professionals and parents discount or ignore the impact of head injuries. They think that a person needs to have a significant loss of consciousness for a prolonged period of time in order for it to do damage. Our brain imaging work, as well as the work of others, is disproving this notion. More on head injuries in Chapter 13.

LACK OF OXYGEN OR TOXIC EXPOSURE

When the brain is exposed to a lack of oxygen or some toxic substance, it is much more likely to show symptoms of ADD. Lack of oxygen can happen with premature babies who have underdeveloped lungs, babies born with the cord wrapped tightly around their necks, and individuals after a drowning accident. Lack of oxygen causes a decrease in overall brain activity. Brain infections, such as meningitis or encephalitis, cause toxic inflammation in the brain and damage tissue. Clearly, fetal exposure to drugs, alcohol, and cigarettes also puts a child at risk for ADD and learning disabilities. Often mothers who use these substances during pregnancy are medicating their own struggles with depression, ADD, or anxiety. The babies inherit vulnerabilities to these problems and in addition experience toxicity to their brains.

In addition, exposure to pesticides, lead, mercury, mold, intrauterine smoking, and other toxins have been associated with ADD. This is very important to understand and evaluate, as the treatment response is generally poorer with a brain exposed to these toxins, and a different approach is often warranted.

MEDICAL PROBLEMS, MEDICATIONS

Certain medical problems, such as thyroid disease, can look like ADD. An overactive thyroid gland may look like Type 1 ADD (feeling hyperactive and inattentive), while an underactive thyroid may look like Type 2 ADD (feeling lethargic and inattentive) or Type 5 Limbic ADD (sad, lethargic, and unfocused). Likewise, certain medications, such as asthma medications, can make people feel and look hyperactive and inattentive. It is important for your doctor to assess the impact of medical problems on behavior.

HORMONAL INFLUENCES

Hormonal influences play a major role in ADD. ADD symptoms are generally worse around the time of puberty in both males and females. In females, ADD symptoms are also exacerbated in the premenstrual period and also around the time of menopause. A number of SPECT studies have shown an overall decrease in brain activity when estrogen levels are low. During perimenopause or menopause, many women who had only mild ADD before now look as if they have major ADD symptoms. Bio-identical estrogen replacement appears to have a positive effect on brain function.

DRUG ABUSE

It is key to assess for drug abuse when evaluating ADD. While ADD and drug abuse commonly occur together, drug abuse can masquerade as ADD. New onset ADD symptoms at the age of fourteen, for example, may signal marijuana abuse. Many drug abusers are not honest (due to feelings of shame or the fear of being found out), so I will frequently order a drug screen to be sure.

Drug screens are not foolproof, but I have found that just the act of ordering the drug screen is helpful. I generally say something like "I want to order a drug screen on you. I know you said that you weren't using drugs, but people who do use drugs often won't admit to it. I want to do a thorough evaluation of you and just want to make sure." If a person says, "I don't believe in drug screens. They are not reliable. I won't do it," that is generally a good indicator that he or she is using drugs. If he or she says, "No problem, I understand," and willingly goes for the test, then it is generally a sign drug abuse is less likely. Of course, I have been fooled, so even if the patient agrees, I send the specimen to the lab.

POOR DIET

In the last thirty years our diet has changed dramatically. These days, children eat a diet high in simple carbohydrates (sugar, white bread, white-flour food products), poor in protein and healthy fat, and positively deficient in vegetables. Think about the great American breakfast. Morning time is often rushed especially when both parents work outside the home, and there is less time to fix a nutritious breakfast. Kids eat Pop-Tarts, sugar cereals, donuts, frozen waffles, pancakes, or muffins. Gone are the days of sausage and eggs (protein), and sugar is in. Try to find bread in the store without sugar or forms of sugar (corn syrup, high-fructose syrup, etc.). In my local supermarket, only one out of about thirty brands of bread available—a dark Russian rye bread—is made without any sugar. Your diet provides the fuel for the brain's work. I have found that a diet high in simple carbohydrates makes attentional problems worse, especially for people vulnerable to ADD. Most ADD children and adults simply do better on a high-protein, low–simple-carbohydrate diet (much more on this later). A lack of protein causes a tremendous problem with focus throughout the day. If a person is vulnerable to ADD, a high-carbohydrate, low-protein diet typically makes their symptoms worse.

LACK OF EXERCISE

Exercise boosts blood flow to the brain. Unfortunately, children and teens get much less exercise than they did thirty years ago. With the advent of video and computer games children are spending more time indoors, doing activities which require little exertion. A sedentary lifestyle makes someone more prone to exhibit ADD symptoms. A study published in the journal *Pediatrics* showed that for every hour of TV a child watches each day—regardless of the content—the risk of having attention problems by age seven goes up 10 percent.

Psychological Factors

Psychological factors fall into the second circle. This includes how we think and talk to ourselves, the running dialogue that goes on in our minds, as well as our self-concept, body image, past traumas, overall upbringing, and significant developmental events. Being raised in a reasonably happy home, getting positive messages growing up, and feeling comfortable with our abilities and our bodies all contribute to psychological health. When we struggle in any of these areas, we are less likely to be successful. If we perceive ourselves as unattractive or less able than our peers, trouble starts to brew. If our thinking patterns are excessively negative, harsh, or critical, that will have a negative impact on our moods, anxiety levels, and ultimately on our ability to focus.

Developmental issues, such as being adopted or experiencing a significant loss or trauma as a child, are also significant. Children often believe that they are the center of the universe and so if something bad

DETAILED CLINICAL ASSESSMENTS

PSYCHOLOGICAL

- Self talk
- Self concept
- Body image
- Upbringing
- Development
- Past emotional trauma
- Past successes
- Past failures
- Grief/loss
- Hope

- Generational histories and issues (i.e., immigrants, survivors of trauma, children or grandchildren of alcoholics)
- Sense of worth
- Sense of power or control

happens, such as if a mother gets cancer, a child may think it is her fault and spend the rest of her life racked with guilt. Past successes and failures are a part of this circle, as are hope and a sense of worth and personal power or control.

If children with ADD are not diagnosed or treated by the age of nine or so, they often experience significant psychological issues, related to feelings of inadequacy, insecurity, and even self-hatred. Many ADD kids have been in trouble every day of their lives, because of their issues with restlessness and impulse control.

EARLY NEGLECT AND ABUSE

Both physical and emotional neglect and abuse contribute to ADD. The brain needs nurturing and appropriate stimulation to develop properly. When a baby is neglected or abused, the brain cannot develop properly and is put at great risk for learning and behavioral problems. An extreme example of neglect occurred during the late 1980s when thousands of Romanian orphans were raised without affection, touching, or nurturing, even though they had food. We have seen hundreds of these children at our clinics. Many of them have developed severe emotional, learning, and behavioral problems. Brain scans showed one of two patterns with these children: 1) overall decreased activity in their brains; without appropriate stimulation, the brain does not make the connections it needs to thrive, 2) overall increased activity, where the brain looks inflamed, either because the immune system is impaired or another insult occurred. Emotional or physical abuse causes a rush of stress hormones and chemicals that poison a baby's or child's brain. Stress hormones damage the memory centers, and chronic stress causes the brain to become hyperalert, leading to severe distractibility and an inability to filter out extraneous stimuli.

NEGATIVE SELF-TALK

Low self-esteem, self-doubt, and a lack of confidence can make some look as if they have ADD. Of course, having ADD makes one more prone to these problems. Negative self-talk often stems from having people talk in a negative way toward you. Type 5: Limbic ADD is often associated with excessive negativity.

LEARNED HELPLESSNESS

Psychologist Martin Seligman coined the term "learned helplessness" to describe what he saw in depressed patients. I often see this phenomenon in people with ADD. Learned helplessness occurs when a person tries to do something important, such as study for school, but performs poorly. Then she tries again, but it doesn't work. She tries yet another time, but it still doesn't work. Finally she gives up. This demoralization contributes heavily to ADD symptoms and, after a while, causes many people with ADD to give up trying.

The Social Circle

The social circle is the next step in a complete evaluation. It includes the current relationships and events in our lives. When we are in good relationships, experience good health, have a job we love, school we care about, and enough money, our brain tends to do much better than when

DETAILED CLINICAL ASSESSMENTS

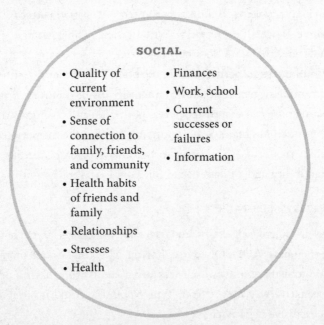

SOCIAL

- Quality of current environment
- Sense of connection to family, friends, and community
- Health habits of friends and family
- Relationships
- Stresses
- Health
- Finances
- Work, school
- Current successes or failures
- Information

any of these areas stress or trouble us. Stress negatively impacts brain function, and dealing with difficult events makes us more vulnerable to illness. Depression is often triggered by current stressful life events, such as school failure, marital problems, family dysfunction, financial difficulties, health problems, work-related struggles, or losses. Plus, the health and habits of the people you spend time with has a dramatic impact on your own health and habits.

In ADD families, the health habits of others are often not the best, because of the impulsivity that is often associated with it. There is a higher incidence of alcohol and drug abuse, smoking, and lifestyle illnesses like diabetes, hypertension, heart disease, and obesity. This is one of the reasons at the Amen Clinics we believe it is essential to evaluate everyone in the family who may have ADD.

SOCIAL SITUATION

Evaluating the current family and social situation is essential to get a complete picture of a person. Who is she living with? What are the relationships like? How is the financial health of the family? Are there any physical or emotional challenges? Is there alcohol or drug abuse in the home?

The Spiritual Circle

Beyond the biological, psychological, and social aspects of our lives, we are also spiritual beings. To fully heal and be your best, it is important to recognize that we are more than just our bodies, minds, brains, and social connections, and we must ask ourselves deep spiritual questions, such as:

What does my life mean?
What is my purpose?
Why am I here?
What are my values?
Do I believe in God or a Higher Power?
How does that manifest in my life?
What is my connection to past generations, future generations, and the
    planet?

DETAILED CLINICAL ASSESSMENTS

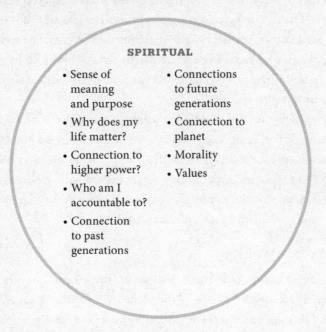

SPIRITUAL

- Sense of
  meaning
  and purpose
- Why does my
  life matter?
- Connection to
  higher power?
- Who am I
  accountable to?
- Connection
  to past
  generations

- Connections
  to future
  generations
- Connection to
  planet
- Morality
- Values

Having a sense of purpose, as well as connections to past and future generations, allows us to reach beyond ourselves to affirm that our lives matter. Without a spiritual connection, many people experience an overriding sense of despair. Morality, values, and a spiritual connection to others and the universe are critical for many people to feel a sense of wholeness and connection, and a reason to get up in the morning and to take good care of themselves.

This is especially important for people with ADD. When they are in a job they love, or learning from a teacher they love, or living a life with meaning and purpose, their attention span and judgment seem better. Love is a drug. Research studies have shown that romantic love works in the same part of the brain as cocaine and Ritalin, boosting dopamine availability. In my experience, when my ADD patients have a deep sense of meaning, purpose, love, and passion for their lives, they are much more able to be successful. In counseling, I talk to my ADD patients about choosing jobs, partners, life missions that give them this deep sense of meaning and purpose. It just seems to work out so much better than choosing to be an accountant for the money when you really wanted to be a writer. Of course, one has to be reasonable with passion—if you cannot support yourself or your family with the job you love, adjustments likely will be needed.

STEP TWO: GET YOUR BRAIN ASSESSED

You can do a great job doing a "Four Circles" assessment and still not fully optimize your brain. You also need to understand how your brain functions. At the Amen Clinics, we have three ways to evaluate brain function:

- Brain SPECT imaging
- Questionnaires
- Online neuropsychological assessments

Brain SPECT Imaging

As mentioned, at the Amen Clinics, we do a study called brain SPECT imaging, which looks at blood flow and activity patterns. SPECT gives a direct look at how the brain works.

In a scientific study we published last year, we found that getting a SPECT scan changed either the diagnosis or treatment plan in nearly eight out of ten patients. Having a scan helps us see more clearly what is happening in the brain that may be the cause of someone's emotional and cognitive struggles, such as when the brain works too hard, not hard enough, or if it has patterns consistent with brain trauma or toxic exposure.

SPECT scans also help us see someone's strengths and vulnerabilities. For example, if someone has a tendency toward impulse control problems, we are more likely to see low activity in the front part of the brain, called the prefrontal cortex. If he tends to be rigid and inflexible, we often see increased activity in an area of the frontal part of the brain called the anterior cingulate gyrus. Researchers from Japan found that brain blood flow in certain areas of the brain was positively correlated with both intelligence and creativity. Protecting the brain's blood flow is critical to having a healthy mind.

Besides helping us make more complete diagnoses, SPECT helps lead us to direct treatment in the context of a Bio/Psycho/Social/Spiritual Assessment. Without a scan or another measure of brain function, it is like throwing medicated-tipped darts in the dark at someone's brain.

At amenclinics.com you can see hundreds of brain SPECT scans and read over 2,800 scientific abstracts on SPECT for a wide variety of behavioral, mood, learning, and mental health issues. In the next chapter I will discuss our work with SPECT and ADD in detail.

Amen Clinics Brain Type Questionnaire

A long time ago I realized not everyone can get a scan, either because of cost or a lack of availability in your area. My books are translated into thirty languages, so if you read one in China or Brazil, odds are you're not going to come to get a scan. So, based on thousands of scans, I developed a series of questionnaires to help people predict what their scans might look like if they could get one. The questionnaires are not as effective as getting the scans, especially when there are complex issues, but many people find them very helpful and they are used by thousands of mental health professionals around the world. Chapter 5 will explain how you can take "Amen Clinics ADD Type Questionnaire" on our website amenclinics.com/healingADDquestionnaire. Based on your answers, we give targeted recommendations, including science-based natural ways to boost the brain. Of course, it is important to talk to your health care provider about any recommendations.

24/7 Brain Gym Assessment

On our coaching website, BrainFit Life, at www.mybrainfitlife.com, we have a 24/7 Brain Gym, where you can test and work out your brain at any time. It starts with a sophisticated thirty-minute computerized assessment to determine the health of your brain. It measures mood, attention span, impulse control, memory, reaction time, and more. This is the same computerized neuropsychological test we use for assessments at the Amen Clinics. Based on your score, the program will give you exercises tailored to enhance your specific brain. Spending ten minutes a day in the 24/7 Brain Gym is a great way to optimize your brain.

STEP THREE: KNOW YOUR IMPORTANT NUMBERS

Another very important part of our assessment program is to know your important health numbers. You cannot change what you do not measure. Here is the list of the key numbers you should know about yourself:

1. BMI
2. Waist to Height Ratio
3. Average hours slept each night, and an assessment of whether you have sleep apnea
4. Blood pressure

1. BMI. BMI stands for "Body Mass Index," a measure of your weight compared to your height. A normal BMI is between 18.5 and 25. Overweight is between 25 and 30, while obese is greater than 30. You can find a simple BMI calculator on the web. Knowing your BMI is important because being overweight or obese has been associated with less brain tissue and lower brain activity, and recently ADD has been associated with obesity, and it is not an association you want to keep. Plus, obesity doubles the risk for Alzheimer's disease and depression. There are probably several mechanisms that create this result, including the fact that fat cells produce inflammatory chemicals and store toxic materials in the body. I want you to know your BMI, because it stops you from lying to yourself about your weight.

2. Waist to Height Ratio (WHtR). Another way to measure the health of your weight is the "waist-to-height ratio." Some researchers believe this number is even more accurate than BMI. The WHtR is calculated by dividing waist size by height. For an example, a female with a 32-inch waist who is 5 feet, 10 inches (70 inches) would divide 32 by 70 to get a WHtR of 45.7 percent. To be healthy your waist size in inches should be less than half your height. So, if you are 66 inches tall, your waist should not be more than 33 inches. If you are 72 inches tall, your waist should not be more than 36 inches.

The WHtR is thought to give a more accurate assessment of health since the most dangerous place to carry weight is in the abdomen. Fat in the abdomen, which is associated with a larger waist, is metabolically active and produces various hormones that can cause harmful effects, such as diabetes, elevated blood pressure, and high cholesterol and triglyceride levels. You have to actually measure your waist size with a tape measure! Going by your pants size does not count, as many clothing manufacturers actually make their sizes larger than they state on the label so as not to offend their customers. In my experience, 90 percent of people will underestimate their waist circumference. Don't lie to yourself.

3. The number of hours you sleep a night. One of the fastest ways to hurt your brain is to get less than seven or eight hours of sleep at night. People who typically get six hours of sleep or less have lower overall blood flow to the brain, which hurts its function. Researchers from the Walter Reed Army Institute of Research and the University of Pennsylvania found that chronically getting less than eight hours of sleep was associated with cognitive decline. Strive to get seven to eight hours a night. There are hypnosis audios to help you sleep on The Amen Solution website. Chronic insomnia triples your risk of death from all causes and is a common problem with people who have ADD.

4. Blood pressure. To keep your brain healthy, it is critical to know your blood pressure. High blood pressure is associated with lower overall brain function, which means more bad decisions. Here are the numbers you should know:

Below 120 over 80: optimal
120 to 139 over 80 to 89: prehypertension
140 (or above) over 90 (or above): hypertension

Check your blood pressure or have your doctor check it on a regular basis. If your blood pressure is high, make sure to take it seriously. Some behaviors that can help lower your blood pressure include losing weight, daily exercise, fish oil supplements, and, if needed, medication.

Get Key Laboratory Tests

Laboratory tests are the next set of important numbers to know. Here are the key lab test numbers you need to know:

- Vitamin D, zinc, and ferritin
- CBC
- General metabolic panel with fasting blood sugar and lipid panel
- Thyroid panel
- C-reactive protein
- Free and total serum testosterone (for adults)

These can be ordered by your health-care professional, or you can order them for yourself at websites, such as www.saveonlabs.com.

1. Vitamin D, zinc, and ferritin (blood test). ADD is thought of as a lack of dopamine being released from brain cells to help nerve cell communication. Inadequate amounts of or poor messages from dopamine are felt to lead to the difficulties with inattention, hyperactivity, and impulsiveness. Many of the medications for ADD are thought to slow the body's recycling of dopamine between neurons, and make more dopamine available for use. One step that limits the amount of dopamine that is made by cells is controlled by a protein (called an enzyme) called tyrosine hydroxylase. One thing tyrosine hydroxylase needs to function well is enough iron. Approximately 80 percent of the global population is iron deficient. Another thing needed to encourage DNA to make the tyrosine hydroxylase protein is vitamin D. In northern climates, vitamin D deficiency is being considered an epidemic. In addition, zinc is needed to help vitamin D bind to DNA and prompt production of the tyrosine hydroxylase protein. Vitamin D deficiency also leads to a lack of absorption of calcium, iron, and zinc.

Testing your ferritin level (the earliest indicator of low iron), vitamin D 25-OH level (the best indicator of vitamin D status), and plasma zinc is an important first step. If you or your child's levels are lower than high average, then they need to be improved (ferritin target of 100ng/ml, vitamin D target of 80ng/ml, and plasma zinc target of 100mcg/dl). Vitamin B6 daily may also be helpful.

2. CBC (Complete Blood Count, blood test). This test checks the health of your blood, including red and white blood cells. People with low blood count can feel anxious and tired, and they can have significant memory problems.

3. General metabolic panel with fasting blood sugar and lipid panel (blood test). This test checks the health of your liver, kidneys, fasting blood sugar, cholesterol, and triglycerides. Fasting blood sugar is especially important. Normal is between 70 to 90mg/dl; prediabetes is between 91 to 125mg/dl; and diabetes is 126mg/dl or higher. According to a large study from Kaiser Permanente, for every point above 85 patients had an additional 6 percent increased risk of developing diabetes in the next 10 years (86 = 6 percent increased risk, 87 = 12 percent increased risk, 88 = 18 percent increased risk, etc.). Above 90 there was already vascular damage and at risk for having damage to kidneys and eyes.

Why is high fasting blood sugar a problem? High blood sugar causes vascular problems throughout your whole body, including your brain. Over time, it causes blood vessels to be brittle and vulnerable to breakage. It leads not only to diabetes, but heart disease, strokes, visual impairment, impaired wound healing, wrinkled skin, and cognitive problems. Diabetes doubles the risk for Alzheimer's disease.

Cholesterol and triglycerides are also important. Sixty percent of the solid weight of the brain is fat. High cholesterol is obviously bad for the brain, but having it too low is also bad, as some cholesterol is essential to make sex hormones and help the brain function properly. According to the American Heart Association, optimal levels are as follows:

- Total Cholesterol 135 to 200 mg/dl, below 135 has been associated with depression
- HDL >= 60 mg/dl
- LDL <100 mg/dl
- Triglycerides <100 mg/dl

If your lipids are off, make sure to get your diet under control, as well as taking fish oil and exercising regularly. Of course you should see your physician. Also, knowing the particle size of LDL cholesterol is important. Large particles are less toxic than smaller particles.

4. Thyroid panel (blood test). Abnormal thyroid hormone levels are a common cause of anxiety, depression, forgetfulness, confusion, and lethargy, and have been associated with ADD. Having low thyroid levels decreases overall brain activity, which can impair your thinking, judgment, and self-control, and make it very hard for you to feel good. Low thyroid functioning can make it nearly impossible to manage weight effectively. To know your thyroid levels, you need to know these figures:

- TSH (thyroid stimulating hormone)
- Free T3
- Free T4
- Thyroid antibodies (thyroid peroxidase and thyroglobulin antibodies)

There is no one perfect way, no one symptom or test result, that will properly diagnose low thyroid function or hypothyroidism. The key is to look at your symptoms and your blood tests, and then decide. Symptoms of low thyroid include fatigue; depression; mental fog; dry skin; hair loss, especially the outer third of your eyebrows; feeling cold when others feel normal, constipation; hoarse voice; and weight gain. Most doctors do not check thyroid antibodies unless the TSH is high. This is a big mistake. Many people have autoimmunity against their thyroid, which makes it function poorly, even while they still have a "normal" TSH. That's why I think measuring the antibodies should also be part of routine screening.

5. C-reactive protein (CRP, blood test). This is a measure of inflammation. Elevated inflammation is associated with a number of diseases and conditions that are associated with mood problems, aging, and cognitive impairment. Fat cells produce chemicals that increase inflammation. A healthy range is between (0.0 to 1.0 mg/dl). This is a very good test for inflammation. It measures the general level of inflammation although it does not tell you what has caused this condition.

The most common reason for an elevated C-reactive protein is a poor diet. The second most common is some sort of reaction to food, either a true allergy, a food sensitivity, or an autoimmune reaction such as occurs with gluten. High CRP levels can also indicate hidden infections.

6. Free and total serum testosterone for adults (blood test). For both men and women, low levels of testosterone have been associated with low energy, trouble focusing, cardiovascular disease, obesity, low libido, depression, and Alzheimer's disease.

Amen Clinics Four Circles Treatment: Biological, Psychological, Social, and Spiritual

Once you know the Four Circles, how your brain works, and your important numbers, treatment is directed toward optimizing the Four Circles:

- Biological interventions may include diet, exercise, supplementation, medication, neurofeedback, sleep apnea evaluations and treatment, and strategies like detoxification if needed.
- Psychological strategies may include different forms of psychotherapy, including cognitive therapy, hypnosis, meditation, interpersonal psychotherapy, and dealing with past traumas or other emotional issues. Building a sense of competence and hope can also be important here.
- Social interventions may include appropriate school or work accommodations, parent training, and social skills training.
- Spiritual interventions include an in-depth conversation on what life means, why you are here, and major life goals. In addition, it may also include discovering connections to past and future generations and the planet.

STEP FOUR: BRAIN RESERVE

The last step in the Amen Method is to always work to boost your "brain's reserve." I coined this term after looking at tens of thousands of scans. Brain reserve is the extra cushion of brain function you have to deal with whatever stresses come your way. The more reserve you have, the better you can cope with stress, loss, hormonal swings, and aging.

Have you ever wondered why two people can be in exactly the same car accident and experienced the same impact and one person walks away unharmed, while the other has serious cognitive or emotional problems. In large part it's due to how much brain reserve they had *before* the accident. Brain reserve starts before you're even born. When you were conceived, if your mother ate well, took her vitamins, and wasn't under a lot of stress, she was building your reserve. But, if she drank, smoked, or ate poorly, you likely started with less reserve. In the same way, throughout the rest of your life you are either building or depleting your reserve. Being raised in a loving, stable, healthy environment strengthened your reserve, while getting a concussion from playing contact sports or being chronically stressed or fed junk food drains your reserve. And, unfortunately, as we age, the brain becomes less and less active, making you more vulnerable to problems. By the time you have symptoms, your reserve is gone and your brain is struggling. But the really good news is . . . that no matter what your age . . . you can boost your reserve and make your brain look and feel younger.

You boost brain reserve by putting three strategies to work in your life.

1. Brain envy. You have to truly want to have a better brain.
2. Avoid anything that hurts your brain: Drugs, alcohol, environmental toxins, obesity, hypertension, diabetes, heart disease, sleep apnea, depression, negative thinking patterns, excessive stress, and a lack of exercise or new learning.
3. Consistently do good behaviors that help your brain: A great diet, new learning, exercise, accurate thinking habits, stress management, and some simple supplements to nourish your brain.

To be at your best it is critical to put all of these pieces into place. Knowing and optimizing your Four Circles, testing and optimizing your brain, knowing and optimizing your important numbers, and boosting your brain's reserve.

This is the approach that we use at the Amen Clinics that has brought us our success. I hope it helps you too.

OTHER THINGS TO LOOK FOR IN ASSESSING ADD

When ADD is present, these other problems should also be evaluated. Sometimes these problems are misdiagnosed as ADD, sometimes they occur with ADD.

Psychiatric/Adjustment Problems: Emotional and adjustment problems can masquerade as ADD, be a result of ADD, or occur together with ADD. Here are samples of the problems:

Adjustment Disorders or Family Problems: Temporarily, family problems or significant stress can cause a person of any age to have problems with concentration or restlessness. The difference between stress and ADD is history and duration of the difficulties. ADD is a long-standing problem that is relatively constant over time. The stress of long-term family problems can cause a child to look as though he or she has ADD. It must be determined, however, whether or not the serious family problems are a result of ADD in one or more of the family members.

Behavioral Problems Not Related to ADD: Some behavior problems have nothing to do with ADD. When parents have ineffective parenting skills, they can actually encourage difficult behavior in their children.

Depression: Depression may be confused with ADD, especially in children. Depressive symptoms include poor memory, low energy, negativity, periods of helplessness and hopelessness, social isolation, along with sleep and appetite changes. Many of these symptoms are also found in ADD. History is the key to proper diagnosis. ADD symptoms are generally constant over time, while depression tends to fluctuate. Many people with ADD experience demoralization (from chronic failure) and may indeed look depressed when ADD is the primary problem. Depression and ADD often occur together.

Manic-Depressive Disorder: Manic-depressive or "bipolar" symptoms may be similar to ADD. Both experience restless, excessive talkativeness, hyperactivity, racing thoughts, and impulsivity. The difference is usually found in the severity, consistency, and course of the symptoms. ADD remains constant; bipolar disorder fluctuates from highs to lows. People who have ADD are consistently distractible, restless, and impulsive. People with bipolar disorder will have periods of those symptoms, but they often fluctuate with depressive episodes and periods of relative calm or normalcy. The manic highs of bipolar disorder are not experienced by people with ADD.

Anxiety Disorders: Anxiety disorders can also present similar symptoms to ADD, including restlessness, hyperactivity, forgetfulness, and an inability to concentrate. Again, the key to proper diagnosis is history. As with depression and bipolar disorder, anxiety disorders tend to fluctuate; ADD symptoms are generally constant. Moreover, having ADD can breed symptoms of anxiety or nervousness. When your mind turns off in the face of stress, it can cause nervousness and fear in work, family, and social situations. It is common for people with ADD to experience significant anxiety from underachievement. These disorders also commonly run together.

Obsessive-Compulsive Disorder (OCD): OCD is marked by a person with obsessions (repetitive negative thoughts) and/or compulsions (repetitive negative behaviors), which interfere with their lives. People with OCD get "stuck" or "locked in" to negative thoughts or behaviors. In my clinical experience, there is a high percentage of people with ADD who also have features of OCD, especially if there is significant alcohol abuse in their family backgrounds. The overfocused subtype of ADD has many features in common with OCD, except serotonin enhancing supplements or medications by themselves often make Overfocused ADD worse. This type of ADD needs both serotonin and dopamine interventions.

Tic Disorders, Such as Tourette's Syndrome: Tic disorders are more common among people with ADD. Tics are abnormal, involuntary motor movements (blinking, shoulder shrugging, head jerking), or vocal sounds (throat clearing, coughing, blowing, and even swearing). Tourette's syndrome occurs when there are both motor and vocal tics that have been present for more than a year. Up to 60 percent of people who have Tourette's also have ADD, and 40 to 50 percent of people with Tourette's have OCD. There is a significant connection between ADD, OCD, and Tourette's.

History of Physical, Emotional, or Sexual Abuse: Abuse in any form can cause learning and behavior problems. Certainly they can also occur together. Many clinicians see an increased incidence of abuse occurring in families with ADD. The increased level of frustration, impulse control problems, and anger found in ADD families causes them to be more at risk. An accurate, detailed history is necessary to distinguish between abuse and ADD. People who have been abused present more clearly symptoms of post-traumatic stress disorder (PTSD), such as nightmares, fearfulness, a tendency to startle easily, flashbacks, feelings of numbness or emotional restriction. Yet, many people who have ADD feel they have a form of PTSD from the chronic dysfunction they have experienced.

Medical Factors: Medical factors also need to be considered in fully evaluating ADD:

- Gestational problems, such as maternal smoking or alcohol, or drug use during pregnancy
- Birth traumas, such as oxygen deprivation or injury
- History of head trauma
- Seizure disorders
- Physical illness/disease, such as thyroid disease or lead exposure
- Severe allergies to environmental toxins or food
- Medications, such as asthma medications.

Learning/Developmental Problems: Learning disabilities occur in approximately 40 percent of people with ADD. Suspect the diagnosis of a learning disability whenever there is long-standing underachievement in school or at work. Medical evaluation and history, family and school history, and clinical observation best evaluate these disabilities. The diagnosis is confirmed by "psychoeducational" testing.

Psychoeducational testing evaluates three areas:

1. IQ and cognitive style (look for discrepancies between verbal and performance scores)
2. level of academic skill (standard achievement tests)
3. evidence of specific learning disabilities or problems (such as auditory processing, reading, writing, social skills).

TREATMENT FOR LEARNING DISABILITIES

The specific treatments for learning disabilities are beyond the scope of the book. When they occur, it is important for the school system to assist with an assessment for special services or special education to evaluate the need for alternative learning strategies and academic accommodations.

CHAPTER 4

Looking into the ADD Brain and the Discovery of the ADD Types

My path to looking into the brain started in an unlikely place: at a military hospital in the middle of nowhere. I did my psychiatric training at the Walter Reed Army Medical Center, now renamed Walter Reed National Medical Center in Washington, D.C. I had been an infantry medic in the early 1970s during the Vietnam War and the GI Bill helped to support me through college and medical school. Walter Reed was the premier military hospital in the world, responsible for the medical care of soldiers, family members, and international political figures. After three years at Walter Reed, I went to Honolulu, Hawaii, to do a child and adolescent psychiatry fellowship at Tripler Army Medical Center. Military training was very practical. Learning about combat psychiatry and taking care of soldiers and their families in times of crises did not leave one with the inclination to become married to any particular psychiatric dogma or tradition. We learned to use what worked, what was helpful, what made a difference—right then and there.

After my formal specialty training in psychiatry, I was stationed at Fort Irwin, forty miles north of Barstow, in California's Mojave Desert. Halfway between Los Angeles and Las Vegas, Fort Irwin was also known as the National Training Center—the place where American soldiers were taught to fight the Russians (and later the Iraqis) in the desert. At the time, I was the only psychiatrist for four thousand soldiers and an equal number of family members. It was considered an isolated assignment. There were problems with domestic violence, drug abuse (especially amphetamine abuse), depression, and ailments resulting from the stress of living in the middle of nowhere. I dealt with many people who suffered from headaches, anxiety attacks, insomnia, and excessive muscle tension.

Shortly after arriving at Fort Irwin, I went through the cabinets in the community mental health clinic to see what instruments and psychological tests my predecessors had left behind. To my delight, there was an old Autogen biofeedback apparatus that measured hand temperature. There was one lecture on biofeedback during my psychiatric training. The concept of biofeedback is fascinating: If you get feedback on the physiological processes in your body, such as hand temperature or heart rate, you can learn to change them through mental exercise and discipline. The problem with biofeedback, as I knew it at that time, was that the training was boring. The needles and dials on the machines were not interesting to patients. Nonetheless, the old machine was dusted off and we used it with patients who had migraine headaches. I taught them how to warm their hands, using only their imagination. It was fascinating to see how patients could actually warm their hand temperature, sometimes as much as 15 to 20 degrees. Temperature training taught patients how to participate in their own healing process.

In late 1987, six months after coming to Fort Irwin, I wrote a request to Colonel Knowles, our hospital commander, to buy the mental health clinic thirty thousand dollars' worth of the latest computerized biofeedback equipment, including ten days of training for me in San Francisco. He laughed at me: He said that the Army didn't have the money (this was at a time when they were spending six hundred dollars on hammers and toilet seats) and that when my assignment at Fort Irwin was over, the equipment would just end up in a closet somewhere, much like the equipment I had found. I dropped the idea but continued using the old temperature trainer. In May 1988, Colonel Knowles called me into his office. He asked if I had kept a copy of the biofeedback proposal. When I said yes, he authorized its funding. In the Army at the time if a unit did not spend its entire annual budget in one year, they lost the unspent portion the next year. We had money left over, and the colonel wanted to make sure he spent it all. I was very excited: Great new equipment, and ten days in San Francisco!

The biofeedback training course in San Francisco changed my life. It was the most stimulating and intense learning experience I had as a physician. The ten-hour days went by in a flash. The new computerized biofeedback equipment was patient-friendly, interesting, and easy to learn. I learned how to help people relax their muscles, warm their hands (much faster than with the old equipment), calm sweat-gland activity, lower blood pressure, slow their own heart rates, and breathe in ways that promoted relaxation.

The lectures on brain wave biofeedback were the most amazing. I was taught that people can learn how to change their own brain wave patterns. What an exciting concept, being able to change your own mental state! I also learned about Dr. Joel Lubar's research at the University of Tennessee on brain wave underactivity in children with ADD. In published research using quantitative electroencephalograms (qEEGs), Dr. Lubar demonstrated that ADD children had excessive slow brain wave activity in the front part of their brain, which worsened when they tried to concentrate. This diminished activity, when compared to a group of people without ADD, made perfect sense to me. Psychostimulants, such as Dexedrine and Ritalin, were the treatment of choice for calming hyperactive children and helping them concentrate. I was taught that these medications exerted a "paradoxical effect": a stimulant calming down a hyperactive child. Understanding Dr. Lubar's research meant that psychostimulants probably corrected the underactivity in the ADD brain—not a paradoxical effect, but rather a direct effect: stimulating the brain's frontal lobe so that the brain could calm and focus the person.

Dr. Lubar's work gave me a critical insight: the importance of looking at the brain in different thought states. He studied people with ADD at rest and while they were doing concentration tasks. After all, people with ADD have problems when they try to concentrate, not when they are at rest.

Dr. Lubar also demonstrated that many children can develop more normal brain wave patterns (and therefore improved focus and behavior) through brain wave biofeedback, also called neurofeedback. In brain wave biofeedback, electrodes are placed on the scalp and connected to computerized biofeedback equipment. The computer screen shows the patient his or her own moment-by-moment brain wave patterns. By knowing these patterns, many patients can learn to change them to more normal, more focused patterns. When I first heard this I was interested, but very skeptical: How can you change your brain? I started talking to other clinicians around the country doing this work who were getting exciting results. Why not change your brain? After all, if you can warm hand temperature by 20 degrees, why can't you increase the amount of focused brain wave activity?

When I returned to Fort Irwin, I tried everything I had learned. I did biofeedback on almost all of the patients who came to see me. I loved it. My patients loved it. I also spent time each day doing it myself. I became a master at breathing with my diaphragm. I could slow my heart rate. And I could even warm my own hands over 15 degrees whenever I felt stressed. I also started to evaluate ADD children with EEG measures. Many of them, although certainly not all, demonstrated the same patterns that Dr. Lubar had written about. Many of them benefited from biofeedback training. I had to learn more.

In 1989 my commitment to the U.S. Army ended and I started a private practice in Fairfield, California. I bought my own biofeedback equipment and continued using it in clinical practice. Also, I became the medical director of the dual diagnosis unit (where patients had both substance abuse and psychiatric problems) at a local psychiatric hospital. I instituted the use of biofeedback throughout the hospital. My interest in biofeedback and evaluating brain function in ADD patients grew each year. In late 1990 and early 1991 it exploded.

In October 1990, Alan Zametkin, M.D., of the National Institutes of Health published an article in the New England Journal of Medicine on brain PET (positron emission tomography) studies in ADD adults. PET studies are sophisticated nuclear medicine studies that evaluate glucose metabolism, blood flow, and activity in the brain. His research showed that when ADD adults concentrate, there is decreased activity in the prefrontal cortex. There was quite a buzz in the medical community. This meant that ADD was real: It is a medical problem you can actually see. For many people this was a paradigm shift. I wasn't quite as excited as many of my colleagues. Dr. Lubar had virtually said the same thing many years earlier, using EEG scalp measurements. But I was excited about the developing new technology to help study our patients. Shortly after Dr. Zametkin's article appeared, I attended a lecture at the hospital by Jack Paldi, M.D., a nuclear medicine physician, who taught us about brain SPECT imaging.

SPECT (single photon emission computed tomography), like PET, is a nuclear medicine study that evaluates brain blood flow and activity patterns. Dr. Paldi said that SPECT was easier to perform, less expensive, and involved less radiation than PET studies. He showed SPECT images of patients with depression, dementia, schizophrenia, and head trauma. He showed brain images before and after treatment. Unlike the PET researchers who felt that their technology was still very experimental, Dr. Paldi said that, in his opinion, SPECT was ready to be used clinically and it could provide useful diagnostic information for psychiatric patients. I was intrigued. When he offered physicians no-cost SPECT scans to try them out, I took him up on his offer. The same day of Dr. Paldi's lecture, I met Sally.

Sally, a forty-year-old woman, had been hospitalized for depression, anxiety, and suicidal ideas. In my clinical interview with her I discovered that she had many ADD symptoms, such as short attention span, distractibility, disorganization, and restlessness. She had an ADD son (a frequent tip-off in diagnosing ADD in adults). She had never finished college, despite having an IQ of 140, and she was employed below her ability.

When I mentioned the possibility of adult ADD to her, she didn't want to think it applied to her and was not open to treatment for it. She had minimized her symptoms. Since I had just heard Dr. Paldi's lecture and read Dr. Zametkin's paper, I asked her if it would be okay to study her brain with SPECT. She was intrigued by the idea. I called the University of Wisconsin, known for research in brain SPECT studies, and asked them how to perform the scans on an ADD adult. They gave us their protocol: a rest study, with the patient doing nothing, and then two days later a concentration study done while the patient performs a series of random math problems.

Sally's concentration study was abnormal. At rest, she had good overall brain activity, especially in the prefrontal cortex. When she performed the math problems, she had marked decreased activity across her whole brain, especially in the prefrontal cortex! This correlated with Dr. Lubar's EEG finding and Dr. Zametkin's paper.

When I showed her the scans she started to cry and said, "You mean it is not my fault?"

"Right," I said, taking the glasses I wear to drive out of my coat pocket, "having ADD is just like people who need glasses. People who wear glasses aren't dumb, crazy, or stupid. Their eyes are shaped funny and we wear glasses to focus. For people who have ADD, they are not dumb, crazy, or stupid. Their prefrontal cortex shuts down, when it should turn on. And they need treatment to keep their prefrontal cortex working properly, so they can focus."

The analogy made sense to Sally, and she had a wonderful response to a low dose of a stimulant medication. Her mood was better, she was less anxious, and she could concentrate for longer periods of time. She eventually went back to school and finished her degree. No longer did she think of herself as an underachiever, but rather as someone who needs treatment for a medical problem. Seeing the pictures were very powerful for Sally. Watching her facial expression when she saw her own scans led me to believe that

Sally's SPECT Studies (Underside Surface Views)

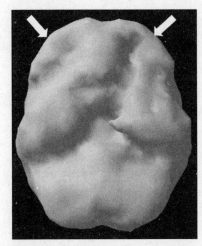 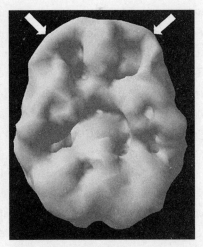

Good activity at rest   *Marked drop-off with concentration*

SPECT may have a powerful application in decreasing the stigma many patients feel when they are diagnosed with a "psychiatric" problem. It makes them realize that these conditions are not just manifestations of a weak will or poor conduct. The scan and her response to medication changed the perception she had about herself. I have seen the reaction Sally had to her scans many, many times over the last twenty-two years.

With Sally's positive response to treatment fresh in my mind, I ordered more SPECT studies, especially on my most difficult patients. I found SPECT immediately useful in a number of different ways. I was able to "see" areas of good brain function and areas of compromised function. I could see areas of the brain that worked too hard and areas of the brain that did not work hard enough. I read everything I could on brain imaging, especially SPECT. A number of my colleagues at the hospital where I worked also ordered SPECT studies on their patients. To my surprise, by early 1991 there was already a very large body of medical literature on SPECT imaging for psychiatric indications.

At this point in the story it is important to understand a bit about SPECT technology. SPECT is a nuclear medicine study that evaluates blood flow and activity in the brain. A radioisotope (which, as we will see, is akin to a beacon of energy or light that emits gamma rays) is attached to a medicine that is readily taken up by the cells in the brain. A small amount of this compound is injected into a vein in the patient's arm, from which it runs throughout the bloodstream and a portion is taken up by cells in the brain. The patient then lies on the SPECT table for about fifteen minutes while a camera rotates slowly around his head. The camera has special crystals that detect where the medicine (signaled by the gamma rays or pieces of light) has gone. The SPECT camera is open and no one feels claustrophobic, which is common with MRI-based procedures. A supercomputer then reconstructs 3-D images of brain activity levels.

The images that result give us blood flow/activity brain maps. With these maps, physicians have been able to identify certain patterns of brain activity that give us specific information on how your brain works.

Nuclear medicine studies measure the physiological functioning of the body and can be used to diagnose a multitude of medical conditions: heart disease, certain forms of infection, the spread of cancer, and bone and thyroid disease. Brain SPECT studies help in the diagnosis of head trauma, dementia, atypical or unresponsive mood disorders, strokes, seizures, the impact of drug abuse on brain function. At the Amen Clinics we have also used SPECT to subtype complex forms of ADD, anxiety, depression, addictions, obesity, aggression, and patients who have failed common treatments.

SPECT can be displayed in a variety of different ways. Traditionally the brain is examined in three different planes: horizontal (cut from top to bottom), coronal (cut from front to back), and sagittal (cut from side to side). What do physicians see when they look at a SPECT study? We examine it for symmetry and activity levels and compare it to what we know a healthy brain looks like. You will see two types of 3-D images in the book. One kind is a 3-D surface image, looking at the blood flow of the brain's outside surface. These images are helpful for picking up areas of healthy activity and low activity. They give insight into the effects of strokes, brain trauma, drug abuse, etc. A normal 3-D surface scan shows good, full, symmetrical activity across the brain's cortical surface.

The other kind is a 3-D active brain image, which compares average brain activity to the most active 15 percent. These images are helpful for picking up areas of overactivity, as seen in active seizures, obsessive-compulsive disorder, bipolar disorder, anxiety problems, certain forms of depression, etc. A normal 3-D active scan shows increased activity (seen by the light color) in the back of the brain (the cerebellum and visual or occipital cortex) and average activity most everywhere else (shown by the background grid). Physicians are usually alerted that something is wrong in one of three ways:

(a) they see too much activity in a certain area;

(b) they see too little activity in a certain area; or

(c) they see asymmetrical areas of activity.

In addition, other SPECT studies were published on dementia, stroke, head trauma, depression, schizophrenia, and drug abuse. In 1992, I went to the American Psychiatric Association's (APA) Annual Meeting in Washington, D.C. To my excitement I met other psychiatrists using SPECT, particularly Thomas Jaeger from Creighton University in Omaha, Nebraska, who had extensive experience with it. Dr. Jaeger and

Healthy SURFACE SPECT Scan

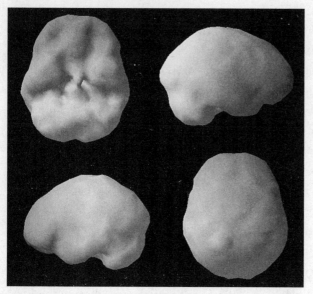

Note full, even, symmetrical activity. Top left image is looking underneath the brain, bottom right image is looking down from the top, the other two are looking at the brain from the sides.

colleagues were presenting an all-day course on how to utilize brain SPECT imaging in child psychiatry. I was very excited.

The day of the course, however, was my first sense that a storm was brewing in the brain-imaging world. I went to hear a lecture by Dr. Zametkin, who had led the PET research on ADD in adults. After the lecture I went up to him and told him that, partially based on his work, I was using brain imaging in my clinical practice and that I found it very helpful. He gave me an angry look and said that the imaging work was just for research: It wasn't ready for clinical use, and we shouldn't use it until people like him gave us the okay. I protested, giving him example after example of how it was helpful, but it was clear he did not want to hear it. I told him about the all-day course by Dr. Jaeger and his group. He said that he should go "crash their party and set them straight." I was livid. There was such a chasm between clinical practice and research-based physicians.

Healthy ACTIVE SPECT Study

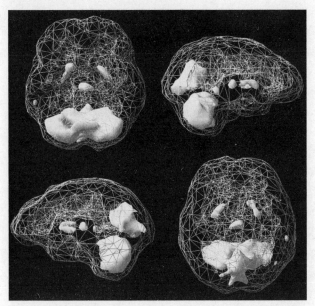

Grey = average activity, white is top 15 percent or most active areas.
Typically in a healthy brain cerebellum the back bottom part of the
brain is most active.

Dr. Jaeger's course was wonderful. He showed all of the different ways SPECT could be applied in a clinical setting: with ADD, depression, bipolar disorder, head trauma, drug abuse, etc. In the APA program abstract Dr. Jaeger wrote, "Regardless of the initial diagnosis, patients who underwent brain SPECT prior to, or during, psychiatric hospitalization had markedly shorter stays than controls. As demonstrated by this clinical database (two thousand patients), brain SPECT may lead to more effective, shorter, safer, and less expensive diagnostic and treatment modes in children and adolescents with suspected neuropsychiatric illness." His experience completely dovetailed with mine.

I wondered, "How can we not look at the brain?" Cardiologists look at the heart, orthopedic doctors have X-rays to examine bones, gastroenterologists look at the gut, pulmonologists look at the lungs, every other medical specialist looks at the particular organ they treat. And, we deal with the most complicated organ in the body. How can we treat it without having any information on how it functions? Psychiatrists are the only medical specialists who never look at the organ we treat!

By 1993, I had ordered several hundred SPECT studies on my patients, and I continued to find them helpful and fascinating. I started to lecture about the findings. I was asked to give grand rounds at local hospitals and then at the University of Colorado School of Medicine. I wrote a research article based on our findings with ADD children.

We performed brain SPECT studies on fifty-four medication-free ADD children and adolescents. We compared this group to eighteen medication-free children and adolescents who did not have ADD. The studies were performed at rest and while the patients were doing a concentration task. Sixty-five percent of the ADD children and adolescents diagnosed with ADD had significant decreased activity in the prefrontal cortex when they tried to concentrate, compared to only 5 percent of those who did not have ADD. Of the nineteen ADD patients (34 percent) who did not suppress their prefrontal lobe activity with concentration, twelve (63 percent) had decreased prefrontal cortex activity at rest.

In 1993, Dr. Jaeger asked me to help teach the brain-imaging course at the 1993 American Psychiatric Meeting in San Francisco. The enthusiasm was growing, as were the naysayers. Within two years of starting our brain imaging work my colleagues and I created a firestorm of criticism among our colleagues. "Psychiatrists don't do this" was something we heard a lot. Being naturally anxious, I hated the criticism. It caused sleepless nights and a general underlying uneasiness. For over a year I stopped talking about the work at our clinic. I was trying to figure out how to handle the conflict.

Then late one night in April 1995, I received a phone call from my sister-in-law Sherrie who was in tears. She told me that Andrew, my nine-year-old nephew and godson, had attacked a little girl on the baseball field that day for no particular reason. The attack was unprovoked and out of the blue. Sherrie told me that for the last year Andrew's behavior had been getting increasingly worse. His personality had changed from a sweet, happy child to someone who was angry and depressed, who had serious suicidal and homicidal thoughts. In his room that day she found two drawings, one of him hanging from a tree, another one where he was shooting other children. I told Sherrie to bring Andrew to see me the next day. His parents drove to my clinic, which was eight hours away.

As I sat with Andrew and his parents I knew something was wrong. I had never seen him look so angry or so sad. He had no explanations for his behavior: "I am just mad all the time." He said no one was hurting or teasing him. He had no idea why he felt the way he did. There was no family history of serious psychiatric illnesses or head injuries. And he had a wonderful family. Unlike most clinical situations, I knew this family. Andrew's parents were loving, caring, and concerned. What was the matter?

The vast majority of my colleagues would have placed Andrew on some sort of medication and had him see a counselor for psychotherapy. Having performed more than one thousand SPECT studies by that time, I first wanted a picture of Andrew's brain. But with the hostility from my colleagues fresh in my mind about the imaging work I asked myself again, *Maybe this was really due to a family problem that I just didn't know about. Maybe this is a psychological problem.* As an aside, if you have extensive psychiatric training you can find dirt in anybody's family. I thought, *Maybe Andrew was acting out because his older brother was a "perfect" child who did well in school and was very athletic. Maybe Andrew had these thoughts and behaviors to ward off feelings of insecurity related to being the second son in a Lebanese family* (I had personal knowledge of this scenario). *Maybe Andrew wants to feel powerful and these behaviors are associated with issues of control.* Then logic took over my brain. Nine-year-old children do not attack other children for no reason. They do not normally think about suicide or homicide. I needed to scan his brain. If it was normal then I could look further into the underlying emotional problems that might be present.

I went with Andrew to the imaging center and held Andrew's hand during the study while he held his teddy bear. As his brain scan appeared on the computer screen I thought a mistake was done in performing the procedure. *Andrew had NO left temporal lobe.* Upon quick examination of the complete study, I realized the quality of the scan was fine. He was indeed missing the function of his left temporal lobe. Did he have a cyst, a tumor, a prior stroke? A part of me felt scared for him as I was looking at the monitor. Another part of me felt relieved that we had some explanation for his aggressive behavior. My research and the research of others had implicated the left temporal lobe in aggression. The next day Andrew had an MRI (an anatomical brain study) which showed a cyst (a fluid-filled sac) about the size of a golf ball occupying the space where his left temporal lobe should have been. I knew the cyst had to be removed. Getting someone to take this serious, however, proved frustrating.

That day I called Andrew's pediatrician in Orange, California, and told him both of the clinical situation and brain findings. I told him to find the best person possible to drain the cyst and relieve the pressure on his brain. He contacted three pediatric neurologists. All of them said that Andrew's negative behavior was probably not in any way related to the cyst in his brain and they would not recommend operating on him until he had "real symptoms." When the pediatrician told me this information I became furious. *Real symptoms!! I had a child with homicidal and suicidal thoughts who loses control over his behavior and attacks people!*

I contacted a pediatric neurologist in San Francisco, who told me the same thing. I then called a friend of mine at Harvard Medical School, also a pediatric neurologist, who told me yet again the same thing. She even used the words "real symptoms." I said to her, "Real symptoms? I have a child with homicidal and suicidal thoughts who attacks people, what do you mean by real symptoms?" "Oh, Dr. Amen," the neurologist replied with a condescending tone, "When I say real symptoms I mean problems like seizures or speech problems." Could the medical profession really not connect the brain to behavior? I was angry and appalled! But I wasn't going to wait until this child killed himself or someone else.

I called the pediatric neurosurgeon, Jorge Lazareff, M.D., at UCLA and told him about Andrew. Dr. Lazareff was famous to me before he was to the world. He is the neurosurgeon who later separated the Guatemalan twins who were connected at the head. He told me that he had operated on three other children with left temporal lobe cysts who were all aggressive. He wondered if it was related. Thankfully, after evaluating Andrew he agreed to drain the cyst.

After his surgery I got two calls. The first one was from Andrew's mother. Sherrie told me that when Andrew woke up from surgery he smiled at her. "Danny," she said. "It was the first time he had smiled at me in a year." The next call was from Dr. Lazareff, who said, "Oh my God, Dr. Amen, Andrew's cyst had been so aggressive and put so much pressure on his brain that it had actually thinned the bone over his left temporal lobe. If he had been hit in the head with something like a basketball it would have killed him instantly. Or the pressure from the cyst could have likely killed him within six months." Andrew was fortunate. He had someone who loved him paying attention to his brain when his behavior was off. He is now twenty-eight, employed, and a wonderful young man. That personal experience gave me the motivation and courage to deal with my critics and do the work I have loved for so long.

Sometimes when I lecture and tell Andrew's story, tears still come to my eyes, even though I have told it hundreds of times. I think of all the children, teenagers, and adults who do terrible things, who we just label as bad, evil, or less than human, even though we have never looked at their brains. We just condemn them. It is so much easier to judge people if you never look at how their brains struggle.

A year after his surgery, Andrew and I were in Hawaii on vacation with our families. When we were on a boat, getting ready to snorkel,

Andrew's Missing Left Temporal Lobe (3-D Underside Surface View)

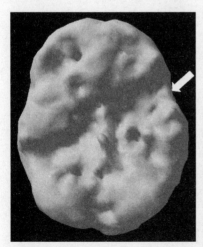 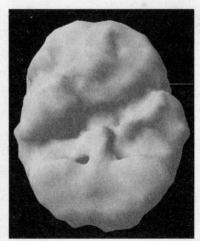

Before   *After surgery*

Andrew looked at me and said, "Uncle Danny, why did I have the cyst and have to go through all those problems?" Feeling a bit overwhelmed, I tenderly looked at Andrew and said, "We'll never really know why, but I think a part of the reason was for me. When I was able to help you, it gave me the courage to tell others about the importance of our brain imaging work without caring about all the people who criticized me. I have to tell everyone I know about it." He didn't fully understand what I was saying to him, but he accepted my response and we had a great time snorkeling.

Now, twenty-two years since I ordered my first SPECT scan there are centers across North America doing this work. The criticism from some academics remain; some people are very slow to change their ways. But we have published studies and collaborated with colleagues, including researchers at UC Irvine, UCLA, University of British Columbia, NYU, University of Pennsylvania, Thomas Jefferson, and Harvard. There is an openness of spirit that represents a major shift in thinking than even five years ago.

SPECT GUIDED BRAIN BASIC TENETS

Here are some of the guiding principles that underlie our work:

- The brain is involved in everything you do, how you think, how you feel, how you act, and how well you get along with other people.
- When your brain works right, you work right.
- When your brain doesn't work right, it is very hard for you to be your best.
- There are many things that hurt our brains, such as injuries, drugs, excessive caffeine, smoking, infections, environmental toxins, poor nutrition, and too little or too much exercise, excessive stress, insomnia, sleep apnea, any physical illnesses, chemotherapy.
- There are things that help the brain, such as proper nutrition, exercise, stress management techniques, new learning, omega-3 fatty acids, meditation, etc.
- Psychiatric illnesses, such as ADD, anxiety, depression, and addictions are not single or simple disorders. They all have multiple types.

Lawrence Left-Sided Stroke
(3-D Underside and Left Side Surface Views)

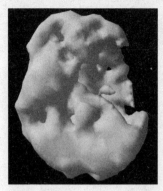   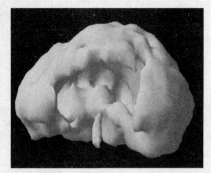

Underside   *Left side*

Steven Head Trauma (3-D Top Down and Left Side Surface Views)

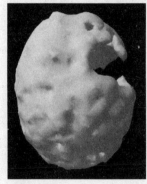   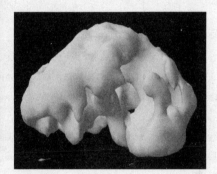

Top down   *Left side*

Kathy Alzheimer's Disease
(3-D Underside and Top Down Surface Views)

Underside   *Top down*

Laura Alcohol Abuse
(3-D Underside and Top Down Surface Views)

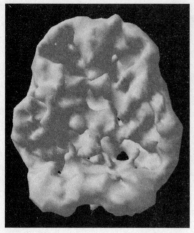   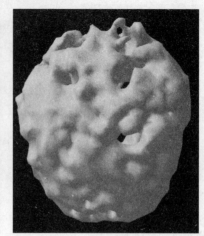

Underside   *Top down*

When I first started imaging I thought that different disorders, such as ADD, would have specific signature patterns, but soon found out that each particular illness, like ADD, actually had many different patterns. This made perfect clinical sense, because someone could meet all of the clinical criteria for ADD, but be made dramatically worse with the standard ADD treatment, stimulant medication. The SPECT scans helped us uncover the specific types.

Here are some examples from our collections of brain SPECT scans. In order to appreciate the functional changes in ADD brains, it's helpful to look at more dramatic examples of brain dysfunction.

Lawrence had a stroke, and since then, his speech has been affected, he has problems with depression, and he has trouble with short-term memory.

Steven fell off a roof onto his head and fractured his skull. He was unconscious for several days. Since the accident, he has had problems with his temper, seizures, and impulse control.

Kathy has Alzheimer's disease. Over the last few years her memory has gotten progressively worse. She gets lost easily and she says inappropriate things to her loved ones.

Laura had been abusing alcohol heavily for ten years. She now complained of memory problems and trouble learning new information.

Due to my personal situation at home, throughout the brain-imaging work I have always had a strong interest in ADD. Initially, as in Sally's case, I thought that ADD was primarily a problem of decreased activity in the prefrontal cortex. My 1993 study showed that 65 percent of ADD patients had decreased prefrontal cortex activity with concentration, but we soon saw other patterns emerge, especially in our more complex patients. As our brain-imaging became better known, the volume and complexity of our cases increased, as did our knowledge and database of scans. We found that there were a number of different brain systems involved. Here is a brief summary of the brain-imaging findings and symptoms for the different types of ADD that I saw. I will devote a chapter to each type with several examples for each.

TYPE 1: CLASSIC ADD

SPECT findings: a generally healthy brain at rest, but during concentration there tends to be decreased blood flow in the underside of the prefrontal

Type 1: Classic ADD (3-D Underside Surface View at Rest and with Concentration)

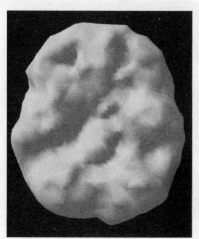 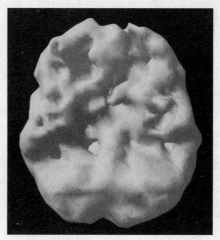

At rest   *With concentration*

cortex, cerebellum, and left and right basal ganglia (structures deep within the brain that help produce the neurotransmitter dopamine). Primary symptoms: inattentive, distractible, disorganized, hyperactive, restless, and impulsive.

This is the easiest pattern to spot. Almost all of the brain-imaging studies performed outside of Amen Clinics have been done on this type of ADD. Typically, prefrontal and cerebellar deactivation can be seen on the scans. This pattern tends to be seen more frequently in boys.

TYPE 2: INATTENTIVE ADD

SPECT findings: a generally healthy brain at rest, but during concentration there tends to be decreased blood flow in the underside of the prefrontal cortex, cerebellum, and basal ganglia.

Primary symptoms: inattentive, disorganization, distractible, but not hyperactive.

This pattern is common in males and females.

Type 2: Inattentive ADD (3-D Underside Surface View at Rest and with Concentration)

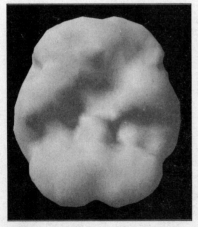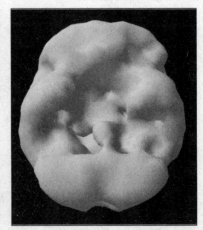

At rest   *With concentration*

Type 3: Overfocused ADD (3-D Active Concentration View, Left Side)

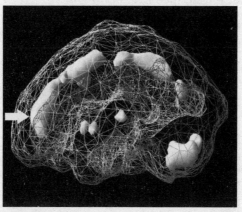

Left-side view

TYPE 3: OVERFOCUSED ADD

SPECT findings: At rest and during concentration there is increased activity in the anterior cingulate gyrus. During concentration there is also decreased activity in the underside of the prefrontal cortex, cerebellum, and basal ganglia. Primary symptoms: inattentive, trouble shifting attention, frequently get stuck in loops of negative thoughts or behaviors, obsessive, excessive worrying, inflexible, frequent oppositional and argumentative behavior. May or may not be hyperactive. This pattern tends to be seen more commonly in children and grandchildren of alcoholics. For personal reasons, families with alcohol-abuse histories were my research interest during training. This is a pattern I discovered within my first year of doing SPECT imaging.

TYPE 4: TEMPORAL LOBE ADD

SPECT findings: At rest and during concentration there is decreased (and infrequently increased) activity in the temporal lobes. During concentration there is also decreased activity in the underside of the prefrontal

Type 4: Temporal Lobe ADD
(3-D Underside Surface Concentration View)

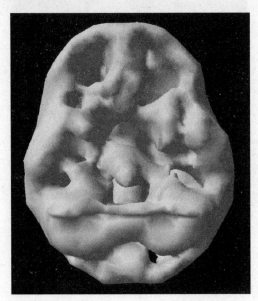

Underside view

cortex, cerebellum, and basal ganglia. Primary symptoms: inattentive, easily distracted, disorganized, irritable, short fuse, dark thoughts, mood instability, memory issues, and may struggle with learning disabilities. May or may not be hyperactive.

A great number of my initial cases involved temporal lobe dysfunction. Early in my imaging education, I discovered how important the temporal lobes are in psychiatric illness, mood instability, violence, and learning disabilities.

TYPE 5: LIMBIC ADD

SPECT findings: At rest there is increased deep limbic activity (thalamus and hypothalamus). During concentration there remains increased deep limbic activity and now there is also decreased activity in the prefrontal cortex, cerebellum, and basal ganglia. Primary symptoms: inattentive,

Type 5: Limbic ADD (3-D Underside Active Concentration View)

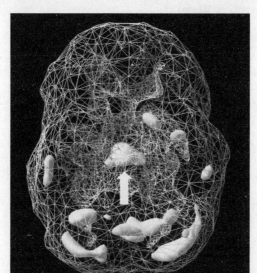

Underside view

easily distracted, disorganized, chronic low-grade sadness or negativity, "glass half empty syndrome," low energy, tends to be more socially isolated, and frequent feelings of hopelessness and worthlessness. May or may not be hyperactive.

Some people say that Limbic ADD is really a combination of ADD and depression. That may be so, but we see this combination very frequently in our ADD patients and it leads us to specific treatments that seem best for this type.

TYPE 6: RING OF FIRE ADD

SPECT findings: At rest and during concentration (often worse during concentration) there is patchy increased uptake across the cerebral cortex with focal areas of increased activity, especially in the left and right parietal lobes, left and right temporal lobes, and left and right prefrontal cortex. In addition there is often increased activity in the cingulate gyrus.

Type 6: Ring of Fire ADD (3-D Top Down Active Concentration View)

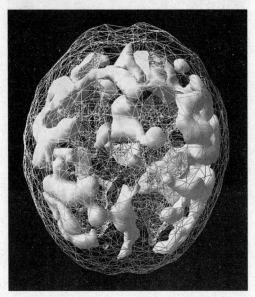

Top-down view

Primary symptoms: inattentive, easily distracted, irritable, overly sensitive, cyclic moodiness, and oppositional. May or may not be hyperactive.

Many of our younger "difficult cases" had this pattern in the brain. Initially, I thought it was related to perhaps an early bipolar pattern. While that may be true, it is more complex and it can also be related to infections, allergies, or inflammation. It is important to note here that young children naturally have very busy brains and this pattern has to be adjusted for age.

TYPE 7: ANXIOUS ADD

SPECT findings: At rest and during concentration there is increased activity in the basal ganglia, an area associated with anxiety. With concentration, there is decreased activity in the underside of the prefrontal cortex and cerebellum. Primary symptoms: inattentiveness, distractibil-

Type 7: Anxious ADD (3-D Underside Active Concentration View)

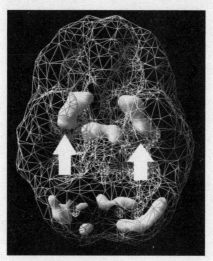

Underside view

ity, disorganization, anxiety, tension, a tendency to predict the worst, freeze in test-taking situations, and a tendency toward social anxiety.

One of the main reasons we have been so successful in both our clinical and brain-imaging work is that they were done in a clinical setting. Being a neuroscientist who studied the brain as well as being a psychiatrist responsible for patient care put me in a unique position to understand what I was seeing in the scans of my patients. They kept me searching, asking questions, and looking for answers.

PART 2

The Seven

ADD Types

CHAPTER 5

The Amen Clinics ADD Type Questionnaire

The widespread use of functional brain-imaging in clinical practice is still, unfortunately, years away. However, I have developed an instrument that allows you and others to take advantage of the information we have learned. Based on tens of thousands of patients and their brain SPECT studies, I have identified seven different types of ADD. Through the years I have developed a questionnaire to help people know their types if they cannot get a scan. It's easy and a good place to start. The Amen Clinics ADD Type Questionnaire is a seventy item self-test, which evaluates the overall ADD syndrome and the seven types I describe in the book. This questionnaire has gone through many revisions as we learn more, but for now I think you will find it useful. Questionnaires like this one have been a part of our evaluations at Amen Clinics for many years.

Self-report questionnaires have certain advantages and limitations. They are quick, inexpensive, and easy to score. One of the dangers is that people may fill them out as they want to be perceived. For example, some people mark every symptom as occurring "very frequently," in essence saying, "I'm glad to have a problem so that I can get help, be sick, or have an excuse for the problems I have." Some people are in total denial: They do not want to see any personal flaws and do not check any symptoms as problematic, saying, "I'm okay. There's nothing wrong with me. Leave me alone." In our clinical experience, most people gauge themselves with reasonable accuracy. Self-report bias is one of the reasons that it is important to have another person fill out the questionnaire as well. This will give you and others a more complete picture.

This questionnaire is an invaluable tool to determine if ADD exists and, if so, which type. It provides the basis for specific effective treatment planning. It's not unheard-of to score as displaying several different types of ADD. A person may have more than one, and some people have four or five types.

It's important to note that this (or any) questionnaire is never meant to be used alone. It is not meant to provide a diagnosis. It serves as a guide to help people begin to identify problems and get further evaluation for them. Please work together with your health care provider to develop the best treatment plan for you or your loved one.

Go to amenclinics.com/HealingADDTypeTest.pdf to download the online assessment and get a personalized look at your type or types of ADD.

CHAPTER 6

Type 1: Classic ADD

Common symptoms include:

Being easily distracted
Difficulty sustaining attention span for most tasks in play, school, or work
Trouble listening when others are talking
Difficulty following through (procrastination) on tasks or instructions
Difficulty keeping an organized area (room, desk, book bag, filing cabinet, locker, etc.)
Trouble with time, e.g., is frequently late or hurried, tasks take longer than expected, projects or homework are "last-minute" or turned in late
Tendency to lose things
Making careless mistakes, poor attention to detail
Forgetfulness
Being restless or hyperactive
Trouble sitting still
Being fidgety, in constant motion (hands, feet, body)
Being noisy, having a hard time being quiet
Acting as if "driven by a motor"
Talking excessively
Being impulsive (doesn't think through comments or actions before they are said or done)
Having difficulty waiting his or her turn
Interrupting or intruding on others (e.g., butts into conversations or games).

When most people think about ADD, they think about Type 1: Classic ADD. Hyperactive, restless, impulsive, disorganized, distractible, and trouble concentrating are Type 1's hallmark symptoms. This type of ADD is usually evident early in life. As babies, Type 1 sufferers tend to be colicky, very active, and they are hard to soothe and hold (they wiggle a lot). They have less eye contact than other children their age and parents have a more difficult time bonding with these children. It is hard to bond with a child who is in constant motion, who struggles to get away when you try to hold her. The hyperactivity and conflict-driven behavior usually gets everyone's attention early. The children are restless, in constant motion, noisy, talkative, and demanding. They also seem to need constant excitement or to see someone get upset. In addition, many of the inattentive symptoms are present as well.

This type is usually the first one to be diagnosed, because children often bring a lot of negative attention to themselves. These children are hard to be around, especially for people who are sensitive to noise. Parents of hyperactive children frequently feel tired, embarrassed, angry, and over-whelmed. As a group, Type 1 ADD individuals have low self-esteem. Due to the hyperactivity, conflict-driven behavior, and impulsivity these children, teens, and adults are in trouble with someone nearly every day of their lives. The brain SPECT findings in Type 1 show normal brain activity at rest and decreased activity, especially in the prefrontal cortex (PFC), during a concentration task. Here are four typical examples of Type 1 ADD (covering ages throughout the life span).

Joey

Mrs. Wilson brought Joey to see me when he was seven years old. He had just repeated first grade. Since preschool, teachers had mentioned prob-lems with Joey. They said he was restless, fidgety, impulsive, and unable to stay focused unless he was really interested. The school had tested his intelligence, which was high normal, and they tested his hearing and vision—also normal. Mrs. Wilson thought that the teachers weren't skilled enough to manage him, but she had to admit she was frequently frustrated with him at home. Ten minutes of homework would take him an hour of unfocused time. He started fights with his older brother and he had to be told to do things over and over. His bedroom was a perpet-ual mess, even right after it was picked up. He needed extra supervision, and dinnertime upset everyone because he wouldn't sit still long enough to eat. Joey had trouble getting to sleep at night because of his restless-ness, and he was hard to get up in the morning. Mrs. Wilson said she had stopped taking him shopping with her because it was too much. Even at the age of seven, he would not stay close, he touched everything, and he asked for treats repeatedly. "He just has no impulse control," she told me. Mrs. Wilson had brought Joey to the pediatrician when he was four years old because of his hyperactivity, but the doctor said he would probably outgrow it in a year or two.

During the evaluation in my clinic, Joey was all over the place. He took books off my bookshelves and played with items on my desk with-out permission. He was in constant motion. His mother appeared upset by his behavior and constant motion. I gave him a computerized test of attention (Conner's CPT), which he scored very poorly on. He had a very impulsive, fast approach to the test. I diagnosed Joey with Type 1 ADD and spoke to Mrs. Wilson about treatment options. A SPECT series was performed to gather the most information possible before treatment.

At rest, Joey's SPECT study showed good, full, symmetrical activity throughout his brain. Two days later, when he tried to concentrate, his SPECT test showed marked decreased activity in the underside of the prefrontal cortex. Typically, in our non-ADD group, when people try to concentrate they get increased activity in this part of the brain: Their brains help them focus by turning on the part of the brain that is largely responsible for focus and follow-through. Joey's brain, however, betrayed him. When he tried to concentrate, his prefrontal cortex shut down rather than turned on. A third study was done with concentration on Adderall. Adderall significantly enhanced prefrontal cortex activity, allowing Joey to have access to the part of his brain that helps him with focus, follow-through, and impulse control.

With a low dose of Adderall, a higher-protein, lower-carbohydrate diet, and regular exercise, Joey had a nice response to treatment. He was more focused, more settled, and over the years, much more successful in school.

Joey's SPECT Series at Rest and Concentration (Underside Surface View)

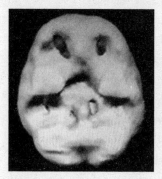 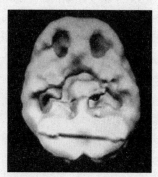

At rest (good activity)

With concentration (decreased prefrontal activity)

Joshua

Sixteen-year-old Joshua found himself in the vice-principal's office. He made an off-color comment in history class and refused to go to the office when he was told to go by the teacher. A scene between Joshua and the history teacher ensued. A small, thoughtless comment turned into a big deal. He and his parents had to meet with the vice-principal, Larry. Fortunately, Larry's wife was a family counselor who was expert in ADD. Rather than lecture Joshua, he asked the parents questions and he took the time to really listen to their answers. Joshua had been diagnosed with ADD when he was six years old. Despite being a bright child, he had always been impulsive, restless, inattentive, and disorganized. He had been on Ritalin as a child, which helped his school performance and behavior. The parents and pediatrician took him off Ritalin at age eleven. They thought everyone outgrew ADD by puberty, and Joshua was not as hyperactive as he once had been. Thinking back on it, his parents said that after fifth grade his school performance deteriorated and he definitely got into more trouble. Larry related to the family that many people with ADD never outgrow the disorder. If Joshua still had problems with impulsivity (obviously), inattention (the mother said homework took him all night to do), and restlessness (he still had trouble sitting still), then he needed another evaluation. Larry recommended the family to my clinic.

We see many, many teenagers like Joshua. As part of the evaluation he had a brain SPECT series, which showed normal activity at rest and markedly decreased activity in the prefrontal cortex during concentration. Showing Joshua and the family the SPECT study was very helpful. Joshua could see that ADD is not some imaginary illness, not an excuse: It is a medical problem that needs treatment. He needed treatment just as someone needs glasses if they have problems seeing. When we were looking at the study, I asked Joshua if he ever woke up and planned to have problem behavior. Joshua's eyes looked down. He said, "No. I never want to get into trouble. I just say stupid things without thinking." I responded that he needed a better internal supervisor. I explained how the prefrontal cortex helps us think about what we say or do before we say something or do something. His prefrontal cortex needed help. I then

showed him some before- and after-treatment SPECT images. His attitude was very positive. He wanted the best brain he could get. His initial
treatment consisted of medication, a higher-protein, lower-carbohydrate
diet, and intense exercise. With the help of treatment Joshua did very
well. In the beginning he was very consistent with his medication, but
less consistent with the diet and exercise. When he turned eighteen he
decided to go into the U.S. Air Force, which had been his lifelong dream.
The Air Force, however, would not take Joshua while he was taking
medication. He had to be off medication for at least a year. He told me
that he really wanted to go off his medication so that he could go into
the military. Having a lot of experience with this scenario, I told him he
had three choices: He could forget about the military and stay on his
medication; he could go off his medication and work hard on natural
treatments; or he could just go off his medication, go into the military,
and take his chances, but the odds were that the ADD symptoms would
get him into trouble. He agreed to work hard at the natural treatments.
He exercised intensely for thirty minutes every day. He ate better, eliminating sugar and simple carbohydrates, such as pasta, bread, potatoes,
and rice. And he took 1,000 milligrams of L-tyrosine twice a day. He did
very well on this combination and entered the Air Force a year later.

Gloria

I met Gloria (forty-five years old) when she brought her twenty-one-year-
old son to our clinic. He was having trouble in college. During the evaluation we had the parents fill out ADD questionnaires on themselves.
Gloria scored very high on her questionnaire. She decided to make an
appointment for herself. All of her life she had felt stupid. Even though
she ended up finishing college, she was labeled a slow learner in elementary and junior high school. She felt that she had to try harder than
everyone else. She needed more time to do her homework than her friends
did. She often didn't go out on weekends because she was overloaded with
schoolwork. Even now, chores around the house took her longer than she
(or her husband) thought they should. Gloria complained of a long-
standing sense of anxiety and restlessness. She did not go to movies. "I
can't sit still for more than fifteen minutes at a time. Getting up all the

time and walking around irritates others," she told me. She had problems with follow-through, and often had to pay late fees on bills. Her husband complained that Gloria was conflict-seeking. "Often I feel like she will just start problems," he said. "If we are having a nice day, she'll start to pick at me or bring something up from the past to be upset about. I don't think we have had a whole month in our twenty-five-year marriage without a fight." In addition, Gloria was disorganized. She told me that her closets were a "disaster area." "You have to wear a hard hat when you go in them" was her husband's comment. She was also frequently late.

As part of a family study, both Gloria and her son were scanned. They showed a similar SPECT pattern: healthy brain activity at rest, but poor activity in the prefrontal cortex during concentration. Gloria had a nice response to treatment. She said her energy was better. She felt more focused and more effective in her day-to-day life. Her anxiety level settled down and she was able to sit through movies without having to get up, missing part of the plot. Her husband said that she was more relaxed, less negative, and less oppositional.

George

Eighty-seven-year-old George made an appointment at our clinic after he saw the improvement in his great-grandson after treatment. He told me that his grandson was just as he himself had been when growing up. He had made too many mistakes in life and wanted to understand why. He also wanted to be able to concentrate better.

He said, "I want to be able to read a book. I have never finished a book even though I like to read." George's family was thrilled when he agreed to an appointment. He had always been difficult. He never sat through a meal, getting up and sitting down several times. He frequently said impulsive things that hurt other people's feelings. No one wanted to go out to a restaurant with George. Invariably he would say something awful to the waitress about the service or the food and embarrass everyone. As part of a four-generational family study, I ordered a SPECT study on George. His study showed normal brain activity at rest with decreased prefrontal cortex activity during concentration. With a low dose of medication (Adderall), a change in his diet, and increased exercise, George felt

George's SPECT Series, Rest and Concentration (Underside Surface View)

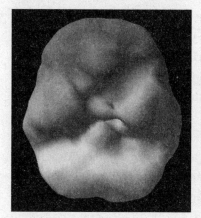
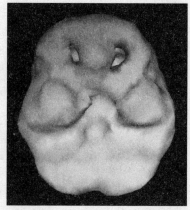

At rest (good activity)   *With concentration (decreased perfrontal activity)*

like a new man. He told me a month later, "I have better energy. I'm more thoughtful and don't upset my family by saying stupid things. My memory appears better, and I can concentrate for the first time in my life. I finished three books this month!" Now six months later, George's family wants to spend more time with him. His grandson, also my patient, told me that Grandpa was easier to be around and that people were not on pins and needles anymore if they went out with him.

THE BRAIN AND TYPE 1 ADD

It appears that Type 1 ADD is likely caused by a relative deficiency of the neurotransmitter dopamine. Dopamine is a chemical heavily involved with attention span, focus, follow-through, and motivation. When its availability in the brain is low, people tend to struggle with Classic ADD symptoms. Too much dopamine causes people to get overfocused or stuck in negative thought patterns or behaviors. The stimulant medications appear to work by enhancing dopamine availability in the brain. Psychiatrist and brain-imaging researcher Nora Volkow from Brookhaven Laboratory in New York State studied the effects of methylphenidate and cocaine on the brain. She injected these substances tagged to a radio-active isotope and watched where they worked in the brain. Both methylphenidate and cocaine worked in the same area of the brain: the head of the caudate nucleus in the basal ganglia (a structure deep in the brain). This is the same area found to be underactive in a number of ADD studies and may be one of the reasons many ADD adults abuse cocaine and methamphetamines. Dr. Volkow concluded in her study that the reason cocaine is addictive and methylphenidate is not is that cocaine is taken up very quickly in the basal ganglia, has a much more powerful effect in releasing dopamine (a high sensation), and is gone quickly (leading to withdrawal). Methylphenidate, on the other hand, is taken up much more slowly, has a weaker effect, and stays around longer (no withdrawal).

The caudate nucleus appears to be an important brain structure in psychiatry, and is involved in motivation, attention shifting, and anxiety control. When it is overactive, people have a tendency to be overfocused or obsessive. When it is underactive, people have trouble paying attention. There are many connections between the basal ganglia and prefrontal cortex. When there is low basal ganglia activity, there is not enough dopamine being produced to drive the prefrontal cortex. The result is primary ADD symptoms.

As I said earlier, almost all of the brain-imaging research on ADD outside of Amen Clinics has been on Type 1. The results consistently point to decreased prefrontal cortex activity, especially in the undersurface of the prefrontal cortex (often termed the inferior orbital prefrontal cortex) and the basal ganglia. Understanding how the key brain structures work helps in appreciating the havoc they can cause when they don't.

The Prefrontal Cortex (PFC)

Occupying the front third of the brain, underneath the forehead, the prefrontal cortex (PFC) is the most evolved part of the brain. It is divided into three sections: the dorsal lateral section (on the outside surface of the PFC), the inferior orbital section (on the front undersurface of the brain), and the anterior cingulate gyrus (which runs through the middle of the frontal lobes). The anterior cingulate gyrus, often considered part of the limbic system, is associated with shifting attention and is often involved with Type 3 (Overfocused) ADD. The dorsal lateral and inferior orbital PFC go by the term "executive control center" of the brain.

Overall, the PFC is the part of the brain that watches, supervises, guides, directs, and focuses your behavior. It contains "executive functions": time management, judgment, impulse control, planning, organization, and critical thinking. Our ability as a species to think, plan ahead, use time wisely, and communicate with others is heavily influenced by this part of the brain. The PFC is responsible for behaviors that are necessary for you to act appropriately, focus on goals, maintain social responsibility, and be effective.

The PFC—especially the inferior orbital PFC—helps you think about what you say or do before you say or do it. It enables you, in accordance with your experience, to select actions among alternatives in social and work situations.

The PFC (especially the dorsal lateral PFC) is also involved with sustaining attention span. It trains your mind to focus on important information while filtering out less significant thoughts and sensations. Attention span is required for short-term memory and learning. The PFC, through its many connections within the brain, keeps you on task and allows you to stay with a project until it is finished. The PFC accomplishes this by sending quieting signals to the limbic and sensory parts

The Prefrontal Cortex

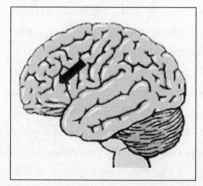

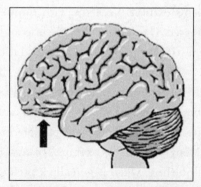

Dorsal lateral prefrontal cortex; outside view   *Inferior orbital prefrontal cortex; outside view*

of the brain. In the face of a need to focus, the PFC decreases the distracting input from other brain areas, inhibiting rivals for our attention. However, when the PFC is underactive, less of a filtering mechanism is available and distractibility becomes common.

The PFC—especially the dorsal lateral PFC—enables you to feel and express emotions: to feel happiness, sadness, joy, and love. Distinct from the more primitive limbic system (responsible for mood and libido) the prefrontal cortex translates the feelings of the limbic system into what we think of as higher emotions, such as love, passion, or hate. Underactivity or damage in the PFC often leads to a decreased ability to express thoughts and feelings. Thoughtfulness and impulse control are also heavily influenced by the PFC. The ability to think through the consequences of behavior is essential to every aspect of human life. Without forethought, it would be awfully difficult to choose a good mate, interact with customers, deal with difficult children, spend money, or drive on the freeway. In all of those kinds of situations, consistent, thoughtful action and inhibition of impulse behavior hold the keys to success.

Within the PFC as a whole, problems in the dorsal lateral prefrontal cortex often lead to decreased attention span, distractibility, impaired short-term memory, decreased mental speed, apathy, and decreased verbal expression. Problems in the inferior orbital cortex often lead to poor impulse control, mood control problems (due to its connections with the limbic system), decreased social skills, and impaired control over behavior.

Problems in the PFC lead to the organization of daily life spiraling into chaos while internal supervision goes awry. People with PFC problems exhibit problems with impulse control, doing things they later regret. They also experience impaired attention span, distractibility, procrastination, poor judgment, and difficulty expressing themselves.

When men have problems in this part of the brain, their emotions are often unavailable to them and their partners complain that they do not share their feelings. This can cause serious problems in a relationship because of how other people interpret the lack of expression of feeling. Many women, for example, blame their male partners for being cold or unfeeling, when it is really a problem in the PFC that causes a lack of being "tuned in" to the feelings of the moment.

The Basal Ganglia

The basal ganglia are a set of large structures toward the center of the brain. Involved with integrating feelings, thoughts, and movement, they also help shift and smooth motor behavior. In our clinic we have noticed that the basal ganglia are involved with setting the body's idling and anxiety levels and modulating motivation. The basal ganglia tend to be underactive in Classic ADD.

The integration of feelings, thoughts, and movement occur in the basal ganglia. This is why you jump when you're excited, tremble when you're nervous, freeze when you are scared, and get tongue-tied when the boss is chewing you out. The basal ganglia allow for a smooth integration of emotions, thoughts, and physical movement. When there is too much input, they tend to lock up and do not allow a smooth transition. When the basal ganglia are overactive (as we have seen in the case of people with anxiety tendencies or disorders), people are more likely to become immobile (in thoughts or actions) in stressful situations and have a tendency to freeze up. When the basal ganglia are underactive (as in this type of

The Basal Ganglia System

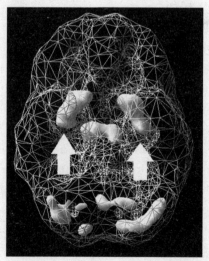

Underside active view

ADD), a stressful situation often moves a person to action. People with ADD are frequently the first ones on the scene of an accident. They respond to stressful situations without fear. I know, for example, that one of my friends who has Type 1 ADD is a lot quicker at responding to crises than I am (I have naturally overactive basal ganglia).

Shifting and smoothing fine motor behavior is another basal ganglia function and is essential to handwriting and motor coordination. Many children and adults who have ADD have very poor handwriting. Their writing often looks choppy or sloppy. In fact, many teens and adults with ADD print rather than write in cursive. They find printing easier because it is not a smooth motor movement but rather a start-and-stop motor activity. Many people with ADD also complain that they have trouble getting their thoughts out of their head and onto paper, a condition called finger agnosia. We know that the medications that help this type of ADD, such as the psychostimulants Adderall, Vyvanse, and Ritalin work by enhancing the production of the neurotransmitter dopamine in the basal ganglia. It is often amazing how these medications improve handwriting and enhance a person's ability to get their thoughts out on paper in an easier way. In addition, many people with ADD say that their overall motor coordination is improved with these medications.

Reversing the low PFC and basal ganglia activity in Type 1 ADD is the therapeutic goal. We'll learn more about that later.

The Cerebellum

At the back bottom of the brain is the cerebellum, which is an incredibly important structure. Even though it occupies only 10 percent of the brain's volume, it has 50 percent of the brain's nerve cells. The cerebellum is involved in physical coordination, but also thought coordination and learning, especially integrating new information.

In addition, it is involved with impulse control, organization, and speed of thought, sort of like clock speed on a computer. The cerebellum is heavily connected to the opposite side prefrontal cortex. For example, if the left prefrontal cortex is damaged, such as in a car accident or stroke, it can turn off the right side cerebellum. Keeping the cerebellum strong is essential to have a prefrontal cortex that works right. Symptoms of

The Cerebellum

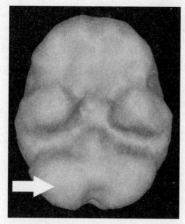

3-D underside active view

cerebellar trouble include coordination problems, slowed thinking and speech, disorganization, poor impulse control, and trouble learning. Coordination exercises can help thinking in many children and adults who have ADD. I especially like dancing exercises and table tennis. Both are great coordination exercises that require some thought. Of course, if you drink while you dance or play beer pong, there is no therapeutic benefit.

CHAPTER 7

Type 2: Inattentive ADD

Common symptoms include:

Being easily distracted

Difficulty sustaining attention span for most tasks in play, school, or work

Trouble listening when others are talking

Difficulty following through (procrastination) on tasks or instructions

Difficulty keeping an organized area (room, desk, book bag, filing cabinet, locker, etc.)

Having trouble with time, for example, frequently late or hurried, tasks take longer than expected, projects or homework are last-minute or turned in late

Having a tendency to lose things

Making careless mistakes, poor attention to detail

Being forgetful

Daydreaming excessively

Complaining of being bored

Appearing apathetic or unmotivated

Being tired, sluggish, or slow moving

Appearing spacey or preoccupied

The second most common type of ADD is Type 2: Inattentive ADD. Unfortunately, many of these people never get diagnosed. Instead they are labeled slow, lazy, spacey, or unmotivated. While Type 1 people bring negative attention to themselves with their hyperactivity, constant chatter, and conflict-driven behavior, Inattentive ADD folks tend to be quiet and distracted. Rather than cause problems in class, they are more likely to daydream or look out the window. They are not often impulsive and are less likely to blurt out inappropriate things. They are frequently thought of as couch potatoes who have trouble finding interest or motivation in their lives. Girls seem to have this type as much as or more than boys. As in Type 1 (Classic) ADD, dopamine is generally considered the neurotransmitter involved in Inattentive ADD—although, in this case, its imbalance is felt by another area of the brain.

Read the following four examples of Type 2 ADD. Seeing what these people went through and how they were helped gives a clear picture of the nature of Inattentive ADD.

Sara

Eight-year-old Sara was brought to our clinic by her mother and father. They were worried about her inability to pay attention. A few minutes of homework often took her three to four hours, with her parents upset at her for taking so long. She appeared spacey, internally preoccupied, and generally in her own world. Her room was usually very messy. She had poor social skills and often ignored children her own age whom her parents arranged to come over to the house to be her playmates. Even though she did not have a defiant attitude at home, she often simply did not do what was asked of her. She said that she had forgotten or didn't hear the request. Her teacher said that she appeared to be a smart child but performed far below her potential. Her mind wandered in class and she had to be reminded to pay attention. She frequently made silly mistakes on tests and homework. Her handwriting was awful. Hearing and vision tests checked out normal, as did thyroid studies done by the pediatrician and tests for learning disabilities by the school psychologist. Sara had all the hallmarks of Type 2 ADD, but the parents were hesitant to start treatment, and wanted further evaluation. We did a SPECT study to evaluate her brain function. Clinically, she appeared to have Inattentive ADD. Sara's SPECT study showed marked decreased activity when she tried to concentrate, especially in the prefrontal cortex. I prescribed a high-protein, low-carbohydrate diet (her diet before the evaluation had been almost entirely carbohydrates), regular exercise, and a regimen of 500 milligrams of L-tyrosine twice a day. Sara's schoolwork and behavior improved within the first week of starting this regimen. Whenever Sara strayed from her treatment, she again became spaced-out and inattentive.

Chris

Ten-year-old Chris was diagnosed as mentally retarded at age six. He was a slow learner and now read at only the first-grade level. After testing Chris, the school psychologist said that he had only limited potential. His parents were very upset with the prognosis given by the school psychologist, because at home they saw flashes of real intelligence. They also saw problems: For example, his room tended to be very disorganized, even though the parents tried to help him. Chris had a low energy level and frequently had to be called on several times before he would answer. A local neurologist ordered a brain MRI, EEG, and blood tests, all of which were normal.

A friend of Chris's mother was a patient at our clinic and suggested that she have Chris evaluated by us. Reviewing his tests, I saw not only that Chris had a low IQ, but also that the psychologist noted that Chris had been very inattentive during the test. In talking to Chris, I found that I had to work hard to make eye contact with him. He gave only limited answers to my questions and seemed easily distracted by the things in my office. I ordered a SPECT study to understand how his brain worked. I believe that all children diagnosed with mental retardation need a functional brain-imaging study. Overall, Chris had very poor blood flow in his brain, especially in the prefrontal cortex. I scanned him again on Adderall to see if it would have a positive effect. On Adderall he had significantly more activity in his brain. Almost immediately the parents noticed a difference in Chris. He was more talkative, more energetic, and more responsive. The next year he picked up three grade levels in reading. A year later, IQ tests were redone and found to be in the normal range. Today, Chris is happy and performing well in school. Prior to treatment, Chris's brain was

Chris's Concentration SPECT Study On and Off Adderall (Underside Surface View)

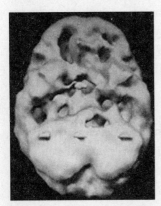

No meds

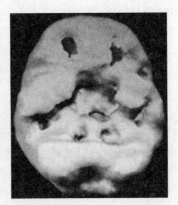

With Adderall

in darkness. Now, with treatment, the lights have been turned on: It was as if we had given a blind person sight.

Gary

Gary, age twenty-nine, came to see me because he had trouble living independently. His parents were still supporting him. Despite his high intelligence, he underachieved in school. Teachers said he didn't care and needed to try harder. He appeared unmotivated, tired, and off in his own world. Even his girlfriend had trouble getting his attention. Even though he worked at several odd jobs and was good at carpentry, he did not make enough money to pay all of his bills. Employers fired him for being late to work or not coming back from lunch on time. Gary's father told him to "get his stuff together" or he would not help Gary anymore.

Even though many people would call Gary lazy, I suspected a medical problem. Gary had symptoms consistent with Type 2 (Inattentive) ADD. Rather than being hyperactive, he appeared underactive. He was spacey, easily distracted, inattentive, and lethargic. His brain SPECT study showed marked decreased activity in the prefrontal cortex when he tried to concentrate. I placed him on a low dose of stimulant medication (Adderall), a higher-protein, lower-carbohydrate diet, and regular, intense exercise. Over the next two years he was able to become more effective in his day-to-day life.

Jenna

Jenna, a fifty-seven-year-old artist, was referred to Amen Clinics by her psychiatrist. She complained of trouble concentrating, distractibility, "fuzzy thinking," disorganization, low energy, difficulty reading, and feelings of life being overwhelming. Facing the day was frightening for her. She would become frozen and panicked by daily tasks, such as opening the mail. She has a beautiful house, but there were piles everywhere. Many of her friends said that she was "too creative" to be organized and focused. Her doctor had tried her on a small dose of Ritalin, which had a significant positive effect on her symptoms. He wanted to send her for a second opinion and for brain-imaging studies to clarify the diagnosis and better target her treatment.

Clinically, Jenna was diagnosed with Type 2 (Inattentive) ADD. Two SPECT studies were performed as part of her workup. The first study, performed without any medication, showed marked decreased activity, especially in her prefrontal cortex. The second study was performed several days later after she took a dose of Adderall. With medication there was significant overall improvement throughout her whole brain, especially in the prefrontal cortex. On Adderall she feels much better. "I feel like I have access to much more of my own brain," she told me, which indeed the SPECT study verified.

Initially, Jenna was very afraid of medication. She wanted to deal with her problems in a "natural" way. In fact, she had tried different diets, exercise, and meditation, with little effect. On medication, she feels more focused, and more organized, with more consistent energy and more brainpower. She still exercises, eats right, and meditates to help keep her brain healthy. She has asked me who the natural Jenna is, the one with the underactive brain or the one with the normal-looking brain. My bias is that she is really herself when her brain works right. Since our first visit in 1998, Jenna has referred most of her family to me because they struggle with very similar issues.

Type 2 ADD is usually very responsive to treatment. As the case studies illustrate, it is often possible to change the whole course of a person's life if the disorder is properly diagnosed and treated.

Jenna's Concentration SPECT Study On and Off Adderall (Underside Surface View)

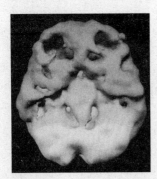

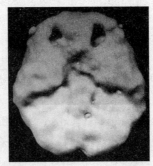

No meds   *With Adderall*

CHAPTER 8

Type 3: Overfocused ADD

ADD core symptoms plus:

Excessive or senseless worrying

Oppositional, argumentative

Strong tendency to get locked into negative thoughts, having the same thought over and over

Tendency toward compulsive behaviors

Tendency to hold grudges

Trouble shifting attention from subject to subject

Difficulties seeing options in situations

Tendency to hold onto own opinion and not listen to others

Tendency to get locked into a course of action, whether or not it is good for the person

Needing to have things done a certain way or you become very upset

Others complain that you worry too much

In my experience Overfocused ADD is the third most common type of ADD. Overfocused ADD patients have all of the core ADD symptoms plus tremendous trouble shifting attention and a tendency to get stuck or locked into negative thought patterns or behaviors. This type of ADD can have devastating effects on families. It is frequently found in substance abusers and in children and grandchildren of alcoholics.

I discovered Overfocused ADD early in my brain-imaging work because it was the one I lived with at home.

My first wife grew up in an abusive alcoholic home. We were teen sweethearts. She was my first love—beautiful, smart, funny, and caring. I had met her when I was fifteen years old working in my father's grocery store. We dated for three years and then, due to having a low draft number, I had to serve in the U.S. Army during the Vietnam War. While I was away, stationed in Germany, Robbin impulsively married someone else, in large part to get away from an abusive household. I was devastated and felt that I lost a part of myself. Her marriage only lasted a few years. She married someone who turned out to be an abusive alcoholic (not uncommon in adult children of alcoholics). When I was discharged from the service I finished college and was accepted into medical school. Shortly after opening my acceptance letter to medical school I called Robbin's mother to tell her the good news. When I was a teen, her mother had been very supportive and spent long hours talking with me about my dreams and goals. She was thrilled for me and, by the way, she said, Robbin had left her first husband and was living in Southern California. I nearly lost my breath. I had never loved anyone like Robbin, my first love. I called her. We dated for several months before I went to Oklahoma for medical school and then we talked every day on the telephone until we were married a year later.

Shortly after our marriage I knew that something was very wrong. Robbin had terrible mood swings. She worried, focused on the negative, had periods of depression, and she had to have things a certain way or she would get very upset. Certain areas of her life were very organized and other areas were very disorganized. I had her see the chief of the department of psychiatry at my medical school—a very kind man who helped her a lot. Unfortunately, when we moved to Washington, DC, for my internship and residency things were not much different. She saw counselors in Washington, but it really didn't help much. Then, while I was studying drug and alcohol treatment at the National Naval Medical Center in Bethesda, Maryland, I attended a lecture on adult children of alcoholics (ACOAs). The lecture brought tears to my eyes. Robbin was suffering with many symptoms attributed to growing up in an alcoholic home: she had trouble trusting others, she often blocked out her feelings, and she had trouble talking about her feelings.

It was only by accompanying Robbin to therapy that I learned about the abusive alcoholic environment she grew up in. While we were dating she never told me about the alcoholism, physical fights, yelling, and abuse going on at home. There was too much shame. When I came home that night I told her about the ACOA lecture. To my amazement, she told me that she felt guilty labeling her father as an alcoholic, but she agreed to go the ACOA meetings. The meetings and new understanding about ACOA issues seemed to help, but many of the problems remained. We then went to Hawaii for my child psychiatry fellowship at Tripler Army Medical Center in Honolulu. I did my research on children and grand-children of alcoholics (I was married to a child of an alcoholic and at the time I had two children who were grandchildren of alcoholics). I found a very high incidence of ADD, obsessiveness, and oppositional behavior. This set the stage for my brain imaging work with these patients a number of years later.

Shortly after we left Hawaii Kaitlyn was born. She was my little hyperactive one. She was diagnosed with ADD at the age of four, even though I had suspicions about it from the time she was eighteen months old. Kaitlyn also had a strong oppositional streak. It seemed that she argued with everything and opposed everything Robbin or I asked her to do. She is the child who taught me a lot about oppositional defiant disorder. She taught me to ask parents this question in diagnosing oppositional defiant disorder: *How many times out of ten when you ask your child to do something will he or she do it the first time without arguing or fighting?* Kaitlyn got a goose egg—it seemed as though she would never comply the first time.

To find out what was normal I sent a questionnaire home to the parents of four hundred children at a school where I was the consultant, asking them that question. Seven times out of ten children from a general population comply the first time without giving their parents grief.

With Kaitlyn, I found that I used reverse psychology a lot. If you asked her to do the opposite of what you wanted her to do you were guaranteed a positive response nearly every time. When Kaitlyn was three years old I had just begun my brain SPECT work.

After seeing how helpful it had been for a number of my patients I decided to scan people I knew to get a good sense of the technology. I scanned my mother, Robbin, all three of my children, including Kaitlyn, and several friends of mine who I thought needed scans. It was so instructive to scan people I knew. Both Robbin and Kaitlyn had excessive activity in the anterior cingulate gyrus and decreased activity in the prefrontal cortex. I was just learning about the anterior cingulate gyrus at the time. It was never even mentioned during my psychiatric training programs. There were brain-imaging studies that suggested there was overactivity in the anterior cingulate gyrus in patients who had obsessive compulsive disorder (OCD). There was a SPECT study in 1991 reporting that Prozac decreased activity in the anterior cingulate gyrus in OCD patients. I saw hyperactivity in the anterior cingulate gyrus in many patients who did not have OCD. But I noticed a common thread with OCD. Patients had trouble shifting attention. Researcher Alan Mirsky wrote a book chapter highlighting the anterior cingulate area of the brain as being involved with shifting attention. In Robbin, Kaitlyn, and many of my patients who had too much activity in the anterior cingulate gyrus I saw this problem of shifting attention: there was a certain cognitive inflexibility that was evident in many of their symptoms. Could it be possible that oppositional children had a similar underlying brain mechanism found in OCD? I was intrigued. Over time the finding proved to be true.

When there is increased activity in the anterior cingulate gyrus a certain cognitive inflexibility is present. This can present as many different symptoms, but the underlying mechanism, trouble shifting attention, remains. The symptom list at the beginning of the chapter is a compilation of what we have seen in these patients. The anterior cingulate area of the brain is heavily innervated with serotonin neurons. We have also found that serotonergic medications seem to be the most helpful in this disorder.

The Anterior Cingulate Gyrus

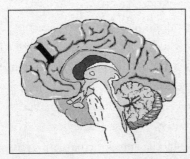

Cingulate gyrus

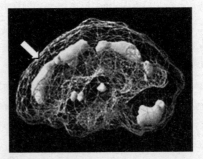

Left side active view

Tammy

Tammy was in fourth grade when she first came to our clinic. Tammy was a stubborn child. If she did not get her way, she would throw mammoth tantrums that could go on for hours. In addition, Tammy was shy around other people, worried a lot, and was having problems in school. She would stare at her work for long periods of time. She craved perfection in her schoolwork, and as a result her papers showed evidence of many erasures. Tammy was distracted easily and had trouble sitting still. While Tammy's attention could easily be diverted from some things, she held on to hurts. If a friend said something she didn't like, her parents would hear about it for weeks. Another child psychiatrist diagnosed Tammy with ADD and put her on Ritalin. But the Ritalin aggravated her, making her moody, irritable, and even more anxious. Tammy's brain scan showed that her anterior cingulate gyrus was very overactive. It was clear from a brain biology perspective that she had trouble shifting her attention.

She needed a calmer cingulate if she was going to improve. Given her poor prior response to medication, the parents and I initially decided to try an herbal approach to treatment. I placed her on St. John's Wort (a

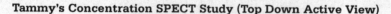

Tammy's Concentration SPECT Study (Top Down Active View)

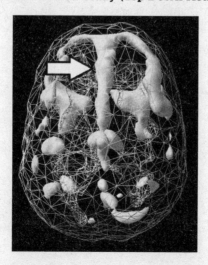

serotonin booster) and had her engage in a daily exercise program. In addition, her parents had to learn to be very firm and prevent her from arguing or opposing them. It took two months for all of the interventions to work together, but they had a significant positive impact on her behavior and academic ability.

Mark

Mark, fourteen years old, was evaluated for anger outbursts and defiant behavior. Psychotherapy and parent training were ineffective, as were many different classes of medication, including stimulants and antidepressants. Prozac made him more aggressive. Mark's parents were ready to send him away to a residential treatment center. The stress on their family was just too much. I ordered a SPECT study. His SPECT study revealed marked hyperfrontality (his anterior cingulate gyrus and lateral prefrontal cortices were very overactive). Mark was unable to shift his attention. He was unable not to be difficult. I placed him on Risperdal, a novel antipsychotic medication, that I have seen calm this part of the brain. He was clearly not psychotic—he wasn't delusional or hallucinating—but we have found this class of medications helpful for this severe hyperfrontality. He had a dramatic response. He was more compliant, happier, and no longer aggressive. One week after I started Mark on Risperdal, his mother came to my clinic, even though she didn't have an appointment. As I walked into the waiting room to greet a patient, I saw her. I wondered why she was there. I smiled at her and she immediately came over to me, grabbed me, and gave me a big hug. She said, "Thank you so much. I have my son back. Mark is doing so much better!" I felt pretty good that day. As the improvement held, and I also added natural treatments, I did two follow-up studies; one study was done a month later, the next one was six months later. There was a progressive calming of the hyperfrontality.

Brandon

Sixteen-year-old Brandon was one of the more difficult children I have treated in my practice. He was negative, surly, argumentative, and oppositional, and would throw long tantrums when he did not get his way.

He did poorly in school. He would not cooperate with teachers, and he did not get along with other students. The parents were at their wits' end when they brought Brandon to see me. Brandon was very opposed to seeing a psychiatrist. "I'm not crazy," he announced to his parents, "and I'm not going to talk to any shrink, so don't waste your money." From the clinical history it was obvious to me that Brandon had anterior cingulate problems. He held true to his word that he wouldn't talk to me, so for a number of months I spent most of my time with Brandon's parents. Brandon refused to take medication and he was threatening to run away from home. The parents and I felt that Brandon might need a residential treatment center where he could get intensive treatment over nine months to a year.

Before I recommended sending Brandon to treatment, however, I ordered a scan to evaluate his brain function and partly to help convince him of the biological need for treatment. Surprisingly, Brandon agreed to the scan without his usual fuss. He was curious and had seen the brain images around our clinic. Brandon's SPECT scan was one of the most abnormal studies that I had ever seen. His anterior cingulate gyrus was on fire. His frontal lobes were completely overactive as well.

Brandon's Concentration SPECT Study (Top Down Active View)

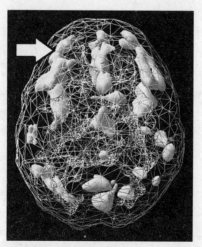

Severe hyperfrontal pattern

As I explained the SPECT results to Brandon, he actually seemed to listen to me for the first time. He asked questions, seemed interested, and asked to see both healthy and dysfunctional brains. By the end of our appointment he had agreed to try some medication. He also agreed to exercise on a regular basis.

The scan seemed to help him shift to a more open emotional place. I placed him on 20 milligrams of Prozac. Three weeks later I had a follow-up appointment with Brandon. I walked to my waiting room, wondering what I would see. I was used to having bad interactions with Brandon. To my surprise Brandon stood up when he saw me, shook my hand, and said, "It's nice to see you again, Dr. Amen. How are you?" My mouth dropped open. I thought to myself, Where is Brandon? Who is occupying his body? Someone must have performed a brain transplant on him. Brandon and his parents came back to my office and told me that about a week after taking the Prozac, Brandon's whole demeanor started to change. He woke up in a pleasant mood. He was more cooperative and even asked if he could help around the house. The tantrums were gone and he was a joy to live with. Over the next several months Brandon's improvement held firm, but he was still having trouble focusing in school. At that point I added a very small dose of Adderall, a psychostimulant medication, to help him focus, as well as some simple supplements and lifestyle interventions. Together, they were the missing pieces of the puzzle and Brandon's schoolwork improved as well.

The first time I saw Brandon's improvement, I wondered, "Who is he really?" What was Brandon's character? What was his soul really like? Over time I learned that Brandon really was a charming, sweet young man who had been trapped inside the circular hell of his brain's inflamed anterior cingulate gyrus. When his anterior cingulate gyrus and his brain worked right, Brandon was able to work right as well.

Sarah

Sarah, twenty-eight, was referred by her therapist because she had failed the bar exam six times. Even though Sarah had graduated from law school, the therapist felt that Sarah had attention deficit disorder because she had trouble with attention span, was distractible, and had poor impulse control.

Sarah had grown up in an alcoholic home. She struggled with periods of depression and obsessive thinking. Many of the people who knew her thought she was selfish, because if things did not go Sarah's way she would get angry. She was rigid, frequently argumentative (while she was growing up her parents told her that she would make a good lawyer because of her tendency to argue), held grudges, and often worried about insignificant matters. Just before the evaluation, Sarah was nearly arrested for an incident on the freeway in which she chased down another driver who had accidentally cut her off. Whenever she took traditional ADD medications, however, she got worse. She overfocused on trivia and became more irritable. To my eye, Sarah had symptoms consistent with Overfocused ADD.

I placed Sarah on Effexor, which is a stimulating antidepressant that increases serotonin, norepinephrine, and dopamine neurotransmitters. Sarah began to feel better within three weeks. She felt more focused, less worried, and more relaxed. Her friends noticed that she was more flexible and didn't always have to have things her way. Today I would have tried her first on supplements to boost both serotonin and dopamine, then evaluated her response before giving her medication. I have often seen that natural treatments can be effective with lower costs and few side effects, which is why I try them first.

Phil

At the age of sixty-seven, Phil was an unhappy, lonely man. He had been divorced three times and his children did not talk to him. Even though he had been somewhat successful in business, he didn't enjoy his life. He was argumentative and negative and worried excessively. He hated to be alone but tended to be rigid, oppositional, and unpleasant whenever he was around others. Anything that did not go his way caused fierce outbursts. He came to see me after his grandson had been helped in my clinic. I ordered two SPECT studies on Phil as part of a family study we were doing. He had significant decreased activity in his prefrontal cortex during concentration and marked increased cingulate activity on both studies. After seeing his scans and listening to his family history, it was clear to me that Phil suffered from Type 3 ADD. He had a deficiency in serotonin and dopamine, causing the brain abnormalities in his prefrontal cortex and cingulate gyrus, which also caused his difficult behavior.

I treated Phil with a combination of medication, dietary interventions, and exercise. It was wonderful to see the difference. Phil became more relaxed, more positive, less argumentative, and more able to love. His children noticed the difference within several weeks and started to enjoy being around him.

GILLES DE LA TOURETTE'S SYNDROME (TS)

TS is a tic disorder that is frequently associated with Type 3 (Overfocused) ADD. Characterized by both motor and vocal tics lasting more than a year, TS provides the bridge between the basal ganglia and two seemingly opposite disorders: ADD and obsessive-compulsive disorder (OCD). Motor tics are involuntary physical movements such as eye blinking, head jerking, shoulder shrugging, and arm or leg jerking. Vocal tics typically involve making involuntary noises such as coughing, puffing, blowing, barking, and sometimes swearing (corprolalia). TS runs in families and there have been several genetic abnormalities found in the dopamine family of genes. SPECT studies, by my clinic and others, have found abnormalities in the basal ganglia of the brains of TS patients. There is a high association between TS and both ADD and OCD. It is estimated that 60 percent of people with TS have ADD and 50 percent of people with TS have OCD. On the surface it would appear that these are opposite disorders: People with ADD have trouble paying attention, while people with OCD pay too much attention to their negative thoughts (obsessions) or behaviors (compulsions). In looking further at both ADD and OCD patients clinically, I have found a high association of these diseases in the two groups' family histories. The medications clonidine and guanfacine can be helpful for the tics, as can the supplements magnesium, zinc, and taurine.

DIFFERENTIATING TYPE 3 (OVERFOCUSED) ADD FROM OCD AND OCPD

I am frequently asked how I differentiate people with this type of ADD from people who have obsessive compulsive disorder (OCD) or obsessive compulsive personality disorder (OCPD). That is easy. All three groups have overfocused tendencies (anterior cingulate issues), but people with Type 3 (Overfocused) ADD also have long-standing core ADD symptoms: short attention span, distractibility, spotty organization, poor follow-through, and poor internal supervision. People with OCD have clear obsessive thoughts and/or compulsive behaviors, such as repetitively checking locks or hand washing. People with OCPD have difficult personality traits—such as emotional rigidity, an "anal" need for sameness, the need to have their way, and compulsive cleanliness—but generally do not have core ADD symptoms. In fact, they usually have the opposite of ADD symptoms: They are overorganized, always on time, never say something impulsively, and must follow through with every task.

CHAPTER 9

Type 4: Temporal Lobe ADD

T he temporal lobes, underneath your temples and behind your eyes are involved with memory, learning, mood stability, and visual processing of objects. Type 4: Temporal Lobe ADD is commonly associated with learning and behavioral problems. It is often seen in people with ADD who struggle with mood instability, irritability, dyslexia, and memory problems.

The SPECT studies seen in Temporal Lobe ADD show abnormalities in the temporal lobes (usually significant decreased activity) along with decreased activity in the prefrontal cortex during concentration tasks. These patients exhibit both prefrontal and temporal lobe symptoms. I saw this type of ADD very early in my brain imaging work, especially with our most difficult patients, and began to see a correlation with earlier head injuries. Associated with domestic violence and suicidal thoughts, this type of ADD can ruin a family.

ADD core symptoms plus:

Memory problems

Learning problems

Auditory processing issues

Irritability

Periods of quick temper with little provocation

Misinterprets comments as negative when they are not

Irritability tends to build, then explodes, then recedes, often tired after a rage

Periods of spaciness or confusion

Periods of panic and/or fear for no specific reason

Visual changes, such as seeing shadows or objects changing shape

Frequent periods of déjà vu (feelings of being somewhere before even though you never have)

Sensitivity or mild paranoia

Headaches or abdominal pain of uncertain origin

History of a head injury

Dark thoughts, may involve suicidal or homicidal thoughts

Kris

The second brain SPECT study that I ever ordered was on Kris. By age twelve, Kris had a long history of emotional outbursts, increased activity level, short attention span, impulsiveness, school problems, frequent lying, and aggressive behavior. At age six, Kris was placed on methylphenidate (Ritalin) for hyperactivity but he became more aggressive and started to have visual hallucinations, so it was stopped. After he attacked a boy at school when he was eight years old, he was admitted to a psychiatric hospital in Alaska where his father was stationed in the military. He was given the diagnosis of depression and started on the antidepressant desipramine (Norpramin). It didn't help. By the age of twelve, Kris had been seen for several years of psychotherapy by a psychiatrist/psychoanalyst in the Napa Valley. His parents were seen by the same psychiatrist as well to help them be more effective in handling Kris's behavior.

The psychiatrist and mother did not get along very well. The psychiatrist frequently blamed the mother as the "biggest part of Kris's problem." It was true that Kris's mother looked angry, but she felt that nothing she did ever worked with Kris. The psychiatrist told her that if only she would get into psychotherapy and deal with her own childhood issues then Kris's problems would go away. Somehow his mother just didn't believe that was true. Before Kris she had not been angry or upset.

Kris's behavior escalated to the point where he became more aggressive and uncontrollable at home. When he attacked another child at school with a knife he was placed in a psychiatric hospital. I was on call the weekend Kris was admitted to the hospital. Seemingly by random chance he became my patient. To connect with my patients on the child psychiatry ward, I often played touch football with them. That day Kris was on my team. Every single play he cheated. When we were on defense, in between plays, he would move the ball three steps back and look at me with an expression that said, "Are you going to yell at me like my mother does?" I decided not to yell at Kris, but rather to scan his little brain to get some clues as to why he acted the way he did. I refused to play his ADD game of "get the adult angry."

Kris's brain SPECT study was very abnormal at rest, showing marked decreased activity in the left temporal lobe. It was 40 percent less active than his right temporal lobe. When Kris performed the concentration task there was marked decreased activity in the prefrontal cortex.

Given the temporal lobe problems, I placed Kris on the anticonvulsant medication carbamazepine (Tegretol) as a way to normalize his temporal lobe. Within a month he was a dramatically different child. He was more compliant, more social, and much more pleasant to be around. On the day he was discharged from the hospital I was on call again. I gathered my patients and we played football. Kris was on my team again. This time, on every single play he talked to me about what we were going to do in the game. His behavior was effective and goal directed rather than conflict driven.

When Kris went back to school his behavior was much better but he still struggled academically. Due to the fact that he had two problems (the left temporal lobe disorder and prefrontal cortex shutdown) I added the stimulant medication magnesium pemoline (Cylert). This helped his attention span and his schoolwork dramatically improved. His mother no

Kris's SPECT Pictures

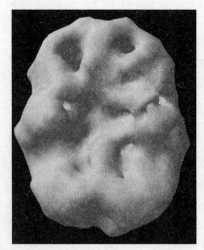 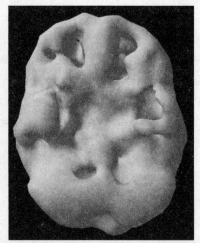

Underside surface view at rest
Mild decreased prefrontal and left
temporal lobe

Underside surface view with concentration
Marked decreased prefrontal and left tempo-
ral lobe

longer looked like "the problem." The positive response to treatment held for many years. Before his graduation from high school years after I met him, I gave a lecture to the teachers at his school. He saw me in the hallway and came up to me to introduce me to five of his friends.

What do you think would have happened to Kris if I hadn't figured out that he had a temporal lobe problem? It is likely that he would have found himself in the California Youth Authority, juvenile hall, a residential treatment facility, or multiple psychiatric facilities. His mother would have continued to feel that she was the cause of his problems. I often feel sad when I think of all the children like Kris who never get the help they need. They get labeled as bad, willful, defiant children who need more punishment, rather than, what I see as the truth, children with medical problems who need treatment.

The temporal lobes play an integral part in memory, emotional stability, learning, temper control, and socialization. On the dominant side of the brain (usually the left side for most people) the temporal lobes are intimately involved with understanding and processing language, intermediate and long-term memory, complex memories, the retrieval of language or words, emotional stability, and visual and auditory processing.

The Temporal Lobes

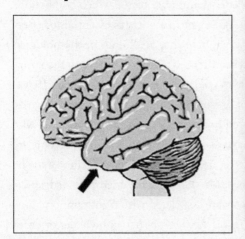

Side view

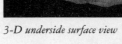

3-D underside surface view

Language is one of the keys to being human. It allows us to communicate with other human beings and it allows us to leave a legacy of our thoughts and actions for future generations. Receptive language, being able to receive and understand speech and written words, requires temporal lobe stability. The dominant temporal lobe helps to process sounds and written words into meaningful information. Being able to read in an efficient manner, remember what you read, and integrate the new information relies heavily on the dominant temporal lobe. Problems here contribute to language struggles, miscommunication, and reading disabilities.

Through our research we have also found that emotional stability is heavily influenced by this part of the brain. The ability to consistently feel stable and positive, despite the ups and downs of everyday life, is important for the development and maintenance of consistent character and personality. Optimum activity in the temporal lobes enhances mood stability, while increased or decreased activity in this part of the brain leads to fluctuating, inconsistent, or unpredictable moods and behaviors.

The nondominant temporal lobe (usually the right) is involved with reading facial expressions, processing verbal tones and intonations from others, hearing rhythms, appreciating music, and visual learning.

Recognizing familiar faces and facial expressions and being able to accurately perceive voice tones and intonations and give them appropriate meaning is critical to social skill. Being able to tell when someone is happy to see you, scared of you, bored, or in a hurry is essential for effectively interacting with others. A. Quaglino, an Italian opthamologist, reported on a patient in 1867 who, after a stroke, was unable to recognize familiar faces despite being able to read very small type. Since the 1940s, more than one hundred cases of prosopagnosia (the inability to recognize familiar faces) have been reported in the medical literature. Patients who have this disorder are often unaware of it (right hemisphere problems are often associated with neglect or denial of illnesses) or they may be ashamed at being unable to recognize close family members or friends. Most commonly, these problems were associated with right temporal lobe problems. Results of current research suggest that knowledge of emotional facial expressions is inborn, not learned (infants can recognize their mother's emotional faces). Yet, when there are problems in this part of the brain social skills can be impaired.

The temporal lobes help us process the world of sight and sound, and give us the language of life. This part of the brain allows us to be stimulated, relaxed, or brought to ecstasy by the experience of great music. The temporal lobes have been called the "Interpretive Cortex," as it interprets what we hear and integrates it with stored memories to give interpretation or meaning to the incoming information. Strong feelings of conviction, great insight, and knowing the truth have also been attributed to the temporal lobes.

Temporal lobe abnormalities occur much more frequently than previously recognized. The temporal lobes sit in a vulnerable area of the brain in the temporal fossa (or cavity), behind the eye sockets and underneath the temples. The front wall of the cavity includes a sharp bony ridge (the lesser wing of the sphenoid bone), which frequently damages the front part of the temporal lobes in even minor head injuries. Since the temporal lobes sit in a cavity surrounded by bone on five sides (front, back, right side, left side, and underside) they can be damaged from a blow to the head at almost any angle.

Model Showing the Base of the Skull

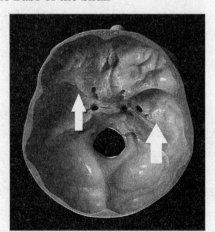

(Thick arrow points to temporal fossa where temporal lobes sit, thin arrow points to sharp edge of the lesser wing of the sphenoid bone)

As with other brain problems, temporal lobe problems can come from many different sources, the most common being genetic (you can get these problems from your parents), toxic or infectious exposure, and head injuries. In my clinic, we will ask you five times whether or not you ever had a head injury. (It amazes us how often people forget they have had head injuries!) Our intake paperwork will ask you if you've ever had a head injury. Our historians, who people see before seeing our physicians, ask this question. Our brain imaging information sheet asks this question. If we see that patients answer no, no, no to this question we'll ask them again. If they say no for the fourth time we'll ask, "Are you sure? Have you ever fallen out of a tree, off a fence, or dove into a shallow pool?" It is not uncommon for people to say, "Oh yeah, now I remember." One man, after saying no four times to this question said, "Oh yeah, I fell out of a second story window. I forgot." Other patients, after saying no four times, have told me about falling out of cars, going through car windshields, falling off porches five feet onto their heads, falling off balconies, down staircases, etc. Your brain is very soft and your skull is very hard. Your brain is more sophisticated than any computer we can design. You cannot just drop a computer and expect things will be okay. The temporal lobes, prefrontal cortex, and cingulate gyrus are the most vulnerable brain areas to damage by virtue of their placement within the skull. They are the most heavily involved parts of the brain in terms of thinking and behavior.

Jake

Jake, age sixty-five, came to see me from Mississippi. His wife heard me on national television and she was sure he had a temporal lobe problem. He was moody, had memory problems, and was often aggressive. Jake often heard bees "buzzing," even though no bees were around. The temper problems seemed to come out of nowhere. "The littlest things seem to set me off. Then I feel terribly guilty," he said. When Jake was fifteen years old, he was in a diving accident where he hit his head on the board and was unconscious for several minutes. After the accident, he had more problems in school and more problems with his temper. His brain SPECT study showed decreased activity in both the front and back of the left temporal lobe (a pattern frequently seen in head injuries) and decreased activity in his prefrontal cortex. Seeing this pattern, it was clear to me that many of Jake's problems came from the poor activity in his left temporal lobe and PFC, likely from the teen accident. I placed him on Depakote (an antiseizure medication known to stabilize activity in the temporal lobes) and Adderall, along with the other Type 4 suggestions given later. When I spoke to Jake and his wife three weeks later they were very pleased. The temper outbursts stopped completely and he felt more focused and energetic. Six years later his temper remains under control.

TEMPORAL LOBE PROBLEMS

Common problems seen with left temporal lobe abnormalities include aggression—internally or externally driven, dark or violent thoughts, sensitivity to slights, mild paranoia, word-finding problems, auditory processing problems, reading difficulties, and emotional instability.

The aggressiveness often seen with left temporal lobe abnormalities can either be externally expressed toward others or internally expressed in aggressive thoughts toward oneself. Aggressive behavior is complex, but in a large study performed in my clinic on people who had assaulted another person or damaged property, more than 70 percent had left temporal lobe abnormalities. It seems that temporal lobe damage or dysfunction makes a person more prone to irritable, angry, or violent thoughts. One patient of mine with temporal lobe dysfunction (probably inherited, as his father was a rageaholic) complains of frequent, intense violent thoughts. He feels shame over having these thoughts and didn't understand where they came from. "I can be walking down the street," he told me, "and someone accidentally brushes against me, and I get the thought of wanting to shoot him or club him to death. These thoughts frighten me." Thankfully, even though his SPECT confirmed left temporal lobe dysfunction, he had good prefrontal cortex function so he is able to supervise his behavior and maintain impulse control over these terrible thoughts. In a similar case, Misty, a forty-five-year-old woman, came to see me for anger outbursts. One day, someone accidentally bumped into her in the grocery store and she started screaming at the woman, which was the reason she came to see me. "I just don't understand where my anger comes from," she said. "I've had sixteen years of therapy and it is still there. Out of the blue, I'll go off. I get the most horrid thoughts. You'd hate me if you knew." In her history she noted that she had fallen off the top of a bunk bed when she was four years old. She was unconscious for only a minute or two. The front and back part of her left temporal lobe was clearly damaged. A small dose of an anticonvulsant medication was very helpful to calm the monster within.

I often see internal aggressiveness with left temporal lobe abnormalities, expressed in suicidal behavior. In a study from our clinic, we saw left temporal lobe abnormalities in 62 percent of our patients who had serious suicidal thoughts or actions. After I gave a lecture about the brain in Oakland a woman came up to me in tears. "Oh Dr. Amen," she said, "I know my whole family has temporal lobe problems. My paternal great grandfather killed himself. My father's mother and father killed themselves. My father and two of my three uncles killed themselves and last year my son tried to kill himself. Is there help for us?" I had the opportunity to evaluate and scan three members in her family. Two had left temporal lobe abnormalities and anticonvulsant medications were helpful in their treatment.

In terms of suicidal behavior, one very sad case highlights the involvement of the left temporal lobes. For years I wrote a column in my local newspaper about the brain and behavior. One column was about temporal lobe dysfunction and suicidal behavior. A week or so later a mother came to see me. She told me that her twenty-year-old son had killed himself several months ago and she was grief stricken over the unbelievable turn of events in his life. "He was the most ideal child a mother could have," she said. "He did great in school. He was polite, cooperative, and a joy to have around. Then it all changed. Two years ago he had a bicycle accident. He accidentally hit a branch in the street and was flipped over the handlebars, landing on the left side of his face. He was unconscious when an onlooker got to him, but shortly thereafter came to. Nothing was the same since then. He was moody, angry, easily set off. He started to complain of 'bad thoughts' in his head. I took him to see a therapist, but it didn't seem to help. One evening, I heard a loud noise out front. He had shot and killed himself on our front lawn." Her tears made me get teary. I knew that her son might well have been helped if someone had recognized that his "minor head injury" likely caused temporal lobe damage and that anticonvulsant medication may well have prevented his suicide. Of interest, in the past twenty years psychiatrists have been using anticonvulsants to treat many psychiatric problems. My suspicion is we are treating underlying brain problems we label as "psychiatric."

In addition to aggression, we have seen people with left temporal lobe abnormalities be more sensitive to slights and even appear mildly paranoid. Unlike people with schizophrenia who can become frankly paranoid, temporal lobe dysfunction often causes a person to think others are talking about them or laughing at them when there is no evidence for it. This sensitivity can cause serious relational and work problems.

Reading and language processing problems are also common when there is dysfunction in the left temporal lobe. It is currently estimated that nearly 20 percent of the U.S. population has difficulty reading. Our studies of people with dyslexia (underachievement in reading) often show underactivity in the back half of the left temporal lobe. Dyslexia can be inherited or it can be brought about after a head injury, damaging this part of the brain. Here are two illustrative cases.

Thirteen-year-old Denise came to see me because she was having problems with her temper. She had pulled a knife on her mother, which precipitated the referral. She also had school problems, especially in the area of reading for which she was in special classes. Due to the seriousness of her aggression and learning problems I decided to order a SPECT study at rest and then again when she tried to concentrate. At rest her brain showed mild decreased activity in the back half of her left temporal lobe. When she tried to concentrate the activity in her left temporal lobe completely shut down. As I showed Denise and her mother the scans, I told Denise that it was clear that the more she tried to read the harder reading would become. As I said this she burst into tears. She cried, "When I read I am so mean to myself. I tell myself, 'Try harder. If you try harder then you won't be so stupid.' But trying harder doesn't seem to help." I told her it was essential for her to talk nicely to herself and that she will do better reading in a setting that is interesting, fun, and relaxed. I sent Denise to see an educational therapist. She taught her a specialized reading program that showed her how to visualize words and use a different part of the brain to process reading.

Carrie, a forty-year-old psychologist, came to see me two years after she sustained a head injury in a car accident. Before the accident, she had a remarkable memory and she was a fast, efficient reader. She said reading was one of her academic strengths. After the accident, she had memory problems, struggled more with irritability, and reading became difficult for her. She said that she had to read passages over and over to retain any information and that she had trouble remembering what she read past just a few moments. Again, her SPECT study showed damage to the front and back of her left temporal lobe (the pattern typically seen in trauma). I had her see my biofeedback therapist to enhance activity in her left temporal lobe. Over the course of four months she was able to regain her reading skills and improve her memory and control over her temper.

In our experience, left temporal lobe abnormalities are more frequently associated with externally directed discomfort (such as anger, irritability, aggressiveness), while right temporal lobe abnormalities are more likely associated with internal discomfort (anxiety and fearfulness). The left-right dichotomy has been particularly striking in our clinic population. One possible explanation is the left hemisphere of the brain is involved with understanding and expressing language and perhaps when the left hemisphere is involved one could express their discomfort. When the nondominant hemisphere is involved the discomfort is more likely expressed nonverbally.

Nondominant (usually right) temporal lobe problems more often involve social skill problems, especially in the area of reading and recognizing facial expressions and recognizing voice intonations. Mike, age thirty, illustrates the difficulties we have seen when there is dysfunction in this part of the brain. Mike came to see me because he wanted a date. He had never had a date in his life and was very frustrated by his inability to meet and successfully ask a woman out on a date. During the evaluation Mike said he was at a loss as to what his problem was. His mother, who accompanied him to the session, had her own ideas. "Mike," she said, "misreads situations. He has always done that. Sometimes he comes on too strong, sometimes he is withdrawn when another person is interested. He doesn't read the sound of my voice right either. I can be really mad at him and he doesn't take me seriously. Or he can think I'm mad, when I'm nowhere near mad. When he was a little boy, Mike tried to play with other children but he could never hold on to friends. It was so painful to see him get discouraged." Mike's SPECT showed marked decreased activity in his right temporal lobe. His left temporal lobe was fine. The intervention that was most effective for Mike was intensive social skills training. He worked with a psychologist who coached him on facial expressions, voice tones, and proper social etiquette. He had his first date six months after coming to the clinic.

Abnormal activity in either or both temporal lobes can cause a wide variety of symptoms including: abnormal perceptions (sensory illusions), memory problems, feelings of déjà vu (that you have been somewhere before even though you haven't), jamais vu (not recognizing familiar places), periods of panic or fear for no particular reason, periods of spaciness or confusion, and preoccupation with religious or moral issues. Illusions are very common temporal lobe symptoms. Common illusions include:

- seeing shadows or bugs out of the corner of the eyes
- seeing objects change size or shape (one patient would see lampposts turn into animals and run away, another patient would see figures move in a painting)
- hearing bees buzzing or static from a radio
- smelling odors or getting odd tastes in the mouth
- feeling bugs crawling on skin or other skin sensations
- Unexplained headaches and stomachaches also seem to be common in temporal lobe dysfunction.

Several of the anticonvulsants are used for migraine prevention, including Depakote and Neurontin. Often when headaches or stomachaches are due to temporal lobe problems anticonvulsants seem to be helpful. Periods of déjà vu (the feeling you've been somewhere before even though you never have) and jamais vu (feeling unfamiliar in familiar surroundings) also are seen in temporal lobe states. Also, unexplained periods of anxiety or fearfulness is one of the most common presenting symptoms with temporal lobe epilepsy. Many patients experience sudden feelings of anxiety, nervousness, or panic. Frequently, many patients make secondary associations to the panic and develop fears or phobias. For example, if the first time you experience the feeling of panic or dread is when you are in a grocery store or at a park, you may then develop anxiety every time you go into a grocery store or go to the park.

Moral or religious preoccupation is a common symptom with temporal lobe dysfunction. I have a little boy in my practice who, at age six, made himself physically sick by worrying about all of the people who were going to hell. Another patient spent seven days a week in church, praying for the souls of his family. He came to see me because of his temper problems, frequently directed at his family, which were often seen in response to some perceived moral misgiving or outrage. Another patient came to see me because he spent hours focused on the "mysteries of life," could not get any work done, and was about to lose his job as a writer for a Bay Area magazine. All of these patients had temporal lobe abnormalities.

Hypergraphia, a tendency toward compulsive and extensive writing, has also been reported in temporal lobe disorders. One wonders whether Ted Kaczynski, the reported Unabomber, didn't have temporal lobe problems given the lengthy, rambling manifesto he wrote, his proclivity toward violent behavior, and his social withdrawal. Some of my temporal lobe patients spend hours and hours writing. One patient, who moved to another state, used to write me twenty- and thirty-page letters, detailing all of the aspects of her life. As I learned about temporal lobe hypergraphia and had her treated with anticonvulsant medication her letters became more coherent and were shortened to two to three pages, saying the same information. Of note, many people with temporal lobe problems have the opposite of hypergraphia; they are unable to get words out of their heads and have a paucity of writing. One of the therapists in my office, who's a wonderful public speaker, could not get the thoughts out of his head to write his book. On his scan there was decreased activity in both of his temporal lobes. On a very small dose of Depakote his ideas were unlocked and he could now write for hours at a time.

Memory problems have long been one of the hallmarks of temporal lobe dysfunction. Amnesia after a head injury is frequently due to damage to the inside aspect of the temporal lobes. Brain infections also cause severe memory problems. Harriet came to see me from New England. She was a very gracious eighty-three-year-old woman who had lost her memory fifteen years earlier during a bout of encephalitis. Even though she remembered events before the infection she could only remember small bits and pieces after the accident. An hour after she ate she would feel full but forgot what she ate. Her daughter heard me lecture in Burlington, Vermont, and told her to come see me. Harriet said, "I left my brain to the local medical school, hoping my problems would help someone else, but I don't think they'll do anything with my brain except give it to medical students to cut up. Plus I want to know what the problem is. And write it down. I won't remember what you tell me!" Harriet's brain showed marked damage in both temporal lobes, especially on the left side, like the virus went to that part of her brain and chewed it away.

Jenny

Jenny, sixteen, tried to kill herself the night before I first met her. Her boyfriend had just broken up with her. He told her that he was tired of the fights she started with him. She told him that she would kill herself if he left. When he started to leave, she took a knife and cut her wrist. He called the police who took her to the hospital. At that time Jenny was also having problems in school. Many of Jenny's teachers said she was not living up to her potential and that she needed to try harder. There were also many fights between Jenny and her parents. Whenever they asked her to do something around the house she would fly into a rage. Over the last year she had broken a window and put several holes in walls and doors. Taking the history, I learned that at the age of eight, Jenny had fallen off her bike face-first onto the cement. She had lost consciousness for about ten minutes. Since the accident, she had complained of headaches and vague abdominal pain. Her pediatrician told her mother that it was just stress. Jenny was also overly sensitive to perceived slights, she frequently saw shadows that were not there, she had periods of anxiety with little provocation, and she had trouble with reading and memory.

Jenny had Temporal Lobe ADD, one of the most difficult behavioral types of this disorder. She had trouble with inattention and impulse control. She was also conflict-seeking and underachieved in school. In addition, she had specific temporal lobe symptoms, such as headaches and abdominal pain, illusions, periods of anxiety for little reason, hyper-sensitivity to others, and memory and reading problems. One of the hall-marks of Temporal Lobe ADD is aggression. She had both external aggression (toward others and objects) and internal aggression (toward herself: the suicide attempt). Her brain SPECT study showed decreased activity in the prefrontal cortex (giving her trouble concentrating) and decreased activity in her left temporal lobe (probably from the head injury that predated the onset of many symptoms). I placed her on the anticonvulsant Neurontin, which stabilized her mood instability and temper, and Adderall, which helped her attention span and impulsive-ness. In addition, she changed her diet and exercised every day. Six years later she remains much better. She has just finished college and has been in a stable relationship for two years.

Jenny

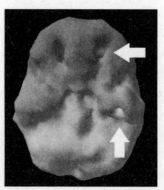

Low prefrontal and left temporal lobe activity

Omar

Omar, thirty-two, was sent to our clinic by his defense attorney after he had been arrested for felony spouse abuse. Omar was Jordanian and he was married to a woman from Lebanon. They had been in the United States for four years. On six occasions in the last four years Omar had lost his temper and assaulted his wife. On the last occasion he broke her ribs and left arm. His explosions seemed to come out of the blue. His wife said that some days he woke up "different." On certain days he had headaches, was overly sensitive, and nothing his wife did was right. All his life he had the core symptoms of ADD. He did poorly in school, despite being of above average intelligence. His teachers said that he was impulsive and had a short attention span. Homework used to take him half the night to do with his mother standing over him to get it done. He was disorganized and frequently late to obligations. Despite his problems, he had risen to a top salesperson in his company and he was responsible for other salespeople at work. Due to his explosive rage he had attended psychotherapy and an anger management class. They did not seem to make much difference. He also had seen a psychiatrist who had diagnosed him with ADD and given him Ritalin. The Ritalin made him feel speedy and irritable.

Our feeling is that anyone who assaults another person should have a brain scan. Omar's SPECT study showed decreased activity in both of his temporal lobes and decreased activity in the prefrontal cortex. He was placed on Neurontin and Adderall and given the dietary and exercise advice for this type. Over the next three months I adjusted his medication dosages and his temper cooled while his ability to focus and organize himself improved. The scans were used in his court case. As part of the plea agreement, Omar had to do community service and see a psychiatrist every month for five years. If he dropped out of treatment he would be taken to prison.

Frequently, stimulants, such as Ritalin or Adderall, make this ADD type worse if they are given without anticonvulsant medication to stabilize temporal lobe function. They cause people to be irritable and sometimes more aggressive. Stabilizing the temporal lobes with anticonvulsant medications, such as Lamictal, Depakote, or Neurontin can literally rescue a life from despair, hatred, and self-loathing. After the temporal lobes are treated, a stimulant medication may be very helpful for concentration.

Jacob

Jacob lived with his grandparents. His mother was a drug addict and unable to care for him. Jacob was exposed to drugs in utero. When I saw him at the age of six he was hyperactive, very impulsive, easily distracted, struggled with learning, and had severe temper problems. His pediatrician had diagnosed him with ADD and put him on a stimulant medication, but four days later he had visual hallucinations. He saw what he described as ghosts (green blobs) floating around him. He also became much more irritable. The pediatrician referred Jacob to me. I ordered a SPECT study to evaluate his temporal lobes and also to see if there was drug damage still evident from his in utero exposure. It was no surprise when I saw overall decreased activity in his brain, especially in the area of the left temporal lobe. Jacob's temper improved on an anticonvulsant. A month later I started Adderall to help his attention span. A year later he was much better.

John

John, a seventy-nine-year-old contractor, had a longstanding history of alcohol abuse and violent behavior. He had frequently physically abused his wife over forty years of marriage and had been abusive to the children when they were living at home. Almost all of the abuse occurred when he was intoxicated. As a boy he had been described as hyperactive, slow in school, and impulsive. At age seventy-nine, John underwent open-heart surgery. After the surgery he had a psychotic episode, lasting ten days. His doctor ordered a SPECT study as part of his evaluation. The study showed marked decreased activity in the left outside frontal-temporal region, a finding most likely due to a past head injury, and decreased activity in his prefrontal cortex. When the doctor asked John if he had ever had any significant head injuries, John told him about a time when he was twenty years old. While driving an old milk truck, that was missing its side-rear mirror, he put his head out of the window to look behind him. His head struck a pole, knocking him unconscious for several hours. After the head injury he had

John's Concentration SPECT Study (Left Side Surface View)

*Left side surface view
(Note marked area of decreased
activity in the left frontal and
temporal region)*

more problems with his temper and memory. There was a family history of alcohol abuse in four of his five brothers, but none of his brothers had problems with aggressive behavior. Given the location of the brain abnormalities (left frontal-temporal dysfunction) he was more likely to exhibit violent behavior. The alcohol abuse, which did not elicit violent behavior in his brothers, did in him. He was placed on carbamazepine and Adderall. His behavior was much more even and he was able to focus better than he had even when he was a child.

Neil

Neil, a seventeen-year-old male, was diagnosed with attention deficit/hyperactivity disorder (ADHD) and left temporal lobe dysfunction (diagnosed by EEG) at the age of fourteen. Before then (from grades one to eight) he had been expelled from eleven schools for fighting, frequently cut school, and had already started drinking alcohol and using marijuana. He had a dramatically positive response to 15 milligrams of methylphenidate (Ritalin) three times a day. He improved three grade levels of reading within the next year, attended school regularly, and had no aggressive outbursts. His grandmother (with whom he lived) and his teachers were very pleased with his progress. However, Neil had a negative emotional response to taking medication. He later said that taking his medication, even though it obviously helped him, made him feel stupid and different. Two years after starting his medication, he decided to stop it on his own without telling anyone. His anger began to escalate again, as did his drinking and marijuana usage. One night, while he was intoxicated, his uncle came over to his home and asked Neil to help him "rob some women." Neil went with his uncle who forced a woman into her car and made her go to her ATM and withdraw money. The uncle and Neil then raped the woman twice. He was apprehended two weeks later and charged with kidnapping, robbery, and rape.

I was asked by Neil's defense attorney to evaluate Neil. I agreed with the clinical history of ADD and suspected left temporal lobe dysfunction because of the chronic aggressive behavior and abnormal EEG. I ordered a series of brain SPECT studies: one at rest, one while he was doing a concentration task, and one on methylphenidate. The rest study showed mild decreased activity in the prefrontal cortex and the left temporal lobe. While performing a concentration task, there was marked suppression of the prefrontal cortex and both temporal lobes. The third scan was done one hour after taking 15 milligrams of methylphenidate. This scan showed marked activation in the prefrontal cortex and both temporal lobes.

After understanding the history and reviewing the scan data, it was apparent that Neil already had a vulnerable brain that was consistent with long-term behavioral and academic difficulties. His substance use may have further suppressed an already underactive prefrontal cortex and temporal lobe, diminishing executive abilities and unleashing aggressive tendencies. It is possible that with an explanation of the underlying metabolic problems and brief psychotherapy on the emotional issues surrounding the need to take medication, this serious problem might have been averted. In prison, he was placed on an anticonvulsant and had no aggressive outbursts for the past two years.

DIFFERENTIATING TYPE 4 TEMPORAL LOBE ADD FROM TEMPORAL LOBE EPILEPSY

I am often asked how to differentiate Type 4 Temporal Lobe ADD from temporal lobe epilepsy. This can be challenging. Both disorders are due to abnormal activity in the temporal lobes. Both disorders are helped with anticonvulsant medication. Temporal Lobe ADD may be a combination of a variant of temporal lobe epilepsy that is comorbid with ADD. In order for the diagnosis to be Temporal Lobe ADD there needs to be long-standing core ADD symptoms in addition to the temporal lobe symptoms. Many people with TLE do not have ADD symptoms and so would not fall into the Temporal Lobe ADD category.

THE TREATMENT DEPENDS ON A COMBINATION OF THE SYMPTOMS AND SCAN FINDINGS

Not everyone who has temporal lobe problems on SPECT needs to be placed on anticonvulsant medication. When there is mood instability, irritability, or temper problems, we tend to use anticonvulsants. When there is learning or memory problems we tend to use supplements, such as gingko, vinpocetine, and phosphatidylserine, or medications, such as Aricept or Namenda—medications originally developed for Alzheimer's disease, to enhance learning and memory. More on this in the medication and supplement chapters.

Type 5: Limbic ADD

Type 5: Limbic ADD is where ADD and depression intersect each other. The ADD core symptoms are present in addition to negativity, moodiness, sadness, low energy, and decreased interest in life. On SPECT we see decreased prefrontal cortex activity both at rest and during a concentration task and we see too much activity in the deep limbic or emotional center of the brain. Depression on SPECT is similar. There is decreased activity in the prefrontal cortex (especially on the left side) at rest, but it improves with concentration. Understanding the deep limbic system is important to understanding Limbic ADD.

THE DEEP LIMBIC SYSTEM

The deep limbic system lies near the center of the brain. Considering its size—about that of a walnut—it is power-packed with functions, all of which are critical for human behavior and survival. From an evolutionary standpoint, this is an older part of the mammalian brain that enabled animals to experience

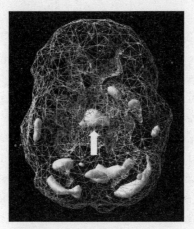

3-D underside active view

and express emotions. It freed them from the stereotypical behavior and actions dictated by the brain stem, found in the older reptilian brain. The subsequent evolution of the surrounding cerebral cortex in higher animals, especially humans, gave the capacity for problem solving, planning, organization, and rational thought. Yet, in order for these functions to occur, one must have passion, emotion, and desire to make it happen. The deep limbic system adds the emotional spice, if you will, in both positive and negative ways.

This part of the brain is involved in setting a person's emotional tone. When the deep limbic system is less active, there is generally a positive, more hopeful state of mind. When it is heated up, or overactive, negativity can take over. This finding actually surprised us at first. We thought that excessive activity in the part of the brain that controlled emotion might correlate with enhanced feelings, not necessarily negative feelings. Yet, we noticed, again and again, when this area was overactive on SPECT, it correlated with depression and negativity. It seems when the deep limbic system is inflamed, painful emotional shading results. New research on depression from other laboratories around the world has borne this out.

Due to this emotional shading, the deep limbic system provides the filter through which you interpret the events of the day. It tags or colors events depending on the emotional state of mind. When you are sad (with an overactive deep limbic system), you are likely to interpret neutral events through a negative lens. For example, if you have a neutral or even positive conversation with someone whose deep limbic structure is overactive or "negatively set" he or she is likely to interpret the conversation in a negative way. When this part of the brain is "cool" or functions properly, a neutral or positive interpretation of events is more likely to occur. Emotional tagging of events is critical to survival. The valence or charge we give to certain events in our lives drives us to action (such as approaching a desired mate) or causes avoidance behavior (withdrawing from someone who has hurt you in the past).

The deep limbic system, along with the deep temporal lobes, has also been reported to store highly charged emotional memories, both positive and negative. If you have been traumatized by a dramatic event, such as being in a car accident or watching your house burn down, or if you have been abused by a parent or a spouse, the emotional component of the memory is stored in the deep limbic system of the brain. On the other hand, if you have won the lottery, graduated magna cum laude, or watched your child's birth, those emotional memories are stored here as well. The total experience of our emotional memories is responsible, in part, for the emotional tone of our mind. The more stable, positive experiences we have, the more positive we are likely to feel. The more trauma in our lives, the more emotionally set we become in a negative way. These emotional memories are intimately involved in the emotional tagging that occurs.

The deep limbic system also affects motivation and drive. Hyperactivity in this area, in our experience, is associated with lowered motivation and decreased drive, which is often seen in depression. The deep limbic system, especially the hypothalamus, controls the sleep and appetite cycles of the body. Healthy sleep and appetite is essential to maintaining a proper internal milieu. Both of these components are often a problem with limbic abnormalities.

The deep limbic structures are also intimately involved with bonding and social connectedness. When the deep limbic system of animals is damaged, they do not properly bond with their young. In one study of rats, when the deep limbic structures were damaged mothers would drag their offspring around the cage as if they were inanimate objects. They would not feed and nurture the young as they would normally do. In people, this system affects the bonding mechanism that enables you to connect with other people on a social level; your ability to do this successfully in turn influences your moods. Humans are not like polar bears, wandering the tundra alone eleven months out of the year. We are social animals. When we are bonded to people in a positive way we feel better about our lives and ourselves. This capacity to bond, then, plays a significant role in the tone and quality of our moods.

The deep limbic system directly processes the sense of smell, the only sense that has so direct a connection. (The messages from all the other senses are sent to a "relay station," the thalamus, before they are sent to their final destination in different parts of the brain.) Considering this, it is easy to see why smells can have such a powerful impact on our feeling states. The multibillion-dollar perfume and deodorant industries count on this fact: beautiful smells evoke pleasant feelings and draw people toward you, whereas unpleasant smells cause people to withdraw. Expensive perfumes and colognes can make you beautiful, sexy, and attractive to others, whereas a disagreeable body odor can make the other person want to rush to the far side of the room.

Research has demonstrated that females, on average, have a larger deep limbic system than males. This gives females several advantages and disadvantages. Due to the larger deep limbic brain, women are more in touch with their feelings and are generally better able to express their feelings than men. They have an increased ability to bond and be connected to others (which is why women are the primary caretakers for children: There is no society on earth where men are primary caretakers for children). Females have a more acute sense of smell, which is likely to have developed from an evolutionary need for the mother to recognize her young. Having a larger deep limbic system leaves a female somewhat more susceptible to depression, especially at times of significant hormonal changes such as the onset of puberty, before menses, after the birth of a child, and at menopause.

The deep limbic system, especially the hypothalamus at the base of the brain, is responsible for translating our emotional state into physical feelings of relaxation or tension. The front half of the hypothalamus sends calming signals to the body through the parasympathetic nervous system. The back half of the hypothalamus sends stimulating or fear signals to the body through the sympathetic nervous system. The back half of the hypothalamus, when stimulated, is responsible for the fight or flight response, a primitive state that gets us ready to fight or flee when we are threatened or scared. This "hardwired response" happens immediately upon activation, such as seeing or experiencing an emotional or physical threat. In this response, the heart beats faster, breathing rate and blood pressure increases, the hands and feet become cooler to shunt blood from the extremities to the big muscles (to fight or run away), and the pupils dilate (to see better). This "deep limbic" translation of emotion is powerful and immediate. It happens with overt physical threats and also with more covert emotional threats. This part of the brain is intimately connected with the prefrontal cortex and seems to acts as a switching station between running on emotion (the deep limbic system) and rational thought and problem solving with our cortex. When the limbic system is turned on, emotions tend to take over. When it is cooled down, more activation is possible in the cortex. Current research on depression indicates increased deep limbic system activity and shutdown in the prefrontal cortex, especially on the left side.

The problems in the deep limbic system often look like depression. Do you know people who see every situation in a bad light? That actually could be a deep limbic system problem. As mentioned, this system tends to set our emotional filter, and when it is working too hard, the filter is colored with negativity. One person could walk away from an interaction that ten others would have labeled as positive, but which he or she considers negative. And since the deep limbic system affects motivation, people sometimes develop an "I don't care" attitude about life and work; they don't have the energy to care. Because they feel hopeless about the outcome, they have little willpower to follow through with tasks.

Since the sleep and appetite centers are in the deep limbic system, disruption can lead to changes, which may mean an inclination one way or the other, too much or too little of either. For example, in typical depressive episodes people have been known to lose their appetites and to have trouble sleeping despite being chronically tired, and yet in atypical depression they will sleep and eat excessively.

DEPRESSION VERSUS LIMBIC ADD

Due to the similarities between the two conditions, it can be hard to distinguish between depression and Limbic ADD: After all, both diseases demonstrate similar symptoms and even somewhat similar SPECT results. Developmental history seems to be the most helpful tool in helping clinicians decide. Depression tends to be a cyclic illness. It may be associated with some of the core symptoms of ADD, but not in a developmental pattern. The cognitive symptoms are only present when the depression is present. By contrast, in ADD, one can see symptoms for a prolonged period of time, usually back to childhood.

In addition, there are subtle SPECT differences. Research has shown that depression is seen on SPECT as decreased activity in the left prefrontal cortex *at rest* with increased limbic activity. When a depressed person tries to concentrate there is usually increased activity in the prefrontal cortex. Limbic ADD, on the other hand, tends to show decreased prefrontal cortex activity *during concentration* in conjunction with increased limbic activity.

Barry

Barry, seventy, came to my clinic for help with a short attention span, poor memory, decreased energy, terrible disorganization, and trouble finishing projects. Barry also complained of problems sleeping, frequent negative thoughts, excessive guilt, and a tendency to isolate himself. His doctor felt that he was depressed, but the antidepressants Prozac and Zoloft made him feel worse. His great-grandson had just been diagnosed with attention deficit disorder and got significant benefit from treatment. He reminded Barry of himself when he was a little boy. Maybe there was still time for him to get help.

Barry had symptoms consistent with Limbic ADD or ADD that also has many depressive symptoms. Hallmark symptoms of Limbic ADD include the typical ADD symptoms (short attention span, distractibility, etc.) plus negativity, sadness, poor energy, social isolation, and feelings of guilt, hopelessness, or helplessness. His brain SPECT study showed decreased activity in the prefrontal cortex plus increased activity in the limbic system (which is the mood control center of the brain). Barry was placed on DL-phenylalanine and L-tyrosine, the amino acid building blocks for norepinephrine and dopamine, the two neurotransmitters implicated in this type of ADD. Within two weeks Barry noticed a significant benefit. He felt more focused, better physical and mental energy, more positive, and more social.

Charity

Charity was thirty-seven when she first came to my clinic, brought in by her husband, a local minister. Both she and her husband wanted help with Charity's negativity, low energy, poor organization, irritability, and short attention span. She also had a poor appetite and had trouble gaining weight. Charity was also very distractible and sensitive to touch. She cut tags out of her shirt and could only be touched by her husband when she was in the mood. Their sex life suffered. Her family physician tried Paxil and Celexa, but they seemed to make her symptoms worse.

Charity had struggles in school since she was a little girl. She was a quiet child who tended to be sad and negative. Her report cards had comments like "needs to try harder" and "needs to work on paying attention." Her organization was a big problem and she remembered being in trouble for her messy room. She remembered that homework was torture and that she would frequently stay up late into the night working on it. Her long-standing symptoms of short attention span, distractibility, disorganization, and poor follow-through were consistent with an ADD diagnosis. In addition, the symptoms of negativity, social isolation, low libido, and poor energy put the ADD into Type 4. Initially Charity wanted to try a "more natural treatment" than prescription medication. I placed her on DL-phenylalanine and L-tyrosine along with The Zone Diet and intense aerobic exercise. Within several weeks Charity felt much improved. Her appetite was better, she was able to gain a few pounds, and she felt more focused and less distracted. Her husband said she was like a new person. Her libido also improved.

Doug

Seventeen-year-old Doug was brought to our clinic by his parents. He was failing in school, despite being tested as being very smart. He had started to talk about feeling hopeless and even suicidal. He was socially isolated, didn't find pleasure in activities other teens enjoyed, and his thought patterns were negative. He smoked marijuana as a way to feel more relaxed and less depressed. He had always struggled in school with a short attention span and distractibility and he was "the master of procrastination" (as he put it). His school problems were worse after he started smoking pot. He had been seen in psychotherapy and had tutors through the years. These interventions did not make much difference. The family doctor put Doug on Prozac, but it only made him less motivated.

Seeing the situation as serious, I ordered a SPECT series. There were a number of findings: He had decreased prefrontal cortex activity at rest that worsened with concentration. He had increased deep limbic activity on both studies, and there was decreased activity in the back half of the temporal lobes (a finding common among marijuana users). I showed Doug his scan and encouraged him to stay away from the marijuana as it was probably damaging his brain. I told him the damage would probably get much better if he stopped. In addition, I put him on Wellbutrin to stabilize his mood and a small dose of Adderall to help him with energy and focus. I also encouraged him to change his diet and to get more exercise. Within two months Doug was feeling much better. He was more optimistic, less negative, more focused, and he was more positive about school. He decided to take the California High School Proficiency Examination to test out of high school and he went to the local junior college. By the age of twenty he earned his AA degree and is now attending a California university.

Doug's case highlights that many people use illegal drugs as a form of self-medication. They have an underlying mood disorder, type of ADD, or anxiety disorder. They use drugs as a means to feel better, more normal. Without proper treatment it is very hard for them to give up the substance abuse.

Stacey's Concentration SPECT Study (Underside Active View)

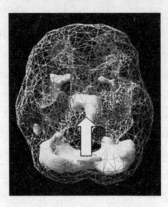

Stacey

At the age of fifteen, Stacey was failing school. She had two D's, two F's, and a C. She had been cutting classes, smoking cigarettes, and arguing with her parents. She had recently become sexually active and just had an abortion before she came for an evaluation at the clinic. Despite being a bright child, she had always struggled in school. Homework took forever to do and she frequently did not turn it in. She had poor handwriting and was easily distracted, very impulsive, and disorganized. She was becoming more negative, irritable, and isolated.

After a full evaluation, it was clear to me that she had Limbic ADD. A SPECT study confirmed the diagnosis. Initially, I tried her on DL-phenylalanine and L-tyrosine, but they were not effective. I then put her on Wellbutrin, a stimulating antidepressant. She had a very nice response to the medication. Within two weeks, her mood brightened, her attention span improved, and she even stopped smoking (Wellbutrin has been approved by the FDA to help people stop smoking).

Sonny

Thirty-eight-year-old Sonny was brought to see me by her husband. She was frequently overwhelmed, irritable, and negative. She had trouble keeping up with her work at home and she constantly complained of being tired. She had a very poor appetite and did not sleep well. She had little interest in sex and was feeling more and more distant from her husband and family. She barely graduated from high school and felt constantly behind in her work. She tended to fall asleep whenever she read. Her husband had read about ADD and found our clinic on the Web. She took our interactive ADD test and found it was likely that she had Limbic ADD. After evaluating her, I agreed. I gave her the options of anti-depressant medication or the amino acid supplements. We started with the supplements, diet, and an exercise regimen. After three weeks she said that the combination was very helpful for her. She could tell within a half an hour if she cheated on the diet. She said, "It's amazing to me that food is as powerful as a drug. When I eat right I feel good. When I don't eat right I feel bad." Her libido improved, as she felt better emotionally and physically.

Limbic ADD is often responsible for failed marriages. The low sexual interest, tiredness, feelings of being constantly overwhelmed, and lack of attention to detail often cause marital conflict. Treating Limbic ADD can literally save families and change a person's life.

Type 6: Ring of Fire ADD

ADD core symptoms plus:

Sensitive to noise, light, clothes, or touch

Cyclic mood changes (highs and lows)

Inflexible, rigid in thinking

Demanding to have their way, even when told no multiple times

Periods of mean, nasty or insensitive behavior

Periods of increased talkativeness

Periods of increased impulsivity

Unpredictable behavior

Grandiose or "larger than life" thinking

Talks fast

Appears that thoughts go fast

Appears anxious or fearful

Irritability, especially when things do not go your way

Ring of Fire," what kind of name is that for an ADD type? Once you understand the underlying physiology seen on SPECT scans, the name makes perfect sense. Rather than have the typical underactive prefrontal cortex activity that is seen in Type 1 and Type 2, these patients have an overall hyperactive or disinhibited brain. There is too much brain activity across the whole cerebral cortex, especially in the cingulate gyrus, parietal lobes, temporal lobes, and prefrontal cortex. It looks like a ring of hyperactivity around the brain. At the Amen Clinic we look at the 3-D active scans in blue (average activity) and red (the most active). The ring of red on the scan of a typical Ring of Fire ADD patient reminds me of the active volcano Kilawea in Hawaii. The behavior in these patients can also be volcanic in nature. Here's an example.

Jarred

Jarred was diagnosed with ADD at the age of eight. He was hyperactive, restless, impulsive, hyperverbal, moody, and oppositional. His parents brought him to the pediatrician on the recommendation of the teacher. In succession, he was tried on three stimulant medications (Ritalin, Dexedrine, and Cylert), but they all made him worse: he was more moody, irritable, and talkative. His parents stopped the medication and refused to bring him back for help. Every bad thing that happens to untreated ADD children happened to Jarred. He dropped out of school in ninth grade. He started using drugs and alcohol at age fourteen. His parents threw him out of the house at age sixteen because of his temper and drug use. He had trouble with the law. He often became violent when he drank alcohol, even though he said that alcohol made him feel better. From the ages of eighteen to twenty, he was arrested ten times for violent behavior, all when he was intoxicated. It wasn't until Jarred was arrested for armed robbery that he came to my clinic.

On the night of the last crime Jarred started drinking about 10:00 P.M. He drank a fifth of peach schnapps within a half-hour followed by forty ounces of malt liquor beer the next half-hour. He then raced a friend down the freeway and crashed his car. He fled the scene on foot. A short while later he flagged down a cab driver. At exactly 12:10 A.M. he pointed a loaded gun at the cab driver's head and demanded all his money. He got twenty-five dollars. The next morning, after sobering up, he turned himself in to the police.

His defense attorney called me to discuss the case. He wondered if the ADD diagnosis would help his defense. I said I didn't think it would help, but wondered why, if he really had ADD, the stimulants made him worse and why he continued to drink despite all of the terrible problems it caused him. Since he seemed to only be aggressive when he drank alcohol, I decided to scan him both sober and drunk.

The first SPECT study was performed drug and alcohol free. The second study was performed after he consumed a fifth of peach schnapps, followed by forty ounces of malt liquor beer (the same brand he drank on the night of the crime consumed in the same time frame). The "non-alcohol" study revealed marked overactivity in the cingulate gyrus, the right and left lateral prefrontal cortices, the right and left parietal lobes, and the left and right temporal lobes (the Ring of Fire pattern). These findings are often associated with anxiety, cyclic mood tendencies, and irritability.

For the alcohol study, his blood alcohol level was 0.2g/dl(percent)—double what is legally drunk in most states. This study showed an overall dampening effect on the hyperactive areas of the brain (prefrontal, parietal, and temporal lobes), with only the cingulate gyrus showing excessive activity (although significantly less activity than on the nonalcohol study). In addition, the right and left prefrontal cortex was now significantly underactive, as were the left and right temporal lobes.

. . . .

Jarred's SPECT Series Off and On Alcohol

(Top 4 images are 3-D active views—notice the Ring of Fire is calmed by alcohol; bottom 2 images are 3-D surface views—notice alcohol crashes brain activity, especially in the prefrontal cortex and temporal lobes.

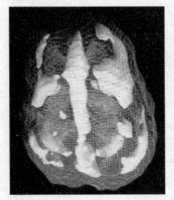

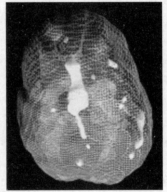

No alcohol
Top down view

Intoxicated
Top down view

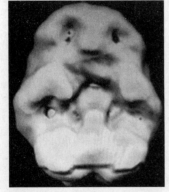

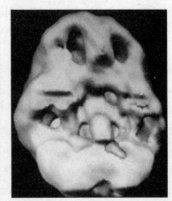

Undersurface view

Undersurface view

Given the marked hyperactivity in his brain in a sober state, along with his report that he felt more relaxed when he drank, it was not unreasonable to assume he may have been using alcohol as a way to settle down his brain and feel more comfortable (self-medication). Unfortunately, by self-medicating, he was inducing a "violent" pattern in his brain. Increased cingulate activity, abnormal left temporal lobe activity, and decreased prefrontal cortex activity is the triad of symptoms that have been found in violent patients. He drank himself into a violent state as a way to medicate underlying abnormalities in his brain.

Jarred had Ring of Fire ADD. Hallmark symptoms of this type include irritability, hyperactivity, excessive talking, overfocus issues, extreme oppositional behavior, and cyclic periods of calm behavior alternating with intense aggressive behavior. The Ring of Fire brain pattern shows excessive activity across the whole cortical surface, as opposed to Classic ADD which shows decreased activity with concentration. Ring of Fire ADD may represent a variant of bipolar disorder mixed with ADD.

Child Psychiatrist Thomas Jaeger from Creighton University in Omaha, Nebraska, has also done pioneering work with brain SPECT imaging. Early in his work he noticed that children and teenagers with bipolar disorder (a phrase for what used to be known as manic-depressive illness) had patchy increased uptake across the cortical surface of the brain. Here is an image of a bipolar patient during a manic episode. Manic episodes are characterized by a cluster of the following symptoms: inflated self-esteem, hyperactive behavior, fleeting attention span, extreme impulsivity (such as in sexual matters or spending foolishly), increased energy, decreased need for sleep, and oftentimes psychotic irrational thinking. The Ring of Fire ADD pattern is very similar to this brain pattern.

We have also seen that psychostimulant medication, such as Ritalin, frequently makes these patients worse. They become more worried, more irritable and more negative. Also, St. John's Wort and medications which increase serotonin, by themselves, often make this type much worse. It is often helped with an elimination diet, supplements that help balance the brain, such as a combination of GABA, HTP, and L-tyrosine, and in more severe cases an anticonvulsant or atypical antipsychotic medication, such as Risperdal.

Bipolar Brain

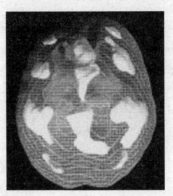

3-D top down active view; note
patchy uptake throughout the cortex

In looking at the SPECT scans for this pattern, we see a number of abnormalities that seem to explain the clinical picture. *Hyperfrontality*, a term for the combined findings of increased cingulate activity and increased left and right lateral prefrontal cortex activity, is associated with severe overfocused symptoms, such as worrying, obsessiveness, oppositional behavior, and cognitive inflexibility. *Increased parietal lobe activity* is often associated with distractibility and hypersensitivity to the environment (extreme sensitivity to sound, touch, taste, smells, and sights). The parietal lobes contain the brain's sensory cortex, which when overactive seems to cause a person to be hypersensitive to incoming information. *Increased lateral temporal lobe activity* often causes problems with mood instability and irritability. This Ring of Fire pattern seems to be the most intense ADD type. It is ADD if the core ADD symptoms are present over a prolonged period of time. It is bipolar disorder if the symptoms occur only in a cyclic fashion. Frequently, we see both patterns. The ADD core symptoms are present over time, the mood problems occur in a cyclic fashion. Some doctors would argue that there are really two separate problems, both ADD and bipolar disorder. We see the Ring of Fire pattern so commonly in our ADD patients that we feel the need to classify it as a separate ADD type. Here are several Ring of Fire ADD examples.

Casey

Casey was described by his teacher as a sweet, endearing boy who tries very hard and always does his best. She also said that even though he does worry too much and gets upset if he makes a mistake, he works with enthusiasm and is a super student. But this is only when he is on his medication; without it he is a horror to be around. When he isn't on his medication he is cruel, combative, angry, and obnoxious. At school, without his medication he often has temper outbursts and will hit other children for little reason. He also has difficulty following rules set by his teacher and will often argue with her or just refuse to obey instructions. At home, without his medication his behavior isn't much better than at school. He is afraid of new situations and usually reacts to change by covering his ears to block out the new experience. At The Amen Clinics he couldn't even flush the toilet because of his inability to function in new situations. He also has difficulty following instructions that his mother gives and will often reply to an order by saying things like: "I hate you," "I wish you were dead," or "I want to kill you." Another common reaction to his mother's orders would be to try to hit her.

Before treatment was started, a SPECT scan was ordered as part of his evaluation. It showed an overactive brain with increased activity in

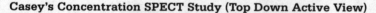

Casey's Concentration SPECT Study (Top Down Active View)

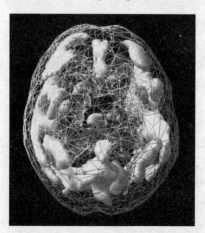

both prefrontal cortices, both parietal lobes, and in the anterior cingulate gyrus. Given the severity of his symptoms I started Risperdal (a novel antipsychotic medication that we have found to be helpful for this pattern) and then Ritalin. Ritalin by itself had made Casey worse, but in combination with a full treatment program, the changes in his behavior have been vast. The effects of treatment were best summed up by his fourth grade teacher when she said, "This year I have only seen two incidents of misbehavior and both times were days he had missed his medication."

Ronny

Ronny was nine years old when his mother brought him to The Amen Clinic. His mother first sensed that something was wrong when, at ten months old, he would begin screaming for no apparent reason, while he was playing alone on the floor. Throughout kindergarten he often hid in the cupboards. Even when he wasn't in the cupboards, he usually refused to participate in class. The few times he did participate, he was a distraction. Toward the end of the year he finally stopped hiding in the cupboards, but he continued to be distracting in class. In the second grade, he and another boy met in the bathroom on several occasions and would touch each other's genitals. Since then, he sexually experimented with several other boys and became obsessed with sex. He also became increasingly oppositional and argumentative to his parents' requests. He would scream and throw temper tantrums nine times out of ten when he was asked to do chores around the house and he refused to sit down to do his homework. Right before his initial evaluation his behaviors became even more concerning. He threatened to kill himself when his mother tried to take a knife away from him.

Ronny's SPECT study showed the Ring of Fire pattern, increased activity in both prefrontal cortices and parietal lobes as well as the anterior cingulate gyrus, and the underside of his prefrontal cortex was noted to be underactive. Before Ronny came to the clinic he had been on Ritalin which had made him more irritable and aggressive. Seeing his scan, the doctor in my clinic put him on Depakote (an anticonvulsant medication often helpful with the Ring of Fire pattern). After some improvement in his behavior

Ronny's Concentration SPECT Study (Top Down Active View)

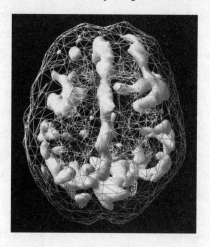

was noticed, a second SPECT study was ordered. His second study, which was performed on Depakote, was calmer overall. His prefrontal cortex was still underactive. Adderall was then added to his regimen. It significantly helped him focus. On his current medication his mood is much better, he has a more even temper, and is less distractible. His oppositional behavior is better (not perfect, but better) and through parent training, exercise, and dietary interventions he continues to improve.

Guy

Nineteen-year-old Guy came to the clinic because he was having problems controlling his temper. He had always had a bad temper and was constantly getting into fights, but he had never tried or even gave any serious thought to hurting anyone with anything more than his fists. This all changed ten months before he first came to Amen Clinics. He got in a fight with someone in a gang. In that fight he took several blows to the head from a pair of nunchakus and went to the hospital with a concussion. While he was in the ER of the hospital he got into *another* fight, this time with a police officer, and was again hit in the head several times—this time with a mag flashlight. Since the incidents of that night ten months before he came to the clinic, Guy has even less control over his temper, especially around figures of authority. He had always been oppositional and had a problem with authority, but now he had no control over his temper around figures of authority. While he was discussing these changes in his temper he told his doctor, "I just don't understand my own brain anymore." He was also experiencing an increase in dark thoughts. Now when he is angry, instead of wanting to hurt someone with his fists, his thoughts have turned homicidal. These new thoughts and urges disturbed Guy who said, "I definitely don't want to hurt anybody or take someone's life, but my thoughts say something different." In addition to his increasingly dark, violent thoughts, he also started to think about suicide. He even knew how he would do it—with a shotgun "to make sure it was over." He said that he wouldn't ever try to kill himself, but the thought hadn't even crossed his mind until his head trauma ten months earlier. His relationships with the people in his life also changed. He would cut people out of his life on a whim without any sorrow or remorse. He stated that his attitude had become "my way or the highway."

Guy has a new son, which is why he sought professional help. He wanted to have more effective and stronger relationships, he wanted to have control over his temper, he wanted to be able to stay on task, to be able to concentrate so he can keep a steady job. A SPECT study was performed as part of his evaluation. It showed increased activity in the cingulate gyrus, left and right prefrontal cortices, left and right lateral parietal lobes, and in the limbic system. There was also decreased activity in the right and left temporal lobes. His doctor put him on a combination of medication (an anticonvulsant, Neurontin, and a stimulating antidepressant, Effexor). In addition, his diet was changed, exercise was increased, and he is seen in weekly psychotherapy to help him deal with the authority issues and to be effective with his son. He has improved greatly. He is less depressed, has control over his temper, and his attention span has improved. Overall he is much happier now and his wife is expecting another child soon.

Michael

Fifteen-year-old Michael came to the clinic with symptoms of ADD, mood swings, impulsivity, and oppositional behavior. He was struggling in school and at home. He was made worse with stimulant medication

Michael Before Treatment

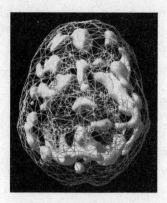

Michael After Treatment

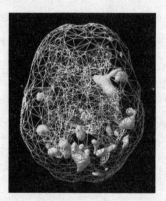

and antidepressants that raise serotonin. His scan showed a Ring of Fire pattern. On a combination of GABA, 5HTP, and L-tyrosine he did much better and after three months his scan was calmer and more normal as well.

PARIETAL LOBES

One brain system not discussed yet is the parietal lobes, toward the back top of the brain. Also called the sensory cortex, it is the part of the brain where touch is processed. We frequently see it overactive in ADD, especially the Ring of Fire ADD. It seems when this part of the brain is too active people become hypersensitive to their environment. They tend to see too much, feel too much, and sense too much. Distractibility is especially heightened in these patients.

DIFFERENTIATING TYPE 6 RING OF FIRE ADD FROM BIPOLAR DISORDER

Differentiating this type of ADD from bipolar disorder is generally difficult in children and easy in adults. Until recently, child psychiatrists didn't think that children had bipolar disorder. They thought that it was a disorder of older adolescence and adulthood. New information has shown that this disorder does occur in children and that it is sometimes very hard to distinguish between it and severe ADD. Bipolar children tend to cycle in their mood and behavior problems. They have times when they are awful, irritable, and aggressive, and they have times when things are relatively normal. Ring of Fire ADD kids tend to have problems on a consistent basis. In order to be diagnosed with bipolar disorder as an adult, the person needs to have a manic episode (pressured speech, trouble sitting still, irritability, decreased need for sleep, grandiose ideas, periods of hypersexuality or hyperreligiosity, extreme impulsivity, and sometimes even psychotic experiences, such as hallucinations or delusions). People with Ring of Fire ADD do not have manic episodes. Their behavior tends to be consistent over long periods of time. People can have both Ring of Fire ADD and bipolar disorder, and some studies suggest that as many as half of the people with bipolar disorder also meet the criteria for ADD.

Type 7: Anxious ADD

ADD core symptoms plus:

Frequently anxious or nervous

Physical stress symptoms, such as headaches

Tends to freeze in social situations

Dislikes or gets excessively nervous speaking in public

Predicts the worst

Conflict avoidant

Fear of being judged

O ver the last thirteen years, I have noticed more and more the combination of ADD and anxiety symptoms running together; and when they do, the ADD symptoms become magnified. In looking at our large dataset of patients, it is very common to see the core ADD symptoms plus fear of being judged, predicting the worst, being conflict avoidant, and having physical stress symptoms, such as headaches and stomachaches. In addition, people with this type tend to freeze in anxiety-provoking situations, especially where they may be judged, such as in test taking.

We often see too much activity in the basal ganglia, those large structures deep in the brain that help produce the neurotransmitter dopamine. Typically, in most types of ADD, the basal ganglia are low in activity, but in this type they tend to be high. Strategies to soothe the basal ganglia and help focus can be so helpful.

In Classic ADD, people tend to be excitement- or conflict-seeking. They tend to have low levels of anxiety that get them into hot water, because they do not think through the consequences of their actions. In Anxious ADD, these people tend to avoid conflict like the plaque and struggle to feel secure.

Clarice

Clarice, nine, struggled in school and was frequently anxious at home. She needed a lot of reassurance and help with her homework. She was often off task, but also nervous about not getting her work done. Her stomach hurt her a lot and she never raised her hand in class. Her mother brought her to our clinic because we had seen her brother, who had the Classic ADD type. Clarice did very well on a combination of relaxation strategies, physical exercise, and the supplements magnesium and theanine, both of which promote relaxation and focus.

Jeffrey

Jeffrey, seventeen, struggled in school and in his social relationships. He was frequently off task, late, and often felt anxious and nervous. He tended to predict the worst and had trouble settling himself down. He smoked marijuana, which helped him feel calm, but it made his focus issues worse. He also tended to be shy and never raised his hand in class

Jeffrey

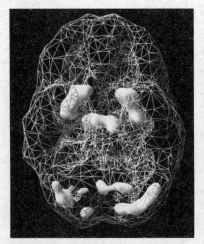

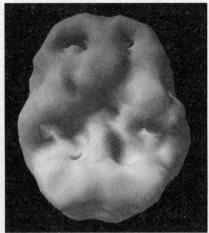

High basal ganglia, low cerebellum   *Low prefrontal cortex*

when he had questions. Jeffrey's mother had been treated at our clinics for an anxiety disorder, which was also common in her family. Jeffrey's SPECT scan showed low activity in his prefrontal cortex and very high activity in his basal ganglia.

He did very well on a combination of supplements I frequently prescribe to support healthy relaxation (theanine, magnesium, Relora, and Holy Basil) and a low dose of a stimulant.

Melody

Melody, thirty-eight, had always struggled in her career and had recently been passed over for a promotion at her job in the banking industry. She struggled to stay focused and organized, but it was her anxiety that interfered most. She avoided conflict at all costs, could not give an oral presentation, and tended to often predict the worst outcome. She often called in sick due to the constant stress she felt. She came to see us because of conflict she was having with her husband. Her SPECT scan showed marked increased activity in her basal ganglia and low prefrontal cortex activity. Her treatment involved teaching her how to soothe herself with cognitive therapy techniques and guided imagery, and she also benefitted from some supplements to calm the anxiety and help her focus, such as theanine, magnesium, Relora, and Holy Basil. After four months she felt significantly better, and eight months later she had a positive review from her boss and achieved her first raise in many years. She told me the treatment was a great investment in her future.

Gary

Gary, fifty-four, initially came to the clinic because he was having trouble with his teenage son, Josh. Gary and Josh always seemed to be fighting over Josh's schoolwork, chores that were not getting done, and issues of disrespect. Gary hated the conflict and tried to avoid it at all costs, but then would explode after it went unaddressed for so long. Gary also struggled with headaches, negative thinking patterns, and often felt sad because he felt he had failed as a father. He felt anxious and nervous most of the time, and struggled to keep up at work.

Josh ended up being diagnosed with Classic ADD. He responded very well to treatment, and his grades and behavior improved. Gary, encouraged by Josh's response, talked more about his own struggles with organization, attention, and procrastination. The anxiety, mixed with the inattentive symptoms, had been negatively affecting Gary since he was a child. On a combination of relaxation training, supplements, and a low dose of a stimulant, Gary felt as though he was a more focused and positive father, and performed better at work.

CHAPTER 13

Soft Brain, Hard Skull

Head-Trauma-Induced ADD

One of the most common causes of ADD-like symptoms outside of genetics is head trauma, especially to the prefrontal cortex. Our brain-imaging work has taught us that head injuries are more important than most physicians have previously believed. SPECT is clearly able to show areas of damage that are not seen in anatomy studies like CAT scans or MRI. SPECT will show early damage, when brain tissue is struggling, while CT or MRI only show up as trouble when the brain tissue has atrophied or died.

With SPECT we can see contra-coup injuries (opposite parts of the brain damaged by the same injury) and old injuries (even damage from birth or forceps deliveries). Why are head injuries so important? Some basic brain facts are in order here.

- **Your brain is involved with everything you do.** How you think. How you feel. How you act. And how well you get along with other people.
- **Your brain is very complex.** Did you know you have one hundred billion nerve cells, or neurons? Every one of your neurons is connected to hundreds and even thousands of other neurons. You have more connections in your brain than there are stars in the universe. Your brain is more intricate, delicate, and complicated than any computer that we can imagine.

- **Your brain is very soft.** It is similar in consistency to soft butter. When I was a little boy working in my father's grocery store I used to see cow brains in little white cups. The cow brains, like human brains, were so soft that they took on the shape of the cup.
- **Your skull is really hard.** Inside your skull there are many rough areas and sharp bony ridges.
- **Your brain is in a closed space.** When you experience a blow to the head, there is no place for the brain to go. It ends up slamming against the walls, ridges, and sharp bony edges in the brain, ripping small blood vessels, causing micro-hemorrhaging (bleeding), and over time small areas of scar tissue.
- **Consciousness is controlled by deep structures in the brain.** The deep structures in the brain may not be injured in a head trauma, but there may be a significant injury to the cortex or surface of the brain, with no loss of consciousness.

Our experience with ADD tells us that when the prefrontal cortex is injured, people have more ADD-like symptoms. The injuries could be from any cause—a damaging forceps delivery; a fall down a couple of stairs or off a bicycle; head-banging as a child; a blow during a fight, a rape, or a robbery; or a motor vehicle accident. Because of higher levels of activity and impulsivity, people with ADD have more head injuries, which may make it hard to determine the real cause of the problematic symptoms.

Frequently patients and their parents forget about head injuries, even though they may have been very significant. When patients come to our clinic, we ask them five times whether or not they have had a head injury. If a patient or his parents repeatedly says no but we see evidence of trauma on the scans, I'll ask again. If they still say no I'll ask, "Are you sure? Have you ever fallen out of a tree, fallen off a fence, or dove into a shallow pool?" You cannot believe the number of people who suddenly remember a significant head injury. I had one man last year who said no four times and then when questioned the fifth time remembered a time at the age of seven when he fell out of a second-story window and had been unconscious for ten minutes. I had another patient who said no five times but later said that ten years earlier (about the time her symptoms started) she was in a car accident and her head had broken the windshield. Due to its location, the prefrontal cortex and temporal lobes are especially susceptible to head injuries. Many people do not fully understand how head injuries—sometimes even "minor" ones, in which no loss of consciousness occurs—can alter a person's character and ability to learn. We see head injuries so often on the SPECT studies we order in our ADD patients that we are tempted to add an eighth type of ADD: Head Injury ADD. Post–head injury symptoms often consist of attention problems, memory difficulties, and decreased energy and motivation. In head-injury-induced ADD, the symptoms follow a significant head injury and frequently look like one of the types of ADD. If the injury just affected the prefrontal cortex, it could look like Type 1 or Type 2. If the injury affected the prefrontal cortex and temporal lobes (common because of the location of the temporal lobes), it could look like Type 4. If the injury damaged the anterior cingulate gyrus, it could look like Type 3. The treatment depends on the clinical picture. We have seen anticonvulsants help to stabilize temporal lobe symptoms, and stimulants or stimulating supplements help prefrontal cortex symptoms.

The brain damage from a head injury has a number of causes. After a head injury, blood vessels may tear or break near the area of injury, causing bleeding, inflammation, and scarring. The blood vessel disruption decreases healthy nutritional supply to an area, and prevents the blood supply from removing the toxic chemicals released from damaged cells. In addition, rotational and shearing effects can also occur from the force of an injury. After an injury, the body's defense system goes into action and recent studies have indicated that the immune system may release substances that are actually toxic to brain cells.

Here are several clinical examples of head-injury-induced ADD.

Brian

When Brian was seven years old he rode his bike full speed into the corner of a brick column. He was wearing a helmet, but it had cracked under the force of the injury. He was unconscious for about a half an hour. His parents did all of the right things, including taking him to the

**Brian's SPECT Study Left Side Surface View
(Before and After Treatment)**

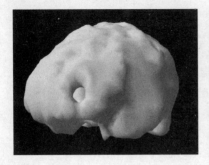 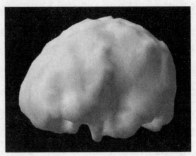

emergency room and having a CT scan done. The emergency room physician just said to watch him. No one said to watch for problems in behavior or learning. After the injury the mother noted changes, subtle at first and then more drastic. By the age of 12, Brian was moody, emotional, irritable, and struggling in school. When he finally came for evaluation at age 16, he was almost failing in school and had just started to experiment with drugs.

Brian's SPECT study showed clear decreased activity in the left lateral prefrontal cortex, underneath the scar from the bicycle accident. His treatment plan included a small dose of Adderall and brain wave biofeedback over his left prefrontal cortex, and natural supplements to help support brain function. Ten milligrams of Adderall enhanced activity in his prefrontal cortex, and the biofeedback was so effective that within eight months he was able to perform in school and at home at a high level without the medication.

Danielle

Danielle, age nine, was a sweet, loving child who was doing well in third grade and got along well with other children. Over Christmas break, while going with her older brother to a family party, she was in a car accident. Danielle had been using a seat belt, but nevertheless, the left side of her head slammed against the rear side window. She was only briefly unconscious. Over about eight weeks Danielle's behavior began to change. She became negative, irritable, and oppositional. She blurted out in class and she had trouble paying attention to her work at school. Homework was hard, where before it had been very easy for her. Over the next year she lost most of her friends because she started trouble with them and often would say things that hurt their feelings.

A year after the accident, Danielle's mother knew that there was something seriously wrong. She brought Danielle to a counselor, who thought the problem was psychological; the counselor thought that Danielle had post-traumatic stress disorder because of the accident, but the counseling didn't help. Her pediatrician thought Danielle was just being oppositional and recommended a tough-love approach. Reluctantly the pediatrician diagnosed her with ADD and tried Ritalin, but it didn't help very much. In fact, it only seemed to make her more moody and aggressive. By the age of fourteen, when she came to our clinic for evaluation, Danielle was failing in school and had many behavioral problems at home. I suspected that her problems were the result of physical damage to her brain from the accident, and her SPECT study bore that out. It revealed marked decreased activity in the prefrontal cortex and temporal lobes. I placed her on a small dose of Neurontin to stabilize her temporal lobes and Adderall to help her focus, along with supplements to help boost blood flow to the brain. The treatment evened out her mood and helped her focus. She was more successful in school, which helped her overall demeanor.

Wes

Wes was fifty-four years old when he sought help. He was depressed, suicidal, lethargic, and had a very short attention span. His volatile temper, a problem for his whole life, had cost him two marriages and alienated his children. Now, he had just broken up with his girlfriend of two years. In the history I discovered that he had done well in school until the eleventh grade. In between tenth and eleventh grades he was in a car accident with a teenage friend. The friend had been drinking and had lost control of the car. Wes wasn't wearing a seat belt and his head cracked the windshield. He did not remember if he lost consciousness. Before the accident, he had been a good student with dreams of going to Stanford, but the next semester he did very poorly and gave up the idea of going

Wes's SPECT Scan Top Down Surface Views

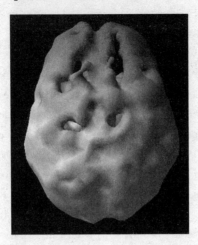

to a top-rung university. He said, "I couldn't pay attention anymore. My mind was always wandering off task." Wes had job security because he worked in his father's business, but he and his father fought constantly. His father wanted him to be on time and stay the whole day. Wes frequently took off and didn't finish the tasks assigned to him.

I ordered a SPECT series to evaluate the underlying metabolic brain issues. His SPECT series was very abnormal. He had decreased activity over the vertex (top) of the brain and decreased prefrontal cortex and temporal lobe activity, especially on the left side of the brain. With concentration, there was further overall decreased activity. Seeing the scan helped Wes understand why he had the struggles he did. On a combination of anticonvulsant and stimulant medication and biofeedback over the left prefrontal and temporal lobe regions, his mood, temper, and attention span stabilized. His girlfriend came back to him when she realized he was dealing with a medical problem, as opposed to just being a difficult person.

Alecia

At the age of twenty-two, Alecia tripped and fell facedown on a slick, rain-soaked ramp at college. She slid fifteen feet before her head struck a concrete wall. She was dazed for most of the day, nauseated for a week, and had a headache for a month. A year later she was referred to me by a therapist who had been seeing her for temper problems. She also had trouble thinking clearly and had to drop out of school. She had energy problems, problems with goal setting, trouble organizing herself, and she spent money foolishly. Her parents were very distressed with the change in Alecia. On SPECT there was marked decreased activity in her prefrontal cortex (especially in the prefrontal pole) and temporal lobes. With Alecia we used a combination of hyperbaric oxygen therapy (HBOT) and natural supplements to help support her recovery.

Alecia's SPECT Study (Concentration, Top Down, Front On, and Underside Surface Views)

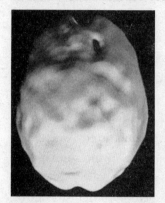

Top down

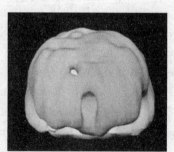

Front

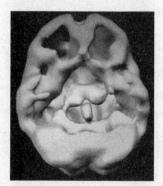

On underside

HYPERBARIC OXYGEN THERAPY (HBOT)

I became interested in Hyperbaric Oxygen Therapy (HBOT) after colleagues who were using it with their patients showed me the before and after SPECT studies. They told me HBOT often helped to boost blood flow to the brain thus speeding up recovery in traumatic brain injuries. HBOT works, as its name implies, by increasing oxygen under pressure. The increased pressure of oxygen signals the DNA in our cells to perform healing tasks that the body normally can't do. Ground zero for this healing activity is the mitochondria, which are the little organelles inside of our cells that convert oxygen and sugar into the gasoline the cells run on (ATP). It doesn't take much to knock mitochondria off-line, and then that cell can't perform the job it was assigned. The mitochondria can be damaged by oxygen deprivation, external toxic exposure, an infection, or trauma. HBOT works by reviving the little mitochondria.

In 2011, my colleague Paul Harch, I, and others published a study in the *Journal of Neurotrauma* on the use of HBOT in sixteen soldiers who had experienced head injuries in Iraq or Afghanistan. Each soldier was thoroughly tested, including having a SPECT study and then given forty sessions of HBOT. After HBOT, the soldiers demonstrated significant improvement in: symptoms, neurological exams, many measures of cognitive and emotional functioning, and even a fifteen-point rise in their IQ. Specifically, we saw improvements in memory, impulse control, mood, anxiety, and quality of life. The SPECT scans also showed improvement in blood flow across many areas of the brain.

Sal

Sal was referred to my clinic by his marital therapist. Sal and his wife had a relationship filled with conflict, tension, and turmoil. Sal's wife complained that he was inattentive, selfish, and incapable of expressing feelings. Sal was a marginally successful attorney who had trouble keeping clients. Like his wife, they found him aloof and seemingly uninterested.

Sal's problems began in high school. He played wide receiver on the varsity football team and his senior year he was being scouted by large universities. That year, he suffered four concussions during games—two on the same night! Sal went to college, but only played football for a year. He found that he had to spend inordinate amounts of time studying just to keep up; he had no time for football. After college, it took him three years to get into law school. He was persistent, but academically did not feel as sharp as he had in the early years of high school.

I suspected that the football head injuries were important in explaining his current symptoms. His SPECT study showed very specific damage to his left prefrontal cortex and left temporal lobe in a pattern consistent with head injury. The outside of the left prefrontal cortex (called the dorsal lateral prefrontal cortex) is the expressive language area of the brain. In Sal's case it had suffered damage and taken with it his ability for empathy and expressive language. I diagnosed him with Alexythymia (a disorder where people do not have access to their own feelings). He cared about his wife, but no amount of therapy helped him to express his feelings. He didn't understand feelings and said that when people talked about feelings it was like a foreign language to him.

I put him on a combination of an anticonvulsant medication, a group of brain enhancement supplements, and we did biofeedback over his left prefrontal cortex. Over several months his wife noticed that he became more expressive and more empathic.

Head injuries, depending on the areas affected, can present as differ-

Sal's SPECT Study (Concentration, Underside, and Left Side Surface Views)

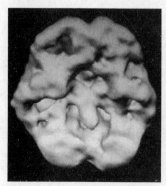

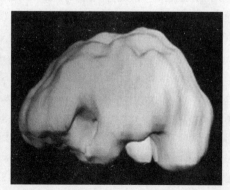

Underside   *Left side*

ent ADD types. ADD symptoms subsequent to head injuries often respond to the same treatments as do the specific ADD types. My SPECT work has taught me how devastating head injuries can be and how important it is to protect your head and the heads of children. After seeing these scans, I would not let my children or grandchildren hit soccer balls with their heads, play tackle football, or snowboard without a helmet. I encourage them to play tennis, golf, Ping-Pong, and track.

AMEN CLINICS STUDY ON ACTIVE AND RETIRED NFL PLAYERS

From 2009 to 2012, Amen Clinics performed the world's largest brain imaging and rehabilitation study on active and retired professional football players. Because of our work with SPECT we had a high suspicion that many players suffered with the effects of chronic traumatic brain injury, and it seemed at the time that the NFL was dragging its feet on understanding and getting the players help.

The results of our study were very clear: A very high percentage of our 135 players had evidence of traumatic brain injury patterns on their scans and they showed the evidence of it in their lives with a high incidence of depression, dementia, obesity, and ADD-like symptoms. In fact, 81 percent of our players complained of attention problems and showed concentration problems on the psychological testing we performed.

The good news came from the second part of the study: After we saw the high level of damage in players, we wondered if their brains could be rehabilitated. I have already shared with you many stories where that, in fact, had occurred. We were hopeful and decided to use lifestyle interventions and sophisticated supplements as our treatments of choice. We taught players how to care for their brains: avoid anything that hurt it and engage in regular brain-healthy habits. In addition, we put them all on NeuroVite +, our high-quality multiple vitamin, high-dose fish oil (5.6 grams of Omega 3 Power), and a brain boosting supplement I designed called Brain and Memory Power Boost that contains seven nutrients to support brain function: gingko and vinpocetine for blood flow; Huperzine A and acetyl-L-carnitine to enhance the neurotransmitter acetylcholine; N-acetylcysteine and alpha lipoic acid, potent antioxidants; and phosphatidylserine to help nerve cell membranes and lower stress hormones. This combination was of significant benefit to 80 percent of our players, including improvements in memory, mood, attention, motivation, and sleep. In addition, we saw that the lifestyle changes and these supplements improved blood flow to their brains.

We were so encouraged by the results that we tested this combination of supplements on two separate groups of reasonably healthy people in double-blind placebo controlled studies (the highest level of scientific evidence) and saw even greater benefits in mood, executive function, memory, reasoning, information processing speed and accuracy. We even saw reduced hostility.

If you have been bad to your brain, have hope. There is high potential for recovery on a brain-smart program.

CHAPTER 14

ADD in Families

SPECT Studies Across
Generations

ADD is a generational disorder, meaning having ADD in a family significantly influences the development of each member. The level of influence is often determined by which parent has ADD, whether it is the father or mother. ADD mothers often have a more negative impact on children than ADD fathers, as they are still often the primary caretakers for children. In addition, ADD influences parenting, job choices, creativity, moves, and legal issues. Here are three examples of ADD across generations.

Tim, Pam, Paul, and Karen

Paul, age twenty, came to see me because he was having trouble finishing his senior year at UC Berkeley. He was having trouble completing term papers, he could not focus in class, and he had little motivation. He began to believe that he should drop out of school and go to work for his father. He hated the idea of quitting school so close to graduation, so he came to see me on a referral from a friend who had a younger brother whom I had helped. Paul told me that he had bouts of depression that had been treated with Prozac with little benefit. Paul's brain SPECT study was consistent with both depression and ADD. He had a wonderful response to a combination of an antidepressant and stimulant medication. He finished college and got the kind of job he wanted. Today, I would have started him on SAMe for Limbic ADD, along with exercise, fish oil, and a higher protein diet, and then evaluated how he did before prescribing the medication.

When Paul's mother, Pam, saw what treatment had done for her son, she came to see me for herself. As a child, she had trouble learning. Even though she was very artistic, she had little motivation for school and her teachers labeled her as an underachiever. As an adult, Pam went back to school and earned her degree in elementary school teaching. In order to student teach, however, she had to pass the National Teacher's Exam. She had failed the test four times. Pam was ready to give up and try a new avenue of study, but Paul's improvement gave her hope that there might be help for her. In fact, she had a brain study very similar to Paul's study and she responded to the same combination of medication. Four months later she passed the National Teacher's Exam.

With two successes in the family, the mother then sent her nineteen-year-old daughter, Karen, to see me. Like her brother, Karen was a bright child who had underachieved in school. At the time she came to see me, she lived in Los Angeles and she was enrolled in a broadcast journalism course. She complained that learning the material was hard for her. She was also moody, restless, easily distracted, impulsive, and quick to anger. Several years earlier she was treated for alcohol and amphetamine abuse. She said that the alcohol settled her restlessness and the amphetamines helped her to concentrate. Karen's brain SPECT study was very similar to her brother's and mother's. Once on medication, she could concentrate in class, and she finished her work in half the time she had before. Karen's level of confidence increased to the point where she could go and look for work as a broadcaster, something she had been unable to do previously.

The most reluctant member of the family to see me was the father, Tim. Even though Pam, Paul, and Karen told him that he should see me, he balked at the idea. He said, "There's nothing wrong with me; look at how successful I am." But his family knew different. Even though Tim owned a successful grocery store, he was reclusive and distant. He got tired early in the day, he was easily distracted, and he was scattered in his approach to work. He was successful at work, in part, because he had very good people who took his ideas and made them happen. Tim enjoyed high stimulation activities, and he loved riding motorcycles, even at the age of fifty-five. Looking back, Tim had done poorly in high school, and he barely passed college, even though he had a very high IQ. He tended to drift from job to job until he was able to buy the grocery store. Tim's wife finally convinced him to see me. She was getting ready to divorce him, because he would never talk with her in the evening. She felt that he didn't care about her. He later told me that by evening he was physically and emotionally drained.

During my first session with Tim he told me that he couldn't possibly have ADD because he was a success in business. But the more questions I asked him about his past, the more lights went on in his head. At the end of the interview I said, "If you really do have ADD, given what you have already accomplished, I wonder how successful you could be if we treat it." Tim's brain study showed the pattern for classic ADD. When he tried to concentrate, the frontal lobes of his brain shut down, rather than turned on. When I told him this, it really sunk in. "Maybe that is why it is hard for me to learn new games. When I'm in a social situation and I'm pressed to learn or respond, I just freeze up. So I avoid these situations."

Tim had a remarkable response to Ritalin. He was more awake during the day, he accomplished more in less time, and his relationship with his wife dramatically improved. In fact, they both said they couldn't believe that their relationship could be so good, after all the years of distance and hurt.

Phillip and Dennis

Nine-year-old Phillip was frightened when the police came to his school to talk to him. His teacher had noticed bruises on his legs and arms and she called Child Protective Services. He wasn't sure if he should tell them that his father, Dennis, had beaten him up, or if he should say that he fell down a flight of stairs or something like that. Phillip did not want to get his dad into trouble and he felt responsible for the beating he received. After all, he thought, his father had told him ten times to clean his room and for some reason, unknown to Phillip, he hadn't done it. Phillip and his father often fought, but it had never been apparent to people outside the home. Phillip decided to tell the truth, hoping that it would somehow help.

Indeed, Phillip's family did get help. The court ordered the father to undergo a psychiatric evaluation and counseling for the family. The father was found to have a short fuse. He was impulsive and explosive in many different situations. He began to have problems with aggressiveness after he sustained a head injury in a car accident six years ago. His wife reported that when Phillip was first born, the father was loving, patient, and attentive, but after the accident, he was irritable, distant, and angry.

In family counseling sessions I noticed that Phillip was a very difficult child. He was restless, active, impulsive, and defiant. When his parents told him to stop doing annoying behaviors, he just ignored them and continued irritating those around him. I soon discovered it was the interaction between Phillip and his father that was the problem and counseling alone would not be helpful. I believed there was some underlying biological or physical "brain problem" that contributed to the abusive interactions. In an effort to further understand the biology of this family's problems, I ordered brain SPECT studies on both Phillip and Dennis.

The brain SPECT studies for both Phillip and his father were abnormal. The father's study clearly showed an area of decreased activity in his left temporal lobe (near the temples), probably a result from the car accident. Several researchers have demonstrated left temporal lobe problems to be associated with people who have a short fuse and a tendency toward violence. Phillip's SPECT study revealed decreased activity in the front part of his brain when he tried to concentrate. This finding is often found in ADD kids who are impulsive, hyperactive, and conflict driven.

After taking a history, watching the family interact, and reviewing the SPECT studies, it was clear to me that Phillip's and his father's problems were, in large part, biological. I placed both of them on medication. The father was put on an antiseizure medication to calm his left temporal lobe, and Phillip was placed on a stimulant medication to increase activity in the front part of his brain.

Once the underlying biological problems were treated, the family was then able to benefit from psychotherapy and begin to heal the wounds of abuse. In counseling sessions Phillip was calmer and more attentive and the father was more able to constructively learn how to deal with Phillip's difficult behavior.

Whenever child abuse occurs, it is a severe tragedy. It may become an even worse tragedy, however, if people ignore the underlying brain problems that may be contributing to the problems, and separate families before getting the proper help. In this case and in many others, it is often the interaction between a difficult child and an aggressive, impulsive parent that leads to the problem. These negative interactions may have a biological basis to them. To be effective in helping these families, it is very important to understand the underlying biological or "brain" contribution to the problem.

Jack and Monica

Jack and Monica had been married eleven years and had two children, ages six and nine. Both parents were physicians: Jack was an emergency room doctor and Monica was an internist. They came to see me from three hundred miles away because of chronic marital problems. There was recent talk of divorce, but they wanted to salvage the marriage for the sake of their children. Jack had been diagnosed with ADD (not uncommon among emergency physicians) by a local psychiatrist several years before they came to my clinic. Jack was disorganized, impulsive, inattentive, distractible, and forgetful. He did not follow through on his promises. He was also bad in business and frequently did not do the paperwork necessary to get reimbursed for his services. Unfortunately, Jack did not have a positive response to Ritalin or Dexedrine. The medications made him moody and irritable.

Monica was angry. She blamed every problem in their marriage on Jack's ADD. There was chronic conflict and tension, exacerbated by the behavior of their youngest child, Matthew. He was hyperactive, impulsive, aggressive, and defiant. It seemed that, with their busy schedules and constant stress, the couple could never connect in a positive way.

During my first session with the couple I sensed that Monica had a cingulate problem. She talked about the same point over and over, held grudges from long ago, worried, and tended to automatically argue with everything that came out of Jack's mouth. When I asked about Monica's family, she told me about her father who "won first prize for overactive cingulate symptoms." He was a physician with whom she shared an office. She described him as angry, rigid, and compulsive. If things didn't go his way he would throw things, and he talked how managed care was ruining medicine at least five times every day. With such a history, I thought it might be a good idea to scan both Jack and Monica—even Monica's dad, if he'd let me. Jack and Monica readily agreed. Monica said if she was part of the problem, she wanted to know about it.

Jack's scan showed decreased activity in the prefrontal cortex and temporal lobes. The temporal lobe problems were probably making the stimulants ineffective. I placed Jack on Aricept, a memory enhancing medication used for Alzheimer's disease that I have also found helpful for ADD adults who complain of memory problems. In addition, Jack exercised intensely, changed his diet, and also took L-tyrosine for focus.

Monica's scan showed marked hyperactivity in the anterior cingulate gyrus. No doubt she was faced with a tough marriage, but her overactive cingulate was not helping her have the needed flexibility to roll with the regular ups and downs of living in an ADD family. I started her on St. John's Wort and exercise.

In addition, I saw their son Matthew. He had Type 3 Overfocused ADD and oppositional defiant disorder. He had decreased prefrontal cortex activity and too much activity in the anterior cingulate gyrus (a combination of mom and dad). I started him on St. John's Wort and Adderall and worked with his parents on developing the parenting skills needed to help him. The parent training really was effective. Up to that point, they just used their parenting style differences as another way to disagree.

Over about six months the family began to heal. There were fewer fights, more loving interactions, and a deeper understanding of the underlying problems. Jack became more focused and his memory was better. Monica became more flexible and able to let go of hurts. Matthew settled down and was becoming happier and more cooperative. After two years I finally got to meet Monica's father. He came to a lecture I gave near his home. After the lecture he came up to me and thanked me for helping his children. He asked if I was doing any family studies. When I said yes, he volunteered for a scan. This delighted Monica very much. She continued to complain about her father's negative behavior. To no one's surprise, not even the father's after he heard my lecture, he had a very overactive anterior cingulate gyrus. He agreed to take St. John's Wort and exercise regularly. Within several weeks Monica e-mailed me, thanking me on behalf of three generations, for making life less stressful. She said her father was more relaxed, more flexible, and not talking anymore about managed care.

ADD in all its types can affect multiple generations. Understanding family history in light of the ADD types can bring healing and hope for generations of families to come.

CHAPTER 15

Self-Medication, Self-Pollution

ADD and Substance Abuse

Drug and alcohol abuse are very common problems in teenagers and adults with untreated ADD. One study from researchers at Harvard reported 52 percent of untreated ADD adults abuse drugs or alcohol. The drugs that they choose to abuse are alcohol and marijuana to settle the internal restlessness they feel, and cocaine and methamphetamines to feel more energetic and focused. Nicotine use (cigarettes, cigars, and chewing tobacco) is much more common in people with ADD, as is the use of large amounts of caffeine. Nicotine and caffeine are mild stimulants.

A very common myth in the lay community is that the use of medication to treat ADD children somehow predisposes them to drug abuse in later life. The theory is that giving children or teens medicine to help their ADD somehow teaches them to abuse substances later on. Both my clinical experience and research shows that, in fact, the opposite is true. Treating ADD actually decreases drug or alcohol abuse later on.

Many people with ADD self-medicate (treat their underlying problems) with substances as a way to feel better, more normal, more focused, more together, less anxious, less depressed, and less overwhelmed. Despite the advantages, substance abuse is always bad medicine. In fact, substance abuse often makes the ADD symptoms much worse over time. Brain imaging work has clearly taught us how harmful drug abuse is to brain function. Cocaine, methamphetamines, alcohol, marijuana, nicotine, and caffeine decrease brain activity over time, sometimes significantly. So when an ADD teen uses alcohol to settle the internal restlessness she feels, the alcohol calms her for the moment, but damages cellular activity, worsening her ADD symptoms in the long run. One study done by Dr. Ismael Mena at UCLA showed that cocaine addicts had overall 23 percent less brain activity compared to a group of people who had never used drugs. Those cocaine addicts in the study who smoked had 45 percent less activity in their brain.

In my clinical experience, people with Type 1 (Classic) ADD and Type 2 (Inattentive) ADD tend to abuse stimulants, such as cocaine or methamphetamine; people with Type 3 (Overfocused) ADD tend to abuse alcohol more frequently; people with Type 4 (Temporal Lobe) and Type 5 (Limbic) ADD tend to be marijuana and stimulant abusers; and people with Type 6 (Ring of Fire) ADD and Type 7 (Anxious) ADD tend to abuse alcohol and marijuana.

Here are several examples:

Cindy

Cindy, forty-two, came to our clinic because she was abusing methamphetamines. She had failed a number of treatment programs, and she was being prevented from seeing her three children because of her drug problems. In addition, she had just lost the third job in a year because of tardiness and poor performance.

Cindy was depressed. She wanted help but felt stuck and out of control. She had begun abusing drugs during high school, and had been off and on ever since then. "When I use speed I feel clear and have energy and focus. I hate coming down and I hate that I have to break the law." It was clear that Cindy had Type 1 (Classic) ADD. As a child she was described as hyperactive, restless, impulsive, disorganized, and thrill seeking. She took Ritalin for a brief period of time, but her parents felt uncomfortable giving her medication and told her that she needed to try harder to do better in school.

When Cindy learned that adults could have ADD, it gave her hope to seek treatment. I changed her diet, gave her a high potency multiple vitamin/mineral complex, high-dose fish oil, and put her on Wellbutrin, a stimulating antidepressant, often helpful for Type 1 ADD. Due to California law at the time, I could not prescribe a substance abuser a controlled medication like Adderall or Ritalin, even though it may be the best treatment. Over the first four months there were many ups and downs, but Cindy stayed with the program and is now fourteen years sober, employed, and able to see her children on a regular basis.

Jim

Jim is a tragic story. He was a close friend of mine when I was in the military. At the age of thirty-six he shot and killed himself. At his funeral his mother told me the following story: As a child, Jim was like three boys in one. He was hyperactive, impulsive, and had a hard time sitting still and staying on task. His mother was called to school frequently during the elementary years. Jim had trouble with his behavior in class and on the playground. As a teenager he got into minor skirmishes with the law, and started using alcohol and marijuana. He barely graduated from high school. His mother said that she had to supervise him nightly until the end of the twelfth grade. "He only graduated because I made him stay at his desk until his homework was done," his mother told me.

During the Vietnam War, Jim was drafted and spent two years in the Army, where he and I met. He was often in trouble with his commander. He had a number of disciplinary actions for insubordination and drug abuse. When he was discharged from the military, he got a job with the local sheriff's office, but he was fired two years later for stealing a shot glass at a local bar when he was drunk. He married and had a child, but he was emotionally erratic, often intoxicated, and his wife left him within three years. His alcohol consumption increased. He got married two more times with the same disastrous results. After he had been fired from a job, the same year his last wife left him, he shot and killed himself. Looking back on Jim's life, through the eyes of a child psychiatrist, I have no doubt he had ADD. When we were together he was fun and impulsive, but I often had to keep him focused and I worked hard to keep him out of trouble. Inside he was a very loving and giving man. He just couldn't be consistent. The alcohol settled his restlessness, but ruined his life.

Jose

In a highly publicized Bay Area case, Jose, a sixteen-year-old gang member, was arrested after he and another gang member beat another teenager nearly to death. They were charged with attempted murder. One evening, when they were in an intoxicated state (from both alcohol and heavy marijuana usage), they approached a boy who was wearing a red sweater walking his dog across the street. They asked him, "What colors do you bang?" (asking him about his gang affiliation). When the boy said he did not know what they were talking about Jose replied, "Wrong answer." You see, Jose's gang claimed the color red. The two gang boys started hitting and kicking their victim repeatedly until he was unconscious. Other gang members described pulling Jose off the boy because "once he started he didn't stop." They were worried he would kill the boy.

The public defender ordered neuropsychological testing on Jose, which found frontal lobe dysfunction and evidence of ADD, depression, and learning disabilities. The psychologist suggested a resting and concentration SPECT series for independent verification. The SPECT series was significantly abnormal. Both studies showed *marked increased activity in the cingulate gyrus*, consistent with problems shifting attention. At rest, his SPECT also showed mildly suppressed prefrontal cortex activity. While doing a concentration task there was marked suppression of the prefrontal cortex and both temporal lobes, consistent with Type 1 (Classic), 3 (Overfocused), and 4 (Temporal Lobe) ADD, learning disabilities, and aggressive tendencies.

Jose had a long history of problems shifting attention. He was described by others as "brooding," argumentative, and oppositional. "Once he got a thought in his head," his father said, "he would talk about it over and over." In prison, he was placed on Effexor (an antidepressant that boosts both serotonin, norepinephrine, and dopamine to calm his cingulate and stimulate his PFC) and an anticonvulsant (to stabilize his temporal lobes). He felt calmer, more focused, and less easily upset.

**Jose's SPECT Results
(Left-Side Active View and Underside Surface Views)**

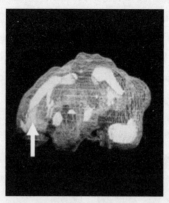

*3-D active side view
Marked increased cingulate (arrow)*

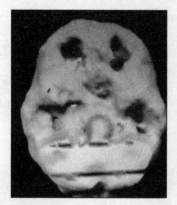

*At rest
Mild decreased PFC activity*

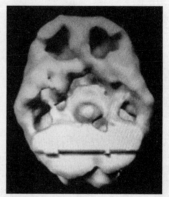

*During concentration
Marked decreased PFC and TL activity*

Walter

Walter, a fifty-seven-year-old physician, came to our clinic after he learned about us at a drug abuse conference. He had abused marijuana for thirty years, and said that he was unable to stop. Whenever he tried to stop he became angry, anxious, and restless. His wife had initially tried to get him to stop; however, she really disliked him sober, so she eventually bought the pot for him. He had tried without success a number of natural remedies to help his addiction. When I asked him about his childhood he said he had struggled in school and homework took him much longer than his friends. He took an extra year to graduate from both college and medical school.

Due to the history we suspected underlying temporal lobe problems. We performed a SPECT series to investigate why he had been unable to stop using pot without feeling very angry, irritable, agitated, and anxious.

Off and On Marijuana

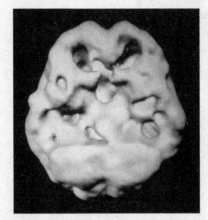

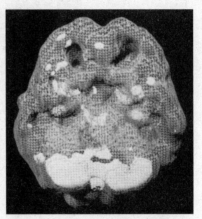

Underside surface view, off THC; Underside surface view, on THC

Decreased PFC and TL activity; Severe decreased PFC and TL

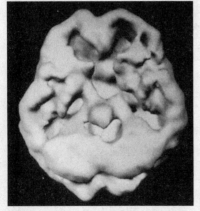

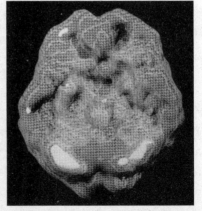

Underside active view, off THC; Underside active view, on THC

Increased deep left TL activity; Overall calming of TL activity

His SPECT showed overall decreased activity, especially in the prefrontal cortex and temporal lobes, but we then learned that in the three days prior to the study he had used marijuana heavily. I convinced Walter to abstain from all drug use for the next month so that we could rescan him to help us understand his sober brain pattern and maybe why he used marijuana. The study without marijuana showed decreased temporal lobe activity (likely from the chronic marijuana usage), but also increased activity in the deep left temporal lobe (often associated with anger, irritability, and anxiety). The study with heavy marijuana usage shows marked overall decreased activity, especially in the prefrontal cortex and temporal lobes (associated with attention, memory, and motivational problems) but also there is a decrease in the overactive areas noted in the "off marijuana" study. This scan series argues for the possibility of "self-medication," but unfortunately this medication caused serious overall decreased activity, even with drug abstinence. Clinically, he did better with anticonvulsant medication to stabilize temporal lobe function and stimulant medication to enhance prefrontal cortex activity, as well as natural treatments to optimize his brain.

David

A close friend of mine came to visit me from another state. He said that he had been having trouble concentrating and his energy was low. I knew that he smoked three packs of cigarettes and drank at least three pots of coffee every day. For a long time I suspected he had ADD (he underachieved in school, did impulsive things, and could never sit still) and that he was medicating himself with the stimulant affects of caffeine and nicotine. He was the CEO of a very successful corporation and not used to taking advice, even from people he knew cared about him. I told him about ADD and said that it would be a good idea to treat it and stop self-medicating. He told me he didn't want to take medication and asked if I there was a natural treatment for it. A bit amazed, I said, "You are doing the natural treatments for ADD—caffeine and nicotine. They will surely kill you eventually. My medication is more effective and when it is used properly it doesn't kill anyone."

I felt SPECT images of his brain might help him see the reality of

David's Concentration SPECT Study (Underside Surface View)

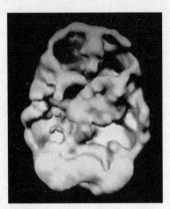

*Marked overall decreased activity,
especially in prefrontal cortex and
temporal lobes*

the situation and encourage him to stop. Even I was surprised by how bad his brain looked. He had marked decreased activity across the whole cortex, especially in the areas of the prefrontal cortex and temporal lobes. I told my friend that he needed to find another way to stimulate his brain. If he didn't stop the caffeine and nicotine he wasn't going to have much of a brain left to enjoy his success. He took my advice for a few weeks, but shortly after he returned home he went back to his old ways. I wondered if his poor temporal lobe activity caused him to be unable to hold the SPECT images in his memory, so he couldn't maintain the importance of them in his mind; or, if his very poor prefrontal cortex activity wouldn't allow him to have the necessary impulse control over his actions. Even though I recommended he try brain stimulants, such as Ritalin or Adderall, he maintained that he wanted to treat his ADD naturally.

SUBSTANCE ABUSE AND ADD TREATMENT ISSUES

ADD treatment issues are often complicated by substance abuse. As mentioned, as many as half of the ADD adults have substance abuse issues. Many physicians feel very uncomfortable prescribing controlled substances like Ritalin or Adderall to people who have addiction problems, as they should. A physician has to be thoughtful and careful with this population. In our practice we weigh the pros and cons of each intervention. If I am going to treat someone who is actively abusing drugs I will not use a stimulant medication until they are in a treatment program and they have clearly shown a prolonged commitment to sobriety. Instead, I'll prescribe stimulating antidepressants, supplements, and dietary interventions. When I do use stimulants I see the patient frequently and only give small amounts of medication.

CHAPTER 16

The Games ADD People Play

L et's Have a Problem"

"I Bet I Can Get You to Yell at Me or Hit Me"

"My Thoughts Are More Terrible than Your Thoughts"

"It's Your Fault and I'm Not Responsible"

"No, No Way, Never, You Can't Make Me Do It"

"I Say the Opposite of What You Say"

"I Say the First Thing That Comes to Mind"

"Let's Call It Even"

"Fighting as Foreplay"

Many people with ADD unconsciously, based on brain-driven mechanisms (not will-driven), play ADD games as a way to boost adrenaline and stimulate their frontal lobes. These games just seem to happen. No one plans for them to happen. Most ADD people deny that they engage in these behaviors, but I have seen these games in my own family and I've heard about them from my patients for many years. Let's look at each of these games in depth.

"LET'S HAVE A PROBLEM"

Without enough stimulation, the brain looks for ways to increase its own activity. Being mad, upset, angry, or negative has an immediate stimulating effect on the brain. Whenever you get upset your body produces increasing amounts of adrenaline stimulating heart rate, blood pressure, muscle tension, and, yes, brain activity. Many people with ADD pick on others to get a rise out of them, to get them upset, to make them crazy. So often family members of my patients tell me they are tired of the problems in their families. They say, "I'm so tired of fighting with my brother [sister, mother, father, son, daughter, etc.]. Why does there have to be this turmoil? Can't he [she] be happy with peaceful coexistence? Why does he [she] always have to fight? He [She] always has to Have a Problem."

Here are three examples of "Let's Have a Problem."

Joshua and Betsy were married for three years before they entered marital counseling. Betsy forced Joshua to get help. Joshua didn't see any problems and initially refused to see the therapist, but Betsy was beside herself. It seemed to her that they fought nearly all the time. She never felt at peace, never felt that they could have an evening or weekend where Joshua didn't complain about something. Even though Joshua was successful in his own business, he frequently complained about his employees. Betsy, who also worked with him, saw that he would regularly select an employee to pick on or engage in some kind of battle. Betsy felt constantly stressed, but Joshua didn't notice a problem. After an extensive intake interview, the therapist saw Joshua's conflict-seeking behavior as only one of his many ADD symptoms, including disorganization, distractibility, and impulsivity. She referred Joshua for a psychiatric evaluation, but also worked with the couple on strategies to recognize and stop this destructive game.

Rosemary and Chrissy, mother and sixteen-year-old daughter, constantly fought. It didn't seem to matter about what: it could be curfew, clothes, music, tone of voice—whatever. I met Chrissy when she was brought to our clinic for evaluation because of trouble at school. During the initial interview with Chrissy and her parents, I watched the two females go after each other. The tone between them was contentious, mutually irritating, and on edge. The father wearily told me, "This is how they live at home. Everything is an issue. Everything is a problem. They both hold on to their own positions and cannot let go. It's as if they have to irritate each other. I often don't want to come home because I know I'll have to listen to their battles." In the evaluation process Chrissy was diagnosed with Overfocused ADD (school struggles, inattention, impulsivity, restlessness, and oppositional and argumentative behavior), as was her mother who grew up in an alcoholic home, struggled in school, complained of low energy, disorganization, procrastination, and forgetfulness. After they were both treated for Overfocused ADD, the tension diminished dramatically. The need for conflict diminished and the father felt less stressed and more comfortable at home.

Wesley and David were brothers, nine and seven. Wesley was diagnosed with ADHD (Classic ADD) at the age of five, but the parents decided against treating him; they were afraid of the side effects of medication. The boys fought all the time. The parents knew that Wesley instigated most of the fights, but they didn't know how to deal with the situation. They came in for family therapy when David started to complain of frequent headaches and stomachaches. When I talked with David alone he told me he felt upset a lot of the time. He said that Wesley punched or kicked him whenever they were in a room alone, he called him names, and he said terrible things about his friends. The parents' decision to withhold Wesley's treatment had a very serious negative impact on David. Through proper education on the risks of not treating ADD, they decided to try medication for Wesley, along with exercise, and dietary changes. David's headaches and stomachaches went away when his brother stopped picking on him all the time.

"I BET I CAN GET YOU TO YELL AT ME OR HIT ME"

A similar game to "Let's Have a Problem" is "I Bet I Can Get You to Yell at Me or Hit Me." Many people with ADD are masterful at getting others to scream, yell, spank, and basically get out of control. They get others so upset, that they cannot help but lose it. These negative behaviors provide quite an adrenaline rush, but frequently lead to serious negative consequences, such as divorce, fights at school, being fired from a job, and even abuse. Again, the game is unconscious, not planned. It seems as if the ADD person senses the most vulnerable issues for others and they work on them until there is an explosion.

Here are three examples.

Bonnie had been diagnosed with Inattentive ADD at age twelve. The only treatment she received was medication, which she took sporadically. Now at age fifteen, she struggled in school and had problems with her parents at home. Her father was frequently upset with her because of her disrespectful tone. She also fought with her mother and a number of her teachers. The parents were very angry at the school because one of the teachers had yelled at her to shut up and sit down in class a number of months earlier. The teacher was disciplined by the school for the outbursts, but she said that she just couldn't take Bonnie's lack of respect and disruptive behavior. During Bonnie's initial evaluation in our clinic her father cried, saying, "I never thought I would have such negative feelings and behaviors toward my own child. I just start screaming at her because she says terrible things. She knows every hot button I have and she pushes them on a regular basis. Sometimes I understand why parents abandon their children. They just can't take the negative feelings, the lack of respect, and the constant fighting."

Jesse, age six, had parents who did not believe in spanking. They were well-educated people who discussed how they would raise their child even before he was born. Yet, even though they didn't want to use spanking, they often found themselves on the edge of losing control. They yelled more than they wanted to, and they found themselves using physical punishment on impulse because they would get so frustrated with Jesse's misbehavior. Jesse was impulsive and seemed driven to turmoil. The parents found out that when they yelled or spanked him his behavior would be better for a while. The mother told me, "If we have a bad morning at home, he has a good day at school. If we have a kind, loving morning at home, then he seems to have a bad day at school." I diagnosed Jesse with Classic ADD; he had the full cluster of symptoms. Besides treating him medically, I worked with his parents on effective parenting strategies. I warned them that as soon as they stopped yelling at Jesse, he would get worse for several weeks. It was as if he was going through adrenaline withdrawal. The parents yelling, screaming, and hitting were stimulating to him, and he, unknowingly, used their anger to feel more alert, which is why he did better in school if they had a bad morning at home.

Evan and Alexa, ages fifteen and twelve, were a brother and sister at war. Evan was diagnosed with Classic ADD when he was ten years old and Alexa had only recently been diagnosed with Overfocused ADD. The parents brought them to our clinic for medication and family therapy evaluations. Both siblings seemed to be masterful at upsetting the other one. There were frequent screaming, shouting, and physical fighting episodes. It seemed to the parents that both of them were involved in starting fights, and they had been at odds for as long as they could remember. On one occasion—the one that precipitated the referral—Evan came into Alexa's bedroom to borrow a CD. Alexa screamed at him to get out. When Evan refused, she threw a speaker at him. When the speaker hit his arm, he attacked her, leaving bruises all over her body.

It is essential to stop playing both "Let's Have a Problem" and "I Bet I Can Get You to Yell at Me or Hit Me" if an ADD person is to live happily with others. One of the more interesting phenomena I've noticed is that when I teach parents, siblings, and spouses to become less reactive, to not feed the need for adrenaline with anger, the ADD person may initially get *worse*. It seems as though the ADD person goes through withdrawal when others become more understanding or more tolerant, at least initially. When they can no longer get the adrenaline anger rush, they go after it full force. Unconsciously, they seem to say to themselves, "I have been able to get my adrenaline fix from you for a long time, I know I can make you yell at me," and then escalate the outrageous behavior. But if a parent, sibling, or spouse can remain nonreactive for a long enough period of time, the conflict-driven behavior usually significantly diminishes. Like a drug addict (I'm talking about adrenaline junkies) they will periodically test the "nonreactive skill" of the people in their environment by seeking intense emotional reactions. Others have to remain on guard to keep these negative behaviors away.

"MY THOUGHTS ARE MORE TERRIBLE THAN YOUR THOUGHTS"

Psychiatrist and brain imaging specialist Mark George demonstrated, in a landmark study, that negative thoughts have an overall stimulating effect on the brain. Using functional brain imaging studies, he looked at brain activity while people were thinking about something neutral, something positive, and something awful. The neutral thoughts did not change brain activity. The positive thoughts actually cooled overall brain activity, especially in the limbic area of the brain (certainly not good for ADD folks who have poor brain activity). The negative thoughts brought overall brain activation, especially in the limbic areas (making them more depressed) and in the prefrontal cortex (helping them focus).

Clinically, I have seen that many ADD people seem to be experts at picking out the most negative thoughts possible and staying focused on them for prolonged periods of time. It is almost as if they need the negativity to have the mental energy to get work done. When I started to talk about this idea to colleagues at my clinic Jonathan, a marriage, family, and child therapist who has ADD, said, "I think I do that myself. I wake up thinking about the most horrific things that could happen during the day. I feel anxious, but it motivates me to get up and get moving."

You have probably noticed the people who play this game at work. If ten good things and one bad thing happen, most of the thoughts are focused on the bad thing. These are the people at work who complain, gossip, find fault, undermine, and pit people against each other. As managers, they are often the ones who notice the negative much more than the positive.

The negativity that is often associated with ADD frequently ruins lives. Few are drawn closer to people who are negative, complaining, or filled with anxious thoughts. Many ADD people who unknowingly play this game end up isolated, lonely, depressed, and even more negative. People who are isolated from others have a higher incidence of both physical and emotional problems.

Some time ago, one of the physicians who worked in my office went through a period during which he was one of the most negative human beings I had ever met. He always had a sour look on his face. Every time I saw him he complained nonstop about office procedures and personnel. He was negative with patients. He hadn't exhibited this behavior when I hired him. I found myself avoiding him in the hallway and feeling frustrated by his behavior. After several weeks of this behavior I told him to come into my office. He started the meeting by complaining about a front office issue, without first wanting to know why I asked to see him. Immediately, I stopped him, saying, "I don't know what is going on with you, but something is different. You complain nonstop about nearly everything. People are avoiding you and patients don't want to see you anymore. I feel we have a serious problem on our hands." The doctor then told me that he had ADD and that he decided to stop his treatment a month ago. He didn't know why he stopped it, but he felt he was struggling more socially and at work. I told him that as his boss I couldn't advise him on his treatment, but if the negativity and complaining didn't stop he would have to leave. I gave him a three-month trial period to straighten out. He immediately started taking his treatment again and the negativity problem subsided.

Many people with ADD, who play the game of "My Thoughts Are More Terrible than Your Thoughts," end up divorced, fired, asked to leave school, isolated, and lonely because the negativity pushes people away. Be careful with negativity. If you use it as a stimulant you might want to get your medication adjusted or increase your exercise. This is a damaging and dangerous game.

"IT'S YOUR FAULT"

Another common game played by many people with ADD is "It's Your Fault." This may be the most dangerous ADD game of all. In this game the ADD person reasons that he (or she) has little, if anything, to do with the problems in his own life; everything is someone else's fault. Frequently, I hear that these people do not perform properly at school, work, or within their families because of "the lousy boss, the ineffective teacher, or the mean brother or sister." This game can completely ruin a life. Whenever you blame someone else for the problems in your own life you become a victim of that other person and you have no power to change anything. Without a sense of personal power people often feel overwhelmed and hopeless.

Billie Jean came into my office complaining about nearly everything in her life. Her husband mistreated her, her children neglected her, her boss was mean to her, and her doctor (not me thankfully) didn't take her seriously. When she was late to an appointment it was because of traffic; when she missed a payment it was because she hadn't gotten her mail. There was just an excuse for everything. Gently, I started to ask her what she could do to make these situations better—with her husband, children, job, and organizing her life. I felt it was critical for her emotional health. Unless she took responsibility for her emotions and reactions, she would always be at the mercy of others. I felt that her tendency to blame was a way to become angry and entitled so that she could use the anger as a stimulant. I began teaching her this concept, which, through therapy, she recognized as a common operant factor in her life. Eliminating blame and asking herself, "What can I do to make the situation better?" was one of the most important parts of her healing process. For example, she used to frequently complain that her children treated her with disrespect. She would yell, scream, cry, and carry on about how badly she was treated. When she asked herself, "What can I do to make the situation better?" she realized that her lax, but hostile parenting style (with poor follow-through—very common in ADD mothers) actually contributed to the problem and that she had to become firmer with the children— without the emotional outpouring that only made the situation worse. By taking responsibility and charge of the situation she was able to make a very positive difference.

It is very important to watch out for the "It's Your Fault" game. It may ruin your life.

"NO, NO WAY, NEVER, YOU CAN'T MAKE ME DO IT"

Opposition probably also increases adrenaline in the ADD brain. Many people with ADD, especially Type 3, tend to be argumentative and oppositional with people in their lives. These negative behaviors often cause tension and turmoil in families, relationships, or at work. Many parents tell me that they are very tired of arguing with their children. This game has one simple rule: The first response or reaction to any request is no, no way, never. I frequently ask my patients this question: "How many times out of ten, when your mother (father, teacher, boss) asks you to do something, will you do it the first time without arguing or fighting?"

Many of my patients tend to look down at the floor when I ask this question. They quietly say, "Not many times, maybe two or three times out of ten." I then ask them why. What is the need to oppose? They tell me they have no idea why they do it. It is not their goal to be oppositional.

Some time ago, I had a very interesting session. I saw a ten-year-old boy for the first time. He came into my office with his mother. He immediately sat down on my blue leather coach and put his shoes on the coach (which didn't bother me, I figure if you see difficult kids you have to have an office that will stand up to them). But the shoes on the coach did bother his mother. She told him to put them down. When he refused, she put them down on the floor. He immediately put them back up on the sofa. She looked at me in frustration and then moved her son's feet back on the floor. He put them up. She put them down. He put them up again. She put them down again and slapped his leg. This went on and on. I watched to see the interaction between them. He wanted his way. She was determined not to give in, but she engaged in the same repetitive ineffective behavior. She would have been better served by cutting the oppositional behavior right away and giving an immediate, unemotional but firm consequence. After about ten minutes of this behavior I asked the boy if it was his plan to upset his mother. He said no. Then I asked him why he had to do the opposite of what she wanted. He said, like so many of these kids do, "I don't know."

The unconscious game of "No, No Way, Never, You Can't Make Me Do It" can ruin someone's life. The level of opposition often drives others away, causing them to make negative judgments about you and emotionally push you away. While writing this book, I went to Israel to speak at an international ADD conference. While at the conference I had the pleasure to spend time with a family who had come to see me in California. The eleven-year-old boy had been depressed when he came to my clinic. Through his history and our scans we were able to properly diagnose him, put him on the right treatment, and help the family with the right behavioral strategies. He made a wonderful improvement. The child and his mother joined my daughter and me on a trip to Jerusalem. We went to the Church of the Holy Sepulcher and traced the steps of Jesus through the Stations of the Cross. The souvenir shops caught the boy's attention. He wanted a chessboard. The mother said no. He asked again. She said no again. This went on for about thirty minutes. I watched. Finally, the boy asked me how he could get his mother to get him a chessboard. I said, "You don't want to hear my answer." He said he really wanted my help. I told him (with his mother listening), "If your mom gets you what you want after she has already told you no fifteen times, then she is teaching you to get your way by irritating other people. You'll be difficult and no one will want to be with you, because you will have to have your way." He put his hands over his mother's ears so she wouldn't hear any more of my advice. Later he said, "Dr. Amen, you are right. I don't like people who are pests. I'll try not to be one."

You cannot let people badger you or irritate you into getting their way. If you allow this game to work, it sets up serious social problems. No one likes someone who argues with everything you say or opposes you most of the time.

"I SAY THE OPPOSITE OF WHAT YOU SAY"

Another destructive ADD game is one I call "I Say the Opposite of What You Say." This game is similar to "No, No Way, Never, You Can't Make Me Do It," but it involves speech more than behavior. The people who play this game take the opposite position as the other person in the conversation, whether they believe in the opposition or not. For example, if your spouse complains that you do not listen to him (her), you deny it and then say that he or she does not listen to you. If a parent tells a child to clean his messy room he is likely to say that his room isn't messy. If a person takes a view on a political position, you will take the opposite position (even if it is against what you really believe). The need to oppose seems to be more important than the truth. The back and forth disagreement brings more adrenaline, stress, and irritation to the table. Watch out for this game. It pushes people away from you.

It seems to me that many politicians are masters at this game. I have often thought that many politicians had ADD. If a Democrat has a good idea, the Republicans will automatically put it down; and if a Republican offers a helpful plan, the Democrats will automatically look for ways to shoot holes in it. Cooperation is so foreign to the political process it is a wonder anything actually gets done. Unfortunately, this same dynamic happens in many ADD homes. The lack of cooperation stresses so many family members.

"I LIKE TO SAY THE FIRST THING THAT COMES TO MIND"

Many of my patients struggle with the game of "I Say the First Thing That Comes to Mind." I have heard a number of my patients say, "I am brutally honest." They wear this trait as if it is a badge of courage. I usually reply to them that brutal honesty is usually not helpful. Relationships require tact.

Recently, I walked into my waiting room to greet an eight-year-old patient. I was about ten minutes late for the appointment. When she saw me she said, "Well it's about damn time." Her mother looked horrified and apologized for the little girl's comment. Living in an ADD household, I know comments like that were just part of the terrain.

This game causes many, many problems. When you just say the first thing that comes to your mind, you can hurt someone's feelings, infuriate a customer, or give away secrets that were entrusted to you. One of my patients was charged with bringing a friend to his surprise party. On the way to the party he inadvertently started talking about how much fun the party would be. When he saw the look on his friend's face he was horrified that he had ruined the surprise.

"LET'S CALL IT EVEN"

It seems that many people with ADD also play a deflection game titled "Let's Call It Even." In this game, whenever someone else has a complaint or criticism, the player also takes on the complaint as his own. For example, if a husband is unhappy that the house isn't clean, the wife may complain that he doesn't help enough. If a wife complains that her husband doesn't listen enough, the husband will complain about the same thing. If a sibling says that her sister goes into her room and takes things, the sister will say she does that because her sister does that too.

"FIGHTING AS FOREPLAY"

Many couples that I have seen through the years have described a fascinating ADD game I call "Fighting as Foreplay." In this game there is an intense fight, then a period of making up, which includes making love. The swing of emotions is quick and dramatic. One minute you are fighting, talking about divorce and ready to leave the relationship, the next moment you are making wild passionate love and feeling blissful. It's confusing to the participants, but makes some biological sense. The fight is needed for stimulation. Once stimulated you are ready for love.

All of these games are very destructive in ADD relationships. The first step in eliminating these games is to notice them, then use the treatment guidelines in this book to feel better and help eliminate the games ADD people play.

CHAPTER 17

The Impact of ADD on Relationships, Families, School, Work, and Self-Esteem

ADD impacts all aspects of life. In this chapter I'll list some of the most common complaints patients and their families bring into my office.

RELATIONSHIPS

As a child, teen, or adult, ADD often has a negative impact on a person's ability to interact with others. Here are some of the reasons:

Social Isolation

Many people with ADD have failed in relationships so many times in the past that they don't want to experience the pain anymore. They avoid relationships or they make excuses to be by themselves.

Teasing

People with ADD are often teased by others. Their behavior brings negative attention to themselves. Additionally, the impulsivity and conflict-driven nature causes them to tease others, sometimes to the point where the other person becomes very upset.

Fighting

Fighting is typical for many people with ADD. It may be related to impulsivity (saying things without thinking), stimulation-seeking behavior, misperceptions, rage outbursts, and chronically low self-esteem. The fighting leads to chronic stress for the person with ADD and those in his or her family.

Misperceptions

Misperceptions often cause serious problems in relationships. Often the parent or spouse of an ADD person has to spend an inordinate amount of time correcting misperceptions that lead to disagreements. Once, on the night before I was leaving on a business trip, I told my wife that I was going to miss her. She heard my words as "I'm not going to miss you" and she was angry at me for the rest of the night, no matter what I said.

Distractibility

Due to distractibility, conversations are often cut short or left uncompleted, leaving the other person feeling unimportant. When a person is distracted, he or she may miss large chunks of conversations and may unconsciously fill in missing pieces with negative information.

Problems Taking Turns

The ADD person's need to have what they want right away often causes problems in situations where they need to take turns, such as in conversations or games.

Speaking Without Thinking

This is perhaps the most damaging problem with ADD in relationships. Just because a person has a thought doesn't mean that it is accurate or that he or she even necessarily believes it. Many people with ADD just say what comes to mind. They then get stuck in defending these statements, which causes further problems.

Problems Completing Chores

Even though the person with ADD wants to finish what he or she starts, distractibility gets in the way and many things may be left half done. This leads to many resentments, arguments, and frustrations felt by others.

Difficulty Playing or Being Quiet

Often the level of activity or noise created by the ADD person causes frustration and irritability in others.

Sensitivity to Noise

At the same time the ADD person may also be sensitive to noise. They often need to escape from others to feel calm or peaceful inside.

Sensitivity to Touch

When the person is sensitive to touch, they often shy away from affection. This can harm a relationship, especially if the person's partner wants or needs affection.

Excessive Talking

Sometimes people with ADD talk for self-stimulation. There is an internal drive to go on and on. This may irritate others, who feel like a prisoner of the conversation because they feel that they cannot get a word in the conversation.

Lack of Emotional Expression

The partners of some ADD people complain that there is little talking or emotional expression in the relationship. "He seems turned off when he comes home" is a common complaint. Often parents will ask their children about their day and the only response they'll get is "Fine" or "Okay." These kids are often called non-elaborators.

Disorganization

This causes problems in a relationship because the ADD person often doesn't live up to their part of the chores or agreements.

Taking High Risks/Thrill Seeking

This type of behavior worries the parents, partners, or friends of the ADD person. Friends often feel pressured to go along with dangerous behavior, causing a rift in the relationship.

Easily Frustrated/Emotional/Moody

Many family members of ADD children, teens, and adults have told me that they never know what to expect from the ADD person. "One minute she's happy, the next minute she's screaming," is a common complaint. Small amounts of stress may trigger off huge explosions.

Tantrums/Rage Outbursts

Some studies have reported that up to 85 percent of people with ADD have rage outbursts, often with little provocation. After this occurs several times in a relationship, the parent, partner, or friend becomes "gun shy" and starts to withdraw from the person. Untreated ADD is often involved in abusive relationships.

Low Self-Esteem

When people do not feel good about themselves, it impairs their ability to relate to others. They have difficulty taking compliments or getting outside of themselves to truly understand the other person. The brain filters information coming in from the environment. When the brain's filter (self-esteem) is negative, people tend to only see the negative and ignore any positive. Many partners of ADD people complain that when they give their partner a compliment, the latter find a way to make it look like they have just been criticized.

Looking for Turmoil

This is a common complaint of people living with someone who has ADD. They say that the person looks for trouble. Rather than ignoring a minor incident, he or she focuses on it and has difficulty letting it go. Things in an ADD house do not remain peaceful for long periods of time.

Chronic Anxiety or Restlessness

As mentioned above, ADD people often feel restless or anxious. This often causes them to search for ways to relax. They may use excessive sex, food, or alcohol to try to calm themselves. I treated one man who had sex with his girlfriend over five hundred times in the last year of their relationship. She left him, because she felt that their relationship was only based upon sex.

Failure to See Others' Needs

Many people with ADD have trouble getting outside of themselves to see the emotional needs of others. They are often labeled as spoiled, immature, or self-centered.

Failure to Learn from the Past

Often people with ADD engage in repetitive, negative arguments with others. They seem not to learn from the interpersonal mistakes from their past and repeat them again and again.

Chronic Procrastination

The ADD person often waits until the very last minute to get things done (bills; buying birthday, anniversary, or Christmas gifts; etc.). This may irritate those around them who feel the need to pick up the loose pieces.

FAMILIES

ADD often causes serious problems in families. I have seen "caring" families fall apart because of the turmoil caused by having an ADD child. I have also seen many divorces between people who "truly loved each other" because of the stress of one or both partners having ADD. Many of the issues listed in the previous section apply here. Here are several other important issues to consider.

Drive Toward Turmoil

ADD children and teenagers are often experts at getting their parents to yell at them. As I mentioned above, the ADD person often has decreased activity in their frontal lobes and they "unconsciously" seek stimulation to feel more awake or alert. In a family, this takes on many forms, such as temper tantrums, noise, and high activity.

Parental Splitting

ADD kids may also be skilled at getting their parents to fight with each other. Splitting parental authority gives children and teenagers too much power and increases the turmoil. Often the scenario is that the mother will blame the father for being "too absent" or "too harsh," and the father will blame the mother for being "too inconsistent" and "too soft." Of course, this goes both ways. I have seen many couples separate, in part, to stop the turmoil they lived in at home.

Negative Expectations

In families with an ADD child, teen, or adult there is often the expectation that there will be problems, so people begin to avoid each other or predict there will be problems. For example, a mother recently told me she expected that her ADD husband wouldn't finish the dinner dishes as he promised. Before he even had a chance to do them, she "resentfully" cleaned them. She was angry at him for the rest of the night, even though she didn't give him a chance to be helpful.

Feelings of Parents:

Denial: "There's nothing wrong with the child! He only needs more time, more attention, more discipline, more love, a better teacher, a better school, a firmer mother, a father who is more available." These are common excuses parents make to deny that any problem exists. Admitting that there is a problem is often so painful that many parents go years and years without seeking help. Denial can seriously harm a child's or teen's chances for success!

Grief: There is often a grieving process that occurs in a family with an untreated ADD person. The parents or spouse often feel the loss of having a "normal" child, teen, or spouse and end up feeling very sad that the situation is not as they expected it would be.

On Guard: For many parents, living with an ADD child is like being in a war zone. They have to be constantly on guard that the child won't run out into the street, won't break something at the store, or won't run off at a park. This chronic watchfulness causes much internal tension for parents.

Guilt: This is a significant issue for many people who live with those who have ADD. The turmoil that an ADD child, teen, or adult causes often brings on bad feelings. Parents or spouses are not "supposed" to have bad feelings toward people they love and so end up burdened by feelings of guilt. In the treatment section, I'll discuss how to break the cycle of guilt.

Anger: Being upset or angry at the teachers, doctors, day care workers, and the other parent is common in parents with an ADD child. The levels of frustration are so high in these families that people look for someone on whom to blow off steam.

Envy: "Why can't we have normal kids? We didn't do anything to deserve the turmoil. It's not fair."

Blame: "You spoil him. How's he ever going to learn if you do everything for him?" "You're too soft on her." "You never say a kind word to him." "If only you would be home more, then we wouldn't have these problems with her." Blame is very destructive and rarely, if ever, helpful. Yet, it is all too common in ADD families.

Isolation: "Everyone thinks I'm a bad parent. No one else has these problems. I can't go anywhere with him, I'm stuck at home." Feelings of isolation are very common. Many parents of ADD children feel that they are the only ones in the world who have these problems. Joining a support group can be very helpful for these people.

Bargaining: "Maybe she'll be okay if we put her in a new school." "Maybe if we put him in outside activities his attitude will improve."

"Maybe if I leave his father, we'll all feel better." Many parents of ADD children attribute their problems to outside forces and feel that making radical lifestyle changes will help. Without the right treatment, however, these changes are rarely helpful.

Depression: "I'm a failure as a parent. I've failed my child. I have no business raising children. I should go to work and leave him with a sitter. I'm so tired that I can't do this anymore." The physical and emotional drain of having an ADD child can often trigger off a significant depression. Watch your moods.

Sibling Issues

Children with ADD often irritate their siblings to the point of causing tears, anger, or fighting. Siblings develop negative feelings toward the ADD child because they are often embarrassed by their outrageous behavior at school or with friends.

Since ADD, for the most part, is a genetic disorder, it is more likely that siblings may also have features of ADD. Having two or more members of a family with untreated ADD can completely disorganize the family.

Oftentimes in families with an ADD child, there is an identified "good" child and a "bad" (ADD) child. Because the parents' self-esteem is so damaged by having an unrecognized ADD child they will often avoid the ADD child and focus a lot of positive energy on the other child and think that they are more "perfect" than they really are. This causes resentment in the ADD child. It also causes the "perfect" child to subvert any progress that the ADD child might make. Corey and Sarah were an example of this "sibling subversion." Here's an example:

Corey, nine, had a severe case of ADD. He would throw three-hour temper tantrums, had problems nearly every day in school, and was chronically noncompliant with his mother. Six-year-old Sarah, with long, curly, red hair, was her mother's angel. She could do no wrong. With treatment, Corey began to significantly improve. But, in therapy, Corey told me that his little sister was "flipping him off" with her middle finger. When he told his mother, she did not believe him, saying, "Sarah wouldn't do that, she's too sweet." I told the mother to watch them secretly when they were playing together. Sure enough, Sarah was using her middle finger to drive Corey crazy. She was having difficulty losing her place in the family as the "perfect" child and she had a stake in Corey remaining a problem.

Feelings of Brothers and Sisters

Embarrassment: Just as parents are blamed by neighbors for unacceptable behavior of their child, so brothers and sisters are often held responsible or ridiculed by their peers for the actions of their ADD sibling.

Anger: An ADD child can evoke intense emotions in his brother or sister.

Resentment: A sibling may feel very resentful at being labeled "weirdo's sister" or having a child come up and say, "Hey, do you know what your brother did?"

Put-Upon: Siblings feel urged to include the ADD child in their play and free-time activities. He or she often has few friends of their own and it's natural for parents to seek relief.

Guilt: Like parents, siblings often feel guilty for emotions they harbor. They care deeply in spite of the behavior they live with.

Out of Control: Brothers and sisters find it difficult to engage the ADD child in play without constant struggles over rules and issues of control. They may strike out at the ADD child as a result of being constantly frustrated.

Jealousy: Siblings often question the double standards that exist in the rules that they are governed by. The ADD child is often rewarded when the behavior does not warrant it as a way of pacifying him or her at the time.

SCHOOL

Whether for children, teenagers, or adults, ADD has a powerful negative impact on a person's ability to do well in school. Except for classes that are small or highly interesting, many people with ADD have significant problems. Here is a list of common school problems.

Restlessness

The hyperactivity that often accompanies ADD in childhood causes obvious problems: the child is restless, out of his or her seat, irritating other kids (not to mention the teacher), and causing turmoil and disruption in his or her path. In teens and adults, the restlessness of ADD often distracts others in class who notice the constant movement (i.e., legs shaking, shifting body posture in seats).

Short Attention Span and Distractibility

Having a short attention span and being easily distracted affects nearly every aspect of school. This will affect a student's ability to follow teachers in lectures, participate in small groups, and perform consistently on tests. The short attention span often causes the ADD student's attention to wander while reading or performing class assignments, causing them to take an inordinate amount of time to finish tasks. Distractibility also may get ADD students in trouble, as they tend to be in everyone else's business.

Impulsiveness

Impulsiveness causes serious school problems. Blurting out answers in class, responding impulsively on quizzes or tests, and saying things without thinking are typical. I've treated many people with ADD who were "tactless" in how they responded to their teachers or professors. One teenager said to her teacher, "You're a lousy teacher! I don't know why you explain things like that, but the other teachers know how to explain things a lot better than you do." All of us have had that thought about certain teachers at one time or another. Most people, however, would never blurt out a statement like that because it would hurt the teacher's feelings and harm their relationship. But with ADD, the mouth is often engaged before the brain.

Procrastination

Many people with ADD wait until the last minute to complete their tasks for school. If it isn't the night before, they cannot get their brain upset enough to get their work done. Many parents have told me about the constant fights they have with their children or teens about starting projects early and working on them over time, rather than the night before. Many adults have told me that they never did term papers in school or they used amphetamines the night before the work was due to get it done. Procrastination in school caused the work to be done poorly or for it to be left undone or incomplete.

Trouble Shifting Attention

As I mentioned above, there is a group of people with ADD who have trouble shifting their attention from one thing to another. They have a tendency to get "stuck" or overfocus. This characteristic can be particularly troublesome in school. Getting stuck on an idea early in a lecture may cause the student to miss the information for much of the lecture. Taking notes for these students is often a disaster. Note taking requires constant shifts in attention: from the teacher to the paper to the teacher to the paper, etc.

Forgetfulness

This symptom often upsets the parents and teachers of ADD students. Forgetting to bring home books, leaving clothes at school, and not turning in homework assignments that were completed are common complaints.

Learning Disabilities

Learning difficulties and disabilities are very common in people with ADD. It is essential to recognize and treat these disabilities if a student is going to perform at his or her potential. Common disabilities are writing disabilities (getting thoughts from the brain to the paper), reading disabilities (shifting or reversing letters or numbers), and visual processing problems and auditory processing problems (trouble accurately hearing what was said).

Unusual Study Habits

Many people with ADD have unusual study habits. Most need a very quiet place to study. My wife used to sit in her car under a streetlight to study. She needed an environment that was absolutely quiet and free from distractions. She had trouble studying at home because she saw all the things that needed to be done and was too easily distracted. Other people with ADD need noise in order to study. Some people have told me they need the TV or radio on, or they need some other sort of noise in order to keep themselves awake and focused.

Timed Situations

Timed testing situations are often a disaster for those with ADD. Whether it is short math exercises, classroom writing tasks, or testing situations, the more time pressure that is put on these people, the worse it tends to get for them.

WORK

Bill, thirty-two, had just been fired from a job he loved. He knew it was his fault, but he just couldn't organize his time to do the work that was expected. He missed deadlines, seemed to drift off in meetings, and he was often late to work. He knew that his wife would be angry with him. This was the third job he had lost in their three-year marriage. As a child, Bill had taken Ritalin for troubles in school, but he was taken off the medication when he was a teenager. His doctor told him that all kids outgrow the problems he was having. That was bad advice. At the age of thirty-two, Bill still suffered from the effects of ADD.

When ADD is left untreated, it significantly affects the workplace. It costs employers millions of dollars every year in decreased productivity, absenteeism, and employee conflicts. Yet ADD remains vastly underdiagnosed, especially in adults.

There is both a positive and negative side to ADD in the workplace. People with ADD often are high in energy, enthusiastic, full of ideas, and creative. If they surround themselves with people who organize them and manage the details, they can be very successful. In my clinical practice, I treat many highly successful ADD executives. Unfortunately, many people with ADD are not fortunate enough to be in positions that maximize their strengths and minimize their weaknesses. These folks often have serious problems at work. Here are some of the difficulties that people with ADD are likely to have at work:

The Harder They Try, the Worse It Gets

Research has shown that the more ADD people try to concentrate, the worse it gets for them. Their brain region responsible for concentrated thinking turns off, not on. When a supervisor or manager puts more pressure on them to perform, they often fall off in their work. Then the boss interprets this decreased performance as willful misconduct, and serious problems arise. I once treated a man with ADD who was a ship welder. He told me that whenever his boss put pressure on him to do a better job, his work got worse (even though he really tried to do better). When the boss told him that he liked his work, he became more productive. In supervising someone with ADD, it is much more effective to use praise and encouragement, rather than pressure.

Distractibility

Distractibility is often evident in meetings. People with ADD tend to look around the room, drift off, appear bored, forget where the conversation is going, and interrupt with extraneous information. The distractibility and short attention span may also cause them to take much longer to complete their work than their coworkers. They are often very frustrating to managers and coworkers.

Forgetfulness

Forgetfulness is common in ADD and a serious handicap on the job. Missed deadlines, forgotten reports, and steps gone undone on a job are just a few examples.

Impulsivity

Often, the lack of impulse control gets the ADD person fired. They may say inappropriate things to supervisors, other employees, or customers. I once had a patient who was fired from thirteen jobs because he had trouble controlling his mouth. Even though he really wanted to keep several of the jobs, he would just blurt out what he was thinking before he had a chance to process the thought. Impulsivity also leads to poor decision making. Rather than thinking a problem through, impulsive people want an immediate solution to the problem and act without the necessary forethought. Similarly, the impulsivity causes these people to have trouble going through the established channels at work. They often go right to the top to solve problems, rather than working through the system. This may cause resentments from their coworkers and immediate supervisors. Impulsivity also may lead to such problem behaviors as lying and stealing. I have treated many ADD people who have suffered with the shame and guilt of these behaviors.

Conflict Seeking

Many people with ADD are in constant turmoil with one or more people at work. They seem to "unconsciously" pick out people who are vulnerable to verbally spar with. They also have a tendency to embarrass others, which does not endear them to anyone. Shades of the grown-up version of the class clown are also evident at work, such as cracking inappropriate jokes in meetings. Conflict may follow the ADD person from job to job.

Disorganization

Disorganization is a hallmark of ADD and it can be particularly damaging in the workplace. Often when you look at the person's work area, it is a wonder they can work in it at all. They tend to have many piles of "stuff"; paperwork is often hard for them to keep straight; and they seem to have a filing system that only they can figure out (and only on good days).

Late to Work

Many people with ADD are chronically late to work because they have significant problems waking up in the morning. I've had several patients who bought sirens from alarm companies to help them wake up. Imagine what their neighbors thought! They also tend to lose track of time, which contributes to their lateness.

Start Many Projects, But Finish Few

The energy and enthusiasm of people with ADD often pushes them to start many projects. Unfortunately, their distractibility and short attention span impairs their ability to complete them.

One radio station manager told me that he had started over thirty special projects the year before, but only completed a handful of them. He told me, "I'm always going to get back to them, but I get new ideas that get in the way."

I also treat a college professor who told me that the year before he saw me he started three hundred different projects. His wife finished the thought by telling me he only completed three.

Moodiness and Negative Thinking

Many people with ADD suffer from moodiness, excessive worrying, and negativity. This attitude comes from their past. They have many experiences with failure, so they come to expect it. Their "sky is falling" attitude has a tendency to get on the nerves of coworkers and can infect the work environment.

Inaccurate Self-Assessment

People with ADD are often not a good judge of their own ability. They may overvalue themselves and think they are better at their jobs than they really are, or they may devalue important assets that they have.

Switches Things Around: Many people with ADD have a tendency to switch things around

This happens with letters or numbers, even phrases or paragraphs. You can imagine the problems this can cause at work. Switching numbers on a phone message can cause many wrong numbers. Reading letters backwards can give different meaning to content. Twisting information from a meeting can cause serious misunderstandings. I once treated a billing clerk who had reversed the amounts on bills she sent out, costing her employer over twelve thousand dollars. I had to meet with the employer to convince him that ADD was a real phenomenon and that the employee was not trying to sabotage his business.

Tendency Toward Addictions

People with ADD have a tendency toward addictions, such as food, alcohol, drugs, even work. Drug or alcohol addictions cause obvious work problems. Food addictions cause health and self-image problems which can impact work. Addiction to work is also a serious problem, because it causes burnout and family problems that eventually show up in the workplace.

Spends Excessive Time at Work Because of Inefficiencies

The symptoms of ADD frequently cause a person to be inefficient on their job. This causes many people with ADD to put in overtime that managers consider excessive. This may result in a poor job evaluation or firing. To avoid these problems, many people with ADD take their work home in order to finish it.

SELF-ESTEEM

By the age of six or seven, ADD often has a significant negative impact on self-esteem. Here are some of the reasons why:

Frequent Conflict

Many ADD sufferers have been in conflict either with their parents, friends, or teachers over and over for years. This causes them to develop negative "self-talk" patterns and low self-esteem.

Negative Input

The difficult behavior associated with ADD often incites negative input from others. "Don't do that." "Why did you do that?" "Where was your head?" "What's wrong with you?" "Your brother doesn't act like that!" "You'd do better if you would try harder." "Shame on you!" These are common phrases many ADD children hear on a regular basis. Constant negative input turns into low self-esteem.

Inaccurate Self-Assessment

As mentioned above, people with ADD are often a poor judge of their own ability. They often devalue their strengths and positive attributes, focusing only on their failures.

Chronic Failure

Most people with ADD have had many failure experiences in life, school, relationships, and work. These failures set them up to expect failure, and whenever a person expects that they will fail, they don't try their best or they don't try at all.

Negative Bonding

ADD often causes negative bonding with parents. Bonding is critical to the emotional health of human beings. Yet, by the time many ADD children are school age, they have such a negative relationship with their parents that they begin not to care about other people, which sets them up for societal problems. Without bonding, people do not care about others, and when a person doesn't care, he or she has no problems hurting others to get what they want.

A Sense of Being Damaged

Due to the many problems that ADD people have experienced throughout their lives, they often have a sense that they are different from others and that they are "damaged."

Tantrums/Rage Outbursts

As I mentioned above, there is a high incidence of rage outbursts in people with ADD. The sense of being out of control wounds the person's self-esteem, making him question why anyone would value someone so volatile.

Brain Filters

When people do not feel good about themselves, it impairs their ability to relate to others. They have difficulty taking compliments or getting outside of themselves to truly understand the other person. The brain filters information coming in from the environment. When the brain's filter (self-esteem) is negative, people tend to only see the negative and ignore any positive. Many partners of ADD people complain that when they give their partner a compliment they find a way to make it look like they have just been criticized.

Negative Thinking Patterns

Thought patterns are the manifestation of self-esteem. Due to difficult past life experiences, many people with ADD have a tendency to think very negatively. They frequently distort situations to make them out to be worse than they really are. They tend to overgeneralize, think in black-and-white terms, predict bad outcomes, label themselves with negative terms, and personalize situations that have little personal meaning. Teaching the ADD person to talk back to negative thoughts is essential to helping them heal.

POINTS TO REMEMBER:
ADD is a neurobiological disorder with
serious psychological and social consequences.

Children, teens, adults, and parents need to know:
It's not their fault,
they didn't cause it,
and there is a lot of hope.

Parents, spouses, and family members
need information and the child, teenager, or adult
with ADD needs good treatment.

PART 3

The Amen Clinics ADD Brain Enhancement Program

CHAPTER 18

Enhancing ADD Brain Function

Effective Interventions for Treating ADD Types, Including Diet, Exercise, Medications, Supplements, and Behavioral Interventions

The Amen Clinics ADD Brain Enhancement Program is geared toward optimizing brain function. The program includes diet, exercise, supplements, medications, neurofeedback, and behavioral interventions. Certainly not everyone needs all treatments, but I believe that it is important for people to know the options available and the pros and cons of each option.

Most people in America have their ADD treated with medication alone. However, research studies by Dr. James Satterfield of Oregon show that medication by itself does not make a lasting difference. To get the best results, the treatment needs to be targeted and comprehensive, including strategies geared toward enhancing brain function, and improving skills at home, at school, in the workplace, and in social situations. In other words, they need treatments geared toward optimizing the brain and reprogramming their lives.

As this book has shown, ADD has clear biological roots and serious psychological and social consequences when it is left untreated. I often use the following computer analogy with my patients. In order for a computer to effectively run any program, its hardware must be sufficient. It must have enough memory and processing speed. Trying to run complex programs on an old computer doesn't work well. Yet many people with ADD do not have enough memory or processing speed in their brains because of the underactivity in the prefrontal cortex and temporal lobes. To run programs effectively you must first optimize the hardware—the brain. But once a computer's hardware is optimized, it still has programming needs. Many people with ADD, because of the hardware (brain) problems, never fully learned the programs (information) they needed. Once the brain is optimized, it is important to input strategies that help people with ADD be more effective within their families, at school or work, and in social relationships.

Earlier we discussed how important it was to assess ADD in the four circles bio-psycho-social-spiritual. Treating ADD is best done in the same way. It is essential to optimize the ADD brain (biology), the mindset of an ADD person (psychology), the interactions between the ADD person and the people in his or her life (social), and developing a deep sense of meaning and purpose (spiritual). Ignoring any of these factors can cause treatment failure. Here is a brief summary of ADD treatments, many of which will be expanded upon in subsequent chapters.

BIOLOGICAL INTERVENTIONS

Eliminate Anything Toxic

Toxic substances can cause and exacerbate ADD-like symptoms. (For example, marijuana use can make someone appear as though they have Type 2 [Inattentive] ADD). Eliminate anything that is toxic to your brain. Given that more than 50 percent of ADD teenagers and adults have or have had problems with drug or alcohol abuse, treatment for abuse is essential to healing ADD.

Caffeine and nicotine have been shown in brain studies to decrease overall blood flow to the brain, which in turn will make ADD symptoms worse over time. In addition, in my experience both nicotine and caffeine decrease the effectiveness of medication and supplement treatments and increase the amount of side effects people have from medication. "But I feel so focused after my coffee in the morning," you say. In the short run caffeine makes you feel more focused. It works on similar neurotransmitters in the brain as does Ritalin and Adderall. Unfortunately, it also decreases brain blood flow and over time can make the ADD symptoms worse. If possible, also stop any medications that contribute to ADD symptoms.

Protect Your Head

As we have seen, head injuries can cause severe ADD-like symptoms. And people who have ADD are more prone to head injuries due to their impulsive nature. Head injuries can take a mild case of Type 2 (Inattentive) ADD and turn it into a severe Type 4 (Temporal Lobe) ADD. Do everything you can to prevent these injuries. Make kids wear their helmets when riding bikes, snowboarding, or rollerblading. Wear your seat belt. Do not engage in activities, no matter how adrenal rewarding they are, if they put you at more risk for head injuries.

Dietary Interventions

This is no small recommendation! As my friend and colleague Barry Sears, PhD (author of *The Zone*) says, "Food is a powerful drug. You can use it to help mood and cognitive ability or you can unknowingly make things worse." All ADD types, except Type 3 (Overfocused) ADD, do better on a higher protein, lower carbohydrate diet, the exact opposite way that most people eat. I will explore dietary interventions for ADD Types in Chapter (19).

Smart Exercise

All ADD types benefit from exercise, especially Types 1, 2, 3, and 5. Exercise boosts blood flow to the brain. Exercise also increases serotonin availability in the brain, which has a tendency to calm cingulate hyperactivity. Tryptophan, the amino acid building block for serotonin, is a relatively small molecule. It does not compete well against the larger amino acids to cross the blood/brain barrier. With intense aerobic exercise the large muscles use the available supply of bigger amino acids to replenish tissue. This decreases competition for tryptophan, which ultimately leads to increased concentrations of it within the brain.

I recommend that my patients do the equivalent of walking for thirty to forty-five minutes four to seven days a week. Walk like you are late. To get the brain benefit, a stroll won't do. Also, lift weights twice a week to optimize muscle mass and hormone function.

Avoid Prolonged Exposure to Video or Computer Games

I recommend no more than thirty to forty-five minutes a day of computer or video games. If you are not careful, they can be harmful and addictive for people who have vulnerable brains. I have had two patients over the past several years who have had seizures while playing video games. They did not have prior seizures. It is a phenomenon called photophobic seizures, which happened to 730 children in Japan several years ago while they were watching the Nintendo *Pokémon* cartoon. I have had other patients who became violent after playing video games. Granted these cases may be extreme, but I cannot see much good that comes from playing these games for hours a day, and I believe they have the potential for harm. My best advice at this point is, be careful and limit the exposure.

Medication

Medication is an emotionally loaded issue for many people. There is a lot of controversy in this area. After doing the brain imaging work for the past twenty-two years it is very clear to me that medication can be very helpful for many patients. Medication is the best-studied and most effective treatment for ADD. Having said that, medication by itself is generally bad treatment. Unfortunately, most people just get medication and ignore the help needed for the psychological and social aspects of ADD. Medication for each ADD type will be discussed in Chapter 21.

Supplements

Even more controversial than medication is using natural supplements for ADD. Much more research is needed in this area. However, our clinical experience has taught us that supplements can be useful when used properly. Yet, because supplements are "natural" people think of them as innocuous, which just isn't true. I am not opposed to natural supplements and I often recommend them. I am opposed to a person being ineffectively treated. A rational, balanced approach to both medication and supplement treatment is needed. Supplement treatment for ADD will be discussed in Chapter 20.

Neurofeedback

A very exciting biological treatment for ADD is neurofeedback. With neurofeedback electrodes are placed on the scalp, electrical brain activity is measured, and the information is fed back to the patient. Areas of increased and decreased activity can be seen. Neurofeedback, like biofeedback, is based on the principle that if one knows the activity in a certain bodily function then one can use techniques to enhance or optimize the activity in the area. Neurofeedback for each ADD type is discussed in Chapter 22.

Sleep Strategies

Sleep disturbances are very common in people with ADD. Many have trouble getting to sleep at night and getting up in the morning. Sleep deprivation leads to overall decreased brain activity. In order to optimize brain function, proper sleep is essential. Effective strategies for getting up and going to bed are given in Chapter 25.

PSYCHOLOGICAL INTERVENTIONS: EDUCATION

Education about ADD—its impact on home, school, family, and the self—is the first step in treatment. The more accurate information you have the more likely you are to get the best help. Robert Pasnau, M.D., past president of the American Psychiatric Association, said that coping requires three things: information, self-esteem, and a sense of control. Obtaining accurate information is the critical first step in treating this disorder.

Correcting Automatic Negative Thoughts

Negativity is one of the hallmark features of ADD. As I've said, many people with ADD use negative thoughts as a form of self-stimulation, but it predisposes them to depression and is harmful to their relationships. In Chapter 26, I will teach you how to identify and rid yourself of the negative thoughts (I call them ANTs—automatic negative thoughts) that invade your life.

Targeted Psychotherapy

For many people with ADD, there are a number of psychological issues that need to be addressed. Without the proper biological treatment, psychotherapy can be a fruitless and frustrating experience for both the therapist and patient. I have consulted with many ADD patients who have been in psychotherapy for years without much benefit. When they were placed on the right medication or supplements and diet, however, psychotherapy brought about dramatic improvement in just several weeks. I'm not dismissing psychotherapy as a necessary component of treatment for children, teens, and adults with ADD. It is often very helpful. It does, however, need to be in combination with the right biological treatment. The following are some psychotherapy themes that are essential in dealing with the ADD patient.

Break Up Erroneous Belief Patterns

Many people with ADD may have erroneous, negative beliefs that prevent them from being successful in the present. For example, they may believe that they'll fail in school (because that was their experience before they were treated) so they will not try. Or, they may believe that they are doomed to have poor relationships (again, because that was their experience before treatment), so they will engage in the same, repetitive behaviors that impair their ability to relate to others. Once medical treatment is successful, it is also important to correct these beliefs, because beliefs drive behavior.

Willie was impotent as an adult. In treatment, I hypnotized him back to the first time he lost his erection with his wife prematurely. He remembered feeling inadequate and ashamed. Still in the hypnotic trance, I asked him to remember the first time in his whole life that he felt inadequate and ashamed. He started to cry and told me of a time when he was six years old. His father was yelling at him and called him "stupid" because he was unable to learn to read! He transferred the feelings of shame and inadequacy to his sexual life as an adult and still felt incompetent. In the hypnotic trance, I educated his unconscious mind about ADD and the erroneous beliefs he carried into adulthood. I told him to rethink his basic assumptions and have his mind help him rather than hurt him. The impotence disappeared within a month.

Along similar lines, Adrianne never played cards. As a child and teenager, she had trouble learning card games because her attention span was so short. When she did play, her impulsiveness caused her to make bad decisions and she often lost, even though she was just as smart or smarter than her opponent. As an adult, she avoided social situations where card games were played. This caused turmoil in her marriage because her husband liked to play cards with other couples and she refused to go with him. After she was placed on medication, she still avoided playing cards until she began talking about this in therapy. When she made the connection between ADD and her underlying belief about card games, she was able to challenge herself to try again. She found that she really liked playing cards, and she began to go with her husband.

The emotional trauma of having ADD, and all that it entails, leaves many people with intense anxiety. I often have my patients undergo EMDR (eye movement desensitization and reprocessing) therapy to help them deal with the emotional pain of the past. EMDR is a specific treatment for patients who have post-traumatic stress disorder and I have found it helpful for many of my ADD patients. In EMDR the therapist has the patient move his eyes back and forth while a traumatic event is remembered. The therapist takes the patient through a series of steps to help relieve the trauma and rid the patient of the underlying beliefs associated with it. Traumas often hinder people from moving their lives forward. EMDR can be very helpful to deal with the psychological fallout of struggling for years with untreated ADD.

Accept the Need for Biological Interventions

Biological interventions, such as medication, supplements, dietary interventions, or neurofeedback, often become a psychotherapy issue. Many people do not want to believe that there is anything wrong with them and taking the medication or supplements may make them feel, in some way, defective. It is critical to talk about these feelings. When these feelings are ignored, children, teens, and adults start missing doses of medication or supplements and then they lose their overall effectiveness.

Justine was an example of this. At age twenty-two, her life was falling apart. She had taken Ritalin as a teenager and it was very helpful for her. However, in the twelfth grade a friend teased her about the medication, and she stopped it. Within the next year, she had been arrested twice for shoplifting, started using drugs, and had dropped out of high school. The next four years were nothing but trouble. After she saw a special on television about adult ADD, she remembered how helpful the medication had been for her and she sought help. After she was placed back on the medication, she was able to start college, maintain stable work, and avoid antisocial behavior.

Focused Breathing

One technique that I have found very helpful for my ADD patients is diaphragmatic breathing. This technique helps impulse control, temper outbursts, anxiety, and clarity of thought. It is easy to learn and when practiced will help you feel in much better control of your own feelings and behavior. This will be discussed in Chapter 27.

Coaching for ADD

One of the most helpful psychological treatments for ADD is personal coaching. Coaching helps a person develop good "internal supervision skills." Coaching involves using another person (a coach) to help you develop goals and the specific skills to meet those goals. I have seen it be very powerful for people with ADD who, as a group, tend to struggle with issues of goal setting, organization, planning, and consistent performance. More on ADD Coaching in Chapter 28.

SOCIAL INTERVENTIONS

Support

Obtaining support for yourself and your family is critical. Many people who have ADD or who have it in their family feel isolated and alone. It's a relief to know there are other people like you. In addition, by interacting with other families with ADD you can share ideas on coping strategies for specific situations. For over a year I wrote a column for an online ADD support site, and was privileged to see the support ADD families offered each other. After I had been writing for about six months, I wrote a letter to the ADD group about a problem I had been having with my ADD son who could not get up in the morning. This was causing him to be late for school and also causing serious turmoil in the house every morning. The next morning I logged on to my e-mail to find seventeen e-mails from other people giving me suggestions on how to deal with this problem. There is no substitute for that kind of support.

There are many ways to get support for ADD. There are support groups online, including on our community site at amensolution.com. A word of caution about the Internet: Because anyone can write on the Internet, check out the information you obtain with your personal health care provider. I once treated a person who used high doses of a cough syrup to treat ADD on the suggestion of a website. He became psychotic and lost his job and his marriage over the bad advice.

Join a local community support group. There are support groups for ADD all over the country. They can be a source of great information. Here are some numbers to contact to get more information:

CHADD (Children [and Adults] with ADD)
(800) 233-4050
CHADD National Office
8181 Professional Place—Suite 150
Landover, MD 20785
chadd.org

LDA (Learning Disability Association of America)
4156 Library Road
Pittsburgh, PA 15234-1349
(412) 341-1515 (412) 344-0224 (FAX)
ldanatl.org

If there are not effective support groups in your area, get online.

Parenting and Family Strategies

As we have seen, ADD is a chronic, stressful medical condition that affects every member of a family. Intervening at a family level is essential to having a happy, healthy family life. In addition, I think of parent training as a primary intervention for ADD children and teenagers. These children are often the most challenging for parents, and parents need superior skills to help their children thrive. Parenting and family strategies are found in Chapter 23.

School Strategies

Children, teens, and young adults spend more than a third of their lives in school or working on schoolwork. Understanding ADD in a school situation and learning proper interventional strategies is an essential part of treatment. Thirty-five percent of untreated ADD teens never finish high school. I have heard it said that graduating from high school is the number one predictor of how a person will do in life. Chapter 24 lays out school intervention strategies for people with ADD.

Interpersonal Strategies

Making and keeping friends is difficult for many people with ADD. It is estimated that at least half of all children and teens with ADD have problems with their peers and up to 75 percent of adults have interpersonal problems. In treating people with ADD of all ages, it is often important to include a social skill component to the treatment. The components of effective social skill treatment often need to include:

- teaching communication skills, including active listening (repeating back the information and feelings you hear before you respond),
- providing an environment for successful peer contacts and positive experiences (encouraging the ADD person to invite peers over to the house to spend time together),
- increasing knowledge about appropriate behavior (look for situations to teach the child about helpful social behavior; discussing interactions that are seen on TV or in stores can be very helpful),

- teaching self-monitoring and internal dialogue techniques (these include techniques that teach people to question what they do before they do it, to stop and think through the consequences to their behavior before they act in a certain way),
- searching for areas of social competence (sports, karate, music) and giving the ADD person healthy doses of these activities, and
- diligently working on decreasing aggressive behavior at home and school (aggressiveness is one of the strongest predictors of peer rejection).

A good place to start social skill training is with the siblings at home. I believe it is essential to expect siblings to be civil and act appropriate with each other. Many psychologists say "let the children work out their own problems, don't interfere." I disagree. Remember what happened to Cain and Abel when their parents didn't intervene? In sibling relationships, clearly state that you expect them to treat each other with respect. When they are positive and appropriate with each other, notice and praise them. When they are inappropriate, condescending, aggressive, or mean with each other, discipline them. When parents lay out the ground rules, siblings are much more likely to get along with each other, which may translate to them behaving more appropriately with others.

Spiritual Interventions

Beyond the biological, psychological, and social aspects of our lives, we are also spiritual beings. So to fully heal and recover, we must recognize that we are more than just our bodies, minds, and social connections, and we must ask ourselves deep spiritual questions, such as the following:

What does my life mean?

What is my purpose?

Why am I here?

What are my values?

Do I believe in God or a Higher Power?

What is my connection to past generations, future generations, and the planet?

Having a sense of purpose, as well as connections to past and future generations, allows us to reach beyond ourselves to affirm that our lives matter. Without a spiritual connection, many people experience an overriding sense of despair. Morality, values, and a spiritual connection to others and the universe are critical for many people to feel a sense of wholeness and connection, and a reason to get up in the morning and to take good care of themselves.

Dietary Interventions for ADD Types

When I initially wrote this chapter, I was in central Oregon, lecturing to mental-health professionals about ADD. When I walked into the large lecture hall, my heart sank as I saw the food in the back of the room. On a table were boxes and boxes of muffins, donuts, bagels, and cinnamon rolls. I thought to myself, Oh no, Daniel, you have to be really good this morning or no one will be able to pay attention in about a half an hour. High-simple-carbohydrate foods are terrible for concentration. These foods are filled with sugar or substances that are easily broken down into sugar in the body. They cause a quick rise in blood sugar followed soon thereafter by an insulin release that lowers blood sugar below normal levels, making people feel tired, spacey, con-fused, and inattentive. Give people a lot of sugar (or high-carbohydrate substances like bread) in the morning, and they will act as if they have ADD. Did you know that if you chew bread long enough, it will actually begin to taste like sugar in your mouth? Your saliva has an enzyme called amylase that breaks down starches into glucose or sugar.

I started my lecture talking about the food in the back of the room. "The food in the back is a good example of what parents unknowingly do to make kids struggle in school. Most children start the day with muffins, donuts, Pop-Tarts, bagels, cinnamon rolls, and sugary cereals. They get virtually no protein in the morning. No wonder teachers com-plain that so many kids cannot concentrate. In order for children or adults to be able to concentrate, they need to have nutritious food that enhances energy and concentration. For most people with ADD, the right diet is a higher-protein, higher-healthy-fat, lower-simple-carbohydrate diet." I was able to keep the group awake, but I wondered about all of the business meetings that start with muffins or donuts and become unproductive halfway through. A better breakfast for the group would have been hard-boiled eggs, nuts, chopped veggies, and fruit (but not fruit juice—too much sugar). I finished my introduction about food by saying, "If you want to concentrate this afternoon and have good energy until dinnertime, have no simple carbohydrates at lunch. No bread, no pasta, no potatoes, no rice, and no sugar. Have something like a stir-fry without the rice, a salmon salad, or a piece of meat and grilled veggies." Many people who took my suggestions about lunch came up to me at the end of the day saying how amazed they were that they felt so good. They said that their energy and concentration were much better than they usually were.

Dietary interventions are very important in treating all types of ADD. Food can be used as brain medicine. It can have a powerfully positive effect on cognition, feelings, and behavior. It can have a very negative effect on these as well. The right diet can actually decrease the amount of medication needed. However, the wrong diet will do the opposite. Joseph Egger reported in the British medical journal *The Lancet* that 116 of 185 hyperactive children had a positive response to a low-allergen diet (higher in protein and lower in simple carbohydrates) supplemented by calcium, zinc, magnesium, and vitamins. Over and over in my clinical practice, I have found that diet matters for treatment and prevention.

When I can convince my patients to eat this way, they notice better mood stability, focus, and stamina, as well as less distractibility, tiredness in the late morning and midafternoon, and less craving for sugary substances. Here are the Amen Clinics Nine Rules for Brain-Healthy Eating. Using these strategies will enhance your brain for better focus and energy, and in some cases can be the primary treatment for ADD.

THE AMEN CLINICS NINE RULES OF
BRAIN-HEALTHY EATING

If you are going to eat right to think right, it is critical to make sure your food is loaded with proper nutrients that your body is able to properly digest and absorb.

Rule #1. Think "high-quality calories" and not too many of them.

The quality of your food matters. Always opt for high-quality food. Also, be careful with calories. Likely due to impulsivity, ADD is often associated with obesity, which has been demonstrated to be bad for the brain. Think of eating only high-quality calories. One cinnamon roll can cost you 720 calories; a small quiche can be more than 1,000 calories. Both will drain your brain. Swap those for a 400-calorie salad made of spinach, salmon, blueberries, apples, walnuts, and red bell peppers, which will supercharge your energy and make you smarter.

If you eat more calories than you need, you will be fatter, sicker, and less productive. In one study, researchers followed a large group of rhesus monkeys for twenty years. One group ate all the food they wanted, the other group ate 30 percent less. The monkeys who ate anything they wanted were three times more likely to suffer from cancer, heart disease, and diabetes, plus researchers saw significant shrinkage in the important decision-making areas of their brains. In addition, the calorie-restricted monkeys had smoother skin and healthier hair.

Rule #2. Drink plenty of water and don't drink your calories.

Your brain is 80 percent water. Anything that dehydrates it, such as too much caffeine or alcohol, decreases your thinking and impairs your judgment. Make sure you get plenty of water every day. To know you are drinking enough water for your brain, a good general rule is to consume half your weight in ounces per day, unless there is significant obesity, and then usually not more than 120 ounces a day.

Rule #3. Eat high-quality, lean protein throughout the day.

Protein helps balance your blood sugar, helps you focus, and provides the necessary building blocks for brain health. Great sources of protein include fish, skinless turkey or chicken, beans, raw nuts, and high-protein vegetables such as broccoli and spinach. I use spinach instead of lettuce in my salads for a huge nutrition boost. Protein powders can also be a good source, but read the labels. Many companies put a lot of sugar and other unhealthful ingredients in their powders. It is important to start each day with protein to boost your focus and concentration skills.

Rule #4. Eat smart carbohydrates (low glycemic, high fiber).

This means eat carbohydrates that do not spike your blood sugar (low-glycemic index), that are also high in fiber, such as vegetables, and fruits like blueberries and apples. Carbohydrates per se are not the enemy; they are essential to your life. But bad carbohydrates *are* the enemy, substances that have been stripped of any nutritional value, such as simple sugars and refined carbohydrates.

Sugar is NOT your friend. Sugar increases inflammation in your body, increases erratic brain cell firing, is addictive, and has been implicated in aggression. In a new study, children who were given sugar every day had a significantly higher risk for violence later in life. I don't agree with the people who say everything in moderation: Cocaine or arsenic in moderation is not a good idea. The less sugar in your life, the better your life will be. Inflammation in the body increases inflammation in the brain.

Get to know the glycemic index (GI). The glycemic index rates carbohydrates according to their effects on blood sugar. It is based on a scale of one to 100+ (glucose is 100), with the low-glycemic foods having a lower number (which means they do not spike your blood sugar, so they are generally healthier for you) and the high-glycemic foods having a higher number (which means they quickly elevate your blood sugar, so they are generally not as healthy for you). In general, I like to stay under 60.

Eating a diet that is filled with low-glycemic foods will lower your blood glucose levels, decrease cravings, and help you focus.

Choose high-fiber carbohydrates. Experts recommend eating 25 to 35 grams of fiber a day, but research shows that most people fall far short of that. Boost your fiber by eating fruits, vegetables, and legumes. When reading a label, look for >5g of fiber and <5g of sugar per serving.

Rule #5. Focus your diet on healthy fats.

Fat is not the enemy. Good fats are essential to your health. The solid weight of your brain is 60 percent fat (after all the water is removed). When the medical establishment recommended we remove fat from our diets, we got fat. However, bad fats, such as trans fats, are the enemy, and should be eliminated. Did you know that certain fats found in pizza, ice cream, and cheeseburgers fool the brain into ignoring the signals that you should be full? No wonder I used to always eat two bowls of ice cream and eight slices of pizza. Focus your diet on healthy fats, especially those that contain omega-3 fatty acids, found in foods like salmon, sardines, avocados, walnuts, flaxseed, chia seed, and dark green leafy vegetables.

Rule #6. Eat from the rainbow.

This means put natural foods of many different colors into your diet; include blueberries, pomegranates, yellow squash, and red bell peppers. This will boost the antioxidant levels in your body and help keep your brain young.

Rule #7. Cook with brain-healthy herbs and spices to boost your brain.

Here is a little food for thought, literally.

- Turmeric, found in curry, contains a chemical that has been shown to decrease the plaques in the brain thought to be responsible for Alzheimer's disease.

- In three studies, a saffron extract was found to be as effective as antidepressant medication in treating people with major depression.
- There is good scientific evidence that rosemary, thyme, and sage help boost memory.
- Cinnamon has been shown to help attention and blood sugar. It is high in antioxidants and is a natural aphrodisiac.
- Garlic and oregano boost blood flow to the brain.
- Ginger, cayenne, black pepper—their hot, spicy taste comes from gingerols, capsaicin, and piperine, compounds that boost metabolism and have an aphrodisiac effect.

Rule #8. Make sure your food is as clean as possible.

As much as possible, eat organically grown or raised foods, as pesticides used in commercial farming can accumulate in your brain and body, even though the levels in each food may be low. Also, eat meat that is hormone free, antibiotic free, and that is free-range and grass-fed. It is critical to know and understand what the things you eat, ate. You are not only what you eat, you are also what the animals you eat, ate. In addition, eliminate food additives, preservatives, and artificial dyes and sweeteners. This means you must start reading the labels. If you do not know what is in something, do not eat it. Now is the time to really get thoughtful and serious about the food you put in your body.

FOURTEEN FOODS WITH THE HIGHEST LEVELS OF PESTICIDE RESIDUES

1. Celery
2. Peaches
3. Strawberries
4. Apples
5. Blueberries
6. Nectarines
7. Cucumbers
8. Sweet Bell Peppers
9. Spinach
10. Cherries

11. Collard Greens/Kale

12. Potatoes

13. Grapes

14. Green beans

SEVENTEEN FOODS WITH THE LOWEST LEVELS OF PESTICIDE RESIDUES

1. Onions

2. Avocado

3. Sweet Corn (Frozen)

4. Pineapples

5. Mango

6. Asparagus

7. Sweet Peas (Frozen)

8. Kiwi Fruit

9. Bananas

10. Cabbage

11. Broccoli

12. Papaya

13. Mushrooms

14. Watermelon

15. Grapefruit

16. Eggplant

17. Cantaloupe

Fish is a great source of healthy protein and fat, but it is important to consider the toxicity in some fish. Here are a couple of general rules to guide you: 1) The larger the fish, the more mercury it may contain, so go for the smaller varieties. 2) From the safe fish choices, eat a fairly wide variety of fish, preferably those highest in omega-3s, like wild Alaskan salmon, sardines, anchovies, and Pacific halibut.

Rule #9. If you're having trouble with your focus, mood, energy, memory, weight, blood sugar, blood pressure, or skin, make sure to eliminate any foods that might be causing trouble, especially wheat and any other gluten-containing grain or food, and dairy, soy, and corn.

Did you know that gluten can literally make some people crazy? There are scientific reports of people having psychotic episodes when they're exposed to gluten, and when they eliminate wheat and other gluten sources (such as barley, rye, spelt, imitation meats, soy sauce) from their diets, their stomachs and their brains are better. One of my patients lost thirty pounds and her moodiness, eczema, and irritable bowel symptoms completely went away when she got wheat out of her diet. Another one of my patients would become violent whenever he ate MSG. When we scanned him on MSG, his brain changed into a pattern more consistent with our aggressive patients.

ADHD-affected and autistic children often do better when we put them on elimination diets that get rid of wheat, dairy, all the processed foods, all forms of sugar and sugar alternatives, food dyes, and additives.

Summary of The Amen Clinics Nine Rules of Brain-Healthy Eating

Rule #1. Think "high-quality calories" and not too many of them.

Rule #2. Drink plenty of water and don't drink your calories.

Rule #3. Eat high-quality, lean protein throughout the day.

Rule #4. Eat smart carbohydrates (low glycemic, high fiber).

Rule #5. Focus your diet on healthy fats.

Rule #6. Eat from the rainbow.

Rule #7. Cook with brain-healthy herbs and spices to boost your brain.

Rule #8. Make sure your food is as clean as possible.

Rule #9. If you're having trouble with your mood, energy, memory, weight, blood sugar, blood pressure, or skin, make sure to eliminate any foods that might be causing trouble, especially wheat and any other gluten-containing grain or food, and dairy, soy, and corn.

There are blood tests you can take to learn more about your sensitivities to food.

FIFTY-TWO BEST BRAIN-HEALTHY SUPERFOODS THAT CAN BOOST YOUR MENTAL ABILITIES

To help you get started on the right path, here is my list of the fifty-two best brain-healthy superfoods. Make sure these foods are organic and, when appropriate, hormone free, antibiotic free, free-range, and grass-fed.

Nuts and Seeds

1. Almonds, raw—for protein, healthy fats, and fiber
2. Brazil nuts—great source of zinc, magnesium, thiamine; high in selenium, healthy fat, and fiber
3. Cacao, raw—loaded with antioxidants and high in flavonoids (substances shown to increase blood flow), magnesium, iron, chromium, zinc, copper, and fiber. Can help decrease cravings and balance blood sugar, plus it can make you happy by stimulating serotonin, endorphins, and phenylethylamine (PEA). (But eat only a small amount of dark chocolate or it will turn into fat)
4. Cashews—rich in phosphorus, magnesium, zinc, and antioxidants
5. Chia seeds—very high in plant-based omega-3 fatty acids, fiber, and antioxidants
6. Coconut—high in fiber, manganese, and iron; low in natural sugars; high in medium chain triglycerides shown to be helpful for brain tissue
7. Hemp seeds—high in protein, contain all essential amino acids and fatty acids; high in omega-3s and healthy 6s, including 6 GLA, which has anti-inflammatory properties; also high in fiber and vitamin E
8. Sesame seeds—high in fiber, help stabilize blood sugar and lower cholesterol. Good source of calcium, phosphorous, and zinc
9. Walnuts—of all nuts, contain the most omega-3 fatty acids to help lower bad cholesterol and may reduce inflammation. Great source of antioxidants, vitamin E, selenium, and magnesium

Legumes (small amounts)

1. Lentils—for fiber
2. Chickpeas—for their high serotonin content (good for Type 3 [Overfocused] ADD)

Fruits

1. Acai berries—for fiber, omega-3s, antioxidants, minerals, vitamins, plant sterols, and phytonutrients. Low glycemic index and sugar
2. Apples—rich in antioxidants and fiber; will help you not to overeat
3. Avocados—high in omega-3 fats; high in lutein (eyesight), potassium, and folate; low in pesticides
4. Blackberries—high in antioxidants, phytonutrients, and fiber; low glycemic index
5. Blueberries—loaded with antioxidants. Anthocyanins, compounds that give blueberries their deep color, may have antidiabetic effects. Labeled "brain berries"; some studies show they help make you smarter
6. Cherries—high fiber, low glycemic index
7. Goldenberry—high in fiber, phosphorous, calcium, and vitamins A, C, B1, B2, B6, and B12. Very high in protein for fruit (16 percent)
8. Gogi berries—rich in antioxidants, fiber, amino acids, iron, and vitamin C. Help lower blood pressure, stabilize blood sugar, and fights yeast
9. Grapefruit—for fiber, nutrients, and lower glycemic index
10. Honey, raw, wild (small amounts only)—rich in minerals, antioxidants, probiotics, all twenty-two essential amino acids. Some types from Hawaii (Lehua and Noni) and New Zealand (Manuka) have antifungal, antibacterial, and antiviral properties
11. Kiwi—for fiber, nutrients, and lower glycemic index
12. Pomegranates—high in fiber and antioxidants; low in calories

Vegetables

1. Asparagus—for fiber and antioxidants
2. Bell peppers—for fiber and vitamin C
3. Beets—high in fiber, phytonutrients, folate, and beta-carotene

4. Broccoli—cruciferous vegetable loaded with sulforaphanes; may increase enzymes that lower the incidence of some cancers

5. Brussels sprouts—high-in-fiber cruciferous vegetable; high in sulforaphanes; may increase enzymes that lower the incidence of some cancers

6. Cabbage—cruciferous vegetable loaded with sulforaphanes; may increase enzymes that lower the incidence of some cancers

7. Cauliflower—cruciferous vegetable, loaded with sulforaphanes; may increase enzymes that lower the incidence of some cancers

8. Chlorella—a blue-green algae rich in chlorophyll; helps detoxify the body and remove dioxin, lead, and mercury; contains high concentrations of B-group vitamins and helps digestion

9. Garlic—from the *Allium* botanical family that can help lower blood pressure, cholesterol, and inhibit growth of some cancer; has antibiotic properties, boosts blood flow to the brain

10. Horseradish—high in calcium, potassium, vitamin C; helps maintain collagen

11. Kale—and other dark leafy greens contain omega-3 fats, iron (especially important for women), and phytonutrients

12. Leeks—from *Allium* botanical family that can help lower blood pressure, cholesterol, and inhibit growth of some cancer; has antibiotic properties

13. Maca root—a South American plant root that is extraordinarily rich in amino acids, minerals, plant sterols, vitamins, and healthy fatty acids

14. Onions—from *Allium* botanical family that can help lower blood pressure and cholesterol; inhibit growth of some cancer; has antibiotic properties and boosts blood flow to the brain

15. Seaweeds—where fish get their omega-3s; high in magnesium

16. Spinach—and other dark leafy greens contain omega-3 fats, iron (especially important for women), and phytonutrients

17. Spirulina—highest concentration of any protein and a top source of iron (don't eat it if your iron is too high); rich in antioxidants and can help you have healthy hair and skin

18. Sweet potatoes—loaded with phytonutrients, fiber, and vitamin A

19. Wheatgrass juice—mineral and vitamin dense; 70 percent chlorophyll and a complete protein with thirty enzymes. Excellent source of phosphorus, magnesium, zinc, and potassium

Oils

1. Coconut oil—stable at high temperatures
2. Grapeseed oil—stable at high temperatures, high in omega-3s
3. Olive oil—use only at room temperature, do not cook with it

Poultry/Fish

1. Chicken or turkey, skinless
2. Eggs—for protein
3. Lamb—high in omega-3s
4. Salmon, wild—loaded with brain-boosting omega-3s
5. Sardine—wild caught are low in mercury, high in brain-boosting omega-3s, vitamin D, and calcium; sustainable

Tea

1. Tea, green is best—protective antioxidants, less caffeine than coffee, metabolism-boosting compound EGCG; also contains theanine, which helps you relax and focus at the same time

Special Category

1. Shirataki noodles—the root of a wild yam plant (goes by brand name Miracle Noodles). This is one of my wife's secret weapons to replace pasta noodles. They are high in fiber and virtually calorie free

HOW TO CONTROL YOUR MIND AND MOOD WITH FOOD

Most people don't know that they can use food to manipulate their minds. Food can help you feel relaxed, happy, and focused, or downright dumb. The way we feed ourselves and our children in this country is backward.

Generally, simple carbohydrates such as those found in pancakes, waffles, muffins, bagels, or cereal boost serotonin levels that help us feel relaxed, calm, and less worried and motivated. Protein, found in meat, nuts, or eggs, boosts dopamine levels and helps us feel more driven, motivated, and focused. Yet, many people eat simple carbohydrates in the morning and have more protein-based meals at night.

For example, it is very common to feed ourselves or our children a breakfast of donuts, pancakes, sugary cereals, or bagels, along with fruit juices (concentrated sugar). Then we ask ourselves and our children to focus. These simple-carbohydrate-based meals spike insulin, which can often cause low blood-sugar levels in a short period of time, causing brain fog. In addition, simple carbohydrates spike serotonin levels in the brain, so we feel happier after the meal. The problem is that serotonin can also decrease our ability to get things done, and for many people can give them a more "don't worry, be happy" attitude. Not exactly the best mindset for school or work. Protein-based meals tend to do the opposite. They can boost dopamine levels in the brain, give us energy, and help us focus. Therefore, it makes sense to eat a protein-rich meal earlier in the day to get started, or at dinner if you still need to get work finished in the evening. If you want to relax in the evening and go to bed early, I recommend decreasing the protein and eating more healthy, fiber-rich, complex-carbohydrate foods such as vegetables.

Often, when kids come home from school, parents give them a few cookies and a soda (a high-simple-carbohydrate-based snack). Then they tell them to do their homework. Unfortunately, the parents have unwittingly diminished their children's ability to get their homework finished, and it causes a night of stress for everyone. Give them an apple and some peanut butter and watch them improve.

Foods to Boost Mood, Focus, Motivation, and Memory

As a reminder, serotonin is a neurotransmitter that helps soothe the brain. It is intimately involved in sleep, mood regulation, appetite, and social engagement. It helps decrease our worries and concerns. Based on research at MIT, foods rich in simple carbohydrates have been found to quickly boost serotonin. They cause a spike in insulin, which lowers most large amino acids with the exception of tryptophan, the amino acid building block for serotonin, thereby decreasing the competition for tryptophan to get into the brain. This is why many people can become dependent on or even addicted to bread, pasta, potatoes, rice, and sugar. They use these as "mood foods" and feel more relaxed and less worried after they eat them. Unfortunately, because they boost serotonin, they can also lower prefrontal cortex function and diminish a person's internal braking ability. I think this is precisely why restaurants serve bread and alcohol before a meal. If you consume them, you are much more likely to order dessert.

Brain-healthy foods that help to boost serotonin include smart carbohydrates such as sweet potatoes, apples, blueberries, carrots, gluten-free steel-cut oatmeal, quinoa, and chickpeas. These cause a more gradual increase in serotonin. It is a myth that foods that contain high levels of tryptophan, such as turkey, actually raise serotonin in the brain. This is because tryptophan is transported into the brain by a system that is geared toward larger protein molecules, and tryptophan, being smaller and less abundant, doesn't compete well against the other proteins to get in the brain. This is one of the main reasons why exercise helps people feel better. Exercise pushes the larger amino acids into your muscles and thereby decreases the competition for tryptophan to get into the brain. If you want to feel happier, grab an apple and go for a walk.

Dopamine is the neurotransmitter involved in motivation, emotional significance, relevance, focus, and pleasure. It helps you get things done. Foods that tend to increase dopamine include beef, poultry, fish, eggs, seeds (pumpkin and sesame), nuts (almonds and walnuts), cheese, protein powders, and green tea. In addition, avocados and lima beans can help. Simple carbohydrates tend to deplete dopamine.

Acetylcholine is the neurotransmitter involved with learning and memory. Liver, eggs, salmon, and shrimp tend to boost these levels.

Heal Your Gut to Boost Your Brain

The gut is often called the second brain. It is loaded with nervous tissue and is in direct communication with our big brain, which is why we get butterflies when we get excited, or have loose bowels when upset. Anxiety, depression, stress, and grief all express themselves with emotional pain (the brain) and quite often, gastrointestinal (GI) distress.

Your gut is one of the most important organs for the health of your brain. It is estimated that the GI tract is loaded with about one hundred trillion microorganisms (bacteria, yeast, and others), about ten times the total number of cells in the human body. To be healthy, the relationship of good bugs to bad bugs needs to be lopsided in the positive direction, around 85 percent good guys to 15 percent bad guys. When it goes the other way and the bad bugs get a foothold, all sorts of physical and mental problems can arise. Keeping the good and bad bugs in proper balance is essential to your mental health.

There is new evidence that friendly gut bacteria actually deter invading troublemakers, such as E. coli, and help us withstand stress. If the friendly bugs are deficient, either from a poor diet that feeds yeast overgrowth (think sugar), or the excessive use of antibiotics (even as far back as childhood) that killed the good bacteria, we are more likely to feel stressed. Disorders ranging from ADD to autism in children, and depression to mental fogginess in adults, have been connected to intestinal bacteria imbalances that cause increased gut permeability.

The intestines provide an important barrier to bad bugs from the outside world. If they become too permeable, often called "leaky gut," inflammation and illness can be created throughout the body. Optimizing the "gut-brain axis" is critical to your mental health.

Factors that decrease healthy gut bacteria:

- medications (antibiotics, oral contraceptives, proton pump inhibitors, steroids, NSAIDS)
- refined sugar intake
- artificial sweeteners
- bactericidal chemicals in water
- pesticide residues in food
- alcohol
- stress, including physiological, emotional, and environmental

- radiation
- high-intensity exercise

The greatest danger from antibiotics does not come from those prescribed by your doctor, but rather from the foods you eat. The prevalence of antibiotics found in conventionally raised meats and vegetables has the potential to throw off the balance of good to bad bacteria. It is estimated that 70 percent of the total antibiotic use in the U.S. is for livestock. It is critical to focus on eating antibiotic free, hormone free, grass-fed, free-range meats.

A Few Good Germs Can Be Good for You

We all need the good bugs in our intestinal tract to boost our immune system, so be careful not to go overboard in keeping your children away from the dirt. Animals raised in a germ-free environment show exaggerated responses to psychological stress. When researchers gave the animals probiotics (healthy bugs), their stress levels normalized.

Stress, all by itself, decreases healthy gut flora. Early abandonment issues can cause increased stress, decreased healthy bacteria, and increased gut permeability. When young rats were separated from their mothers, the layer of cells that line the gut became more permeable, allowing bacteria from the intestine to pass through the bowel walls and stimulate immune cells to start attacking other organs. "In rats, it's an adaptive response," reports Dr. Emeran Mayer of the UCLA Collaborative Centers for Integrative Medicine. "If they're born into a stressful, hostile environment, nature programs them to be more vigilant and stress responsive in their future life." Dr. Mayer says that up to 70 percent of the patients he treats for chronic gut disorders had experienced early childhood traumas like parents' divorces or deaths, or chronic illnesses. "I think that what happens in early life, along with an individual's genetic background, programs how a person will respond to stress for the rest of his or her life."

What does this mean for you? Follow the brain-healthy food guidelines in this chapter carefully, especially by eliminating most of the simple sugars from your diet that feed the bad bugs. Focus on eating smart carbohydrates (low glycemic, high fiber), which enhance healthy flora. Also, consider taking a daily probiotic to give the good bugs a head start. Be careful with antibiotics, and if you had a lot of them in the past, a probiotic and healthy diet becomes even more important to the health of your brain.

TYPE 3 (OVERFOCUSED) ADD

As we have seen, Type 3 (Overfocused) ADD is associated with low serotonin and dopamine levels. It is often associated with worrying, moodiness, emotional rigidity, and irritability. A higher-protein, higher-healthy-fat, lower-carbohydrate diet (that enhances focus) may cause people with Overfocused ADD to focus even more on the things that bother them. Remember, the problem in this type is not that they can't pay attention, it is that they can't stop paying attention and they tend to get stuck in negative thoughts or behaviors. Dietary interventions need to be geared toward naturally increasing serotonin and dopamine.

Diet matters. Pay attention to it.

CHAPTER 20

Supplement Strategies for ADD Types

Through the years, many people have asked me about natural treatments for ADD. At least once a month a parent tells me about an amazing new treatment for ADD. Vitamins, herbs, fish oil, amino acids, grapeseed extract, and magnets to name a few. With three ADD children of my own, I've kept an open mind. I want to know about everything that works to help this disorder. Through the years, I have tracked each of these treatments, kept up on what little scientific literature exists, and constantly stay on the lookout to see what works. Wading through the claims, parental excitement, and failures is challenging. The good news, however, is that many of these treatments are helpful, especially if you target the interventions to specific ADD types.

A word of caution: Ignoring ADD type can cause some of these interventions to backfire and make things worse. Just because something is natural does not mean it's innocuous. Here's an example:

Seven-year-old Justin was brought to see me by his mother. He had symptoms of ADD (short attention span, restlessness, and impulse-control problems) along with temper problems. A month before I met Justin, his mother read a magazine article on St. John's Wort. It said that it helped with mood and temper problems. She gave it to her son. Within a week Justin's behavior was much worse. He was more hyperactive, angrier, and he started to have dreams of decomposing bodies. When she stopped the St. John's Wort, his symptoms lessened. During Justin's evaluation at my clinic, I did a SPECT scan. It showed decreased activity in his left temporal lobe. I have often seen that serotonergic interventions, such as selective serotonin reuptake inhibitors or St. John's Wort, make temporal problems worse. It was clear to me that Justin needed something to help his temporal lobes. He had a very positive response to the anticonvulsant Depakote and Adderall.

Always check with your doctor before adding supplements to medication. Some supplements will interact with medication, so caution is needed.

In this chapter I will go through each ADD type and tell you what supplements I have seen to have clinical benefit. I'll give you the rationale and dosage protocols that I suggest to my patients. If you decide to use these supplements instead of medication, as many people do, make sure you keep tabs on their effectiveness. I only want my patients to take something that is clearly beneficial to them. I also want them to consider medication if the supplements are not effective. Many parents say that they want to try the natural supplements before they try medication. I'm not opposed to that, but I worry that if the supplements are not fully effective that they will not pursue more effective treatments. Follow through to find what works for you or your child. Be open to new ideas, and persist until you get the best brain and life functioning.

NO MATTER WHAT TYPE—100 PERCENT MULTIVITAMIN AND MINERAL SUPPLEMENT

I recommend a daily 100 percent multiple vitamin and mineral supplement for all types. When I was in medical school, the professor who taught our course in nutrition said that if people eat a balanced diet, they do not need vitamin or mineral supplements. I have seen that balanced diets are a thing of the past for many of our "fast-food families." In my experience, ADD families in particular have problems with planning and tend to eat out much more frequently than non-ADD families. Protect yourself and your child by taking a vitamin and mineral supplement that provides 100 percent of your daily allowances. In a study published in the British medical journal *The Lancet*, ninety children between the ages of twelve and thirteen were divided into three groups. One group took no tablet, one group took a typical multivitamin and mineral tablet, and the last group took a tablet that looked and tasted just like the vitamin and mineral tablet, yet contained no vitamins or minerals. The result of this well-controlled study was that the group who took the vitamin and mineral tablet had a significant increase in nonverbal intelligence, while the other two groups showed no difference at all. The subclinical vitamin and mineral deficiency may have been contributing to these students performing below their abilities.

OMEGA-3 FATTY ACIDS

Omega-3 fatty acids have been found to be helpful in children with ADD in a few studies, plus people with ADD have been found to have low levels of omega-3 fatty acids in their blood. Omega-3 fatty acids have two major components: EPA and DHA. EPA tends to be stimulating while DHA tends to be sedating. For Types 1 and 2, I recommend a higher EPA component of fish oil, and for the other types a combination of EPA and DHA. For adults, I recommend they take 2,000 to 4,000 milligrams a day; children should take 1,000 to 2,000 milligrams per day.

Here is a summary of several recent studies: In a study from Sri Lanka, one hundred children (ages six to twelve) who were resistant to treatment with Ritalin and behavior therapy for more than six months were given a combination of omega-3/6 fatty acids or a placebo. Outcome was measured at three and six months after treatment using a self-assessment checklist completed by the parents. Significant improvements were found in the treatment group compared with the placebo group in the following measures: restlessness, aggressiveness, completing work, and academic performance. Statistically significant improvement with inattention, impulsiveness, and cooperation with parents and teachers was not found at three months of treatment, but was evident at six months of treatment. **This means you have to be patient and give the omega-3 fatty acids time to work.**

In a study from Sweden, ninety-two ADHD children (ages seven to twelve) were given 500 milligrams of EPA omega-3s or a placebo for fifteen weeks. The EPA group improved their attention scores and had less oppositional behavior. The children who responded best had lower EPA levels to start.

In a study from the UK, researchers tested the level of omega-3 fatty acids in seventy-two children, twenty-nine with ADHD and forty-three without. Callous-unemotional (CU) traits were found to be significantly higher in the ADHD children with lower EPA levels. EPA levels were lower in the ADHD group. The findings report lower omega-3 levels in children with ADHD who had antisocial traits.

In an analysis of ten studies, researchers summarized ten trials involving 699 children. Omega-3 fatty acid supplementation demonstrated a small but significant effect in improving ADHD symptoms. EPA dose within supplements was significantly correlated with supplement efficacy. They concluded that omega-3 fatty acid supplementation, particularly with higher doses of EPA, was modestly effective in the treatment of ADHD.

TYPE 1 (CLASSIC) ADD AND TYPE 2 (INATTENTIVE) ADD

There are a number of stimulating herbs and supplements that my patients have found helpful for Classic and Inattentive ADD, including rhodiola, ginseng, ashwagandha, green tea, grapeseed extract, acetyl-L-carnitine, and L-tyrosine. We did a study with rhodiola and found it boosted blood flow to the brain.

As mentioned, these types seem to be due to deficiencies of the neurotransmitter dopamine. I frequently prescribe the amino acid L-tyrosine in doses of 500 to 1500 milligrams two to three times a day for adults and 100 to 500 milligrams two to three times a day for children under

10. L-tyrosine is the amino acid building block for dopamine. It is reported to increase the level of phenylethylamine (PEA), a mild stimulant that is found in higher concentrations in chocolate. Many of my patients have reported that it is helpful for them. It is softer in its effect, but nonetheless they notice a positive effect. Because of absorption patterns, I recommend that they take it on an empty stomach (a half hour before meals or an hour after meals). I have not seen any side effects with L-tyrosine, except for mild weight loss. L-tyrosine does not work well by itself in treating Type 3 (Overfocused) ADD because it tends to increase the intensity of overfocused symptoms. Symptoms of tyrosine deficiency— which leads to low dopamine levels—include hypothyroidism, low blood pressure, low body temperature (cold hands and feet), and restless leg syndrome.

Phil had been treated for Type 1 ADD for several years. He was taking Ritalin, which would work for a while and then seem to wear off. The up-and-down effectiveness of the medication frustrated him. He tried Adderall, but it seemed to have the same effect. I stopped the stimulant medications, put him on 1,000 milligrams of L-tyrosine three times a day, was firm about dietary guidelines, and encouraged Phil to walk fast for an hour five times a week. Within a week he said he felt better. He has maintained the regimen for four years now.

Grapeseed or pine bark extract has also shown some mild benefit for Type 1 and Type 2 ADD. Grapeseed and pine bark extract are proanthocyanidin compounds. These compounds have been found to increase blood flow and act as superantioxidants, twenty to fifty times as powerful as vitamin E. There are no published studies on the use of grapeseed or pine bark extract for treating ADD, but there are a number of published case reports. (There is a body of medical literature that says these compounds are very helpful for people with varicose veins. If you have ADD and varicose veins, then grapeseed or pine bark extract may be for you.)

Crystal, age forty-eight, came to the clinic for symptoms of ADD. Her whole life she had been restless, inattentive, easily distracted, terribly disorganized, and impulsive. After her third child, she also developed terrible varicose veins, which I had noticed in the initial interview. When we talked about treatment options for her Type 1 (Classic) ADD, she said that she wanted to try the grapeseed extract, then she would see about other options. After three weeks she noticed that she felt she had more energy and her legs looked and felt better. Eventually we added L-tyrosine to give her more help with focus, but the regimen has worked well for her over the past several years.

TYPE 3 (OVERFOCUSED) ADD

This type of ADD seems likely due to a relative deficiency of both serotonin and dopamine. I have seen that a combination of St. John's Wort and L-tyrosine is often very helpful. St. John's Wort comes from the flowers of the St. John's Wort plant (*wort* is Old English for *plant*). It got its name either from the fact that it blooms around June 24, the feast day of St. John the Baptist, or the red ring round the flowers that, when crushed, looks like blood—the blood of the beheaded John the Baptist. St. John's Wort seems to be best at increasing serotonin availability in the brain. The starting dosage of St. John's Wort is 300 milligrams a day for children, 300 milligrams twice a day for teens, and 600 milligrams in the morning and 300 milligrams at night for adults. Sometimes I'll go as high as a total of 1800 milligrams a day in adults. The bottle should say that it contains 0.3 percent hypericin, which is believed to be the active ingredient of St. John's Wort. I have done a number of before and after SPECT studies with St. John's Wort, and I have no doubt that it decreases anterior cingulate gyrus hyperactivity for many patients. It also helps with moodiness and trouble shifting attention. Unfortunately, I have also seen it decrease prefrontal cortex activity. One of the women in the study said, "I am happier, but I'm dingier." When anterior cingulate symptoms are present with ADD symptoms, it's important to use St. John's Wort with a stimulating substance like L-tyrosine or a stimulant such as Adderall. It has been reported that St. John's Wort increases sun sensitivity (you could get sunburned more easily and need to be careful in the sun). Also, don't use it if temporal lobe symptoms are present, without first stabilizing the temporal lobes.

Elaine, age sixteen, had always been a worrier. She also had problems with anger at home. If things did not go her way, she would explode at her parents or at her younger sister. As a student she was a perfectionist, which caused her to spend excessive time on assignments. Her mother, a school principal, brought her to my clinic after she heard me lecture. She told me that she was sure Elaine had Overfocused ADD. Elaine's SPECT study showed marked increased activity in her anterior cingulate gyrus. She also had mild decreased activity in her prefrontal cortex. I placed her on 600 milligrams of St. John's Wort in the morning and 300 milligrams at night. I also had her take 500 milligrams of L-tyrosine two to three times a day. Within a month Elaine was much better. She was more relaxed, less reactive, and did much better in her classes. She said that studying was easy because she no longer felt the need to have everything just so. She still wanted to excel, but didn't have to copy pages over three and four times until things were perfect.

L-tryptophan (the amino acid building block for serotonin) and 5-HTP (also a serotonin building block) are other ways of increasing cerebral serotonin. L-tryptophan was taken off the market a number of years ago because one contaminated batch, from one manufacturer, caused a rare blood disease and a number of deaths. The L-tryptophan actually had nothing to do with the deaths. L-tryptophan is a naturally occurring amino acid found in milk, meat, and eggs. I have found it helps patients improve sleep, decrease aggressiveness, and improve mood control. In addition, it does not have side effects—a real advantage over the antidepressants. L-tryptophan was recently reapproved by the Food and Drug Administration and is now available by prescription. One of the problems with dietary L-tryptophan is that a significant portion of it does not enter the brain. It is used to make proteins and vitamin B3. This necessitates taking large amounts of tryptophan. I recommend L-tryptophan in doses of 1,000 to 3,000 milligrams taken at bedtime.

5-HTP is a step closer in the serotonin production pathway. It is also more widely available than L-tryptophan and it is more easily taken up in the brain. Seventy percent is taken up into the brain, as opposed to only three percent of L-tryptophan. 5-HTP is about five to ten times more powerful than L-tryptophan. A number of double-blind studies have shown that 5-HTP is as effective as antidepressant medication in treating depression. 5-HTP boosts serotonin levels in the brain and helps to calm anterior cingulate gyrus hyperactivity ("greasing" the anterior cingulate, if you will, to help with shifting of attention). The dose of 5-HTP for adults is 50 to 300 milligrams a day. Children should start at half dose. Take 5-HTP and L-tryptophan on an empty stomach for better absorption. The most common side effect of 5-HTP is an upset stomach. It is usually very mild, but it's best to start with a low dose and work your way up slowly.

There have also been some recent studies with inositol, a vitamin from the B family, which is available at health food stores. In doses of 12 to 20 grams a day, it has been shown to decrease moodiness, depression, and overfocus issues.

Do not take St. John's Wort, L-tryptophan, or 5-HTP with prescribed antidepressants, without the knowledge and close supervision of your physician.

SEROTONIN PATHWAY

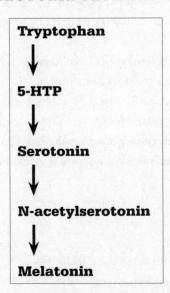

Tryptophan

↓

5-HTP

↓

Serotonin

↓

N-acetylserotonin

↓

Melatonin

TYPE 4 (TEMPORAL LOBE) ADD

Temporal lobe ADD is a combination of temporal lobe dysfunction and poor prefrontal cortex activity. Strategies geared toward temporal lobe stabilization and enhancement have proven valuable for this ADD type. In my experience, antiseizure (also called anticonvulsant) medications seem to be the most helpful. We suspect that these medications that work for Type 4 enhance the availability of the amino acid gamma-aminobutyric acid (GABA), an essential neurotransmitter in the brain. Formed in the body from glutamic acid, GABA calms neuronal activity and inhibits nerve cells from overfiring or firing erratically. GABA can be taken as a supplement. It acts like an anticonvulsant and also as an antianxiety agent. In the herbal literature, it is reported to work in much the same way as tranquilizers, but without fear of addiction. I have seen it have a nice calming effect on people who struggle with temper, irritability, and anxiety (all which may be temporal lobe symptoms). The doses of GABA range from 100 to 500 milligrams a day for adults, half that for children. Magnesium can also be helpful to stabilize nerve cell firing, and has been used to help calm anxiety and irritability. Eighty percent of the population has been found to be low in magnesium. I often start patients taking 200 to 400 milligrams of magnesium citrate or magnesium taurate twice a day.

Many people with temporal lobe problems suffer from memory problems. I have found a number of natural substances helpful to enhance memory, including: gingko and vinpocetine for blood flow; Huperzine A and acetyl-L-carnitine to enhance the neurotransmitter acetylcholine; N-acetylcysteine and alpha lipoic acid, both potent antioxidants; and phosphatidylserine to help nerve cell membranes and lower stress hormones.

TYPE 5 (LIMBIC) ADD

Limbic ADD has many symptoms of mild depression, including negativity, sadness, feelings of hopelessness, and an overabundance of ANTs (automatic negative thoughts). Frequently I have seen stimulants make people who have this type of ADD more negative and moody. The supplements that seem to help this type of ADD best are DL-phenylalanine (DLPA), L-tyrosine, and S-Adenosyl-Methionine (SAMe).

DLPA is the amino acid precursor for norepinephrine. In a number of studies norepinephrine and epinephrine (adrenaline) have been shown to be low in ADD and depression. The antidepressants imipramine, desipramine, and a new one, Reboxitine, work by increasing norepinephrine in the brain. DLPA, by boosting norepinephrine's precursor, can have a positive impact on mood and focus. In fact, in a number of studies DLPA has been found to be helpful for depression, energy, and pain control. I have used it for fifteen years as a mild antidepressant in children, teens, and adults. It is more mild in its effect than prescribed antidepressants, but it also has significantly fewer side effects. People who have PKU (phenylketonuria) should not take DLPA, as they do not have the enzyme that metabolizes it. I recommend doses of 400 milligrams three times a day on an empty stomach, half that dose for children.

Victor, a seventeen-year-old high school senior, came to see me at his own request after I did an assembly lecture at his school. He said that he often felt negative, had too many ANTs, and was always disorganized. He didn't want to take medication, but wanted to know if there were "natural things" he could do. I had him exercise, eat a more balanced diet, and take 400 milligrams a day of DLPA. Within two weeks he called me and said that he felt much better, more focused, more energetic, and more positive. He recently wrote me from college saying he had remained faithful to his regimen and continued to feel well three years later.

Another effective supplement for treatment of Type 5 ADD is SAMe. Involved with the production of many important brain compounds, such as neurotransmitters, SAMe's unique chemical action (it's called a methyl donor, a rare property) helps the brain to function properly. Normally, the brain manufactures all the SAMe it needs from the amino acid methionine. In depression, however, this synthesis has been found to be impaired. Supplementing the diet with SAMe increases the neurotransmitters involved with depression and improves cell membrane fluidity. SAMe is one of the best natural antidepressants available, and a number of recent studies have shown that it is as effective as antidepressant medication. SAMe has also been found helpful for people who suffer from fibromyalgia, a chronic muscle pain disorder. Fibromyalgia and ADD commonly coexist. I think the chronic stress associated with ADD is in part responsible for the muscle pain. *People who have bipolar disorder or manic-depressive illness or Type 6 (Ring of Fire) ADD should not take SAMe.* There have been a number of reported cases of SAMe causing manic or hypomanic episodes (excessively up or happy moods, extreme impulsivity in sexuality or spending money, pressured speech, or decreased need for sleep). I think these reports highlight that SAMe is an effective antidepressant, as all of the prescription antidepressants have that capability as well. The dosage of SAMe is between 200 and 400 milligrams two to four times a day, half that for children.

TYPE 6 (RING OF FIRE) ADD

Type 6 (Ring of Fire) ADD is often associated with fierce ADD symptoms, such as intense hyperactivity and distractibility, severe impulsiveness, hypersensitivity to the environment, pressured speech, and cyclic mood changes. This type of ADD may be related to bipolar disorder. Stimulants tend to make it worse. However, we have seen that GABA, 5-HTP, and L-tyrosine, plus fish oil have a positive effect on Type 6 (Ring of Fire) ADD. As discussed, GABA has a calming effect on nerve cells, 5-HTP, helps calm the anterior cingulate hyperactivity, and L-tyrosine helps to balance brain function.

Here's an example of how the right supplements can literally change someone's life. Sam was fourteen years old when he first came to see us. His father had a friend who came to our clinic and bought him a copy of the first version of this book. The father saw the Ring of Fire pattern in Sam. He was argumentative, angry, moody, inattentive, hyperactive, easily distracted, and very sensitive to noise in the environment. He had tried a number of traditional treatments without success. His SPECT study showed a very severe Ring of Fire pattern with diffuse cortical hyperactivity. We put him on a combination of GABA, 5-HTP, L-tyrosine, and omega-3 fatty acids. Within two months he was dramatically different. The repeat SPECT study was significantly improved.

TYPE 7 (ANXIOUS) ADD

The supplements most effective to help this type of ADD are those that help calm and soothe the brain. B vitamins help support healthy relaxation, especially B6 and inositol, as does L-theanine from green tea (200 milligrams two or three times a day). Relora (750 milligrams two to three times a day) is another favorite of mine, as it helps to block the release of cortisol, the main stress hormone. Magnesium (100 to 300 milligrams two to three times a day) is another calming supplement that can be very helpful, especially for sleep and muscle twitches. Holy Basil (200 to 400 milligrams a day) is an adaptogenic herb that we have also found useful to help people focus and feel more relaxed.

CHAPTER 21

Medication for ADD Types

Medication is often an important ADD treatment option to consider. There is clearly a biological component to ADD, and medication is one of the biological options for treatment. Sometimes the other biological therapies discussed (supplements, neurofeedback, exercise, etc.) can replace the need for medication, but sometimes medication can be lifesaving. I think optimal brain function is the goal, not whether to be on or off medication.

Whenever medication is started or considered, it's essential to have clear goals in mind for its use. Some examples of ADD medication treatment goals include:

- increasing attention span and learning
- decreasing distractibility
- decreasing restlessness or high activity levels
- decreasing impulsiveness and increasing thoughtfulness
- decreasing irritability
- increasing motivation
- overall, improving functioning at school, at work, at home, in relationships, and within yourself.

Medication needs to be targeted to each individual ADD type. The wrong medication can make things worse; ineffective treatment is not innocuous. When treatments fail, individuals and families get discouraged. The discouragement leads to discontinuation of treatment. The earlier treatment is effective, the more people are willing to follow through with treatment.

TYPE 1 (CLASSIC) ADD & TYPE 2 (INATTENTIVE) ADD

Stimulants are the first-line medications for treating Type 1 and Type 2 ADD. Our current understanding of these medications is that they increase dopamine output from the basal ganglia and increase activity in the prefrontal cortex and temporal lobes. Here is a table that highlights the current available stimulant medications:

It is essential not to take stimulants with citrus juices (orange, grapefruit, lemon) or anything with citric acid in it (read the labels: citric acid is used in many things as a preservative). It tends to lessen the effect of medication. Likewise, decrease caffeine intake when taking a stimulant.

Generic name	Brand name	Side Effects	Notes
Amphetamine and amphetamine salt combinations	Dexedrine (regular/ sustained release SR), Adderall (regular/SR), Vyvanse (SR)	Some loss of appetite, weight loss, sleep problems, irritability, tics. Short-acting meds may need to be given frequently and have more rebound effect. Long-acting medicines are convenient but may have greater effects on appetite and sleep.	Adderall is my personal favorite because it lasts longer than Ritalin and is gentler as it wears off. Also, the tablets are double scored. This makes it easy to quarter them and fine-tune the dose.
Methylphenidate-based products	Ritalin (regular/SR), Concerta (SR), Focalin (regular/SR), Metadaet (regular/SR), Methylin (regular/SR), Ouillivant (SR), Daytrana Patch (SR)	Some loss of appetite, weight loss, sleep problems, irritability, tics. Short acting meds may need to be given frequently and have more rebound effect. Long-acting medicines are convenient but may have greater effects on appetite and sleep.	Watch for rebound when it wears off with the short-acting products.

Caffeine and stimulants together tend to overstimulate the nervous system.

Common Questions and Answers on Stimulants

Here is a list of common questions about stimulant medications in general.

1. *What are the indications for stimulant medications?*
Stimulant medications have several uses in medicine. Most commonly, they are prescribed for ADD. They are also used for narcolepsy (sudden sleep attacks); as an adjunctive treatment for depression; in chronic obesity; and to help thinking, concentration problems, and appetite problems in the elderly.

2. *How can stimulant medications help?*
They can improve attention span, decrease distractibility, increase ability to finish tasks, improve ability to follow directions, decrease hyperactivity and restlessness, and lessen impulsivity. Handwriting often improves with this medication. Schoolwork, homework, and overall work performance often improves significantly. Improved listening and communication skills often occur, along with a decrease in stimulation or conflict-seeking behaviors.

3. *How long does the medication last? What is the usual dosage?*
Ritalin and Dexedrine usually last three to four hours, but in some people they last as little as two and a half hours or as long as six hours. There are also slow-release preparations that last six to twelve hours and may help you or your child avoid taking a late morning or noontime dose. The slow-release form of Ritalin has a reputation for being somewhat erratic. For some people, it works great, for others, not so good. Often you just have to try it to see. The slow-release form of Dexedrine, Adderall, and Vyvanse seem to be somewhat more reliable.

In addition to weekday morning doses, I usually prescribe medication for my patients in the afternoon and on weekends. During those times, people with ADD still need to do work, homework, or housework and interact with other people.

Everyone is different in his or her need for medication. Some people need small doses of stimulant medication twice a day; some need it four or five times a day. Others need larger doses of stimulants. I have found that response often does not correlate with body weight or age. Trial, supervision, and observation are the keys to finding the right dose.

4. *How will the doctor monitor the medication?*
In my practice, I initially see patients every couple of weeks until we find the right medication and dosage. During appointments I ask about progress (at home, school, and work) and check for any side effects of the medication. I'll keep a check on weight and height and occasionally check blood pressure. In addition, I often ask teachers to fill out follow-up rating scales to see the effectiveness of the medication. For adults, I often ask that their spouses come to the appointments so that I can get another opinion on the patients' progress.

5. *What side effects can these medications have?*
Any medication can have side effects, including allergies to the medication (usually exhibited by a rash). Because each patient is different, it is important to work together with your physician to find the best medication with the least amount of side effects. The following list may not include rare or unusual side effects. Talk to your doctor if you or your child experiences anything different after starting the medication.

Common Side Effects
As the medication wears off, there may be a rebound effect where the hyperactivity or moodiness becomes worse than before the medication was started. Dosage adjustment usually helps rebound.

Lack of appetite. Encourage a good breakfast, and afternoon and evening snacks; give medication after meals, rather than before. Some children and teens become hungry near bedtime. Unfortunately, some parents think that the child's hunger is no more than a manipulative ploy to stay up later, and they engage the child or teen in a battle. The medication really does affect appetite. If the child or teen is hungry later on and they did not have much to eat at dinner, it is often a good idea to give them a late evening meal or snack. For some people, a lack of appetite is a significant problem and the medication may need to be changed or adjusted. Some of my patients use nutritional supplements to make sure they get enough calories and nutrients.

Trouble falling asleep. Some people experience insomnia. If they do, I either give them a lower dose in the late afternoon or eliminate the last dose. In cases where there are problems when the last dose is eliminated, I may try giving a small dose of the stimulant right before bedtime. This works especially well for the hyperactive group. The medication settles them down so that they can go to sleep. Typically I will try this on a Friday night the first time to make sure it doesn't keep someone up all night. For insomnia, I often recommend a concoction of 6 ounces of warm milk with a tablespoon of vanilla and a tablespoon of sugar or honey. This seems to have a nice sedating effect for many people. I also use melatonin or our Restful Sleep preparation.

Headaches or stomachaches. Patients may complain of headaches or stomachaches. These typically go away after several weeks. Acetaminophen or ibuprofen can be helpful for the headaches; taking the medication with food often decreases the stomach problems.

Irritability, crankiness, crying, emotional sensitivity, staring into space, loss of interest in friends. Some patients experience moodiness and minor personality changes. These side effects often go away in a week or two. If they don't, the medication often needs to be changed. Sometimes Wellbutrin or Strattera is a good option when this occurs.

Less Common Side Effects
Tics. Some patients develop tics (such as eye blinking, throat clearing, head jerking) on the medication. If that happens, it is important to discuss it with your doctor. Sometimes the tics go away on their own; sometimes higher doses of the medication may improve the tics; and sometimes the medication has to be stopped. If the stimulant is very helpful, I

might add another medication (such as clonidine) along with the stimulant to help with the tics.

A complicating factor with tics is that a high percentage of patients with tic disorders, such as Gilles de la Tourette's Syndrome (manifested by having both motor and vocal tics), have ADD. Sometimes it is hard to know if the medication caused the tics or if the tics were already present but worsened by the medication.

Slowed growth. There used to be a concern about stimulants stunting growth, but the long-term studies show that even though they may slow growth for a period of about a year, in the long run children usually catch up to where they should be.

Rapid pulse or increased blood pressure. If a patient notices chest pain or a heart flutter, it is important to notify the physician.

Nervous habits. Picking at the skin, stuttering, and hair pulling can sometimes occur with these medications.

Keep in mind that the side effects of having untreated ADD are usually worse that those caused by the medication.

6. *What could happen if this medication is stopped suddenly?*
There are no medical problems due to stopping the medication suddenly. A few people may experience irritability, moodiness, trouble sleeping, or increased hyperactivity for a few days if they have been on daily medication for a long time. Often it is better to stop the medication gradually over time (a week or so).

7. *How long will the medication be needed?*
There is no way to know how long a person may need to take the medication. The patient, doctor, parent, teacher, and spouse need to work together to find out what is right for each person. Sometimes the medication is only needed for a few years, sometimes it is needed for many years.

8. *Does this medication interact with other medications?*

It is a good idea to check with your doctor before mixing any prescription medications. Make sure he or she knows every medication—including over-the-counter preparations and dietary supplements—that you are taking. When stimulants are used with tricyclic antidepressants, an occasional side effect may occur, such as confusion, irritability, hallucinations, or emotional outbursts. Sometimes, however, combining stimulants with antidepressants can be a powerfully positive combination. I have done this in many patients without bad effects, but remember, everyone is different.

It is not a good idea to combine stimulants with nasal decongestants (such as medications that contain pseudoephedrine or related medications), because rapid pulse or high blood pressure may develop. If nasal decongestion is severe, it is better to use a nasal spray.

Many patients with ADD may become cranky or more hyperactive on antihistamines, such as Benadryl. If medicine for allergies is needed, ask for one of the antihistamines that does not enter the brain, such as Hismanal. Check with the pharmacist before taking over-the-counter medication with stimulants.

9. *Does this medication stop working at puberty?*

Not usually. For most people it continues to work into adulthood. If it does lose its effectiveness, the dose may need to be increased; alternately, switching to another stimulant may be helpful. However, for the vast majority of people with ADD, medication does not stop working at puberty.

10. *Why does this medication require a special prescription? (This information varies from state to state)*

Stimulants sometimes require special prescriptions for controlled substances that must be filled within a certain period of time. Some adults have been known to abuse stimulants, so caution is always advised. In my experience, children who are adequately treated for ADD have a lower percentage of drug abuse as teenagers and adults than those kids with ADD who were never treated with medication.

11. *What if my child or I have problems remembering to take the medication?*
Remembering to take medication three times a day can be difficult, even
for people who do not have ADD. Forgetfulness is a common symptom
of ADD, and when the medication has worn off, the person is fully ADD
again. If forgetfulness is a chronic problem, don't assign blame or be
upset. Look for solutions. Here are two I recommend: try switching to a
slow release form of the medication, or get an alarm system (such as a
digital watch that has five alarms) to help you remember.

12. *What about the negative news media reports on these medications?*
It is critical to get your medical information from your doctor, not solely
from the media that often reports only sensational findings. Many people
have erroneous ideas about stimulant medication. If you hear things that
worry you, check with your doctor before making any decisions.

For a period of a year, I kept a log of comments my patients told me after
I started them on stimulant medication for Type 1 and 2 ADD. Here is
a brief sample from the log.

"I experienced an increased awareness of the world around me. I saw
the hills for the first time when driving to work. I saw the bay when I
crossed over the bridge. I actually noticed the color of the sky!"

"A dramatic difference! I am really amazed."

"I experienced a 180-degree difference in my attitude."

"I left your office a skeptic. I came back converted."

"My husband said he doesn't have a knot in his stomach anymore."

"I look at my children and say 'Aren't they cute,' rather than complaining about them."

"I could enjoy the moment. My thoughts are calmer, quieter, easier
to live with."

"I could sit and watch a movie for the first time in my life."

"I am able to handle situations where I used to be hysterical. I am
able to see when I'm starting to overreact."

"The lens on my life is much clearer."

"I was tremendously overscheduled. No sane person would do that!"

"It amazes me that a little yellow pill [5 milligrams of Ritalin] can take me from wanting to jump off the bridge to loving my husband and enjoying my children."

"It is like being given sight!"

"I'm not running at train-wreck speed."

"For the first time I felt in charge of my life."

"I'm better able to keep things in perspective."

"I used to think I was stupid. It seemed everyone else could do more things than me. I'm starting to believe that there may be intelligent life in my body."

"My appetite is more normal."

"I sleep much better. Can you believe I'm taking a stimulant and it calms me down?"

"I'm out of the damned black hole I was in."

"I used to be the kind of person who would go walking by myself in downtown Detroit at 2 A.M. Now on the medication I would never do something so stupid. Before, I just wouldn't think about the consequences."

"Now I can give talks in front of groups. Before, my mind would always go blank. I organized my life around not speaking in public. Now my brain feels calmer, clearer."

"I feel like I think everyone else feels."

"I'm not as intimidated by others like I used to be."

"My husband may not be as happy as before I was on medication. Now I can think and he doesn't win all of the arguments. I'm going to have to retrain him to not always expect to get his way."

"I'm not losing my temper."

"It's like waking up after being asleep your whole life."

"Night and day!"

"I feel totally in control of my life."

"Six months ago there was no way I would drive on L.A. Freeways. Now I can drive on them no problem."

"I can't stand useless confrontation when I used to thrive on it!"

When stimulant medications do not appear to work for Type 1 or 2 ADD I may try a medication such as Strattera, Provigil, Wellbutrin (the stimulating antidepressant medication listed under Type 5 Limbic ADD), or one of several blood pressure medications, such as clonidine or guanfacine. The blood pressure medications have been found to be helpful for hyperactivity, aggressiveness, and impulsivity. They are not usually helpful with the attentional symptoms. Mixing them with a stimulant medication can produce excellent results.

Clonidine and guanfacine are also used as primary treatments for tic disorders such as Gilles de la Tourette's Syndrome. When I use clonidine in addition to a stimulant medication I will order a screening EKG. There have been several reports that this combination may cause problems, even though personally I have found it to be an effective, safe combination. These medications have also been used to treat insomnia, which is very common in ADD.

TYPE 3 (OVERFOCUSED) ADD

Type 3 (Overfocused) ADD is most likely due to a deficiency of both serotonin and dopamine. Medication interventions need to be targeted at enhancing both of these neurotransmitters. If one neurotransmitter is enhanced by itself it may make this type worse. For example, when stimulant medications are given to people with Type 3 (Overfocused) ADD, they often become overstimulated and stuck on certain issues. In addition, they tend to be anxious and worried. Serotonin medications by themselves (such as Prozac or Zoloft) tend to help with the overfocus but eventually cause more problems with focus and motivation. A balance is needed.

Effexor, Pristique, and Cymbalta are my first drugs of choice for Type 3 (Overfocused) ADD. They increase serotonin (helping to shift attention) and norepinephrine and dopamine (stimulating neurotransmitters). Often they can be used alone without the need for a stimulant medication. When these medications are ineffective or not well-tolerated I often prescribe an SSRI (selective serotonin reuptake inhibitor). These medications only increase serotonin availability in the brain so I often need to add a stimulant medication like Adderall to fully treat this type of ADD.

In our experience, people who have temporal lobe problems may experience an increase in angry or aggressive feelings on serotonin enhancing medications and even supplements. Therefore, we are careful to screen for these before placing someone on these medications. If there are side effects on any medication, it is important to contact your doctor and discuss them. Unlike stimulants, these may take several weeks to a month to be effective and even three to four months to see the best benefit.

TYPE 4 (TEMPORAL LOBE) ADD

The medications used to treat Type 4 (Temporal Lobe) ADD are classified as anticonvulsant medications. We have seen that they are good at stabilizing temporal lobe activity and they tend to significantly help symptoms of aggression, mood instability, headaches, and in some cases learning problems. Treating Type 4 ADD often involves combining them with a stimulant medication. Even though these medications are classified as anticonvulsant or antiseizure medications, we are not saying that Type 4 patients have a seizure disorder. Rather, they have dysfunction in a part of the brain commonly associated with seizures. In treating ADD, we often use much lower doses than used to combat seizures. Sometimes even very small doses are all that is necessary. Anticonvulsants strive to enhance the neurotransmitter, GABA, which has a calming or inhibitory effect on nerve cells. In the last twenty years, psychiatry has come around to using these medications for many different conditions. Anticonvulsants are almost equally prescribed by psychiatrists and neurologists.

Typically, I tend to prescribe Neurontin for anxiety, irritability, and pain; Lamictal for resistant depression; and Depakote or Tegretol for aggression.

In addition to anticonvulsants, I often use memory-enhancing medication for people with temporal lobe problems. Memory problems are very common in this ADD type. Donepezil (Aricept) is a medication indicated for Alzheimer's disease that works by increasing the amounts of acetylcholine in the brain. Acetylcholine is a neurotransmitter that is known to be involved in laying down new memories. I have seen this medication be very helpful for many patients with Type 4 (Temporal Lobe) ADD. One woman wrote me that after she took Aricept it was like going from 4 megabytes of RAM in her head to 128 megabytes. In addition, Piracetam, a medication that is difficult to obtain in the U.S., but not in Europe or Canada, has been shown in a number of studies to help memory. A number of my patients through the years have written away for it and found it beneficial without side effects. Mark, a seventeen-year-old patient with learning disabilities stemming from memory problems, was placed on Piracetam. In three weeks he noticed that he felt that he was mentally clearer and his memory was better. His school performance improvement has lasted for the three years that he has taken Piracetam.

TYPE 5 (LIMBIC) ADD

Wellbutrin is my favorite medication for Type 5 (Limbic) ADD. Researchers think it works by increasing dopamine. It has also been found to be effective in helping people stop smoking. When Wellbutrin was first released in the United States, a number of people developed seizures on it. It was then pulled from the market in the early 1980s. The manufacturer figured out the dosage pattern was wrong and the FDA allowed them to rerelease it with a different dosage regimen. Do not take more than 150 milligrams at a time of the regular release preparation or 300 milligrams of the slow release preparation. Imipramine is another option for this type. I also use it for anxiety disorders and bedwetting.

TYPE 6 (RING OF FIRE) ADD

I typically start with supplements for this type, usually a combination of GABA, 5HTP and L-tyrosine. If I prescribe medication I typically start with one of the anticonvulsants listed under Type 4 ADD, and may add a stimulant medication later on. Stimulants by themselves often make this type worse. When used alone, serotonergic medication also seem to make this type worse. If the anticonvulsants do not seem to work, I may very cautiously use one of the novel antipsychotic medications, such as Risperdal. Often the dosages of the anticonvulsants or antipsychotic medications are much smaller than needed for seizure disorders or psychotic illnesses. In selected cases, the antipsychotic medications can be very effective. Some of my teenage patients have been kept out of the hospital or residential treatment centers using these medications. However, one of the problems with these medications is weight gain. I have a number of patients who have gained twenty to thirty pounds in less than a year. The amazing response to the medication is the only reason I persisted with the medication. The anticonvulsant Topamax is known to promote weight loss in some patients and I have used it successfully in some of my Ring of Fire patients. The blood pressure medicines guanfacine and clonidine can also be helpful. These tend to calm overall hyperactivity seen in this type.

TYPE 7 (ANXIOUS) ADD

For this type I like to presbribe the tricyclic antidepressants imipramine or desipramine, both of which have been shown to be helpful for anxiety symptoms, depression, and ADD. I have also successfully used Neurontin plus a stimulant to help this group.

Combinations

Sometimes a combination of medications is needed to obtain the full therapeutic effect. I particularly like the combination of stimulants and antiobsessive medications for children of alcoholics. Sometimes a person may have three or four different subtypes of ADD and may be on a sophisticated combination of medications. If that is the case for you, I recommend an evaluation by a specialist in the field.

REMEMBER:
The goal needs to be the best functioning,
not to be off medication!

Many people have the misguided belief that it is better if they only take a "little bit" of the medication. Often this attitude causes the medication to be ineffective. I give patients the following metaphor:

When a person goes to the eye doctor because he or she is having trouble seeing, they want a prescription for the glasses that will help them see the best. They don't ask for "just a little bit of a lens." They want to see clearly!

So it is with ADD: Everyone is different in the quantity of medication they require to function at their best. For some people, it is 5 milligrams of Adderall one to two times a day. For others, it is 20 milligrams of Adderall three times a day. Everyone is different.

ONE MORE IMPORTANT QUESTION

Many of my patients are rightfully concerned about the side effects of medication for ADD, as they should be. It is also important to ask yourself about the side effects of not being effectively treated. Given all we know about the poor outcomes of people who have never been treated or only received ineffective treatment for ADD, it is worth asking. My bias is to start with supplements if possible, but when they are only partially effective or ineffective, medications are worth considering.

CHAPTER 22

Neurofeedback Strategies for ADD Types

I n late 2012, the American Academy of Pediatrics recognized neurofeedback as a Level 1: "Best Support" Intervention for ADD on par with medication. Over the past thirty years, Joel Lubar, Ph.D., of the University of Tennessee, and many other clinicians have reported the effectiveness of brain wave biofeedback, also known as neurofeedback, in the treatment of ADD in children and teenagers.

In 2013, in a high-quality study from Spain published in the prestigious journal *Biological Psychiatry* researchers compared forty sessions of neurofeedback to Ritalin. Behavioral rating scales were completed by fathers, mothers, and teachers at pre- and post-treatment, and at two- and six-month follow-up. In both groups, similar significant reductions were reported in ADHD symptoms by parents and teachers. However, significant academic performance improvements were only detected in the neurofeedback group.

Biofeedback, in general, is a treatment technique that utilizes instruments to measure physiological responses in a person's body (such as hand temperature, sweat gland activity, breathing rates, heart rates, blood pressure, and brain wave patterns). The instruments then feed the information on these body systems back to the patient who can then learn how to change them. In neurofeedback, electrodes are placed on the scalp, measuring the number and type of brain wave patterns.

There are five types of brain wave patterns:

- *delta waves* (1 to 4 cycles per second), very slow brain waves, seen mostly during sleep
- *theta waves* (5 to 7 cycles per second), slow brain waves, seen during daydreaming and twilight states
- *alpha waves* (8 to 12 cycles per second), brain waves seen during relaxed states
- *SMR* (sensorimotor rhythm) *waves* (12 to 15 cycles per second), brain waves seen during states of focused relaxation
- *beta waves* (13 to 24 cycles per second), fast brain waves seen during concentration or mental work states

In evaluating over twelve thousand children with ADD, Dr. Lubar has found that the basic issue for these children is their inability to maintain beta concentration states for sustained periods of time. He also found that these children have excessive theta daydreaming brain wave activity. Dr. Lubar found that through the use of neurofeedback, children could be taught to increase the amount of beta brain waves and decrease the amount of theta or daydreaming brain waves. They can train their brains to be more active.

The basic neurofeedback technique asks the patient—child, teen, or adult—to play games with their minds. The patient's brain is hooked up to the computer equipment through electrodes placed on the head. The computer feeds back to the patient the type of brain wave activity it's monitoring. For Type 1 (Classic ADD), the patient is rewarded for producing concentration or beta waves, and the more beta states he or she produces, the more rewards accrued. On the neurofeedback equipment, for example, a child sits in front of a computer monitor and watches a game screen that reflects the composition of his or her brain waves. If the child increases the "beta" activity and/or decreases the "theta" activity, the game continues. The game stops, however, when the child is unable to maintain the desired brain wave states. Children find the screen fun and many are able to gradually shape their brain wave patterns to a more normal one.

From experience, clinicians know that this treatment technique is not an overnight cure. Children often have to do neurofeedback for thirty to forty sessions to see a significant benefit. In my experience with neurofeedback and ADD, many people are able to improve their reading skills and decrease their need for medication. Also, neurofeedback has helped to decrease impulsivity and aggressiveness. It is a powerful tool, in part, because we are making the patients part of the treatment process by giving them more control over their own physiological processes.

SPECT HELPS TO FOCUS NEUROFEEDBACK

Through SPECT we have seen that ADD is a complex condition. Therefore successfully treating it requires more than one neurofeedback treatment. The figure below shows standard electrode placements. For people interested in neurofeedback, here is a list of training sites that we use in our office for the different ADD types. Share them with the neurofeedback professional in your area.

Joey, age seven, was brought to our clinic by his mother for hyperactivity, restlessness, impulse control problems, inattention, and distractibility. She heard about our work with neurofeedback and wanted an alternative to medication. Joey did neurofeedback twice a week for two years. After six months we began seeing significant changes, including less hyperactivity and longer ability to focus. In addition, his interest in reading significantly increased. After he stopped the neurofeedback, he continued to do well in school and at home. He maintained an exercise program and a higher protein, lower carbohydrate diet.

TYPE 3 (OVERFOCUSED) ADD

In Overfocused ADD there is excessive activity in the anterior cingulate gyrus. It is helpful to do the neurofeedback training over the front central part of the brain between FZ and CZ. This training helps people shift attention and feel more settled, less worried, and more compliant. It also enhances attention span. The training consists of enhancing high alpha activity (relaxed but focused).

Figure 22-A, B (Top Down View, Left Side View)
Standard Electrode Placement Areas:

FP = frontal poles,
F = frontal lobe areas,
C = central areas,
P = parietal lobe areas,
T = temporal lobe areas,
O = occipital lobe areas.

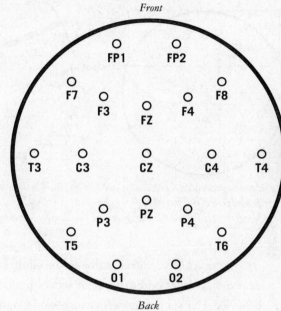

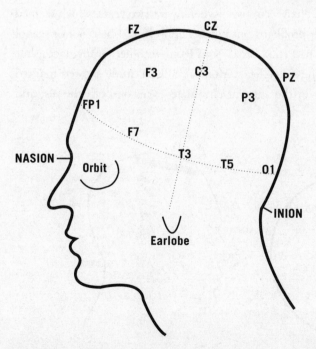

Type 1 (Classic) ADD and Type 2 (Inattentive) ADD

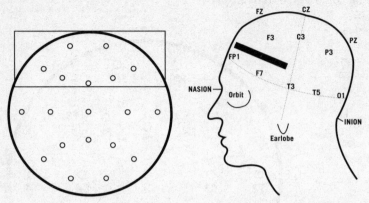

Classic and Inattentive ADD show decreased activity (excessive theta activity and poor beta activity) in the prefrontal cortex. It is helpful to do the neurofeedback training as close to the prefrontal poles as possible. The training consists of enhancing prefrontal beta activity and decreasing prefrontal theta activity.

Monica, age seventeen, came to the clinic for problems with anxiety, worrying, temper outbursts, poor school performance, and oppositional behavior. Her symptoms were much worse right before the onset of her menstrual period. She was in psychotherapy for two years, which seemed to help her temper problems but not her oppositional behavior or school performance. She had tried Prozac and Paxil with her family doctor but she did not like the side effects. Monica's SPECT study showed marked increased activity in the anterior cingulate gyrus on both the rest and

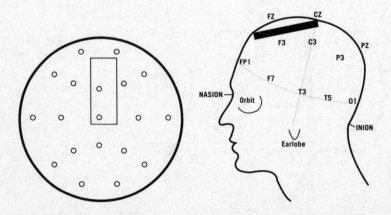

concentration studies. When she learned about neurofeedback, she liked the idea of learning how to control her own brain (sort of an "anterior cingulate control thing"). We did neurofeedback over her anterior cingulate gyrus twice a week for six months. In the first month she noticed less worrying. By the end of six months she felt more focused, less anxious, and overall more cooperative, an assessment her family validated. Nevertheless, she still had a hard time right before her period. I placed her on a small dose of St. John's Wort (300 milligrams twice a day) which seemed to smooth out her menstrual mood swings.

TYPE 4 (TEMPORAL LOBE) ADD

In Temporal Lobe ADD there is usually decreased activity (excessive theta activity) over the temporal lobes on one or both sides. Neurofeedback training over the affected temporal lobe seems to do the most good. We have seen this training help people have better mood stability, improved reading ability, and improved memory. The training consists of enhancing SMR activity and suppressing theta activity over the affected temporal lobe.

Marty, age fourteen, came to see us for temper outbursts, memory problems, poor reading skills, inattention, disorganization, and language problems (he had problems finding the right words and he often misunderstood people). His SPECT study showed significantly decreased activity in his left temporal lobe at rest. When he concentrated, the temporal

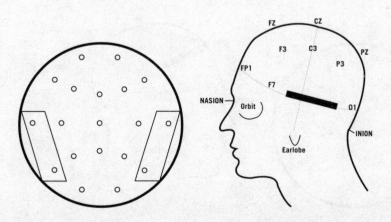

lobe activity decreased even further along with his prefrontal cortex activity. He had had a poor response to Ritalin and the parents were hesitant to try an anticonvulsant medication. They wanted to try non-medication options first, and they liked the idea of neurofeedback. We started neurofeedback training over Marty's left temporal lobe. Within two months we noticed that his reading was starting to improve and his temper was better. After six months there was more mood stability. At that point, we started training his prefrontal cortex to be more active. He learned quickly. After eighteen months of training, Marty felt more in control of himself and much improved. In addition to training, he also exercised regularly and ate a consistent simple carbohydrate-free diet.

TYPE 5 (LIMBIC) ADD

In Limbic ADD there is decreased activity in the left prefrontal cortex and increased activity in the deep limbic areas. Since the deep areas are too deep in the brain to do neurofeedback training, we have found that teaching the patient to increase beta activity over the left prefrontal cortex has the most beneficial effect. This training helps improve focus and mood while decreasing negativity and negative thoughts. Of interest, a relatively new treatment for depression termed transcranial magnetic stimulation (TMS) uses powerful magnets to increase blood flow in this part of the brain. TMS has been shown to be very effective in resistant depression.

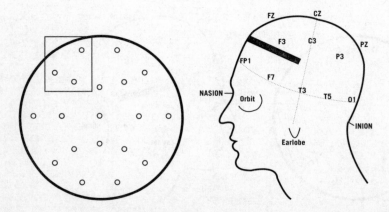

Robbie, forty-two, came to see me after he had lost his job and was nearly homeless. He was disheveled, lethargic, and demoralized. His history and SPECT studies clearly indicated Limbic ADD. His whole life he had underachieved in school and barely finished high school even though he had been tested as having an IQ of 120 (bright normal). He was disorganized, inattentive, and easily distracted. Teachers used to say that he did not live up to his potential and that he would do better if he tried harder. There were also teacher comments on his report cards that he should try to be more cheerful and positive. His SPECT study showed decreased left prefrontal cortex activity both at rest and with concentration and increased deep limbic activity on both studies.

He wanted to do neurofeedback instead of medication. Robbie trained his left prefrontal cortex to be more active. At first the training was very slow. It took him six months to be able to tune into his own brain wave patterns. But once he caught on to how to do the neurofeedback, the training went much faster. Within a year he felt better energy and he was more positive. He went to junior college and enrolled in an airline mechanics course. He got straight A's in the course and was very proud of his abilities. He surprised himself by discovering a hidden artistic side, and he started bringing us sculptures and drawings. At the end of three years of neurofeedback training, he was significantly improved. Five years later he remains so.

TYPE 6 (RING OF FIRE) ADD

The neurofeedback protocol for this type of ADD is unknown at this time. Due to the diffuse nature of the cerebral hyperactivity, we doubt that one training site will work. It's possible that multiple training sites

will be helpful, such as SMR training over the parietal and lateral prefrontal areas and high alpha training over the anterior cingulate area, but it is yet to be determined.

TYPE 7 (ANXIOUS) ADD

In Anxious ADD we often see excessive beta activity in the right prefrontal cortex. The neurofeedback protocol for this type of ADD is to calm this part of the brain, but not too much, so we do high alpha training over this area.

Audio-Visual Stimulation (AVS)

A similar treatment to neurofeedback is something called Audio-Visual Stimulation. This technique was developed by Harold Russell, Ph.D., and John Carter, Ph.D., psychologists at the University of Texas, Galveston. Both Drs. Russell and Carter were involved in the treatment of ADD children with neurofeedback, but they wanted to develop a treatment technique that could be available to more children. They based their technique on a concept termed "entrainment," in which brain waves tend to pick up the rhythm in the environment around them. They developed special glasses and headphones that flash lights and sounds at specific frequencies that help the brain "tune in" to be more focused. Patients wear these glasses for thirty to forty-five minutes a day.

I have tried this treatment on a number of patients, with some encouraging results. One patient, who developed tics on both Ritalin and Dexedrine, tried the glasses for a month. His ADD symptoms signifi-

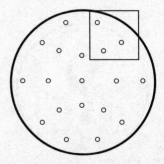

cantly improved. When he went off the Audio-Visual Stimulator, his symptoms returned. The symptoms again subsided when he retried the treatment.

Trigeminal Nerve Stimulation (TNS)

Another potentially interesting and helpful treatment for ADD is something called Trigeminal Nerve Stimulation (TNS). It is a noninvasive treatment already approved in Europe and Canada for refractory epilepsy and major depression. A study of twenty seven- to fourteen-year-old children presented at the 2013 Annual Meeting of the American Psychiatric Association reported that use of TNS resulted in robust improvements in ADD symptoms and executive function, as well as on computerized testing of cognitive measures. Ian Cook, M.D., of UCLA said there is great excitement over the potential of this treatment.

"The trigeminal nerve is one of the twelve cranial nerves, and stimulation of this one nerve can enhance functions such as attention, emotional processing, concentration, anxiety, and seizure generation," Dr. Cook said. Using positron emission tomography (PET) scans, these researchers had previously shown that electrical stimulation of trigeminal nerves using an adhesive patch on the forehead attached to a stimulator resulted in increases in blood flow within sixty seconds in areas such as the frontal lobes.

During studies of the system in refractory epilepsy and treatment-resistant depression, Dr. Cook said, they noticed that patients also reported that they were able to focus their attention better, which led to current study. TNS is not yet approved in the United States, but may be soon, and is worth watching.

Neurofeedback, AV stimulation, and TNS hold significant promise as non-pharmacological treatments for ADD.

PART 4

Optimizing

The ADD Life

CHAPTER 23

Parenting and Family Strategies

Even those with the best parenting skills deteriorate when they're up against the day-to-day stress of ADD kids, and intervention with the parents and family is crucial to a healthy outcome for these children. Having an ADD child or teenager is often extremely stressful on a family system. Siblings are often embarrassed by the child's behavior, and parents often feel guilty for struggling so much with these children. One of the most helpful things I have done for these families is to lead a weekly parent education and support group. When I help parents become more effective with these children, the entire household does better.

Before undertaking parent training, it is important to screen parents and other siblings for ADD. Untreated ADD in parents or siblings sabotages treatment. Untreated ADD parents are often unable to follow through on their homework. Untreated siblings often disrupt the progress of the child or teen in treatment.

Here is a summary of the important points from the parenting course:

- **Be focused.** Set clear goals for yourself as a parent and for your child. Then make sure that you act in a way that is consistent with your goals.
- **Relationship is key.** With a good parent-child relationship, almost any form of discipline will work. With a poor parent-child relation-

ship, any form of discipline will probably fail. Relationships require two things: time and a willingness to listen.

- **Spend some "special time" with your child each day, even if it's only ten to fifteen minutes.** Being available to the child will help him or her feel important and enhance self-esteem.

- **Be a good listener.** Find out what the child thinks before you tell him or her what you think.

- **Be clear with what you expect.** It is effective for families to have posted rules, spelling out the values of the family. For example, "We treat each other with respect, which means no yelling, no hitting, no name calling or put-downs. We look for ways to make each other's lives easier."

- **When a child lives up to the rules and expectations, be sure to notice him or her.** If you never reinforce good behavior, you're unlikely to get much of it.

- **Notice the behaviors you like in your child ten times more than the behaviors you don't like.** This teaches them to notice what they like about themselves, rather than to grow up with a critical self-image.

- **Mean what you say.** Don't allow guilt to cause you to back down on what you know is right.

- **Don't tell a child ten times to do something.** Expect a child to comply the first time! Be ready to back up your words.

- **Never discipline a child when you're out of control.** Take a time-out before you lose your cool.

- **Use discipline to teach a child rather than to punish or get even for bad behavior.**

- **See misbehavior as a problem you're going to solve rather than "the child is just trying to make you mad."**

- **It's important to have swift, clear consequences for broken rules, enforced in a matter-of-fact and unemotional way.** Nagging and yelling are extremely destructive, ineffective, and tend to be addictive for the ADD child.

- **Give a child choices between alternatives, rather than dictating what they'll do, eat, or wear.** If you make all the decisions for your child, he or she will be unable to make their own decisions later on.

- **Parents need to be together and support each other.** When children are allowed to split parental authority, they have far more power than is good for them.
- **Keep promises to children.**
- **Children learn about relationships from watching how their parents relate to each other.** Are you setting a good example?
- **Children live up to the labels we give them.** Be careful of the nicknames and phrases you use to describe your children.
- **Parents need time for themselves.** Parents who are drained do not have much left that is good for their children.
- **Teach children from your own real-life experiences.**
- **In parenting, always remember the words "firm but kind."** One parent used the phrase, "tough as nails and kind as a lamb." Try to balance them at the same time.
- **Do not yell at, hit, or berate an ADD child.** The more emotionally intense you get, the more they will make you get emotionally intense.

GET RID OF GUILT

Perhaps the biggest roadblock to effective discipline of ADD children and teens is *guilt*. Too often parents allow guilt to get in their way and render them totally ineffective in dealing with the difficult child.

Here is *the guilt cycle* that often perpetuates bad behavior.

PARENT EXPLODES

(because they can't take the bad behavior anymore)

PARENT FEELS GUILT

(because they overreacted or were excessively harsh)

PARENT ALLOWS THE CHILD TO GET AWAY WITH MISBEHAVIOR

(because of their guilt over the explosion toward the child)

PARENT FEELS TENSION BUILDING UP

(because they are not effectively dealing with the misbehavior)

PARENT EXPLODES

(and the cycle starts all over again)

It's very important when dealing with the ADD child to break the guilt cycle. The best way to do this is by dealing with difficult behavior whenever it occurs and not allowing the tension to build up in you to the point where you explode.

STEPS TO SHAPING POSITIVE BEHAVIOR

Retraining difficult behavior patterns is an essential part of the treatment for ADD. As I've mentioned, having this disorder causes faulty learning in many areas of life. For example, many children with ADD are repeatedly given the message that they're stupid (i.e., by parent or teacher complaints, being teased by other children). Too often, they begin to believe they really are stupid. As such, they stop doing their work, believing it is too hard for them.

Behaviorally, many children, teens, and adults learn to get other people upset with their difficult behavior. They learn, on a purely unconscious and biological level, that when there is turmoil between people, it stimulates their brain, making them feel more alert and awake. They do not know this on a conscious level and would, in fact, deny that they ever do it. But when you watch these people with their parents or in social situations, their behavior seems goal-directed toward turmoil. After listening to hundreds of mothers, I'm convinced that this is a technique to treat underlying brain deactivation with turmoil, as an alcoholic may treat underlying restlessness or anxiety with alcohol.

Retraining behavior patterns or behavior modification involves several clear steps:

Step One: Define the desired and undesirable behaviors specifically.
Step Two: Establish a baseline period.
Step Three: Communicate the rules and expectations clearly.
Step Four: Reward desired behavior.

Step Five: Give clear, unemotional consequences for the negative behavior.

Step One

Define the desired and undesirable behaviors specifically. Before you can
shape behavior, it is critical to clearly know what behaviors you want and
what behaviors you don't want. Examples of desirable behaviors might
include doing what parents say the first time or doing homework before
going out to play. Hitting another person and talking back are examples
of undesirable behaviors.

Step Two

Establish a baseline period of how often either negative or positive behavior occurs. Take some time (a week to a month) to keep a log on how
many times a behavior occurs. For example, if the desired behavior is
getting homework done before a child or teen goes out of the house, keep
a log on how many times that actually occurs during the baseline period.
Doing this will allow you to know whether or not your interventions are
effective.

Step Three

Communicate rules and expectations clearly. Establishing clear, written
rules and expectations is the next step in effective behavior modification.
These rules need to give direction for the child's behavior. When the
child knows what is expected, he or she is much more likely to be able
to give it. Too often, parents believe that children should know how to
act without the rules being clearly communicated to them.

Another reason to have the rules written is that children respond to
symbols of rules in the environment (traffic signals, posted rules at the
pool, etc.). My nephew Andrew went through a time when he was three
years old during which he was afraid of monsters in his room at night.
Week after week, Andrew's parents searched the room with Andrew,
trying to prove to him that there were no monsters in his room. They
looked under the bed, in the closet, behind the door, and under the covers. Finally, they realized that they were only making the fear worse by

exploring the room for the monsters. Andrew's mother decided that they would make a sign saying that monsters were not allowed in Andrew's room. She and Andrew drew a picture of a monster and then drew a red circle around it with a slash across the monster. Underneath the picture they wrote NO MONSTERS ALLOWED. Amazingly, Andrew's fear of monsters in his room vanished because he knew the sign kept them away.

Written rules have power! They let children know what is expected of them in a clear way. They allow you to know when the children are following the rules and they give you a basis for reinforcing them. They keep the standards of good behavior unambiguous and serve as a touch point for clear, unemotional consequences.

Here is a set of rules that I've found helpful, both for my own household and for my patients'. Post them up where the family can see them every day.

FAMILY RULES

TELL THE TRUTH

TREAT EACH OTHER WITH RESPECT
(which means no yelling, no hitting, no kicking, no name calling, and no putting down)

NO ARGUING WITH PARENTS
(as parents, we want and value your input and ideas, but arguing means you have made your point more than one time)

RESPECT EACH OTHER'S PROPERTY
(which means we ask permission to use something that does not belong to us)

DO WHAT MOM AND DAD SAY THE FIRST TIME
(without complaining or throwing a fit)

ASK PERMISSION BEFORE YOU GO SOMEWHERE

PUT THINGS AWAY THAT YOU TAKE OUT

LOOK FOR WAYS TO BE KIND AND HELPFUL TO EACH OTHER

These rules set the tone and "values" for the family. They clearly state that there is a line of authority at home, and that it is expected that children will follow the rules and respect their parents, their siblings, and the family's property. These are good social expectations and teachings. When you tell someone what you expect, you're much more likely to get it.

In establishing expectations at home, it's often important to use visual clues, such as pictures or short printed directions. Try to minimize verbal directions since people with ADD may have trouble processing verbal input (especially in a noisy environment). Writing expectations down also has the advantage of being able to refer to it later when the ADD person denies that you ever told him about it.

Step Four

Reward desired behavior. After clear expectations are given, it is essential to praise and reward the behavior that meets those expectations. When positive behavior goes unnoticed, it often ceases to exist. Most children, teens, and even adults enjoy being noticed by others. Rewards or reinforcers may take many forms. As adults, we often work for monetary gain. The more financial benefit, the harder we'll work. But we also work for praise from our boss or spouse. Our personalities often determine the rewards we're interested in working toward. Children are the same way—some children will work hard to comply for the verbal praise of their parents, while others need different types of rewards. Here is a list of different reinforcers.

Social rewards: verbal praise ("I really like it when you . . . "); physical affection, such as hugs or looks
Material rewards: toys, food ("Clean your room before your snack."), little presents, or surprises
Activity rewards: sports, trips to library, park, arcade
Token rewards: star or point systems, money

Here are some simple principles in rewarding good behavior:

- Use many more rewards than punishment
- Reward as soon as possible after a child fulfills your expectations

- Focus your energy on catching them being good
- Look for ways to reinforce them
- Reward the child in a way he or she likes (all children are different; use what works!)
- Be consistent
- Make it to the child's benefit to behave.

Many parents object to the use of reward systems when it comes to reinforcing good behavior. They say, "I'm not going to bribe my child to behave. They should do it anyway." I respond that the definition of a bribe is to give someone something of value to encourage them to do something illegal. Behaving is not illegal! Generally, adults would not go to work if there was not some sort of payoff. It is important to think that children also work for goals and payoffs that turn them on. For difficult kids, it is often necessary to set up a token system or a point system to help keep them on track.

Here is a simple five-step "point" or "chip" system that has worked well for hundreds of parents.

1. **Choose**
   - three chores (such as doing the dishes, cleaning their room, vacuuming, feeding the animals, etc.)
   - three behaviors (such as treating their sister well, getting ready for school on time, doing what Mom and Dad say the first time, etc.).

2. **Assign a point (or poker chip) value to each chore and behavior,** depending on how difficult each is for the child to accomplish. If the child has a lot of trouble doing something, make it worth more points or chips than something he can do easily. Add up the possible points or chips the child can get each day if he or she has a perfect day. Also, let the child know that he or she can earn bonus points or chips for especially cooperative and pleasant behavior. Tell the child that points or chips will only be given for chores and behaviors done on the first request. If you have to repeat yourself, the child will not get any points or chips and will still have to do it.

3. **Establish two lists of rewards:**
   - one for future incentives the child wishes to work for (toy, having a friend spend the night, a special trip to restaurant or arcade, renting a video, etc.)
   - another list for everyday rewards (watching TV, playing with friends, playing video games, staying up an extra half hour, etc.).

4. **Determine the point value necessary to redeem each reward.** About half should be spent on everyday rewards. This allows a child, if they have a really good day, to save about half of their points or chips for special rewards down the line.

5. **Add up the points every day.** Allow the child to use his or her rewards to buy everyday privileges and keep a "savings account" for points or chips to be used later on. This works to teach them the value and need for saving.

Note:
   - Initially, make the system very reinforcing so that children will want to participate. Then slowly tighten the reins on it as their behavior improves.
   - You can use the rewards for almost any behavior you like.
   - Reward as quickly as possible.
   - Do not give chips or points away before the actual behavior or chore is done. In this system, there is no credit!

FAT FREDDY'S & CHANGING BEHAVIOR

For decades I have collected penguins. I now have over two thousand five hundred penguins—more than I could ever want or need. Penguins remind me of the need to shape behavior in a positive way. I used to live in Hawaii. On the island of Oahu, there is a place by the name of Sea Life Park. At Sea Life Park they had a penguin show, and the penguin's name was Fat Freddy. Freddy could do amazing things. He could jump off a twenty-foot board, he could bowl with his nose, he could count—he even jumped through a hoop of fire. I was really taken with this penguin. I remember watching Freddy's show with my son, Antony, who was seven at the time.

Toward the end of the show the trainer asked Freddy to go get something. Freddy went and got it and brought it right back. I was taken aback when I saw this. I thought to myself, "I ask this kid to get me something and he wants to have a discussion with me for twenty minutes and then he doesn't want to do it. What's the difference? I know my son is smarter than this penguin." We went up to the trainer after the show and I asked her how she got Freddy to do all of those really neat things. The trainer looked at my son and then she looked at me and she said, "Unlike parents, whenever Freddy does anything like what I want him to do, I notice him, I give him a hug, and then I give him a fish."

Even though my son didn't like fish, the light really turned on in my head: Whenever he did things that I liked, I paid no attention to him at all because I'm a very busy guy. But whenever he did something I didn't like, I gave him a ton of attention because I don't want to raise bad kids. Well guess what I was doing: I *was encouraging him to be a pain in the neck.* By misbehaving he got noticed more and more by me!

So I collect penguins as a way to remind myself to notice the good things about the people in my life a lot more than the bad things about them. This is the essence of shaping behavior.

Step Five

Administer clear, unemotional consequences for the negative behavior. In order for consequences to be effective, they must be used with the other steps in shaping behavior, i.e., clear expectations and positive reinforcement. Consequences by themselves change nothing, but when used in conjunction with the other steps of the program they can be very powerful in helping to parent the difficult child.

I once saw an interaction between a mother and her four-year-old son in a grocery store that turned my stomach. After the child ran off for the third time, the mother jerked him by the arm, picked him off the ground, and whacked him so hard his little body flew into the air. She then slammed him down into the cart and said, "You little brat, do what I say!" With a panicked look, he held his little arms up to hug her, at which point she turned and looked away from him. He then started to cry.

Too often parents punish children as a reaction to the anger they feel inside and when they're out of control of themselves. This type of punishment causes the child to feel frightened and angry and the parent to feel guilty and frustrated.

It's important to distinguish between punishment and discipline. Punishment means to inflict a penalty for wrongdoing. Discipline, from the root word *disciple*, means to teach or train. It's critical that we use discipline to teach children how to be good, rather than inflict punishment when they're not.

As I mentioned above, reinforcing good behavior is a much more effective change agent than giving consequences to bad behavior. Yet, there still are times when consequences are needed.

Here are eight components of effective discipline:

1. **A good relationship with a child is a prerequisite to effective discipline.** When parents have a good relationship with a child, almost any form of discipline is effective. When the relationship is poor, however, almost no form of discipline works well. Never discipline children in a way that damages your relationship with them.

2. **You must be in control of yourself.** If you feel like you're going to explode, take a time-out: Take several deep breaths, count to fifty, hit a pillow, take a walk, call a friend, do anything to avoid exploding at the child. It's impossible to discipline effectively when you're out of control, and it does more harm than good.

3. **Don't yell, nag, or belittle!** What happens inside you when someone yells, nags, or belittles you? If you're like me, you immediately turn them off. These are very ineffective techniques, and they harm the relationship more than help the situation. Also remember: Some kids get unconsciously "turned on" by turmoil. When you feel like yelling, talk softly (the difference in your behavior will get their attention).

4. **Have a goal in mind for the behavior you're trying to change**. For the mother in the grocery store, the goal was to get the child to stay near her. She would be more effective if she gave him a lot of positive attention for the time he stays near her, rather than giving him a lot of negative attention for when he goes away. By viewing the process to change the behaviors you don't like in a positive light, you're more likely to be helpful to your child.

5. **Develop a plan for discipline before you're actually in the situation**. This also prevents you from overreacting. Discipline should be as immediate as possible and should be a reminder to the child on how to change his or her behavior. It should not be an assault. I often recommend a short time-out method for younger children and a slightly longer one for older children. Parents can also have their children write lines or essays on how they'll change their behavior.

6. **Whenever possible, use *natural* and *logical* consequences**. Ask yourself, *What's the natural or logical consequence to the misbehavior?* If the child refuses to do his homework, then he goes to school without it. If the child is acting up at dinner, then he or she doesn't get to finish dinner if everyone else is done. If the child refuses to put away his or her toys, then it is logical that they will be taken away for several days. Using these natural or logical consequences help children learn cause and effect and teaches them that they are responsible for their behavior.

7. **Attitude is everything**. Many parents ask my opinion on spanking. I generally tell them that whether or not you spank a child has nothing to do with effective discipline. How you discipline, not the method, is what's important. When you mildly spank a child on the buttocks when you're in control of yourself, for a specific reason, and afterwards give the child a hug, then spanking can be very effective. However, most parents don't use it that way. They spank a child when they're angry and on the verge of being out of control themselves. Use discipline for teaching. You and your child will both feel better.

8. **Never withhold love, affection, or time from a child who has misbehaved**. When children are in trouble, they need you the most. Let them know it's their behavior you're disciplining, but you still love them very much.

A TIMEOUT METHOD THAT WORKS

When used properly, Timeout is an extremely effective discipline technique for children two to twelve years of age. Use the following guidelines:

- **Give clear commands**. For example, "Antony, take out the trash now." And then count to five or ten seconds to yourself. If you count out loud you teach the child to cue off your voice.

- **Expect immediate compliance**. We teach our kids when to respond to us. When we repeat ourselves ten times and then get serious with a child, we're teaching them not to listen to us until the tenth time we say something. Expect your child to obey you the first time you say something. When they do comply, notice and appreciate them. (In our example, "Thanks Antony, I really like it when you do what I say the first time.")

- **When the child doesn't comply, warn them only once and give them the choice to comply**. In our case, "Antony, I told you to take out the trash now (spoken in a firm, but not hostile tone). You have a choice; you can take it out now or you can spend ten minutes in Timeout and then you can do it. It's up to you."

- **If the child still doesn't comply *immediately*, put him or her in Timeout!**

- **Timeouts are best served in a neutral, boring corner of the house**. Don't use the child's bedroom because you have probably gone to great lengths and expense to make their bedroom a nice place to be. Use a Timeout chair, because there may be times when the child has to be in it for a while. Also, with a chair you can set the rule that in order for them to be in Timeout, both buttocks need to be on the seat of the chair.

- **The time in Timeout should be their age in minutes or twice their age in minutes for more severe offenses**. For example, if the child is five years old, the Timeout should be five minutes long (or ten minutes if it was a particularly bad offense). It's often good to get a timer to clearly set the time.

- **A child's time starts when he or she is quiet.** Children should not be allowed to badger you when they are in Timeout. It is a time for them to think about their behavior, and they can't think about it when their mouths are going! If they start to cry, whine, or nag you, simply reset the timer. Say very little: Difficult kids may try to engage you in a fight, but don't take the bait.

- **Don't give in to their protests about being in Timeout**. The first few times you use this method, your child may become extremely upset. Expect it. But *know* you're going to follow through! In unusual situations, a child may cry, fight, or whine for several hours. The child believes if he or she irritates you enough, then you'll give in to their tantrum. Whatever you do, do your best to hang in there. Simply repeat: "Your time starts when you are quiet," and nothing else. If you go for two hours the first time and hold firm, it's likely the next time will be only an hour, then a half hour, then pretty soon the child will go to Timeout without a fuss. The first time you use Timeout, don't do it when you're in a hurry to go somewhere. Be sure to leave yourself enough time to be able to do it right.

- If the child refuses to stay in Timeout, you have several choices.

(1) You can tell the child that he or she will get two spankings on their buttocks for leaving Timeout. (Make sure you're in control of yourself before you use this method.)

(2) You can take away points or chips if they are on a token system.

(3) You can ground them from activities they enjoy.

- In order for the child to get out of Timeout he or she must promise to do the thing they were asked to do and apologize for not doing it the first time they were asked. If the child refuses to do it, they remain in Timeout until they do. It's very important to give the child the message that *you're serious and that you mean what you say!* If the child can't do what was asked or they broke a rule such as "No hitting," the child must promise not to do it again. The apology your child gives you must be sincere. It's important that we teach children the value of "conscience" and feeling sorry when they do things that are wrong.

- If the child is bothered or teased by a sibling while he or she is in Timeout, have the sibling take the child's place in Timeout. This is a very effective technique in keeping the other kids from further inflaming the situation.

For teenagers, it is more effective and less humiliating to use "response cost" methods. When they break a rule or fail to comply with a request, the negative "response" costs them something important to them, such as privileges, money, phone time, going out on the weekends, etc. Make sure the consequence fits the crime. I've treated some teenagers who were grounded for the summer. By July they became depressed.

Make discipline a time for teaching and reshaping behavior.

FAMILY EFFECTIVENESS STRATEGIES

Families often fall victim to undiagnosed or untreated ADD. Involving the whole family in treatment is often essential for a healthy outcome. Here are some important family treatment issues to consider.

Screen Other Family Members for ADD

ADD usually has genetic underpinnings. When one member has ADD, it is likely that another person may have it as well. Trying to effectively treat one family member while others in the family have untreated ADD invites frustration and failure. It is helpful to do some screening on every member of the immediate family. I have found that when parents have untreated ADD, they have trouble following through on medication schedules for their children or the parent training suggestions given as part of therapy. When a sibling goes undiagnosed, he or she often sabotages the process by his or her own conflict-seeking behavior.

Communication Issues

Families with one or more persons with ADD often have serious communication issues. These families tend to misinterpret information, react prematurely, or have emotional outbursts over real or imagined slights. It is essential to teach families how to listen, clarify misunderstandings, and avoid mind reading. It is also essential to teach families with one or more ADD members to communicate in a clear, unemotional manner. Emotionality decreases effectiveness in communication.

Calm the Drive Toward Turmoil

As I've mentioned many times now, ADD children, teenagers, and adults are experts at getting others to yell at them. It is essential, therefore, to teach families how to calm volatile situations. Teaching simple breathing techniques to all family members can be very valuable in calming disagreements. Also, the use of family Timeouts can be helpful when a situation starts to escalate. In family Timeouts, everyone in the family goes to a quiet part of the house for a designated period of time (ten to fifteen minutes), whenever voices are raised or someone is losing control. Of course, family Timeouts need to be set up ahead of time if they are going to work in calming difficult situations.

Get Rid of Guilt

Guilt is an issue for many in an ADD family. Resentment, bad feelings, and anger are common in family members. However, parents, spouses, or siblings feel that they are not "supposed" to have bad feelings toward people they love. They end up burdened by feelings of guilt. These resentments are normal, given the difficulties in the family. Explaining

the biological nature of ADD to family members often helps them understand the turmoil and have more compassion toward the person with
ADD, while alleviating any guilt they might feel.

Dealing with Embarrassment

Embarrassment is a common feeling among ADD family members. The
outrageous behavior and public displays of turmoil often lead family
members to want to hide from the outside world. Siblings complain that
their friends tease them at school because of their brother's or sister's
behavior; parents are frequently subjected to disapproving looks from
store clerks or other parents who have "perfect" kids. Understanding
ADD helps families deal with the embarrassment.

Good Guy Versus Bad Guy

In families with ADD, people often get a "good guy" versus "bad guy"
label. Children with the disorder often find that their behavior causes
them to be outcasts or "black sheep." Whenever there is trouble, parents,
unconsciously, look to them first. This "good guy" versus "bad guy" perception also applies to parents. A parent who has ADD often gets labeled
by the other parent as emotional, irrational, or troubled. By doing this,
the ADD parent may be stripped of his or her authority, causing resentment and turmoil. Treating the disorder in all family members who have
it, along with teaching the family to share power, is essential to treating
this "good guy" versus "bad guy" phenomenon.

Split Families

Divorce is more common in ADD families. This may be due to many
factors, such as the increased turmoil caused by ADD children or the
interpersonal problems of the ADD adults. Thus, the issues of divorce,
custody, and stepfamilies often need to be addressed in treatment.

Parents of an ADD child often blame each other for the problems
and begin to pull apart. Who wants to work all day and then come home
to a house filled with tension? Who wants to be in a battle zone all day
and then have a spouse come home who doesn't want to hear about all of
the problems of the day? After a while, people get burned out and they

may look elsewhere for some satisfaction in their lives. This dynamic may make them more vulnerable to becoming workaholics or having extramarital affairs.

Because of the higher divorce rate, child custody often becomes an issue. I have done many child custody evaluations in my practice. I look for the parent who is best suited to help the child have a good relationship with both parents, rather than a parent who vilifies the other one.

Stepfamily issues are also very important for many of these families. All members of the families need to be educated about ADD, its effects on families, and its treatment. A positive attitude and open communication between families are also essential to establishing a healthy situation. Considering the ADD person's drive toward turmoil, the child or adult may unconsciously seek conflict, and stepfamilies are often more vulnerable to misunderstandings and tension.

What to Do About Dad

Unfortunately, men are often the last people to admit that there are emotional or family problems. They often delay treatment, for their children or themselves, until there has been a negative effect on self-esteem or functioning. I have heard many men tell me that there is nothing wrong with their son, even though the child may have been expelled from school on numerous occasions three years in a row. A typical comment I hear is "He is just like I was when I was young, and I turned out okay."

Why men are less likely to see emotional or family problems is the subject of many debates. Here are some possibilities:

- many men have trouble verbalizing their feelings
- many men have difficulty getting outside of themselves to see the needs of others
- men tend to be more action oriented than women, and they want to solve the problems themselves
- societal expectations seem to teach men that they can handle problems on their own and they are weak if they seek help

- men aren't allowed to cry or express any negative feelings, so they often do not learn to seek help or talk through their problems.

Whatever the reason, men in ADD families need education about the disorder, and they need to be part of the treatment process if it is to have the best chance of being successful. To this end, it is important for wives, mothers, and the therapist to engage the father in a positive way, encouraging him to see his valuable role in helping the whole family heal. ADD is a family problem and needs the support of everyone to be successful.

It is ineffective (and may turn into a disaster) to blame the man or make him feel like he is the cause of all the problems. Approach him in a positive way and there is likely to be cooperation. Approach him in a negative way and there is likely to be resistance. In general, men are more competitive than women are and they need encouragement, as opposed to badgering, to be helpful. In my experience, once a resistant father becomes part of the treatment, he often takes much more responsibility for healing in the family.

Living with a Partner with ADD

When one or both partners in a marriage (or other living situation) has ADD, it is important to understand the couple dynamics and the treatment process. Here are important issues to consider:

- Have empathy for the ADD person and try to see the world through their eyes of frustration and failure.
- Go to at least some appointments with the doctor together. When I treat adults with ADD, I prefer to see both partners together, at least some of the time, to gather another perspective on the treatment progress. I'm often amazed at the different perspective I get from a person's partner.
- Both partners need clear education on ADD, its genetic roots, how it impacts couples, and its treatment.
- After the initial diagnosis, take a step back from the chronic turmoil that may have been present in the relationship. Look at your relationship from a new perspective and, if need be, try to start over.

- Set up regular times for talking and checking in.
- Keep lists to avoid resentments for chores and tasks not done.
- Assume the best about the other person.
- Set clear goals for each area of your life together and review them on a regular basis. Evaluate whether your behavior is getting you what you want. For example, I want a kind, caring, loving, and supportive relationship with my wife. But, sometimes her behavior irritates me beyond belief. I can impulsively respond in an angry way (which has never been helpful) or I can choose to respond in a loving, helpful way, which more closely matches my goals with her. When you know what you want, you are much more able to make it happen.
- Set clear individual goals and share them with each other. Then look for ways to help the other person reach their own personal goals.
- Avoid stereotyped roles of "caretaker" and "sick one."
- Talk out issues concerning sex in a kind and caring manner.
- Frequently check in with each other during social gatherings, to see the comfort level of each partner.
- Get away alone together on a regular basis. This is especially important when there are ADD kids in the family.
- Work together in parenting children. Children with ADD put a tremendous strain on relationships. This is magnified even further when one of the parents has ADD. See yourselves as partners, not adversaries.
- Praise each other ten times more than you criticize!
- Get rid of the smelly bucket of fish (hurts from the past) that you carry around. Many couples hold on to old hurts and use them to torture each other months to years later. These "smelly fish" are destructive and stink up a relationship. Clean them out of your life.
- If the ADD person refuses to get help, even after repeated encouragement to do so, the partner must consider whether or not to stay in the relationship. Many people with ADD have such a wounded sense of themselves that they refuse to acknowledge any problems, and refuse to accept any help or treatment. At this point, the spouse or lover should not protect or cover for the ADD person, since this

only makes them more dependent and less likely to seek help. In fact, I have seen many occasions where the spouse's leaving the relationship led the ADD person to seek treatment. "Codependency" is not just a term for spouses of alcoholics: it applies to those who protect and help adults with ADD, thus preventing them from having to grow up on their own.

CHAPTER 24

School Strategies

Finding the best classroom and homework strategies are critical to school success for people with ADD. Here are lists of the strategies I give my patients:

THE TEACHER

The teacher is a major determining factor on how well the child or teen will do in school. Choose carefully! Look for a teacher who:

- understands ADD or is at least willing to learn about it
- will keep in regular contact with you about your child's progress
- protects the child's or teen's self-esteem and will not put him down in front of other children or allow other children to make fun of him (Singling out a child sets him or her up to be teased by their peers!)
- has clear and consistent rules, so that the child or teen knows what to expect
- cannot be manipulated easily and who is firm yet kind
- will motivate and encourage
- realizes the tremendous effort these children and teenagers need to put out in order to be average

- has an exciting and stimulating presentation style, using multisensory, teaching methods (visual, auditory, and kinesthetic)
- gives directions slowly and clearly, and is willing to repeat them if necessary and check to see if the ADD child or teen is following them correctly
- will make adaptations as necessary, such as decrease the size of an assignment, allow more time for tasks, allow for the use of calculators, etc.
- will not undermine the treatment you have with your doctor (I've known some uninformed teachers who had the nerve to tell parents, "I'm really opposed to medication.")

I realize that it's unlikely to find a teacher who possesses all of these traits, but look for teachers who have an open mind and know or are willing to learn about ADD. Having a helpful, positive teacher is often the difference between success and failure for your child.

THE LEARNING ENVIRONMENT

Here are some tips I frequently give to parents and teachers to make the environment, pacing, and total school experience more conducive to learning. Parents, I suggest you show this section of the book to your child's teacher. Oftentimes the secret to a successful learning experience for an ADD child is a well-prepared teacher.

- Keep the walls simple: Do not cover every wall with artwork, posters, and pictures. (Visually stimulating material may distract ADD students.)
- Usually it is best to seat the ADD child up front, near the teacher, with his or her back to the rest of the students, away from the door; this decreases distractions.
- Reduce or minimize distractions (both audio and visual): Do not place an ADD student near the air conditioner, heater, high traffic areas, doors, or windows.

- Make earphones available to allow children to decrease auditory distractions.
- Allow for cooling-off periods when the student (or teacher) becomes upset.
- Use written, displayed rules in the classroom.
- Surround ADD students with "good role models."
- Encourage cooperative and collaborative learning, and give the non-ADD students praise and reinforcement for helping out.
- Help the ADD student feel comfortable seeking help. Many of these students won't ask questions for fear of appearing stupid to their peers, and they need to be "brought out" and encouraged.
- Most fights and "acting out" behavior at school occurs in the cafeteria because of the noise and confusion. Providing a quiet place for lunch may decrease the number of lunchtime problems for these children.
- ADD children often come in from recess or lunch "wound up." Have the entire class walk around the room, then pretend to be palm trees swaying in the breeze. "How slowly can you sway?" is a calming-down exercise that will help start the late-morning or -afternoon session off right.
- If lines are a problem for the child, place him or her at the end of the line where people will not be brushing up against their body: many of these kids are sensitive to touch.

Pacing
- Adjust time for completion of projects.
- Allow frequent breaks and vary activities often.
- Omit assignments requiring copying in a timed situation.
- Give only one assignment at a time.

Increasing Attentiveness
- Pause after a question and look at different students before calling on anyone to answer.
- Alert students that you are going to ask a question (e.g., "I am going to call on someone soon—I don't know who yet.").

- Encourage students to look at the student who is answering.
- Create a level of uncertainty that requires more than passive receptivity (e.g., "What do you think will happen next?").
- If a teacher sees a student's attention wandering, call his name and ask a simple question he can answer.
- Use "attention recording sheets" for self-monitoring: The student marks a plus each time he realizes he has been paying attention and a minus each time he realizes his mind has wandered.
- Have students record time taken to complete tasks (e.g., note starting time at the top of the page and ending time at the bottom; actual time is not important, but the process of self-monitoring is crucial). A watch with a stopwatch and an alarm can be very helpful.
- Have students grade their own papers and tests. This instills a habit of reviewing their own work.
- Use nonverbal or secret cues to keep the child on track.

Presentation of Subject Matter

- Emphasize teaching approach according to learning style of student (audio/ visual/ tactile/ multisensory).
- Increase class participation in lectures.
- Make the material highly interactive, interesting, novel, and stimulating.
- Foster individual or small group discussions.
- Provide taped lectures for replay.
- Use demonstrations to illustrate points.
- Utilize "hands-on" activities.
- Emphasize critical information: teach "The Big Picture."
- Preview new concepts and vocabulary at the beginning of the lesson and highlight them again at the end of the lesson to reinforce learning.
- Use advanced organizers.
- Use computers to help present material.
- Provide visual clues.
- Maintain good eye contact.
- Present more difficult lessons early in the day: Children and teens with ADD fatigue more easily than others; also, their medication

often wears off in the late morning (if they are taking the regular form of Ritalin or Dexedrine).

- Make auxiliary materials available
  1. taped texts
  2. highlighted texts/study guides
  3. supplementary materials as needed
  4. note taking assistance; copies of notes from excellent students
  5. typed notes from the teacher
  6. calculators or computer word processors
  7. adapted or simplified texts
  8. graph paper for math problems, handwriting, etc.

Assignments

- Give directions in small, distinct steps.
- Allow copying from paper or book.
- Use written backup for oral instructions.
- Lower reading level of assignment if necessary.
- Adjust length of assignment.
- Change format of assignments to best fit need of child.
- Give assignments in chunks, or a series of smaller assignments; this is especially helpful for longer projects.
- Reduce pencil and paper tasks.
- Read directions/worksheets to students.
- Give oral/visual clues or prompting.
- Allow assignments to be typed or dictated.
- Adapt worksheets/packets.
- Maintain an assignment notebook.
- Avoid penalizing for spelling errors.
- Encourage the use of dictation or word processing for those with writing difficulties.
- For people with visual processing problems, you may have them read their material into a tape recorder and then listen to the material over and over.

Reinforcement and Follow-Through

- Use reward systems for positive behavior.
- Use concrete rewards.
- Check often for understanding and review.
- Request parental reinforcement if it is a positive experience for the student and parent.
- Have the student repeat the instructions.
- Make/use vocabulary files.
- Teach study skills.
- Teach organizational skills, and supervise their implementation on a regular basis.
- Use study sheets to organize material.
- Reinforce long-term assignment timeliness (cut into short chunks).
- Use behavioral contracts/daily or weekly report cards.
- Arrange for tutoring.
- Have regular conferences with student and parents, emphasizing the positive as well as giving feedback on the negative.

Testing Adaptations

- Give some tests orally (some students need most tests orally due to other learning disabilities).
- Have someone read the test to the student if there are reading problems.
- Reduce the reading level of the test if necessary.
- Adjust time for test completion.
- Short answer/multiple choice questions are best for many ADD students.
- Shorten the length of test.
- Test for knowledge, not attention span.

Grading

- Modify weights of examination.
- Give extra credits for projects.
- Credit for appropriate class participation.

- Increase or eliminate time limits.
- Shorten length of exams.

Encourage Questions

- Take time to encourage the child or teen to ask questions when he or she feels confused or lost.
- Establish a positive feeling about asking questions. Most students do not ask questions for fear of appearing stupid. If they can overcome this barrier, it will serve them well for the rest of their academic career.
- Praise the child for asking appropriate questions.

Discipline

- "Firm and kind" are the words to remember.
- When you say something, mean it; and be willing to back it up, but in a kind, caring tone.
- Be very careful not to discipline a child when their misbehavior is the result of confusion or misunderstanding instructions.
- Use discipline for teaching, not punishment.
- Never discipline a child when you feel you're out of control.
- Show disapproval of the behavior, not the child.
- Stay calm and unemotional. (Remember, ADD children are often trying to get a rise out of you!)
- Have well-thought-out consequences to certain behaviors ahead of time. (Anticipation is the key to success).
- Focus 90 percent of your efforts with the child on noticing behavior you like, to set a positive tone.
- Have frequent contact with the parents. (They need to be allied with you if discipline is going to be effective.)

Finger Agnosia

"Finger agnosia" is a term for students who struggle with the mechanics of writing. When they try to write, their mind often goes blank. This is very common in people with ADD and occurs in part because the person has to concentrate so hard on the actual physical act of writing that they forget or are unable to formulate what they want to write.

Common symptoms of finger agnosia include:

- messy handwriting
- trouble getting thoughts from the brain to the paper
- staring at writing assignments for long periods of time
- writing sentences that don't make sense
- frequent spelling and grammatical errors
- many erasures and corrections
- difficulty with timed writing assignments
- printing rather than writing in cursive.

Here are some helpful suggestions for dealing with finger agnosia:

- Allow the student to print as often as possible. (For many students it's easier and uses less effort.)
- Encourage early use of typing and computer word processing programs. (Mavis Beacon Teaches Typing is an excellent computer typing program for children and teens.)
- Try out different types of pens and pencils to see which ones work best. Some are easier to use than others.
- Break down assignments and long reports into pieces, and work on them over time, rather than all at once (such as on the night before they are due).
- Before an actual writing project is done, encourage students to write an outline of the assignment to help keep them on track.
- Encourage students to write down their ideas before worrying about spelling/grammar.
- If it helps, have students dictate their answers or reports first. This often helps them add ideas and substance to the article that would not have been present through writing alone.
- Use a binder/organizer to keep written assignments together.
- Modify writing workloads at work and school as needed.
- Avoid timed situations; give tests orally if necessary.
- Avoid having other students grade the work, as this may set up embarrassment and teasing.

Homework

Here are some suggestions for taking the nightmare out of homework:

- Provide a "special" quiet spot without distractions in which to do homework.
- Break assignments into short segments of about fifteen to twenty minutes; set a timer to structure work periods.
- Intersperse physical activity between segments.
- Check assignment sheets and notebooks on a regular basis.
- Continually work on good communication between home and school.
- Reward positive homework behavior.
- If problems continue, use a daily report system to ensure compliance.

Useless and/or Harmful Strategies

- Tell the child or teen to try harder. (The harder they try, the worse it gets.)
- Lecture a student about showing his "true" ability.
- Notice only the negative.
- Compare the student to other students.

DAILY PROGRESS NOTE (DPN)

Supervision is the key to helping students with ADD or other students who are having difficulty adapting to the rigors of school. They often have not developed the internal discipline to be successful day-to-day at school and with their homework. I use this system for both children and teenagers. Even though teenagers may balk at this system, many teens in my practice have used it very successfully. I'm convinced that many students have graduated from high school because we kept them on track with this system! ADD students tend to do much better if they know someone is watching.

Directions

Every school day the child or teen is to bring the Daily Progress Note to school for the teacher or teachers to fill out (at the end of the day if there is only one teacher, at the end of each class for those who have multiple teachers). The teacher (or teachers) rates the student on a scale of 1 to 5 (1 = best, 5 = worst) in four different areas: homework, class participation, class work, and peer interactions. After rating the child in each area, the teacher then puts his or her initials at the bottom of the form. (It is important to emphasize to the teacher the importance of giving an accurate assessment. Some teachers give out "good" marks just to be nice and then put the real grades down on the report card, shocking the student and parents.)

At the end of the day, the child or teen brings the DPN home. This note provides the student, parents, and teacher with immediate feedback on performance and helps everyone track progress throughout the year. Good performance is noticed and reinforced. Mediocre or poor performance is observed and necessary corrective measures can be put into place. When the child or teen brings the DPN home, it is helpful if parents first look for something they like. (Too many parents only notice the negative.) If the child or teen's marks are particularly poor, the parents need to question the reasons behind the difficulties of the day.

After the discussion, the parent assigns points for the day.

Here is a sample point system:

1 = 5 points
2 = 2 points
3 = 1 point
4 and 5 = 0 points

In the system listed above (for students with one teacher a day), there is a total of 20 possible points that the child can earn (a score of 1 [5 points] multiplied by 4 areas = 20 points).

The points are then spent in two different ways; one, on daily wants and needs, the other for future privileges. Earning points for daily wants and needs is significant, as these reinforce and discipline behavior on a more immediate basis. To do this, the parent and child make up a list of the things he or she likes to do on a daily basis, such as watching television, playing outside, having a friend over, playing a video game, talking on the telephone, etc. Half of the possible points (10 in the example above) should be spent on daily privileges. This lets the child know that he or she can't just blow a day at school and expect everything to be okay at home. For example, points needed for daily wants may be as followed

2 = 1/2 hour of television
2 = 1 hour of playing outside
3 = having a friend over for an hour
2 = playing a video game
3 = 1/2 hour of telephone privilege

The other half of their points can be saved for special treats and privileges as they earn enough points (such as a special toy, a trip to their favorite restaurant, having a friend spend the night, or being able to stay up past their bedtime). It is important to make up a wish list of the things the child or teen is willing to work for. The child or teen needs to develop this list in order to more fully buy into this program.

In some cases, children will intentionally lose their DPN or forget to have their teacher sign it if their performance that day was poor. In the case where the child claims to have lost the DPN or they say that the teacher didn't fill it out, they lose all of their points for the day (or portion of points if multiple teachers are involved). The child or teen must take responsibility! On a day where the child earns little or no points for various privileges, the child is to be encouraged to do better the next day and he or she is simply allowed to read books or play in his or her room.

Almost all children find this system to be very rewarding after they have used it for several days. Some children refuse to participate initially, but if the parents persist, the child will adapt. One of the advantages of this system is that some children become "miserly" with their points and will often give up watching television and playing video games to save points for other things they are interested in. In addition, many begin to develop a more positive attitude toward school because of their ability to earn extra privileges for performing well in school.

Some parents have asked me if the DPN does not single out the child for teasing from peers. I have rarely found this to be the case. In fact, this helps the child to modify their behavior in school, which in turns helps their interactions with peers.

Daily Progress Note

Name: _____ Date: _____

Please rate this child/teen in each of the areas listed below as to how he/she performed in school today, using ratings of 1 to 5. (1 = excellent; 2 = good; 3 = fair; 4 = poor; 5 = terrible or did not do the work.

Class Periods

Subjects	1	2	3	4	5	6	7
Homework	☐	☐	☐	☐	☐	☐	☐
Class Participation	☐	☐	☐	☐	☐	☐	☐
Class Work	☐	☐	☐	☐	☐	☐	☐
Peer Interactions	☐	☐	☐	☐	☐	☐	☐
Teacher's Initials	☐	☐	☐	☐	☐	☐	☐

GET SCHOOL RESOURCES INVOLVED EARLY

Under the law (PL 94-142), all students are entitled to an educational setting in which they can learn. If they are handicapped, the school system must make proper modifications so that they can receive an education. As you have seen, ADD often handicaps a child or teen from taking advantage of education. Due to a lack of funding and personnel, however, many schools overlook children with ADD and learning problems unless they are forced to take action. Parents need to be the prime force that gets the child appropriate help.

Parents need to *advocate* for their children and not just rely on the overworked principal, counselor, or school psychologist. To that end, parents must be educated on ADD and know the proper school interventions. I often tell my parents that they are the ones who need to intervene when things are not going well at school. The squeaky wheel gets the grease! Don't give in to a school administrator who tries to intimidate or condescend to you!

If you are not the "assertive type," consider obtaining a school advocate for your child. A school advocate is someone who has experience in dealing with the school system to ensure the child gets all the help he or she needs. To get the name of an advocate in your area, contact the local chapter of CHADD (a national support group for parents of children with ADD, with local chapters) or look online.

Most school systems are willing to test preschool children if there is a suspected learning or speech problem. Contact your local school counselor or principal for more information on special testing. The earlier you address problems, the more hope there is for successful interventions.

CHAPTER 25

Sleep Strategies for Getting Up and Going to Bed

Eva was a thirty-eight-year-old government employee who had significant problems getting up in the morning. When she first came to see me she had just been put on probation for being chronically late to work. She was very frustrated because she loved her job, but felt so sleepy in the mornings that she slept through four alarms. She was so scared that she actually went out and bought a siren to get her up in the morning. Even though that helped her, she had made all of her neighbors mad at her, and now she was threatened with eviction from her condominium.

Getting up in the morning and going to sleep at night are frequently significant problems for people with ADD. Sleep-cycle problems can interfere with relationships, work, school, and overall energy level. Chronic sleep deprivation makes ADD worse.

GETTING UP

Mornings are difficult for many people with ADD. Here are some common statements people with ADD say as they're trying to get out of bed:

"Later . . ."

"Just a few more minutes."

"I'll get up in a little bit."

"Leave me alone."

"My alarm is set" (even though it already went off).

"I'm too tired to get up."

"Okay, I'm up" (only to lie back down for several hours).

Many people with ADD feel very groggy or fuzzy-headed in the morning. The harder they try to get out of bed, the worse it gets. One teenager I know had such a hard time getting out of bed that she almost got fired from her summer job. Her boss told her if she was late one more time she was gone. She had three alarm clocks and she had two of her friends call her in the morning. Many high school students are frequently late for school because of the trouble getting up. Adults with ADD also have this problem. Have you ever heard of adults who say that they have to have a couple of cups of coffee in the morning to get going? Coffee contains the stimulant caffeine. (Stimulants are common treatment for ADD.)

Parents complain that they have to wake up ADD children and teen-agers three, four, five, six, even ten times before they get out of bed. This can cause a lot of family turmoil in the morning. When parents have to tell a child over and over to get out of bed, they can get pretty irritable. They may start yelling, threatening, or using force to get the child mov-ing. Some parents we know use water or ice to help the child or teen get up. The morning grogginess causes many people with ADD to be chron-ically late, which stresses out everyone in the morning, especially if the parent has to get to work or has other children to get to school.

The child or teen who wakes up to parent hostility starts the day off in a bad mood. It's hard to concentrate in class when you have just been yelled at, threatened, or grounded because you couldn't get out of bed on time. This also leads to other problems. For example, if you can't get up on time, you may miss the bus, get a speeding ticket, end up in the tardy tank, or just cut class so that you're not late again. Starting the day off on the wrong foot can affect your mood and attitude for the whole day.

Many ADD people say that when they get up on their own, they tend to do better than if someone is screaming at them to get out of bed. It often becomes a battle of wills. Both people end up feeling terrible.

Without parents hassling kids, some children and teenagers don't get out of bed until noon, 1:00, 2:00, or even 3:00 P.M.. This can cause serious problems. When kids get up late, they will have trouble going to sleep at night. Getting up late causes a large part of the day to go by without participating in it. Many parents complain that their kids are wasting the day.

HELPFUL HINTS FOR GETTING GOING IN THE A.M.

1. Go to bed at a reasonable time. (See bedtime suggestions below.)
2. Set the alarm clock to play the kind of music that gets the person going. (Some people like fast rock music to wake them up, others like rap, some even like country music.) Try different forms of music to see what works best.
3. Keep the alarm clock (or clocks) across the room so that the person has to get out of bed to turn it off. Don't have the kind of alarm that turns itself off after thirty seconds. Have one that keeps going, and going, and going.
4. Take your medicine a half hour before you're supposed to get out of bed. Keep it by the bed with a glass of water. Set two alarms: One to take your medicine and one to get up.
5. Have something for the ADD person to do that motivates him or her in the morning. Sometimes having a girlfriend or boyfriend call you can be great motivation. Some people enjoy working out with weights in the morning as a way to get their bodies (and brains) feeling alive.
6. Stay away from early classes and early morning jobs if possible. In college, many of my patients don't start class until after 10:00 A.M. Being late irritates teachers and bosses, which is the last thing someone wants to do if he or she want to do well in school or in a job!
7. Watch the body's own cycle. Some people are good in the morning and some later on. Fit your schedule to your body's rhythms.

GOING TO BED

Many people with ADD have sleep problems. Some "go and go" all day until they drop from exhaustion. Others have difficulty getting asleep, or they wake up frequently throughout the night. Some are even hyper in their sleep and constantly on the move. Getting a restful night's sleep helps you feel calmer in the morning. After a poor night's sleep, the ADD person has even more trouble awakening.

Here are some of the things people with ADD have said about their sleep problems:

"I have to count sheep to get to sleep, but the stupid sheep are always talking to me."

"When I try to get to sleep, all kinds of different thoughts come into my mind. It feels like my mind spins when I try to calm it down."

"I feel so restless at night. It's hard to settle down, even though I'm tired."

"The worries from the day go over and over in my head. I just can't shut my brain down."

"I have to sleep with a fan to drown out my thoughts. I need noise to calm down."

Sleep disturbances can cause many other problems, in addition to the obvious problems of difficulty waking up and morning grogginess. If it is hard to settle down at night, it might make parents angry, because they know too well about the morning problems. Not getting enough sleep continues the cycle of feeling tired and wanting to sleep during the day.

One teenager I know had such trouble sleeping that he could never go to bed before three o'clock in the morning. This caused terrible problems: He couldn't get up in the morning and had to drop out of school. This caused him to feel isolated from other people his age. He even went to the Stanford University Sleep Center for help with his problem. In the end, medication was needed to help his sleep cycle.

Doctors aren't sure why people with ADD have more sleep problems. Some doctors think it has to do with serotonin, the neurotransmitter most closely tied to types 3 and 6 ADD. However, we all depend on serotonin to fall asleep, and when there is not enough of it, getting to sleep can be an awful chore.

THIRTEEN WAYS TO GET TO SLEEP

Here are thirteen ways to make it easier to go to sleep. No one suggestion will work for everyone, but keep trying new tactics until you find what works for your situation:

1. Don't watch television one to two hours before bedtime, especially any program that may be overstimulating (i.e., the shows you most like). This includes news programs, as people with ADD tend to ruminate on the bad things that happened that day in their own world and the world at large.
2. Stimulating, active play such as wrestling, tickling, teasing, etc., should be eliminated for one to two hours before bedtime. Quiet activities such as reading, drawing, or writing are more helpful in the hours before bedtime.
3. Some people try to read themselves to sleep. This can be helpful. But read boring books. If you read action-packed thrillers or horror stories you are not likely to drift off into peaceful never-never land.
4. Try a warm, quiet bath.
5. A bedtime back rub in bed may be soothing. Starting from the neck and working down in slow, rhythmic strokes can be very relaxing. Some children and teens say that a foot massage is particularly helpful (although it may be hard to find someone to give a teen a foot massage if they haven't showered or taken a bath before bed).
6. Soft, slow music often helps people drift off to sleep. Instrumental music, as opposed to vocal, seems to be the most helpful. Some people with ADD say that they need fast music in order to block out their thoughts. Use what works.
7. Nature-sounds tapes (rain, thunder, ocean, rivers) can be very helpful. Others like the sound of fans.
8. Some people with ADD say that restrictive bedding is helpful, such as a sleeping bag or being wrapped tightly in blankets.
9. A mixture of warm milk, a teaspoon of vanilla (not imitation vanilla, the real stuff), and a teaspoon of sugar can be very helpful. This increases serotonin to your brain and helps you sleep.

10. We make hypnosis and guided imagery audios to help. These can be so powerful.

11. Learn self-hypnosis. Self-hypnosis can be a powerful tool for many different reasons, including sleep. Here's a quick self-hypnosis course:

     Focus your eyes on a spot and count slowly to twenty. . . . Let your eyes feel heavy as you count, and close them when you get to twenty.

     Take three or four very slow, deep breaths.

     Tighten the muscles in your arms and legs and then let them relax.

     Imagine yourself walking down a staircase while you count backwards from ten. (This will give you the feeling of "going down" or becoming sleepy.)

     With all of your senses (sight, touch, hearing, taste, smell) imagine a very sleepy scene, such as by a fire in a mountain cabin or in a sleeping bag at the beach.

12. Seek sleep control therapy. Here are the tips many sleep experts give to chronic insomniacs to help them get to sleep on a regular basis.

     Go to bed only when sleepy.

     Use the bed and bedroom only for sleep.

     Get out of bed and go into another room when you are unable to fall asleep or return to sleep easily, and return to bed only when sleepy.

     Maintain a regular rise time in the morning regardless of sleep duration the previous night.

     Avoid daytime naps.

13. I often use our Restful Sleep formula (with regular and slow release melatonin, magnesium, valerian, and GABA) to help quiet the ADD busy mind.

     Getting up and going to sleep can hinder the success of a person with ADD. Use the techniques in this chapter to help. Be persistent. If one technique doesn't work for you, don't give up: Try others.

CHAPTER 26

Killing ADD ANTs

Thinking Skills for
Overcoming Past Trauma,
Fear, and Failure

C hildren, teens, and adults with ADD often develop erroneous thought patterns, based on the numerous failures they have experienced in their lives. It often helps to investigate the way an ADD person thinks and then teach them to correct any erroneous thought patterns.

Here are some examples of common negative thoughts:

"I'm a terrible student."
"I'm always messing things up."
"No one ever wants to be with me."
"Anybody could have done that. I'm not so special."
"The teacher (or boss) doesn't like me."
"I will fail at this."
"I feel you don't love me."
"I should do better."
"I'm so stupid."

These thoughts severely limit a person's ability to enjoy his or her life. How people think "moment by moment" has a huge impact on how they feel and how they behave. Negative thoughts often drive difficult behaviors and cause people to have problems with their self-esteem. Hopeful thoughts, on the other hand, influence positive behaviors and lead people to feel good about themselves and be more effective in their day-to-day lives.

Most ADD children, teens, and adults have lots of negative thoughts. These thoughts come from many sources. Some of the negative thoughts come from what other people have told them about themselves (i.e., "You're no good! Why can't you ever listen? What's the matter with you? You make me crazy!"). Other negative thoughts originate from experiences where the person is continually frustrated, either at home, school, or work. They begin to think thoughts such as, "I'm stupid. I can't ever do anything right. It will never work out for me."

In many ways, our brain works like a computer. When a person receives negative INPUT about themselves, they STORE it in their subconscious mind, and the input becomes EXPRESSED as negative thoughts, feelings, or behaviors. Unless people are taught how to talk back to these harmful thoughts and messages, they believe them unconditionally. This is a critical point. Most people never challenge the thoughts that go through their heads. They never even think about their own thoughts. They just believe what they think, even though the thoughts may be very irrational. Their behavior is often based on false assumptions or false ideas.

Unfortunately, many ADD children carry these negative thought patterns into adulthood, causing them to have problems with their moods and behavior. These negative thoughts affect their moods and in many children become the seeds of anxiety or depression later on in life. It's critical to teach people about their thoughts and to teach them to challenge what they think, rather than just accepting blindly the thoughts that go through their heads. Unfortunately, when you're a child, no one teaches you to think much about your thoughts or to challenge the notions that go through your head, even though your thoughts are always with you. Why do we spend so much time teaching kids about diagramming sentences and so little time teaching them how to think clearly? Most people do not understand how important thoughts are, and leave the development of thought patterns to random chance. Did you know that thoughts have actual weight and mass? They are real! They have significant influence on every cell in your body (more detail on this in a little bit). When a person's mind is burdened with many negative thoughts, it affects that person's ability to learn, his or her ability to relate to other people, and his or her physical health. Teaching people with ADD how to control and direct their thoughts in a positive way can be helpful in all areas of their lives.

Here are the actual step-by-step "positive thinking" principles that I use in my psychotherapy practice with children, teens, and adults. When people truly learn these principles, they gain more control over their feelings and their behavior.

Did you know . . . ?

STEP #1: Every time you have a thought your brain releases chemicals. That's how our brain works:

- You have a thought
- your brain releases chemicals
- an electrical transmission goes across your brain, and
- you become aware of what you're thinking.

Thoughts are real and they have a real impact on how you feel and how you behave.

STEP #2: Every time you have a mad thought, an unkind thought, a sad thought, or a cranky thought, your brain releases negative chemicals that make your body feel bad. Whenever you're upset, imagine that your brain releases bubbles with sad or angry faces, looking to cause problems. Think about the last time you were mad. What did you feel inside your body? When most people are mad, their muscles get tense, their heart beats faster, their hands start to sweat, and they may even begin to feel a little dizzy. Your body reacts to every negative thought you have.

STEP #3: Every time you have a good thought, a happy thought, a hopeful thought, or a kind thought, your brain releases chemicals that make your body feel good. Whenever you're happy, imagine that your brain releases bubbles with glad or smiling faces, making you feel good. Think about the last time you had a really happy thought (such as when you got a good grade on a test or cuddled a child). What did you feel inside your body? When most people are happy their muscles relax, their heart beats slower, their hands become dry, and they breathe slower. Your body also reacts to your good thoughts.

STEP #4: Your body reacts to every thought you have! We know this from polygraphs or lie detector tests. During a lie detector test, you are hooked up to equipment which measures:

- hand temperature
- heart rate
- blood pressure
- breathing rate
- muscle tension, and
- how much the hands sweat.

The tester then asks questions, such as, "Did you do that thing?" If you did the bad thing your body is likely to have a "stress" response and it is likely to react in the following ways:

- Your hands will get colder
- your heart will go faster
- your blood pressure will go up
- your breathing gets faster
- your muscles get tight, and
- your hands sweat more.

Almost immediately, the body reacts to what you think, whether you say anything or not.

Now the opposite is also true. If you did not do what they are asking you about, it is likely that your body will experience a "relaxation" response and react in the following ways:

- Your hands will become warmer
- your heart rate will slow

- your blood pressure will go down
- your breathing will become slower and deeper
- your muscles become more relaxed, and
- your hands become drier.

Again, almost immediately, your body reacts to what you think. This not only happens when you're asked about telling the truth; your body reacts to every thought you have, whether it is about school, friends, family, or anything else.

STEP #5: Thoughts are very powerful! They can make your mind and your body feel good or they can make you feel bad! Every cell in your body is affected by every thought you have. When people get emotionally upset, they actually develop physical symptoms, such as headaches or stomachaches. If you can think about good things you will feel better. It worked for Abraham Lincoln. He had periods of bad depression when he was a child and adult. Some days he didn't even get out of bed. In his later life, however, he learned to treat his bad feelings with laughter. He learned that when he laughed, he felt better.

STEP #6: Unless you think about your thoughts, they are "automatic" or "they just happen." Since they just happen, they are not always correct. Your thoughts do not always tell you the truth. Sometimes they even lie to you. I once knew a boy who thought he was stupid because he didn't do well on tests. When we tested his IQ (intelligence level), however, we discovered that he was close to a genius! You don't have to believe every thought that goes through your head. It's important to think about your thoughts to see if they help you or they hurt you. Unfortunately, if you never challenge your thoughts, you just "believe them" as if they were true.

STEP #7: You can train your thoughts to be positive and hopeful or you can just allow them to be negative and upset you. Once you learn about your thoughts, you can choose to think good thoughts and feel good, or you can choose to think bad thoughts and feel lousy. That's right, it's up to you! You can learn how to change your thoughts and you can learn to change the way you feel.

One way to learn how to change your thoughts is to notice them when they are negative and talk back to them. If you can correct negative thoughts, you take away their power over you. When you just think a negative thought without challenging it, your mind believes it and your body reacts to it.

STEP #8: As I mentioned above, negative thoughts are mostly automatic. They "just happen." I call these thoughts Automatic Negative Thoughts. If you take the first letter from each of these words, it spells the word "ANT." Think of these negative thoughts that invade your mind like ants that bother people at a picnic. One negative thought, like one ant at a picnic, is not a big problem. Two or three negative thoughts, like two or three ants at a picnic, and it's more irritating. Ten or twenty negative thoughts, like ten or twenty ants at a picnic, can cause real problems.

Whenever you notice these automatic negative thoughts (ANTs), you need to crush them or they'll begin to ruin your whole day. One way to crush these ANTs is to write down the negative thought and talk back to it. For example, if you think, *Other kids will laugh at me when I give my speech*, write it down and then write down a positive response—something like *The other kids will like my speech and find it interesting*. When you write down negative thoughts and talk back to them, you take away their power and help yourself feel better.

Some kids tell me they have trouble talking back to these negative thoughts because they feel that they are lying to themselves. Initially they believe that the thoughts that go through their mind are the truth. Remember, thoughts sometimes lie to you. It's important to check them out before you just believe them!

Here are nine different ways that our thoughts lie to us to make situations out to be worse than they really are. Think of these nine ways as different species or types of ANTs (automatic negative thoughts). When you can identify the type of ANT, you begin to take away the power it has over you. I have labeled some of these ANTs as red, because these ANTs are particularly harmful to you. Notice and exterminate ANTs whenever possible.

ANT #1: "All or nothing" thinking. These thoughts happen when you make something out to be all good or all bad. There's nothing in between. You see everything in black or white terms. The thought for children, "There's nothing to do," is an example of this. When children say "There's nothing to do" they feel down and upset, bored, and unmotivated to change the situation. But is, *There's nothing to do,* a rational thought? Of course not: It's just a thought. Even on a day when it's raining outside and children have to stay in, they can probably list twenty things to do if they put their minds to it. But if they never challenge the thought, *There's nothing to do,* they just believe it and spend the rest of the day feeling crummy. Other examples of "all or nothing thinking" include thoughts such as, *I'm the worst ball player in the city* and *If I get an A on this test, I'm a great student, but if I do poorly, then I'm no good at all.*

ANT #2: "Always" thinking. This happens when you think something that happened will "always" repeat itself. For example, if your wife is irritable and she gets upset, you might think to yourself, *She's always yelling at me*, even though she yells only once in a while. But just the thought *She's always yelling at me* is so negative that it makes you feel sad and upset. Whenever you think in words like "always," "never," "no one," "everyone," "every time," "everything," these are examples of "always" thinking. There are many examples of "always" thinking: *No one ever plays with me. Everyone is always picking on me. You never listen to me. You always give her what she wants.* This type of ANT is very common. Watch out for it.

ANT #3 (red ANT): Focusing on the negative. This occurs when your thoughts only see the bad in a situation and ignore any of the good that might happen. For example, if you have to move and you're sad to leave your friends, you don't think of the new places you'll see and the new friends you'll make. It's very important, if you want to keep your mind healthy, to focus on the good parts of your life a lot more than the bad parts. I once helped a child who was depressed. In the beginning, he could only think about the bad things that happened to him. He had recently moved and told me that he would never make new friends (even though he already had several). He thought he would do poorly in his new school (even though he got mostly good grades), and that he would never have any fun (even though he lived near a bay and an amusement park). By focusing on the negative in his new situation, he was making it very hard on himself to adjust to his new home. He would have been much better off if he looked at all the positives in the situation rather than the negatives.

ANT #4 (red ANT): Fortune telling. This is where you predict the worst possible outcome to a situation. For example, before you have to give a speech in front of a class or work meeting, you might say to yourself, *Other people will laugh at me or think I'm stupid.* Just having this thought will make you feel nervous and upset. This is a red ANT because it can do real damage to your chances for feeling good.

I once treated a ten-year-old boy named Kevin who stuttered in class whenever he read out loud. In private he was a wonderful reader, but whenever he started to read in class he thought to himself, *I'm a lousy reader; the other kids will laugh at me.* Because he had these thoughts, he stopped raising his hand to volunteer to read. In fact, this thought made him so upset that he started getting sick before school, and missed nearly a month of school before his mother brought him to see me. He also stopped answering the telephone at home for fear that he would stutter whenever he said hello. When he told me about his thoughts in class and at home, I understood the problem. When you predict that bad things will happen, your mind then often makes them happen: the classic self-fulfilling prophecy. The treatment for Kevin was to get him to replace those negative thoughts and pictures in his head with the image of him being a wonderful reader in class. Learning breathing techniques (we'll cover this later) and being the designated person to answer the telephone at home also helped his confidence. Whenever you're afraid of unreasonable things, such as answering the telephone or reading in class, it is important to face your fears. Otherwise, fears develop power over you. Over the next couple of weeks, Kevin was able to go back to school, and he even volunteered to read. His mother told me that at home he ran to answer the telephone whenever it rang. If you are going to predict anything at all, it is best to predict the best. It will help you feel good and it will help your mind make it happen.

ANT #5 (red ANT): Mind reading. This happens when you believe that you know what another person is thinking when they haven't even told you. Many people do mind reading, and more often than not it gets them into trouble. It is the major reason why people have trouble in relationships. I tell people, "Please don't read my mind; I have enough trouble reading it myself!" You know that you are doing mind reading when you have thoughts such as, "Those people are mad at me. They don't like me. They were talking about me."

I once treated a teenager, Dave, who had this problem so badly that he would hide in clothes racks at the shopping mall so that other kids wouldn't see him. He told me, "If they see me, they'll think I look funny and then they'll want to tease me." He became very nervous around other people because he worried about what others thought of him. He finally realized that other teenagers were more worried about themselves and they really spent little time thinking about him. Avoid reading anyone's mind. You never know what others are thinking.

ANT #6: Thinking with your feelings. This occurs when you believe your negative feelings without ever questioning them. Feelings are very complex, and, as I mentioned above, feelings sometimes lie to you. But many people believe their feelings even though they have no evidence for them. "Thinking with your feelings" thoughts usually start with the words "I feel . . ." For example, "I feel like you don't love me," "I feel stupid," "I feel like a failure," "I feel nobody will ever trust me." Whenever you have a strong negative feeling, check it out. Look for the evidence behind the feeling. Do you have real reasons to feel that way? Or are your feelings based on events or things from the past?

Here's an example: Matt, age ten, had a problem learning and he got expelled from his school for fighting. He felt that he was stupid and that he was a bad boy. When I first met him, I diagnosed ADD and started him on medication. He also went to a new school. He did wonderful! He did so well, in fact, that his old school (which was a better school) was willing to take him back. When his mother told him this good news, he became very upset. He said that he felt that he would fail and have lots of problems. He was letting the "old" feelings from the past mess up his chances for a new start. When he corrected his negative feelings by talking back to them, he was able to return to his old school. He even made the honor roll!

ANT #7: Guilt beatings. Guilt is not a helpful emotion. In fact, guilt often causes you to do those things that you don't want to do. Guilt beatings happen when you think with words like "should," "must," "ought to," or "have to." Here are some examples: *I should be nice to my younger brother. I must never lie. I ought to call my grandmother. I have to do my homework.* Because of human nature, whenever we think that we "must" do something, no matter what it is, we don't want to do it. Remember the story of Adam and Eve: The only restriction that God put on them when he gave them the Garden of Eden was that they shouldn't eat from the Tree of Knowledge. Almost immediately after God told them what they "shouldn't" do, they started to wonder why they shouldn't do it. Well, you know the rest of the story. It is better to replace "guilt beatings" with phrases like *I want to do this . . . It fits my goals to do that . . . It would be helpful to do this. . . .* So in our examples above, it would be helpful to change those phrases to *I want to be nice to my younger brother. It's helpful for me not to lie, because people will trust me. I want to call my grandmother. It's in my best interest to do my homework.*

ANT #8: Labeling. Whenever you attach a negative label to yourself or to someone else, you sabotage your ability to take a clear look at the situation. Some examples of negative labels are "nerd," "jerk," "idiot," "spoiled brat," and "clown." Negative labels are very harmful. Whenever you call yourself or someone else a spoiled brat or an idiot, you lump that person in your mind with all of the "spoiled brats" or "idiots" that you've ever known and you become unable to deal with them in a reasonable way. You begin to expect the worst of them (or yourself). Stay away from negative labels.

ANT #9 (the most poisonous red ANT): Blame. People who ruin their own lives have a strong tendency to blame other people when things go wrong. They take little responsibility for their problems. When something goes wrong at home, school, or work, they try to find someone to blame. They rarely admit their own problems. Typically, you'll hear statements from them like, "It wasn't my fault that . . . ," "That wouldn't have happened if you had . . . ," "How was I supposed to know . . . ," "It's your fault that . . ."

The bottom-line statement goes something like this: "If only you had done something differently, then I wouldn't be in the predicament I'm in. It's your fault, and I'm not responsible."

Blaming others starts early. I have three children. When my youngest, Katie, was eighteen months old she would blame her brother, who was eleven, for any trouble she might be in. Her nickname for him was DiDi, and "Didi did it," even if he wasn't home. One day she spilled a drink at the table while her mother's back was turned. When her mother turned around and saw the mess and asked what had happened, Katie told her that "Didi spilled my drink." When her mother told her that her brother was at a friend's house, Katie persisted in saying that "Didi did it."

Whenever you blame someone else for the problems in your life, you become powerless to change anything. Many kids play the "Blame Game," but it rarely helps them. Stay away from blaming thoughts and take personal responsibility to change the problems you have.

SUMMARY OF ANT TYPES:

1. "All or nothing" thinking: thoughts that are all good or all bad.
2. "Always" thinking: thinking in words like *always, never, no one, everyone, every time, everything*.
3. Focusing on the negative: only seeing the bad in a situation.

4. Fortune telling: predicting the worst possible outcome to a situation with little or no evidence for it.

5. Mind reading: believing that you know what another person is thinking even though they haven't told you.

6. Thinking with your feelings: believing negative feelings without ever questioning them.

7. Guilt beatings: thinking in words like *should, must, ought,* or *have to.*

8. Labeling: attaching a negative label to yourself or to someone else.

9. Blame: blaming someone else for the problems you have.

Whenever you notice an ANT entering your mind, train yourself to recognize it and write it down. When you write down automatic negative thoughts (ANTs) and talk back to them, you begin to take away their power and gain control over your moods.

Here are some examples of ways to kill these ANTs:

ANT	Species of ANT	Kill the ANT
There's nothing to do.	"all or nothing"	There are probably lots of things to do if I think about it for a little while.
No one ever plays with me.	"always" thinking	That's silly. I have played with lots of kids in my life.
The boss doesn't like me.	mind reading	I don't know that. Maybe she's just having a bad day. Bosses are people too.
The whole class will laugh at me.	fortune telling	I don't know that. Maybe they'll really like my speech.
I'm stupid.	labeling	Sometimes I do things that aren't too smart, but I'm not stupid.
It's my wife's fault.	blame	I need to look at my part of the problem and look for ways I can make the situation better.

Your thoughts and the thoughts of your children matter. Teach them to be positive and it will benefit their mind and their bodies. Take time to teach yourself and your kids how to think positive and feel good.

CHAPTER 27

Focused Breathing

The Immediate ADD Salve

Temper problems, anxiety, impulsivity, rest-lessness, insomnia, and lack of focus are very common problems in people with ADD. I have found that a very simple biofeedback breathing technique helps to combat these problems. It is so simple, in fact, that many of you will be skeptical in how helpful it could be and not use it. Big mistake. Let me tell you why.

Like brain activity, breathing is also involved in everything you do. Breathing is essential to life. The purpose of breathing is to get oxygen from the air into your body and to blow off waste products such as carbon dioxide. Every cell in your body needs oxygen in order to function properly. Brain cells are particularly sensitive to oxygen, as they start to die within four minutes when they are deprived of oxygen. Slight changes in oxygen content in the brain can alter the way a person feels and behaves. When a person gets angry, his or her breathing pattern changes almost immediately. His or her breathing becomes more shallow and the rate increases significantly (see diagram below). This breathing pattern is inefficient and the oxygen content in the angry person's blood is lowered. Subsequently, there is less oxygen available to a person's brain and they may become more irritable, impulsive, and confused, causing him or her to make bad decisions, such as to yell, threaten, or hit another person.

To correct this negative breathing pattern, I teach my patients to become experts at breathing slowly and deeply, mostly with their bellies.

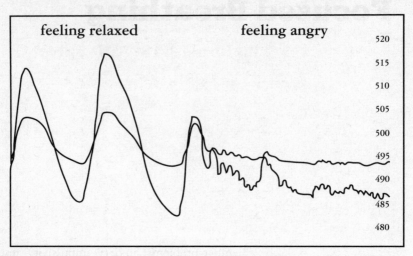

feeling relaxed   feeling angry

520
515
510
505
500
495
490
485
480

Breathing Diagram: The large waveform is a measurement by a gauge attached around the belly during abdominal or belly breathing; the smaller waveform is a measurement by a gauge attached around the upper chest during chest breathing. At rest, this person breathes mostly with his belly (a good pattern), but when he thinks about an angry situation his breathing pattern deteriorates, markedly decreasing the oxygen to his brain (common to anger outbursts). No wonder people who have anger outbursts often seem irrational!

In my office I have some very sophisticated biofeedback equipment that uses strain gauges to measure breathing activity. I place one gauge around a person's chest and a second one around her belly. The biofeedback equipment then measures the movement of the chest and belly as the person breathes in and out. Many people, especially men, breathe exclusively with their chests, which is an inefficient way to breathe. If you watch a baby or a puppy breathe, you notice that they breathe almost solely with their bellies. That is the most efficient way to breathe. If you expand your belly when you breathe in, it allows room for your lungs to inflate downward, increasing the amount of air available to your body. I teach patients to breathe with their bellies by watching their pattern on the computer screen. In twenty to thirty minutes, most people can learn how to change their breathing patterns, which relaxes them and gives them better control over how they feel and behave.

To do this at home, lie on your back and place a small book on your belly. When you breathe in, make the book go up, and when you breathe out, make the book go down. Shifting the energy of breathing lower in your body will help you feel more relaxed and in better control of yourself.

You can use this breathing technique to help you be more focused and less anxious and have better control over your temper. It is easy to learn and it can also be applied to help with the sleep problems so common in ADD.

Here's an example of how helpful this technique can be. Twenty-two-year-old Bart came to see me for ADD symptoms and problems with anxiety and temper. During my first session with him, I noticed that he talked fast and breathed in a shallow, quick manner. One of my recommendations was for Bart to do three sessions of breathing biofeedback. He was amazed at how easy this form of breathing was and how relaxed he could make himself in a short period of time. He noted that his level of anxiety improved and he had better control of his temper.

Ever since I learned this technique fifteen years ago, I have used it personally. I use it when I feel anxious, angry, or stressed. It sounds so simple, but breathing is essential to life and when we slow down and become more efficient at it most things seem better.

CHAPTER 28

ADD Coaching

With Master ADD Coach Jane
Massengill M.S.W.

A powerful treatment for many people with ADD is something called "coaching." ADD coaching is a specific set of interventions that help people set and reach their goals in life. It helps develop structure and skills that can reduce problems with focus and procrastination. In this chapter I have asked my good friend, colleague, and ADD coach, Jane Massengill, to help me write a synopsis of ADD coaching. Jane is a licensed clinical social worker and a certified professional coactive coach. Together we will address how a coaching relationship works. We will delineate the responsibilities of both the coach and the client, as well as how someone with ADD can expect to benefit by having an ADD coach.

Although there is a tremendous amount of variety in how people do ADD coaching, at our clinic, the general format looks like this. An initial meeting is scheduled for two to three hours, in person if possible. It can be done over the phone if distance is a factor. The client is given a workbook with numerous tools. This is the beginning: a place to record how they want to create change in their life. Some of the key topics in the workbook include the following: Action List, Habits, Commitments, Time Management, Organization, Goals, Vision, Values, Skills, and Money Management.

During the initial meeting, clients identify several areas that they want to keep as the focus of the work with the coach. They overview where they are in life and begin to identify goals and habits that will move them towards where they want to be. This is also a place where the coaching relationship will be designed. Clients identify how they are best motivated and how they have been most successful in the past.

Here's what we ask:

1. **Be honest**. Honesty is the best policy in coaching—in fact, the only policy! You must be honest with your coach about whether you completed an assignment or tried something you were challenged to. If you don't, you are sabotaging your chances for making the relationship work. In coaching, everything is celebrated, including successes and failures! If you aren't willing to fail, you aren't willing to succeed! Your coach creates a very safe environment where you can be honest about even your most difficult areas.

2. **Give your coach permission to be honest with you**. Sometimes it's hard to hear things about ourselves that other people notice. And yet, that's part of the power of coaching. Your coach must have your full permission to tell you when they notice you are moving away from rather than towards your goals. This is done without judgment and solely for the sake of your learning.

3. **Be willing to work at change**. You have to have a desire to change yourself when you enter a relationship with a coach. You are the one who will be taking action and creating new habits. Therefore, it has to be something that's important for you, not your spouse, your parent, or your employer.

The coaching sessions after the initial meeting generally take place over the phone for thirty minutes a week. Some clients prefer meeting in the office for an hour once a week, or twice a week for fifteen or thirty minutes. Some coaches include a daily check-in period via phone, e-mail, or fax to help with accountability.

To illustrate how powerful coaching can be, we'll take you through someone's real-life coaching experience. . . .

Thomas wanted to work with an ADD coach for help with being more disciplined. He had been diagnosed with ADD about three years before and was not feeling he was doing all that he could to control his symptoms. He owned his own business and was financially successful, but he felt he was poor at keeping commitments and being organized, both personally and professionally. He was very critical of himself, despite his professional achievements. Thomas attributed his financial success to good fortune rather than any intentional effort. He was not convinced that he could re-create this same success anywhere else in his life.

BALANCE

The first thing we looked at was the overall "balance" in Thomas's life. Balance is the way we choose to divide ourselves among the different areas of our life: home, family, work, etc. Although we think of "being in balance" as an equal division among these areas, the truth is that balance is never completely equal. It is always in motion. Stand on one foot and try to balance yourself and you will see that even though you are balanced, you are never completely still. Although clients come to coaching for specific issues, a coach helps them develop the skills to look at their whole life and be able to see how they divide their time. We call this "seeing The Big Picture." The coach's role is always to be looking for whether their client is moving towards or away from balance in his life.

Using a scale from 1 to 10, with 10 being the greatest degree of satisfaction and 1 being the lowest. Thomas's life looked like this:

career: 5
money management: 3
physical health: 3
family and friends: 5
significant other/romance: 5
personal growth: 6
fun and recreation: 6
physical environment: 5

By having a visual tool to help Thomas see The Big Picture, he was able to recognize which areas of his life needed the most attention. He also could see which area, if brought to a 10 first, would have the most impact on the other areas. Physical health was the area that Thomas saw as having the greatest effect on the other areas of his life. When he gets regular exercise, he feels clearer, and more connected to the rest of the world. Ultimately, he will have better relationships with friends and family and more energy to pursue his other goals.

PRIMARY FOCUS

During the initial session, clients are asked to list those things that they want to have as their focus while they are in this coaching relationship. This gives both the coach and the client some clarity about what is expected.

Thomas chose several areas to have as his primary focus of coaching:

1. to create and follow a regular schedule for routines, both personally and professionally
2. to be more in control of rigid thought patterns
3. to better follow through on commitments
4. to create and follow a consistent exercise program.

The coach's role is to hold the focus for the clients in creating a way to get what the clients want. Often a client with ADD will forget why he came to coaching in the first place or why he even wanted to make changes in his life. A coach helps to keep him pointed towards his goals and reminds him, especially when the going gets tough, of what he is trying to create for himself. When a client brings up issues that seem unrelated to his primary focus, the coach helps by asking questions that explore how the current issue may or may not relate to what he wants.

VALUES

Our values are a thumbprint of who we are. They are those things in life that we hold sacred, that would be intolerable to live completely without. Love, family, humor, joy, honesty, and spirituality are examples of values.

When we allow values to be honored in our life, our true self shows up: not who we would like to be, but our unique selves, the selves that appear when we are being authentic in expressing and relating to ourselves and others. Our values are like an arrow, pointing us in the direction of knowing when we are being true to ourselves. They can be turned to when making decisions, when trying to understand interpersonal relationships, and when problems with procrastination occur.

Discovering one's values is a starting point in coaching that gives the client a sense of direction and ownership. During our first meeting, we helped Thomas identify his most important values. We did this through exploring peak moments in his life and looking for times when he felt completely fulfilled and totally alive. We also looked at his biggest arguments and what values were getting squished. The list took shape like this:

1. family
2. freedom
3. integrity/ honesty
4. joy
5. spirituality
6. emotional and physical health
7. humor
8. sensuality
9. service/ contribution

Once we identified values that were important to him, we looked at how much he was honoring these values by the actions in his life. Thomas was pleased to see that the majority of his key values were indeed being given attention. What he needed to focus on more was finding ways to honor his values of family, spirituality, physical health, and integrity. These were used as a springboard for action in the coaching relationship. By the end of the first session, Thomas agreed to take on a daily habit of spending fifteen minutes every evening planning for the next day. He also committed himself to find a place to keep his wallet, which he frequently lost at home. For the longer term, he agreed to begin the process of developing a social schedule with several of his friends. He asked to be held accountable to all these things, to be reviewed on the first call.

GREMLINS

For the first several weeks, Thomas was on a roll, accomplishing most things to which he set out to be held accountable. Then the real change began. Thomas was beginning to hit roadblocks for the bigger areas that he wanted to work on, such as organizing his desk, sticking to a routine, and exercising. He was stuck in a cycle of belief that he was incapable of being able to do these things because of his past performance, his ADD, and his procrastination to make a commitment. It was time to go "gremlin hunting"! The "gremlin" is a concept used in coaching to identify the voice within us that holds us back from being who we want to be. It sabotages our growth and keeps us from taking action. Richard Carson, in his book, *Taming Your Gremlin*, provides a format to help become aware of the gremlin and how to control it. The concept of the gremlin is one of the most powerful tools someone takes away from coaching.

Thomas agreed to "polish his gremlin radar" for the week, simply noticing when it was present. He would notice where in his body his gremlin liked to live, in what situations he was most likely to show up, and what his favorite sayings of sabotage were. Best of all, he could begin to fantasize about how he would like to get rid of him! For someone who values humor, this could be fun!

The following week, Thomas was in amazement about how his gremlin was controlling him! He realized that the tightness in his neck and shoulders were part of his gremlin, telling him to work harder because nobody believed he could keep up. He also began to see that his belief system was being controlled by his gremlin. He heard messages such as, *You can't be organized, You are too old to exercise consistently,* and *Why try to follow a routine? You never stick to anything anyway!*

Thomas developed an imaginary jail to send his gremlin to when he noticed he was acting up as a way of learning to control him. Once the gremlin was aside, Thomas was instructed to ask himself this question: *I've noticed my gremlin has a judgment or an opinion here. What are my choices in this situation?* This gave the control back to Thomas to make his own decisions and not let his gremlin decide for him. We tied his values into his decision-making process, choosing actions that included integrity, spirituality, and family. Thomas's self-esteem started to take off at this point!

VISION

Having an idea of what you want your future to look like is an important part of coaching. Before you can set goals and work towards them, it helps to have a mental picture of what you want to create. The most commonly asked question in coaching is, "What do you want?" Lots of time is spent developing the skill of "metaview," meaning seeing things in The Big Picture. This is an area that tends to be weak for people with ADD, especially the Overfocused subtype. We use metaphors like gardening to help clients get an image of what they want the "landscape" to look like, what type of flowers they want to plant, and what sort of care the garden is going to require. Clients often find that they are spending too much time nurturing a flower they don't even like or studying one part of the garden while not seeing that another section is dying.

For Thomas, this vision started with an assignment to write out his idea of a perfect day, from start to finish. He had full permission to be as creative as he wanted, as long as he completed the task. He faxed it before the next session. We compared his vision of a perfect day to his list of values. When exercise was missing, we looked for what there might be to learn from that. For Thomas, there was a gremlin lurking with his message about not being able to get his body in shape at this age. Once he realized that, Thomas was able to look at his choices and make a commitment to include exercise in his perfect day because of the benefits he knew it would give him both physically and mentally.

Thomas also created a two-year vision for the areas of his life that matched his values. He became very specific about what he wanted his life to look like, including how much he wanted to weigh, what he wanted his office to look like, how often he will take trips with friends and family, and what he wanted his net worth to be. From this, we created a list of goals and prioritized which one would have the biggest impact on his life once completed. We also worked on raising his awareness about The Big Picture of his life. We did this by imagining jumping into a helicopter together and spying on his life to see what we could see from a distance. Thomas's coach gave him the question, "What am I choosing right now?" to ponder for the week and see what he could learn from it.

GOALS

Reaching a goal that you never imagined you could reach is one of the best feelings in the world! Ask anyone who has been told they will never walk again and what they felt like when they took their first step. Wow! Most people come to coaching with fear that they will not be able to be organized or to be successful in a job due to their ADD. They believe that because of their programming, change is impossible. One of the most significant moments for most people in ADD coaching is when they are asked the following question: "Okay, you have ADD. How do you want to *be* with it? How do you want to show up in life, given that you have this? You have some choices here. What do you want?" Once a client sees that they do indeed have some choices about their attitude and the language they use in dealing with their ADD, goals begin to flow naturally.

Breaking things down into baby steps is very helpful in reaching goals. People with ADD tend to have trouble looking at The Big Picture and seeing a path to the goals. There is a feeling of being overwhelmed, sensory overload, and then defeat. In coaching, we teach people how to approach goal setting and then keep them accountable to doing what they say they are going to do. Clients learn to take on a 360-degree view of what it will take to accomplish their goal. They look at the following questions:

What will I have when the goal is accomplished?
What am I saying "yes" to by working toward my goal?
What do I need to say "no" to by working toward my goal?
What resources do I need to obtain or develop?
What habits do I need to have in place?

In the past, what has gotten in the way of obtaining my goal?

What are three things I can do differently from what I have tried in the past?

What is the action I will take on a daily basis that will move me closer towards my goal?

By what date do I wish to accomplish my goal?

For Thomas, we mapped out all the steps that needed to be done to accomplish one particular goal. At the end of his road map, he would have a clean desk at home and at work. He began by looking at what got in his way in the past. Distractions seemed to be the number one problem in both places. He broke the steps of this goal down like this:

1. Review material on organizing for executives.
2. Decide which organizational system I want to choose.
3. Purchase baskets and files needed for desk organizing system.
4. Spend ten minutes a day at my desk to organize materials, standing up! (Keep my attention focused! I will use a timer as an auditory reminder when my time is finished.)
5. Ask my daughter if she wants to spend one hour a week to file materials. I will pay her for this.

Simply having a system in place seemed to reduce procrastination. Thomas also liked the idea of standing as it was something physical he could do to be more in charge of his distractions.

LIFE PURPOSE

A life purpose statement, often referred to as a mission statement, is a way to describe one's intention in life. It is a statement about how you will make a difference on the planet, both in your life and in the lives of others. When clients are living their life with the knowledge of their life purposes, they are living intentionally, not by accident. They are focused on paths with direction.

In coaching, we ask clients this key question: "What needs to change on the inside to create change on the outside?" It isn't just about setting up good systems or structures. Lasting change comes from the understanding of what our life purposes are, who we are, and how we uniquely impact the people around us. Knowing one's purpose is like the battery that drives the motor. Over and over, it drives clients in coaching to look at whether the choices they are making are consistent with The Big Picture of their lives.

Defining Thomas's life purpose was quite meaningful for him. We spent several weeks working on the idea of who he is and how he impacts the world. He was very clear on this in his role as a father and husband, but not so with the rest of his life. Once he took the time to explore it, he began to acknowledge himself for his gifts and talents, while at the same time following the vision of the life he was creating for himself. He began to realize that he wasn't just lucky in how his life was turning out. It was because of who he is in the world, his attitude, his drive, his caring about others. We tapped into the things in life that give him passion, such as community outreach, spending quality time with his kids, and stopping to say hello to a stranger. He started to see how he could make choices that would give him more of a sense of fulfillment and balance in his life.

SKILLS

Skill building is an art. The two most important parts of developing a skill are practice and commitment. During this awkward stage of development, there is usually a period of ups and downs, being excited, testing the waters, retreating because of failure, moving forward with fear, and finally making a commitment to succeed. Most people find relief in knowing that a coaching relationship is a safe place to practice these skills, without worry of being judged or measured. This gives them permission to practice the skills in ways that are unfamiliar to them. For people with ADD, this is refreshing, exciting, and stimulating.

Here are several skills used in ADD coaching:

Awareness

One of the biggest pieces of building any skill is the awareness of when and where to use the skill. Awareness is a common issue for most people with ADD. "Feeling fuzzy" is the way one client describes what gets in the way of making decisions and following routines. Another client calls it his "deer in the headlights" feeling. For him, this is when he is immobile, even with the knowledge of impending disaster. A third person refers to it as "the twirls." "I go from room to room, not even sure why I went there in the first place." In ADD coaching, building one's awareness is imperative to success. The client develops an internal awareness monitor through the coach's use of questions. Questions like, "How do I know when I am fully present?" and "What am I choosing right now?" as well as, "Where is my awareness?" are ways for clients to be reminded of when they are on or off track. We set up systems to help them ask these questions, such as visual or auditory reminders on watches, clocks, computers, etc.

Thomas chose several ways to develop his awareness. First of all, he implemented a system of using timers to keep him on track. He put a timer on his desk at work, on his watch, and in his home office. He used the timer to get him started on a job he didn't feel very motivated to do, like clean his briefcase or pay the bills. Once the timer ran for fifteen minutes, he had the choice to continue or quit. Usually he chose to continue. Getting started was the hardest part for him. Secondly, he used the timers to stay on task and not get too far distracted. For example, when he wanted to surf the Internet at night, he would set the timer for one hour to set boundaries for himself to go to bed. He also developed a system of stickers as a reminder to get present and look at his choices in the moment. He placed the stickers in places where he found himself most often distracted such as on the phone, in his car, his computer screen, and his planner. Thomas had to change the stickers about once a month, otherwise he got used to them and would not see them. He found them helpful in bringing him back to reality when he was daydreaming and reminding him to focus on what was important just then.

Habits

The definition of a habit, according to the *Random House Dictionary* is this: "an acquired behavior pattern regularly followed until it has become almost involuntary." We have come to believe that our habits are a part of our personality and therefore, impossible, or at least gruelingly difficult, to change. And yet, most people come to coaching with a genuine desire to change and get rid of the struggles they experience. A coach—being with you in the journey, and there to pick you up when you fall and cheer you at the finish line—believes that you can change your habits. Although there is an acknowledgment that the symptoms of ADD are difficult, a coach understands that with practice and commitment, change is possible. Coaching is most powerful when the client is committed to the belief that habits can be changed, and that means getting the gremlin out of the way. There are several techniques we use to strengthen this commitment. One is "stepping over the line." The client literally steps over a threshold to symbolize that they are leaving behind what they do not want and "stepping into" a new place where they will take action to get what they do want. We also use a technique called a "yes/no" board. This is a poster board with YES on the left and NO on the right. Clients write out the things in their life that they are saying yes to as well as the things to which they are saying no in order to achieve their goals. For example, saying yes to taking a continuing education class might mean saying no to a regular night out with friends. This tool helps in visualizing what they must give up in order to gain something else. We find that these types of tools aid in memory as well as offer an opportunity to acknowledge consistency or to look at what got in the way of success.

Thomas had daily and weekly habits that he recorded. For most people, habits change throughout the course of coaching. After they achieve the first few, others are added. At the beginning of coaching, Thomas's list included these items:

1. Take fifteen minutes before bed to plan for the next day.
2. Spend ten minutes in some type of spiritual reflection daily.

3. Exercise three times a week.

4. Do something nice for my wife weekly.

As Thomas developed these items to his satisfaction, he would add new things to be tracked. After a year in coaching, his list looked like this:

1. On Sunday night, spend fifteen minutes planning for the week.

2. Exercise daily.

3. Listen to thirty minutes of spiritual music or tapes while commuting, three times a week.

4. Spend one hour of quality time with wife and/or kids daily.

By developing the skills he wished to incorporate into his life, Thomas was able to rearrange his thinking about how he could run his business. Eventually, he made choices that allowed him more time for the things in his life that were the most important to him.

The biggest change in coaching for Thomas was when he honestly believed that he could change his habits. Despite having ADD, he did have some control in his life over his ability to be organized and focused. This was truly a time to be celebrated! It was from this point forward that his energy and momentum took off!

Perspective and Choice

When ADD clients seek out a coach, they are desperate to be relieved of their pain. They feel out of balance and stuck, unsure which way to turn and unsure of their abilities to be able to succeed. One thing that makes coaching so powerful is the questions asked by the coach to help clients look at their life from different perspectives or angles. We often choose the perspective we have for a good reason. We get stuck in believing that there is only one way, based on the experiences we've had or the knowledge we currently hold. For example, one client saw no hope for herself in passing a medical board exam. She had failed on several occasions. From her perspective, that meant she was incapable of ever passing it. After several sessions of exploring her current perspective, the client realized that by not passing the exam, she was validating her feelings about herself as a loser. She recognized that past attempts at test taking did not include all that she could do to pass such as having a study partner and creating a review schedule. Once she saw that her gremlin was the one who actually held her in this perspective, she was able to move forward with zest in her belief that she was indeed a winner and fully capable of taking and passing this exam! Even if she never passed, she gained a perspective about herself that was liberating and gave her a choice to be whoever she wanted to be. The transformation was breathtaking!

In coaching, we are always looking for other perspectives that the clients can choose. "Choice" is an important word here. What makes coaching work is the client's ability to choose what will work for them. Being able to choose gives you a sense of power and fulfillment like nothing else! It takes you out of a role of being a victim and places you in the role of being an "owner" as described by Steve Chandler in his book *Reinventing Yourself.* "Owners create and victims react. Taking ownership is the highest form of focus." When you are intentional in your choices, you are living a life that has clarity and fullness. You are living on purpose, not by accident.

Throughout his course in coaching, Thomas had many opportunities to look at what perspective he was holding and see what other ones he could choose. This is one habit that develops for most clients in coaching. An inner voice pipes in to encourage them to see things from different perspectives—just for the fun of it, if nothing else. A coach might ask how Elmer Fudd would look at this situation or what a blind man might say about it. From this comes a lightness about choice instead of the well-known heaviness that is often experienced. There is also an acknowledgment about the fear that gets in the way of making choices. For Thomas, when this fear got in the way, he was challenged to wear a sticker that said, "I can handle it." In this way, he was creating a mantra for himself that gave him freedom to take risks and make mistakes, all with the greater goal in mind of getting what he wants for himself in life.

THE PROCESS OF THE PATH

As for most people in coaching, there are roadblocks that get hit while they are in the process of change. Many don't even see these blocks because they have become so ingrained in who they are. Our gremlins want us to believe that these blocks are absolutely impossible to move. In coaching, we get right in the face of the roadblocks and try to look at them from as many different perspectives as we can to see what we can learn about them. We even try to experience the feelings that arise when we imagine the worst thing that could happen. Some of the most common roadblocks include fear of failure, fear of success and responsibility, loneliness, rejection, sadness, emptiness, and commitment. We look at the associations clients have with these words and how they hold certain beliefs as the absolute truth about them. By actually experiencing these emotions in coaching sessions, clients begin to see the absurdity of their beliefs and how maintaining the belief only holds them back in life. In this way, they face their fears. The power the roadblock had over them is dissipated.

Coaching invites people to be challenged in a way that holds them in a soft, friendly light. The coach creates an environment where exploration is safe and where curiosity wins out over judgment. No one loses. Risk-taking is celebrated, no matter what the outcome is. It demonstrates that the client is taking action and moving in the direction of their path. This is a tremendous relief for people with ADD who have had what feels like a long list of failures. By breaking through a roadblock that they thought was impossible to move, they develop a greater sense of confidence in their abilities. This in turn gives them momentum to move forward with their goals. Because of the drive for stimulation, once they find a goal that has meaning, they are difficult to stop!

One area in which Thomas got stuck was in his belief that he could not be organized due to his biology of having ADD. Whenever he sat down at his desk, he was overwhelmed by the quantity of papers and the tasks that lay ahead. He would turn off and do something that would distract him from his desk. Often this was getting on the Internet or calling business associates to discuss ideas. But this wasn't getting him what he wanted: a clean desk! So, we explored what feelings come up for Thomas when he sits down at his desk and wants to dive into his work but instead flounders. All he saw was a big black hole. We "got curious" about this hole, visualized jumping in, and enveloped ourselves in what it was like. After several minutes "in the hole," Thomas realized that he had a negative association with perfectionism. In his mind, perfectionism was equal to exposure. If he tried to be organized and orderly, people would discover that he was not as smart as he appeared. They would see that he wasn't a great speller and didn't graduate from the best college. This would negate him in their eyes and consequently, he would lose his business and end up poor and rejected. With the coach's acknowledgment of Thomas's strengths, accomplishments, and values, he was able to see the absurdity of his association with perfectionism and how it impacted his energy to be organized. He became more committed to himself at this point and started to tackle his daily habits with enthusiasm and a belief that he could succeed!

ENDINGS

The length of coaching varies. Clients are asked to make a three-month commitment to the process, primarily to acknowledge that long-term change takes time. For most clients, six months seems to be a minimum. At this writing, Thomas has been in coaching for one year and has recently lengthened the time between sessions to once a month to test his abilities to maintain his habits. Many clients choose to stay in a coaching relationship over time, perhaps talking once or twice a year. Because coaching is primarily done over the phone, distance is not an issue. When someone moves, the relationship does not have to be terminated. It's calming to know that there is always a place to go where you will be accepted for whoever you are, where your failures will be celebrated just as much as your achievements, and where you can be reminded of The Big Picture of your life. Here are some of the comments clients have made about ADD coaching:

"I feel like I lost weight in a whole different way!"
"I am living a life of intention."
"This is more powerful than any therapy I've ever done."

"When someone else believes in you, you start to believe in yourself."
"I feel so much more focused and aware of the choices I make."
"The myths I had about myself being disorganized have disappeared!"
"You aren't just an ADD coach, you are a life coach."

Coaching is about action and learning. Both pieces must be present if coaching is to take place. The best learning occurs when the coach gets out of the way and asks questions that will generate the client's own deductions and intuitions. The client learns not to look to the coach for the answers but rather, looks inside him- or herself. Clients will often say to their coach, "I know what to do. I just don't do it!" This is the basis on which coactive ADD coaching is built. When clients come up with their own answers, they develop a genuine awareness of themselves and their abilities that allows them to acknowledge who they are and the gifts they have. Yes, there is still some frustration with piles and lists, even when the coaching relationship winds down. But what is in its place is an ability to be focused on the things in life that are truly important. The piles may take on less meaning or may be completely under control, depending on what the client values. The important part is that the clients leave the coaching relationship realizing that they have a choice about the piles and how they want to see them. They may have begun to dream of even bigger "piles" to tackle, such as starting a business or going after a career they were always afraid to pursue. This is the exhilarating part of coaching: watching people go headfirst in life, with confidence, in enthusiasm, with passion, and intention.

Picture a world where all "disabilities" are seen as gifts.
Picture a world where everyone has permission to experiment with being
    who they really are, without judgment.
Picture a world where there are no more victims, only owners.
Picture the power of ADD coaching!

In a recent study published in the Journal of Attention Disorders,[xix] researchers studied ADD coaching in a sample of 148 college students over a five-year period, using a method similar to what was described here. Students who received an eight-week coaching program showed significant improvement in their ability to study and learn and on measures of self-esteem and satisfaction with school and work. These results were consistent across different semesters and time of semester, and with a variety of different coaches.

CHAPTER 29

Self-Hypnotic Reprogramming for Success

With Emmett Miller, M.D.,
Author of *Deep Healing: The
Essence of Mind/Body Medicine*

Dr. Miller is a world-renowned expert in the field of hypnosis, cognitive reprogramming, and achievement. He has a private practice in Nevada City and he used to be on staff at Amen Clinics.

PROGRAMMING AND THE HUMAN BRAIN

To some people the idea of "programming" or "reprogramming" sometimes sounds somehow cold and calculating. Science fiction books and movies often portray evil mind-control tyrants as using "programming" to turn susceptible people into robot-like subjects. The truth is that the human brain acquires information and makes decisions based upon the instructions it has been given, just like a computer. And many of the instructions for how to interpret the world and how to react to it were trained into us when we were children, and we had no say over what programs were being implanted. These programs persist as our beliefs. Often, especially for people with ADD, these beliefs, especially about themselves, can be very harmful.

What we see and feel as we confront the challenges of everyday life is dramatically affected by what we believe. A little trick one of our college roommates used to do was to wet his hands, then, while walking behind another student, let out a huge sneeze, flicking the water over the back of the neck and head of his unsuspecting mark. The reaction of the student to what he felt was often dramatic and hilarious. The reaction would have been very different had he realized that someone was just flicking some clean, cold water on the back of his head and neck.

The reaction of a seven-year-old Palestinian child shown a photograph of first an Israeli soldier and then an Arab "freedom fighter" would be very different from the reaction one would expect from a Jewish child of exactly the same age who grew up in Israel. Each child would see one as an ultimate expression of goodness and love and the other as a potential threat. Each would be quite certain of his beliefs, and would feel emotions relevant to those beliefs. In other words, each, because of his beliefs, would have a tremendously different behavior in response to the pictures, never recognizing how utterly arbitrary the belief with which he interpreted these pictures was, for their beliefs had simply been "programmed" into their minds by the families and cultures that had formed their thinking apparatus.

In an equally profound way, the programming each of us has received has served to convince us that certain of our beliefs about the world are "true," even though they may become completely arbitrary. For example, if a talented, attractive student tries out for the school play, but he believes that he is not very attractive or talented, he has little chance of getting the part. Many of our convictions about ourselves—whether we feel like a success or failure, whether we feel lucky or unlucky, whether the glass is half empty or half full—are simply just beliefs, and can all be changed. If they are not changed, they become self-fulfilling prophecies. Many people with ADD have been programmed into believing they can't change the problems that are holding them back from being successful in their lives. This negative belief system is one of the first things that must change before you can have true success in your life. A person with ADD often finds himself experiencing failure: failure to perform to his highest potential, failure to be able to sit still, failure to concentrate well, failure to organize well, failure to avoid distraction and addictive tendencies. This can lead to intense feelings of shame, guilt, fear, anxiety, and anger. Your attitudes about yourself or the things that people said to you in the past created an internal set of beliefs that hold you back. If you can recognize that these thoughts are just beliefs and that they belong to you, you can change them and convert them into positive beliefs that support you.

Common negative beliefs developed by people with ADD are:

"People are mad at me."

"I am an annoying person."

"I mess things up."

"For some reason, no one can ever understand me."

"I'm not worth very much."

"The world is very overwhelming to me."

"No matter how hard I try, I just can't get organized (be on time, focus for a long period of time, avoid distractions, etc.)."

The process you learn here will enable you to recognize both that you have these beliefs and that you can change them. You will learn how, through self-hypnosis, you can replace the faulty beliefs with positive, helpful ones.

CHANGING YOUR BELIEFS WITH SELF-HYPNOSIS

The good news is that your brain and your mind belong to you. You have the right and the power to look at the beliefs, feelings, and behaviors that run your life, and to decide which you want to keep and which you want to change. One of the most powerful tools for doing this is the tool known as *self-hypnosis.* The techniques of self-hypnosis are widely used by psychologists and psychiatrists in clinical settings, and by peak performers such as athletes, musicians, actors, and public speakers, whose success depends upon their using their minds and brains at peak efficiency. Self-hypnosis is simply a tool, a powerful tool that can be used to dramatically change your beliefs and your life.

The fundamental steps of self-hypnosis are:

1. entering a state of deep relaxation
2. positive affirmations
3. visualizing success
4. leaving the state of deep relaxation, and returning to a more usual, wakeful, state of consciousness

STEP ONE: ENTERING THE DEEPLY RELAXED (SELF-HYPNOTIC) STATE

To enter the state of deep relaxation, you will first learn how to use auto-suggestion to separate yourself from all the fears, tensions, stresses, and confusions of the outside world for a few minutes. This is done by letting go of mental and physical tension, by focusing on the present moment, and allowing yourself to experience inner silence, stillness, and mental and physical relaxation. The technique we will use is counting to twenty, allowing the eyes to close, sending waves of relaxation throughout your body, then going to your own special place, your "haven." The first few times you do this, you may not find yourself relaxing as deeply as the words seem to suggest. This is merely because you need practice. The world has trained most of us to be tense. After you have done this a number of times, you will find it easier to quickly enter a deep state of relaxation.

STEP TWO: POSITIVE AFFIRMATIONS

The second step is to hear positive self-talk. Most of us talk to ourselves each day, but much of what we say is negative, e.g., "I'm such a dolt," "I'll never be successful," "Everybody else is doing better than I am." The statements you will read to yourself on the tape (more on this later) will replace these negative statements with positive ones. These will then begin to create positive beliefs about yourself to replace the negative, harmful ones. Our goal is to create confidence where there was shyness, focus where there was disorganization, self-confidence where there was self-doubt, self-awareness where there was denial, self-acceptance where there was self-criticism, self-control and empowerment where there was helplessness.

STEP THREE: VISUALIZING SUCCESS

One of the most powerful learning tools is the human imagination. When children are playing house or building a fort in the backyard, they are actually learning very important skills. They are willfully suspending their disbelief and allowing themselves to pretend, to temporarily believe that they are actually parents or soldiers. Wise teachers know how to use imagination and pretend to teach valuable lessons. We will use imagination in a very similar way. If we asked you to close your eyes, and imagine sitting in your living room you would be able to point to the window, to the front door, and to reach over and pretend to flip on the light. In order to do this, you would be holding in your mind an image, a kind of mental model, then referring to it to give your responses to the questions. This is an example of mental imagery, or visualization. Even though we may use the word *visualization*, do not think it is absolutely necessary to "see" a clear "picture" in your mind. Fifty percent of adults and most children can "see" mental images in this way. It is helpful but not necessary for our purposes here. In the same way you can make this mental model of your living room, you can make a mental model of your workplace (where your desk is, where your boss's office is, where the phone is, etc.), or your child can make a mental model of his/her classroom. Your goals will be to:

1. mentally picture a challenging situation that might occur in the future—one in which you might have used inappropriate behavior (anger, distraction, fear, avoidance, etc.) *in the past,* and
2. visualize the kind of behavior you would use if you truly believed the positive affirmations you have just given yourself.

As you go through this scene, you will imagine yourself actually being there, and carrying out the most successful behavior you can imagine. This will serve to be a kind of "post-hypnotic suggestion" to your deeper mind.

STEP FOUR: DEHYPNOTIZING YOURSELF

No matter how deeply you relax, you will always have the ability to wake yourself up if there is an emergency or some other situation you need to respond to. You are not "under a spell," and can wake up even faster than if you had been sleeping! On the other hand, we strongly recommend that you awaken yourself slowly whenever possible. The deeply relaxed state is a very sensitive one. Your vulnerable inner mind is exposed, much as it was when you were a young child. Most of the time you keep this part of you protected by your "ego," allowing it to be openly available only when you know you are in a safe, secure situation. In the deeply relaxed state you have dropped your guard, so to speak, and when you return to your normal waking state it is best to do it gradually. In this way you will be able to reestablish the ego protections you need to be able to function smoothly as you go about your next activities. If you rouse yourself too quickly, you may feel a bit groggy, half asleep, or even a little anxious. If this should happen, simply sit or lie down and relax briefly, then bring yourself back into full activity more slowly.

A MOST REMARKABLE TOOL

Technically, once you have learned how, you can enter the hypnotic state by just speaking silently to yourself with your eyes closed. In the beginning, however, it is too difficult to remember all the steps in the right order while still remaining relaxed. The act of trying to remember creates tension, which directly contradicts what you are trying to do. So what you need is a way to be guided through this experience. One way is to have someone read the instructions to you. If you are working with your child, you may choose to read these instructions out loud some of the time, and if you are the subject, it is a virtual necessity. What you need is a way to easily have the words spoken to you whenever you want. The most remarkable tool for accomplishing this lies right at your fingertips: the tape recorder! By following through with the very simple steps in this chapter, you will create a most powerful and effective tool for gaining control of your physiology, your mind, your behaviors, your brain, and your life.

PREPARING YOUR SCRIPT

Get a pad and pencil and settle back in your easy chair. Open a page and title it, "Wise Messages to Myself." As you read the rest of this chapter, make notes on the things that come to you as you read each of the steps below. Then, using this chapter together with your notes, you will create a custom-designed self-programming recording.

Create a statement of purpose, a single sentence that describes why you will be listening to this tape. For example: "The purpose of this deep relaxation and imagery experience is to help my conscious and subconscious mind function better, to improve my organization, to improve focus, to stabilize my emotions, and to create patience. Its goal is to self-program at every level the wisest thoughts, feelings, and behaviors that will lead to ever higher degrees of success."

Read the section below entitled "Script" and familiarize yourself with the instructions. When you reach the section entitled "Positive Affirmations," if there are any that you do not want to become true for you, draw a line through them and don't read them into the tape. Likewise, if there are certain affirmations that are especially appropriate for you (or your child), you may add them. Feel free to consult with your therapist, teacher, or other trusted advisor about which statements they might think it would be most valuable to include. But only include those that you feel very certain that you would like to believe. Do not use suggestions that hurt other people. Stay positive.

Make any changes to the script that you are sure will make it more effective for you. Most people will find the wording we have given here perfect just as it is, but don't feel constrained if you have strong feelings in any way. (Sometimes folks with strong religious or spiritual convictions will want to put in certain statements of gratitude to a Higher Power. This tape is you talking very intimately and personally to yourself or to your child.)

When you reach the imagery about "Your Special Haven," make notes or write out in detail (whichever you like) a description of a place you associate with relaxation. This may be a place you have been on vacation, a place you would like to visit someday, or even a completely imaginary place. If you find the imagery of the beach satisfactory, you may use the words written there.

Many people find the tape to be more enjoyable and effective if music plays in the background. If you want music, set up a separate tape deck or CD player nearby, so you can control the volume from your chair. Locate a long piece of relatively slow music that you find relaxing. (Many people find that a tempo of about sixty beats per minute, the speed of the resting heart, is about right.) During the relaxation phase, play very slow music such as Bach's "Air for the G String," Pachelbel's "Canon," or slow New Age music. The only requirement is that the music be slow, gentle, relaxing, and appealing to you. You may play this throughout the entire tape, or, if you wish, you may substitute a more upbeat piece near the end, as you are visualizing success in the future, as you are awakening. Most of the time, it is best to use only instrumental music, so the words of the songs won't compete in any way with the positive words you are reading to yourself.

Place a tape recorder next to a comfortable chair. Use a tape recorder that will clearly record your voice. Use your voice on the tape. It is better to use a separate microphone, rather than to use the one physically built into your recorder. Place the microphone in a holder about one to two feet in front of your mouth.

INSTRUCTIONS FOR READING THE SCRIPT YOU PREPARE

It is probably best to think of your first attempt to record as a practice session. This way you can listen to what you have done, closing your eyes and following the instructions to see if the speed, the volume of the music, and other aspects of your recording are just right. Play it back and make a note of changes you want to make in it.

Speak the words clearly, directly toward the microphone. Speak slowly and clearly, enunciating each word carefully, but not so stiffly as to sound rigid. Try for a gentle, flowing sound, one that is soothing yet filled with confidence and enthusiasm. During step one, deep relaxation, your tone should be similar to one you would use to lull a child to sleep. Then, for the affirmations and imagery, you may want to shift your tone slightly to one that is a little bit more upbeat, the kind a coach or support person might use.

Most of the time it is a very good idea to personalize the tape by speaking the name of the person for whom you are making the tape several times throughout the tape. So you might begin with "Let yourself sit comfortably back in your chair, Johnny, and listen carefully. . . . ," or "Now, Mary, picture yourself walking into your class feeling confident, and as you see your teacher, Mr. Wilson, you feel even better. . . ." Later you might say, "Each time you listen to this tape, Tommy, you will feel more and more confident in yourself."

If you are making this tape for a child, it is almost always a good idea to include the child's name a number of times. If you are making a tape for yourself, you need to decide whether or not you will feel comfortable hearing your own voice say your name on several occasions.

Turn on your tape recorder, wait about five seconds for the leader tape to pass, then immediately start the background music you're going to play. Let about ten or fifteen seconds of music play on the tape before you begin to speak. As you begin to speak, try to get your voice to flow along with the music, even fitting into the tempo of the music if possible. The music should be played at a low volume, so that it is just gently audible behind your speaking voice, which should be recorded quite a bit louder on the tape than the music. The music is there to help mask background sounds and create relaxation only, and should never be allowed to interfere with the intelligibility of the words you speak.

If you make a mistake, stop the tape recorder and the music. Rewind the tape recorder to the place where the error was made. (If you make sure to leave pauses every couple of sentences, there will always be an easy point for you to go back and edit.) Next, rewind the music approximately the same amount of time. It is not essential to start the music at the exact same passage you were in. The music will be very soft in the background, and the change will barely be noticed, if at all. Start the music, then start the tape recorder and continue reading from where you left off. If you need to pause at any point to read the instructions, you can do so: this is a lot to get through at a single reading. You may pause, and, just as you would do if you made a mistake, follow this procedure.

After completing the recording, take a short break, have a glass of water, or take a little walk. When you come back, sit back and listen to what you have done, following the instructions. Have a pad and pencil in your hand so you can make notes on changes you want to make in your final recording. Do not be surprised or critical when you hear your voice sounding different over your small tape recorder. It sounds very different from what you hear inside. It's important to remember that when you listen to your speaking voice, you have a stereophonic, high-fidelity connection augmented by the bass reflex subwoofer of your chest and the echo chamber of your sinuses. It's never going to sound that good coming out of that little speaker. Everyone tends to react with disappointment when they hear the sound of their recorded voice. Just ignore any tendency toward self-criticism. When you listen to the tape, you will become rapidly so relaxed, you will forget the sound of the voice, and focus on the sound of the words. Change is going to occur within you; get used to listening to your own voice. (A parent's voice is often soothing and acceptable to a child. If you are doing this for your child, modify the instructions as appropriate.)

You may end up making three or more versions before doing one you feel comfortable with. Don't be a perfectionist. You are making a tape for yourself, not something you are entering into a contest. Even a sloppy tape will work fine. Be reasonable.

SCRIPT: SELF-HYPNOTIC REPROGRAMMING FOR SUCCESS

Turn off the phone, put a DO NOT DISTURB sign on the door, and turn off all the noise possible, especially extraneous alarms like washers, timers, cell phones, beepers, etc. Find a comfortable chair. Many people prefer a reclining or lounge chair so their head is supported. Some people prefer to lie flat, perhaps with something supporting the knees and under the head. If you find that you tend to go to sleep while listening to the tape, then it is probably better to sit up—and if you still fall asleep, sit in a straight-backed chair. The actual script to read into the tape recorder is in boldface type.

STEP ONE: ENTERING THE DEEPLY RELAXED (SELF-HYPNOTIC) STATE

Hello, [put in your name]. . . . We are here to clear your mind, relax your soul, break through old barriers, and program success. Pick

a spot on the wall a little above your eye level and stare at it. [You may find it helpful to put a little thumbtack there to look at.] As you focus on this spot, become aware of the fact that there's no other place that you need to go at this moment, nothing else that you need to do, and there's no problem that you need to solve right now. Therefore, you can give yourself permission to relax. Continue to look at that point, and as you do, I am going to begin to count, slowly, from one to twenty.

As I count, say the number to yourself, silently, in your mind. You may find it helpful to picture each number as you count it.

[Leave a couple of seconds between each number.]

One . . . two . . . three . . . four . . . five . . . six . . .

Notice your eyelids beginning to feel heavier and heavier. . . .

Seven . . . eight . . . nine . . . ten . . . eleven . . . twelve . . .

Notice how that spot in the distance is fading out of focus and your eyelids are feeling still heavier and heavier. . . .

13 . . . 14 . . . 15 . . . 16 . . . 17 . . . 18 . . .

Your eyelids are feeling so heavy, they feel as though they really want to close.

19 . . . 20 . . .

Take a deep breath in . . . and as you let that breath out, let your eyelids slowly close.

[Some people may actually find that they relax more if they leave their eyes open through the entire experience. If you choose to do this, simply keep them focused on that spot and don't be concerned that your eyes stay open in spite of your voice saying they are growing heavier. After a while, you may find that your eyelids *will* prefer to close.]

In a moment, I'm going to ask you to take three deep breaths, and with each breath in, feel relaxation flowing in like pure, white light. And with each breathing out, let yourself feel the feeling of letting go. With each breath in, say, silently, to yourself, "With each breath in, I breathe in relaxation," and with each breath out, say the words, "With each breath out, I let my body breathe out all tension and all the things that might interfere with my becoming totally relaxed and comfortable."

Now take a deep breath in, repeating to yourself, "With each breath in, I breathe in relaxation."

And as you let this breath out, repeat, internally to yourself, "With each breath out, I let my body breathe out all tension and all the things that might interfere with my becoming totally relaxed and comfortable."

[Take a few slow, deep breaths in and out, and get a sense of the speed with which you will need to read these words to yourself.]

Now take another deep breath in, feeling the coolness of the air as it enters through your nostrils, and repeat silently, "With each breath in, I breathe in relaxation."

And as you let this breath out, let it be a feeling of letting go and repeat, "With each breath out, I let my body breathe out all tension and all the things that might interfere with my becoming totally relaxed and comfortable."

Now take a deep breath in, repeating to yourself, "With each breath in, I breathe in relaxation." As you let it out, imagine you are a balloon letting out all the air, becoming completely flat and relaxed, and saying to yourself, "With each breath out, I let my body breathe out all tension and all the things that might interfere with my becoming totally relaxed and comfortable."

Now let the air do the breathing for you, just as it does when you're asleep at night, and feel how your chest and abdomen gently rise and fall with each breath, letting each breath continue to relax you from head to toe.

Now, as your body continues to relax, close your eyes really tight, as though you were trying to keep soap out of them. Hold them tense for just a few seconds, and feel the tension in your eyelids.

Now, slowly let the muscles of your eyelids relax . . . relax . . . more and more relaxed with each breath. [Five second pause]

Notice how much your eyelids have relaxed already. They will continue to relax. And perhaps you will notice your eyes gently rolling upward behind your eyelids, and your eyelids feeling so relaxed, they just don't want to open at all. Now, as your eyelids become more and more relaxed, imagine ripples of relaxation flowing outward from your eyelids, like ripples flowing outward from a stone thrown into the water . . . flowing into your forehead . . . through all the muscles of your face . . . relaxing your jaw muscles and your lips . . . and flowing down through your neck and into your shoulders. Feel your shoulders releasing any tension; you may even feel them lower just a tiny little bit as the muscles relax.

Now feel the relaxation flowing down through your shoulders and your arms . . . flowing through your chest and through all the rest of your body. With each rising and falling of your chest and abdomen, your chest becomes more relaxed and all your internal organs are becoming more relaxed. Feel that relaxation flowing through the pelvis, relaxing all your pelvic organs . . . and flowing down through your thighs and your knees . . . your legs and your ankles and your feet . . . all the way down to the tips of your toes. Imagine your body is resting in a soft tub filled with soothing, warm water, that your muscles are melting . . . all the tension is being absorbed by the warmth of the water.

YOUR SPECIAL SAFE HAVEN

[Next, describe a special place . . . your special place . . . a special haven that you can go to in your imagination. Maybe a place you've been in the past or a place you've always wanted to go but only seen pictures of. There might have been a time in the past when you were on vacation. . . . It might even have been a time early in your childhood. It can be a real or an imaginary place: The idea is to create a place where you feel completely relaxed and comfortable. Describe this place clearly to yourself, and slowly so that it will make it easy for you to visualize it.

[As you describe it, describe the sensations in all your senses—what you see; the sounds around you; the temperature of the air; the movement of your body if you're moving, or its peaceful stillness if you are not; the smell of the air; even the tastes if there are any tastes there. Use as much detail as you can. You may take from four to eight minutes for this description. Sometimes people have a long description at first when they are learning to relax, then later make another tape with a description of only one or two minutes in length. As you listen to the tape more often, your ability to relax quickly will increase. For children, ask them ahead of time what scene they would like to go to. They often like the beach, the mountains, or a beautiful park. Just as an example, we will give you a description of walking along the sand at the edge of the ocean. Here's an example. . . .]

Imagine you are on a magic carpet or in a time machine travel-ing through space and time—relaxing as you travel. Imagine you are traveling to a beautiful beach, perhaps on a peaceful tropical island. Even before you see the gentle waves out on the ocean you can begin to feel the warm sand beneath your feet. Feel the pleasant dryness of the warm sand beneath your feet. And as you move first one foot and then the other from side to side, you can feel the warm sand on the sides and the tops of your feet. As you push your toes gently into it, you can feel the dry granules of sand between your warm toes. Gradually you can begin to see this beautiful beach . . . dimly at first, then more and more clearly. Now, let yourself look down the beach . . . and see the warm, glowing, golden-white sand. Let your eyes follow the beautiful expanse of sand . . . and as you lift your eyes and look down this beautiful sandy beach . . . off to one side you can see the deep blue-green of the ocean. Listen . . . you can hear the sounds of the ocean waves rolling slowly to shore and see them breaking into watery white fingers of foam that glide smoothly over the wet sand. Walk over to the edge of the damp sand, and see the bright reflection of the sky in the thin film of water left behind as each wave strokes the wet surfaces and then rushes back down the slope. Feel the damp sand beneath your feet. White crests of waves slowly follow each other in toward the shore. And as you enjoy the deep, rich color of the ocean . . . perhaps you can feel the salty breeze blowing in, gently cool on the surface of your body. Take a deep breath in, savoring the pleasant fragrance, the smell of the sea. Perhaps even taste the slightly salty taste on your lips and tongue. And floating directly above you, you can see the cottony fluffs of pure white clouds . . . and a bird gliding through vast expanses of blue. Behind you is the bright sun, shining and pleasantly warming the skin of your back. Feel the warmth on the surface of your back, sinking deep into all the muscles of your back, relaxing you even more. And now, if you wish, you can go for a walk or a run down the beach. Perhaps you'd like to run on the firm damp sand, or on the soft warm sand. Or if you like, you might like to wade into the water and feel its pleasant temperature. Immerse your body in it. Maybe you'd like to swim. Whatever you'd like to do, let yourself do it now . . .

[Pause for fifteen to thirty seconds]

[After you have completed your description of your haven, your special place, say:]

As you listen to the rest of this tape, imagine yourself spending time in your haven, perhaps walking about, exploring it, enjoying it in any way that you wish.

[These first few steps should take about five to ten minutes. After you have finished with these initial steps, read the following affirmation phrases into your tape recorder, modifying them to better suit your situation or that of your child. Read them slowly and clearly with a firm feeling of certainty: Read it with a voice that sounds as though you truly believe it, whether you do or not at this moment in time. Soon you will begin to believe it, and as you believe it, it will happen!]

STEP TWO: GIVING YOURSELF POSITIVE AFFIRMATIONS

With each breath in, breathe in warmth and relaxation . . . and with each breath out, release all the tensions and worries that disrupt life. Say to yourself:

"Day by day, I'm feeling better and better in every way. I'm feeling more control in my life.

- I have clear goals for my relationships: to develop and nurture kind, caring, loving relationships.
- I have clear goals for my work (or school): to do the best I can every day.

- I have clear goals for my physical health and mental health: to always do things to keep my mind and my body healthy.
- I focus energy every day on accomplishing my goals.

I expect to succeed in whatever I do. I am able to see myself succeeding at tasks before I start them. In this way, I program myself for success . . . and I see success. I understand that successful people sometimes make mistakes and have failures along the way. I do not expect perfection, but I learn from each mistake.

Every day, in every way, I am becoming the best person I can be. I learn from others. By learning from others, I expand my horizons on a daily basis.

I prepare carefully for each of my tasks and projects. I set myself up to win and I have let go of the old pattern of putting off tasks and thereby setting up failure. Every day I'm becoming more and more organized. . . . Organization is becoming a vital part of my nature. I realize that when I put something in its right place in the beginning, I am more likely to find it when I need it.

Every day I am becoming more focused, more alert, more wide awake, and more filled with energy. Every day I'm becoming more interested in what I am doing, in whatever is going on around me, and the people around me. I work smart as well as hard, focusing my energy on the goals I have set for myself.

I am more flexible . . . more adaptable . . . more willing and able to change as needed. At the same time, I am more disciplined . . . more thoughtful.

My environment matters . . . I will seek to be a positive force in my environment every day. I surround myself with positive people, and people who believe in me. Similarly, I am more positive with those around me. I can step outside myself and understand the feelings of others, and I see things from their perspective as well as my own. I am free of fear of competition with others. I feel wonderful when I win; when I do not win, I learn. Competition spurs me on to be as good as I can be.

More and more, I accept myself as I am and I accept others as they are . . . I accept things as they are, not as I think they should be. I compromise when it is necessary. I eliminate the ANTs and bad thoughts whenever they enter my mind. I own me, and I am in control of me . . . and I live with the inner voices that help and uplift me. I erase any voice that would try to tear me down. When I find anxiety, I am able to turn it into positive energy for creativity and positive change.

I have let go of the habit of giving up on myself. Instead, I give my best effort toward reaching the goals I have set for myself . . . and no matter what . . . I keep pursuing my fondest dream in my life.

[If you've decided to put a little more active music on at this time, you may do so.]

STEP THREE: VISUALIZING SUCCESS

Now visualize yourself in some future situation, perhaps a test or challenge or meeting that is coming up in the near future. Choose the kind of situation you might have had trouble with in the past, but this time, as you go through it, visualize yourself applying all the positive beliefs you've just repeated to yourself in your mind, and watch yourself being personally successful, no matter what the outcome of the situation is.

Visualize yourself there, clearly and vividly; see and hear everything that is going on around you, and feel your body and your voice responding in the way you really want to . . . and the way that is healthy and wise . . . and see yourself being successful.

[Pause for about a minute or two, and then begin to read again.]

STEP FOUR: DEHYPNOTIZING YOURSELF

Now, as I count from ten down to zero, gradually feel yourself becoming more and more awake. [Again, leave about three or four seconds between each two numbers.]

Ten, nine, eight . . .

Feeling yourself coming up, growing more and more awake.

Seven, six, five . . .

Feeling alert and full of energy.

Four, three . . .

Bringing the feelings of energy and relaxation with you as you come up . . . filled with energy and ready to do whatever you want to do next.

Two, one, zero.

Take a deep breath in. As you let it out, let your eyelids open and think to yourself, *Wide awake* . . .

Feel your body beginning to stretch and move.

Now get up and walk around the room, and make sure you're fully wide awake before you do anything else.

The total time of the tape will be from fifteen to thirty minutes, depending on the pace of your voice, images, etc.

Now that you have made the tape for yourself or your child, listen to it once every day. This is important: The first few times you will find out how your body will react to the relaxation. Some people become so relaxed that they doze off to sleep for a bit. If that happens to you, great! Listen to the tape before you go to bed, or when you can catch a nap. Some people find that it takes them awhile to be fully with it; they remain very relaxed for several minutes afterward, as if they were waking up from sleep. If the tape affects you that way, you want to make sure that you're clearly awake before you do anything that requires full concentration, like driving a car. Others can listen to the tape anytime, anywhere, and feel a relaxed energy flow through their body.

The most important thing is that you listen to your tape every day. You can change the content of the tape in any way that you think will be beneficial to you. This is your tape. Use it to strengthen your life.

Information on other self-hypnosis cassettes can be found at our website at amenclinics.com or on Dr. Miller's website at DrMiller.com.

CHAPTER 30

How to Find the Best Help

A Resource Guide

our questions that I am frequently asked are: When is it time to see a professional about ADD? What to do when a loved one with ADD is in denial about needing help? How do I go about finding a competent professional? When do you order a SPECT study? This chapter will attempt to answer these questions.

WHEN IS IT TIME TO SEE A PROFESSIONAL ABOUT ADD?

This question is relatively easy to answer. I recommend people seek professional help for ADD for themselves or their child when their behaviors, feelings, or thoughts interfere with their ability to reach their potential in the world, whether in their relationships, in their work, or within themselves. If you see persistent relationship struggles (parent-child, sibling, friends, romantic), it's time to get help. If you see persistent school or work problems, it is time to get professional help. If you see continued monetary problems, it's time to get help. Many people have told me they cannot afford to get professional help. I respond that it is much more costly to live with untreated ADD than it is to get appropriate help. If you see persistent self-esteem problems, or mood or anxiety problems it's time to seek help. In my experience, if ADD remains untreated past the age of nine-years-old there is a very high chance of self-esteem and mood problems.

GAINING ACCESS TO YOUR OWN GOOD BRAIN

The internal problems associated with ADD can ruin lives, relationships, and careers. It is essential to seek help when necessary. It is also critical for people not to be too proud to get help. Pride often devastates relationships, careers, and even life itself. Too many people feel they are somehow "less than others" if they seek help. I often tell my patients that, in my experience, it is the successful people who seek help when they need it. Successful businesspeople hire the best possible outside consultants when they are faced with a problem that they cannot solve or when they need extra help. Unsuccessful people tend to deny they have problems, bury their heads in the sand, and blame others for their problems. If the ADD symptoms are sabotaging your chances for success in relationships, work, or within yourself, get help. Don't feel ashamed: feel as though you're being good to yourself.

In thinking about getting help, it is important to put ADD in perspective. First, I have patients get rid of the concept of "normal versus not normal." "What is normal anyway?" I ask. I tell my patients who worry that they are not normal, that "normal" is the setting on a dryer. Or that Normal is a city in Illinois. Actually, I spoke in Normal, Illinois, at a major university several years ago. I got to meet Normal people, shop at the Normal grocery store, see the Normal police department and fire department, and even be interviewed on the Normal radio station. I met Normal women. They were a very nice group, but really not much different from those folks in California. The Normal people seemed to have their share of ADD—which is why I was asked to speak.

I tell my patients about a study sponsored by the National Institutes of Health, where researchers reported that 51 percent of the U.S. population suffers from a psychiatric illness at some point in their lives. Anxiety, substance abuse, and depression were the three most common illnesses. At first, I thought this statistic was too high. Then I made a list of twenty people I knew (not from my practice). Eleven were taking medication or in therapy. Half of us at some point in our lives will have problems. It's just as normal to have problems as to not have problems. Again, it is the more successful people that will get help first. The same study reported that 29 percent of the population will have two separate, distinct psychiatric diagnoses and 17 percent of us will have three different psychiatric diagnoses. In my experience, very few people are completely without these problems. In fact, in doing research, one of the most difficult challenges is finding a "normal" control group.

One of the most persuasive statements I give patients about seeking help is that *I am often able to help them have more access to their own good brains.* When their brains do not work efficiently, they are not efficient. When their brains work right, they can work right. I often will show them a number of brain SPECT studies to show them the difference on and off medication or targeted psychotherapy, as a way to help them understand the concept. As you can imagine, after looking at the images in this book, when you see an underactive brain versus one that is healthy, you want the one that is healthy.

J.C. was the nineteen-year-old son of a Bay Area physician. His mother brought him to see us because he had problems in school and problems with his behavior. He was angry, resentful, oppositional, and moody. He had been in psychotherapy with three different therapists over the past twelve years. His mother thought that medication might be helpful. J.C. was opposed. "I don't want medication," he said, "I want to be myself. It's not my problem." His SPECT study revealed marked decreased temporal lobe activity, increased anterior cingulate activity, and decreased prefrontal cortex activity. I showed him his brain on the computer monitor. After he understood the scan, his first comment to me was, "Can you give me something to help my brain?" I gave him medication to stabilize his temporal lobe, and supplements to calm his anterior cingulate gyrus and stimulate his prefrontal cortex. He felt better within several weeks. He was compliant with treatment because he wanted to have optimal access to his own brain.

WHAT TO DO WHEN A LOVED ONE IS IN DENIAL ABOUT NEEDING HELP

Unfortunately, the stigma associated with ADD or "psychiatric illness" prevents many people from getting help. People do not want to be seen as crazy, stupid, or defective. They often do not seek help until they (or their loved one) can no longer tolerate the pain (at work, in their relationships, or within themselves). Men are especially affected by denial.

Many men, when faced with obvious problems in their marriages, their children, or even themselves, refuse to see problems. Their lack of awareness and strong tendency toward denial prevent them from seeking help until more damage has been done than necessary. Many men are threatened with divorce before they seek help. Often, with ADD, many men had been diagnosed as children with hyperactivity and had been on medication. They hated feeling different than the other kids and resented taking medication, even if it was helpful for them.

Some people may say it is unfair for me to pick on men. And indeed, some men see problems long before some women. Overall, however, mothers see problems in children before fathers and are more willing to seek help, and many more wives call for marital counseling than husbands. What is it in our society that causes men to overlook obvious problems, to deny problems until it is too late to deal with them effectively or until significant damage occurs? Some of the answers may be found in how boys are raised in our society, the societal expectations we place on men, and the overwhelming pace of many men's daily lives.

Boys most often engage in active play (sports, war games, video games, etc.) that involves little dialogue or communication. The games often involve dominance and submissiveness, winning and losing, and little interpersonal communication. Force, strength, or skill handles problems. Girls, on the other hand, often engage in more interpersonal or communicative types of play, such as dolls and storytelling. When my wife was little, she used to line up her dolls to teach them. Fathers often take their sons out to throw the ball around or shoot hoops, rather than to go for a walk and talk.

Many men retain the childhood notions of competition and that one must be better than others to be any good at all. To admit to a problem is to be less than other men. As a result, many men wait to seek help until their problem is obvious to the whole world. Other men feel totally responsible for all that happens in their families and admitting to problems is to admit that they have in some way failed.

Clearly, the pace of life prevents some men from being able to take the time to look clearly at the important people in their lives and their relationships with them. When I spend time with fathers and husbands and help them slow down enough to see what is really important to them, more often than not they begin to see the problems and work toward more helpful solutions. The issue is not one of being uncaring or uninterested: It is not seeing what is there.

Many teenagers also resist getting help, even when faced with obvious problems. They worry about labels and do not want yet another adult judging their behavior.

Here are several suggestions to help people who are unaware or unwilling to get the help they need:

1. Try the straightforward approach first (but with a new brain twist). Clearly tell the person what behaviors concern you. Tell them the problems may be due to underlying brain patterns that can be tuned up. Tell them help may be available—help not to cure a defect but rather help to optimize how their brain functions. Tell them you know they are trying to do their best, but their behavior, thoughts, or feelings may be getting in the way of their success (at work, in relationships, or within themselves). Emphasize access, not defect.

2. Give them information. Books, videos, articles on the subjects you are concerned about can be of tremendous help. Many people come to see me because they read a book of mine, saw a video I produced, or read an article I wrote. Good information can be very persuasive, especially if it is presented in a positive, life-enhancing way.

3. When a person remains resistant to help, even after you have been straightforward and given them good information, plant seeds. Plant ideas about getting help and then water them regularly. Drop an idea, article, or other information about the topic from time to time. If you talk too much about getting help, people become resentful and won't get help to spite you. Be careful not to go overboard.

4. Protect your relationship with the other person. People are more receptive to people they trust rather than to people who nag and belittle them. I do not let anyone tell me something bad about myself unless

I trust the other person. Work on gaining the person's trust over the long run. It will make them more receptive to your suggestions. Do not make getting help the only thing that you talk about. Make sure you are interested in their whole lives, not just their potential medical appointments.

5. Give them new hope. Many people with these problems have tried to get help, and it did not work or it even made them worse. Educate them on new brain technology that helps professionals be more focused and more effective in treatment efforts.

6. There comes a time when you have to say enough is enough. If, over time, the other person refuses to get help, and his or her behavior has a negative impact on your life, you may have to separate yourself. Staying in a toxic relationship is harmful to your health. Staying in a toxic relationship often enables the other person to remain sick. Actually, I have seen the threat or act of leaving motivate people to change, whether it is about drinking, drug use, or treating ADD. Threatening to leave is not the first approach I would take, but after time it may be the best approach.

7. Realize you cannot force a person into treatment unless they are dangerous to themselves, dangerous to others, or unable to care for themselves. You can only do what you can do. Fortunately, today there is a lot more we can do than we could have done just ten years ago.

FINDING A COMPETENT PROFESSIONAL WHO USES THIS NEW BRAIN SCIENCE THINKING

At this point, we get many calls and e-mails a week from people all over the world looking for competent professionals in their area who think in ways similar to myself and the principles outlined in this book. Because the principles in this book are still on the edge of what is new in brain science, these professionals may be hard to find. Still, finding the right professional for evaluation and treatment is critical to the healing process. The right professional can have a very positive impact on your life. The wrong professional can make things worse. There are a number of steps to take in finding the best person to assist you.

- **Get the best person you can find**. Saving money up front may cost you in the long run. The right help is not only cost-effective but saves unnecessary pain and suffering. Don't just rely on a person who is on your managed-care plan. That person may or may not be a good fit for you. Search for the best. If he or she is on your insurance plan— great. But don't let that be the primary criteria.

- **Use a specialist**. ADD diagnosis and treatment is expanding at a rapid pace. Specialists keep up with the details in their fields, while generalists (family physicians) have to try to keep up with everything. If I had a heart arrhythmia, I would see a cardiologist rather than a general internist. I want someone to treat me who has seen hundreds or even thousands of cases like mine.

- **Get information about referral sources from people who know about your problem**. Sometimes well-meaning people give very bad information. I have known many physicians and teachers who make light of ADD and discourage people from getting help. The following is a quote from a family physician to one of my patients: "Oh, ADD is a fad. You don't need help. Just try harder." In searching for help, contact people who are likely to give you good information, such as child psychiatrists, CHADD coordinators, Internet ADD medical support groups. Often support groups have members who have visited the professionals in the area, and they can give you important information about subjects such as bedside manner, competence, responsiveness, and organization.

- **Once you get the names of competent professionals, check their credentials**. Very few patients ever check a professional's background. Board certification is a key credential. To become board certified, physicians have to pass additional written and verbal tests. They have had to discipline themselves to gain the skill and knowledge that is acceptable to their colleagues. Don't give too much weight to the medical school or graduate school the professional attended. I have worked with some doctors who went to Yale and Harvard who did not have a clue on how to treat patients appropriately, while other doctors from less prestigious schools were outstanding, forward thinking, and caring.

- Set up an interview with the professional to see whether or not you want to work with him or her. Generally you have to pay for their time, but it is worth spending time getting to know the people you will rely on for help.
- Read the professional's work or hear the professional if possible. Many professionals write articles or books or speak at meetings or local groups. If possible, read their writings or hear them speak to get a feel for the kind of person they are and their ability to help you.
- Look for a person who is open-minded, up-to-date, and willing to try new things.
- Look for a person who treats you with respect, who listens to your questions and responds to your needs. Look for a relationship that is collaborative and respectful.

We maintain a list of people who have taken our affiliate training on our website at amenclinics.com/aaec/about-referrals/referral-network.

I know it is hard to find a professional who meets all of these criteria who also has the right training in brain physiology, but these people can be found. Be persistent. The caregiver is essential to healing.

WHEN TO ORDER A SPECT STUDY; QUESTIONS ABOUT SPECT

Here are several common questions and answers about SPECT.

Will the SPECT study give me an accurate diagnosis? No. A SPECT study by itself will not give a diagnosis. SPECT studies help the clinician understand more about the specific function of your brain. Each person's brain is unique, which may lead to unique responses to medicine or therapy. Diagnoses about specific conditions are made through a combination of clinical history, personal interview, information from families, diagnostic checklists, SPECT studies, and other neuropsychological tests. No study is "a doctor in a box" that can give accurate diagnoses on individual patients.

Why are SPECT studies ordered? Some of the common reasons include:

1. evaluation of seizure activity
2. evaluation of blood-vessel diseases, such as stroke
3. evaluation of dementia and distinction between dementia and pseudo-dementia (depression that looks like dementia)
4. evaluation of the effects of mild, moderate, and severe head trauma
5. suspicion of underlying organic brain condition, such as seizure activity contributing to behavioral disturbance; prenatal trauma; or exposure to toxins
6. evaluation of atypical or unresponsive aggressive behavior
7. determination of the extent of brain impairment caused by drug or alcohol abuse
8. typing of ADD when clinical presentation is not clear
9. determination of the type of anxiety, depression, addiction, or obesity when the clinical presentation is not clear
10. general health screening.

Do I need to be off medication before the study? This question must be answered individually between you and your doctor. In general, it is better to be off medications until they are out of your system, but this is not always practical or advisable. If the study is done while on medication, let the technician know so that when the physician reads the study, he or she will include that information in the interpretation of the scan. In general, we recommend patients try to be off stimulants at least four days before the first scan and remain off of them until after the second scan, if one is ordered. Medications such as Prozac (which stays in the body four to six weeks) are generally not stopped because of practicality. Check with your specific doctor for recommendations.

What should I do the day of the scan? On the day of the scan, decrease or eliminate your caffeine intake and try to not take cold medication or aspirin. (If you do, please write it down on the intake form.) Eat as you normally would.

Are there any side effects or risks to the study? The study does not involve a dye and people do not have allergic reactions to the study. The possibility exists, although in a very small percentage of patients, of a mild rash, facial redness and edema, fever, and/or a transient increase in blood pressure. The amount of radiation exposure from one brain SPECT study is approximately the same as one abdominal X-ray.

How is the SPECT procedure done? The patient is placed in a quiet room and a small intravenous (IV) line is started. The patient remains quiet for approximately ten minutes with his or her eyes open to allow their mental state to equilibrate to the environment. The imaging agent is then injected through the IV. After another short period of time, the patient lies on a table and the SPECT camera rotates around his or her head. (The patient does not go into a tube.) The time on the table is approximately fifteen minutes. A concentration study is done the same way except that the patient does a concentration task while the medicine is being injected into their arm. If a concentration study is ordered, the patient returns on another day.

Are there alternatives to having a SPECT study? In my opinion, SPECT is the most clinically useful study of brain function. There are other studies, such as quantitative electroencephalograms (QEEGs), Positron Emission Tomography (PET) studies, and functional MRIs (fMRI). PET studies and fMRI are considerably more costly and they are performed mostly in research settings. QEEGs are very useful and provide a different type of look at brain function. Sometimes we do both.

Does insurance cover the cost of SPECT studies? Reimbursement by insurance companies varies according to your plan. It is often a good idea to check with the insurance company ahead of time to see if it is a covered benefit in your case.

Is the use of brain SPECT imaging accepted in the medical community? Brain SPECT studies are widely recognized as an effective tool for evaluating brain function in seizures, strokes, dementia, and head trauma. There are more than a thousand research articles on these topics. In our clinic, based on our experience over twenty-two years, we have developed this technology further to evaluate aggression and non-responsive psychiatric conditions. Unfortunately, many physicians do not fully understand the application of SPECT imaging and may tell you that the technology is experimental, but over five thousand medical and mental health professionals have referred patients to us for scans.

CHAPTER 31

What to Do When Treatment Doesn't Work

We have been able to help thousands of patients who were previously resistant to treatment through the new brain-based model given in this book. Although treatment failures are less common using this model, sometimes treatment doesn't seem to work or doesn't seem to alleviate a patient's symptoms completely. Patients who do not get well, and those who get a little better but who continue to experience significant symptoms in spite of what appears to be good treatment, are known as "treatment resistant patients." The most common reasons for treatment resistance can be grouped into six categories: problems with the diagnosis; medication issues; interfering factors; poor patient follow-through with treatment recommendations; trying to cut corners; and those things for which we do not have an explanation.

PROBLEMS WITH THE DIAGNOSIS

When a condition is misdiagnosed as ADD, treatment will be ineffective and often makes things worse by delaying treatment of the underlying illness. A classic example is thyroid illness. Hypothyroidism is a condition in which the thyroid gland is underactive. The decreased amount of thyroid hormone available to the body causes symptoms that mimic decreased focus, fatigue, and lack of motivation. This condition can be easily mistaken for ADD and will not respond to stimulating supplements, medication, or neurofeedback. On the other hand, an overactive thyroid gland can cause symptoms of anxiety, agitation, and increased heart rate that resemble hyperactivity or anxiety disorders.

The list of medical conditions that affect brain function and attentional issues is extensive and crosses all specialties from cardiology to dermatology. Medical conditions should always be excluded as the underlying cause of symptoms before a psychiatric diagnosis is made.

Comorbidity is the presence of more than one condition, and it is one of the more common reasons for poor treatment outcome. Substance abuse disorders are one of the most common comorbid conditions we treat. Marijuana, inhalants, pain medications, and alcohol abuse interfere with the action of medications or supplements used to treat ADD. Substance abuse disturbs brain function and can disrupt brain development. Almost everyone knows this is true for babies exposed to substances during development, but most people don't realize that teenagers and young adults are still vulnerable because the brain is still developing into young adulthood.

Self-medication with drugs and alcohol is a vicious cycle. Emotional and physical pain cause people to abuse substances or misuse prescription medications in an attempt to get relief, but intoxication and withdrawal states only aggravate the underlying conditions. Substance abuse issues must be dealt with for treatment to be effective.

Finally, doctors do not always get all the information necessary to make a correct diagnosis or to make treatment decisions. Sometimes patients do not tell us about underlying medical conditions, substance abuse, other medications they are taking, or the amount of stress they have in their lives. The reasons people withhold information are as unique as the people are themselves. Many times people feel shame over things in their past; think we won't treat them if they have a substance abuse problem; are embarrassed by their thoughts; believe they will be judged if they reveal they are HIV positive; are concerned about what will be written in the medical record; and so on. Other times people forget about a prior head injury or cannot remember the names and dosages of the medications they are taking. All of this information is important for the accurate rendering of a diagnosis and formation of an effective treatment plan.

MEDICATION ISSUES

Think of your treatment plan as a recipe and your supplements or medications as one of the ingredients in the recipe. If you leave things out, make additions or substitutions, or if your timing is off you may not get what you planned for. But if you follow your recipe, you will have a better product. Medications and supplements work best when they are taken on schedule. They work less well if they are taken randomly. And they don't work at all when doses are frequently missed. Why do people miss doses of medications or supplements? Complicated dosing schedules are sometimes a problem, and this is the reason we try to use medications and supplements that can be taken once or twice daily. We also try to minimize the number of medications or supplements a person is taking to further simplify things. The very young, very old, and people with ADD may not remember to take all their doses. Teenagers sometimes skip doses intentionally, and unfortunately, some parents who are divorced or separated victimize their children by withholding medication to get back at the other parent.

Medications and supplements must be taken at the correct dose to be effective. Every day in our practice we are amazed by the number of "treatment resistant" patients who are simply underdosed on their medications or supplements. Taking only half the dosage necessary to help your brain will not work any better than using half the heat necessary to bake your bread. Additionally, many doctors who are not specialists in the field of psychiatry do not prescribe high enough dosages of supplements or medications.

Other prescription medications, over-the-counter drugs, and herbs and supplements can interfere with the action of supplements and medications prescribed to treat ADD. Examples of medications that may cause such interference include: some of the antihistamines, asthma medications, and medications used to treat heart conditions. Caffeine is known to aggravate some of the stimulant side effects. Medications used to treat high blood pressure cross over into brain tissue and worsen mood issues. It is extremely important to always inform all your doctors of every medication and supplement you take.

We have also seen generic medications cause treatment problems and confusion, and we know generic medication works differently from brand-name medication. Sometimes it works better, sometimes worse. For example, one of my daughters responded very nicely to a specific generic for Ritalin, but not others.

One factor that few physicians consider is the difference between how females and males process supplements and medication. Very few drug trials involve women, and therefore finding the therapeutic dose for women is often a process of trial and error. Hormonal factors affect the action of supplements and medications in women. Many women also have a higher percentage of body fat than men and that may affect drug distribution. These and other factors mean that women may need a different dose of the same supplement or medication we use to treat men, or else an altogether entirely different protocol.

INTERFERING FACTORS

Your treatment plan is a prescription for health, and when prescribed lifestyle changes are not made, the entire plan can be sabotaged. We prescribe dietary changes to help brain function, boost supplement or medication effectiveness, and to normalize energy levels. Patients eating a high-carbohydrate diet will continue to experience blood sugar and insulin level fluctuations that aggravate their mood, energy levels, and ability to concentrate. Excessive caffeine and any nicotine use will interfere with the action of many supplements and medications, including stimulants. Because the effects of caffeine and nicotine are so short-lived, they cause people to be irritable and sometimes more unfocused. Citrus juices slow down the ability of the body to process some supplements and medications.

A problematic or difficult environment (such as at home, work, or school) also contributes to treatment failures. You can have the right diagnosis and right treatment protocol, but if you are in a chronically difficult marriage, have difficult parents or teachers, or have siblings who are abusing you, treatment will appeared flawed and frequently fail. The environment needs to support the treatment.

One of the most important aspects of the treatment plan is the therapeutic relationship. The doctor-patient relationship is in itself an instrument of healing. Patients work hard to find care providers who are not only experts in their field, but who are also good communicators. Conflicts and miscommunication in doctor-patient or patient-therapist relationships lead to poor outcomes. Patients need to inform all medical providers of any change in their medical or psychological status and report any medications, supplements, herbs, and over-the-counter medications they are taking.

Poor Follow-through

Lack of patient follow-through with treatment is what doctors and therapists call lack of compliance. Doctors spend a lot of time trying to figure out why patients become noncompliant with treatment protocols. We've compiled our own list of common reasons:

- Patients expect supplements or medications to work too quickly and discontinue their use before the medications have a chance to be effective.
- Doctors, especially those who are not specialists in neuropsychiatry, change patient supplements or medications prematurely, or do not push doses high enough to be effective. Patients need to see specialists for treatment of their disorders.
- Supplement or medication dosing schedules are complicated and patients become confused or frustrated.
- Side effects occur and patients were not told to expect them and/or the doctor does not know how to treat the side effects.
- Patients stop supplements or medications as soon as they start to feel better and relapse.
- Well-meaning family members and friends undermine the treatment plan by reassuring patients that "they don't really need treatment," and suggesting alternatives such as meditation, exercise, and religion. We believe these are essential elements of a treatment plan, but alone may not be enough.

- Popular media and the Internet are rife with sensational stories and hype that scare patients into prematurely discontinuing their treatment.
- Sometimes patients expect too much from supplements or medications. There are no magic bullets and medications are only one part of a prescription for health.
- Patients are not willing to discontinue the use of drugs and/or alcohol, participate in therapy, or make other lifestyle changes that are necessary to achieve the best outcomes.

To increase the likelihood that our patients will derive the best possible benefit from treatment, we stress the importance of strict compliance with the full treatment plan. A full treatment plan is a prescription for health that encompasses many areas of your life and requires your active participation on a daily basis. Communication with your doctor about your concerns and to modify the plan as needed is essential. Patience and persistence are keys to success.

Impatience and thoughtlessness can have dire consequences.

Cutting Corners

We've all heard the phrase "you get what you pay for." Unfortunately, we usually hear it after we've written the check for something we were sure was a good bargain only to realize we had a "lemon" on our hands the day after the warranty ran out. No one wants to spend money needlessly and everyone wants to make a good investment. The best investment you can make is in your health, especially your brain health. This truly is an investment for life—your own life and the lives of your children.

Most of us complain less about the cost of clothing, food, and automobiles than we do about the health care we purchase. Many of us spend money excessively on entertainment, large homes, vacations, and even things that are not good for us—such as cigarettes, excessive alcohol, and too much food.

Some patients are treated by nonspecialists and do fine on generic drugs. But if you are among those who are becoming frustrated because you are not getting better, you need to see a specialist. You might benefit from technology that can image your brain and guide diagnosis and treatment. You might need a more sophisticated combination of supplements and medications. This might require some people to pay out-of-pocket, or go outside their insurance plan. The cost of a consultation with a specialist, with or without tests, and getting the correct treatment prescribed is enormously less expensive than the costs of repeated visits to other doctors, medication trials and errors, and long-term disability resulting from poorly treated symptoms.

The Unknown

Poor compliance, premature discontinuation of treatment, active substance abuse, and untreated medical illnesses are some of the factors that contribute to the risk of continued symptoms of ADD. Untreated sleep disturbances are known to increase the risk of cognitive impairment. Every patient has the risk of relapse or recurrence, yet it is higher for patients who are treated only until their symptoms respond as opposed to those who are treated until their symptoms are in remission. In other words, patients who discontinue their treatment on their own as soon as they start to feel better are at much higher relapse risk than those who remain on treatment until they complete a full course (usually several years). Further, once in remission, the chance of relapse and recurrence can be further reduced by maintaining a healthy lifestyle.

There are countless factors that influence the neurochemical state of the mind and body. We are only beginning to understand some of these influences and there is much we do not know. I look forward to the continued development of imaging techniques to study the brain, to guide treatment, and to follow the course of treatment.

References and Further Reading

The information in *Healing ADD* is based on hundreds of references and sources, including scientific studies, books, interviews with medical experts, statistics from government agencies and health organizations, and other reliable resources. I have decided to place them exclusively on the amenclinics.com website. I invite you to view them at amenclinics. com/healingADDreferences.

Acknowledgments

This book is the product of many years, many friendships and collaborations. I am grateful to the best teachers a physician could have—my patients. I wish to acknowledge and thank the staff at the Amen Clinics, especially through our growth over the past twenty-four years. In addition, I wish to thank Jane Massengill and Emmett Miller, who have made significant contributions to this book. I am also thankful to the many professionals who have helped me develop and spread this work, including Earl Henslin, Joseph Annibali, Kristen Willeumier, Larry Momaya, Ari Darmal, Garrett Halweg, Tim Earnest, Brad Johnson, Jennifer Love, Mona Karimpour, Jay Faber, Bob Alpern, Riz Malik, Liz Stuller, Bob Licata, Martin Waugh, Lilly Somner, Manuel Trujillo, Sandi Lowe, Jeff Ditzell, Mittsi Crossman, Ted Henderson, Rob Tarzwell, Phil Cohen, John Thornton, Howard Schneider, Mike Uszler, Dennis Alters, Rick Lavine, Sheila Krystal, Terry McGuire, Dan Pavel, Rob Kohn, Joseph Wu, Karen Lansing, Rick Gilbert, Leon and Linda Webber, Bill Klindt, David Smith, Jack Felton, Mark Kosins, and Jayson Graves.

I also wish to thank Faith Hamlin and the wonderful people at Sanford J. Greenberger Associates who have represented me around the world for more than fifteen years, and my editor at Berkley, Denise Silvestro.

I also wish to thank my children, Antony, Breanne, Kaitlyn, and

Chloe who not only give me great stories, but have given me love and affection, and are a continual source of pride. And, of course, my amazing wife, Tana, who has supported and loved me during the revision of this book and the writing of many others.

Index

ABOUT DANIEL G. AMEN, M.D.

Dr. Amen is a physician, psychiatrist, teacher, and multiple *New York Times* bestselling author. He is widely regarded as one of the world's foremost experts on applying brain imaging science to clinical psychiatric practice. He is a board certified child and adult psychiatrist and a Distinguished Fellow of the American Psychiatric Association. He is the medical director of Amen Clinics, Inc., in Newport Beach and San Francisco, California; Bellevue, Washington; Reston, Virginia; Atlanta, Georgia; and New York, New York. Amen Clinics have the world's largest database of functional brain scans, totaling nearly eighty-five thousand scans on patients from ninety-three countries.

Dr. Amen is widely regarded as a gifted teacher, taking complex concepts in neuropsychiatry, neuroimaging, and brain health to make them easily accessible to other professionals and the general public. Dr. Amen is the lead researcher on the world's largest brain imaging/brain rehabilitation study on professional football players, which not only demonstrated significant brain damage in a high percentage of retired players, but also the possibility for rehabilitation in many with the principles that underlie his work. Under the direction of Pastor Rick Warren, Dr. Amen together with Drs. Mark Hyman and Mehmet Oz, is one of the chief architects on Saddleback Church's "Daniel Plan," a fifty-two-week program to get churches healthy, physically, emotionally, and spiritually.

Dr. Amen is the author of fifty-five professional articles, the co-author of the *Comprehensive Textbook of Psychiatry*'s chapter on Functional Imaging in Clinical Practice, thirty books, including: *Change Your Brain, Change Your Life*; *Magnificent Mind at Any Age*; *Change Your Brain,*

Change Your Body; *Use Your Brain to Change Your Age*; and *Unleash the Power of the Female Brain*. He is also the author of *Making a Good Brain Great*; *Healing the Hardware of the Soul*, and coauthor of *Unchain Your Brain*; *Healing Anxiety and Depression*; and *Preventing Alzheimer's*.

Dr. Amen is the producer of eight highly popular shows about the brain, which have raised more than fifty million dollars for public television.

A small sample of the organizations Dr. Amen has spoken for include: the National Security Agency (NSA), the National Science Foundation (NSF), Harvard's Learning and the Brain Conference, Franklin Covey, the National Council of Juvenile and Family Court Judges, and the Supreme Courts of Delaware, Ohio, and Wyoming. Dr. Amen's work has been featured in *Newsweek*, *Parade Magazine*, *New York Times Magazine*, *Time*, *Washington Post*, *Men's Health*, and *Cosmopolitan*.

Dr. Amen is married to Tana, is the father of four children, and is grandfather to Elias, Julian, Angelina, Emmy, and Liam. He is an avid table tennis player.

About Amen Clinics, Inc.

Amen Clinics, Inc., (ACI) was established in 1989 by Daniel G. Amen, M.D. It specializes in innovative diagnosis and treatment planning for a wide variety of behavioral, learning, emotional, cognitive, and weight problems for children, teenagers, and adults. ACI has an international reputation for evaluating brain-behavior problems, such as ADD, depression, anxiety, school failure, brain trauma, obsessive-compulsive disorders, aggressiveness, marital conflict, cognitive decline, brain toxicity from drugs or alcohol, and obesity.

Brain SPECT imaging is performed in the clinics. ACI has the world's largest database of brain scans for emotional, cognitive, and behavioral problems. ACI welcomes referrals from physicians, psychologists, social workers, marriage and family therapists, drug and alcohol counselors, and individual patients.

Amen Clinics Southern California
3150 Bristol St., Suite 400

Costa Mesa, CA 92626
(888) 564- 2700

Amen Clinics, Inc., San Francisco
1000 Marina Blvd., Suite 100
Brisbane, CA 94005
(888) 564- 2700

Amen Clinics, Inc., Northwest
616 120th Ave. NE, Suite C100
Bellevue, WA 98005
(888) 564-2700

Amen Clinics, Inc., DC
1875 Campus Commons Dr.
Reston, VA 20191
(888) 564- 2700

Amen Clinics New York
16 East 40th St., 9th Floor
New York, NY 10016
(888) 564- 2700

Amen Clinics Atlanta
5901-C Peachtree Dunwoody Road, N.E., Suite 65
Atlanta, GA 30328
(888) 564-2700

amenclinics.com

Amenclinics.com is an educational, interactive website geared toward mental health and medical professionals, educators, students, and the general public. It contains a wealth of information and resources to help you learn about and optimize your brain. The site contains more than three hundred color brain SPECT images, thousands of scientific abstracts on brain SPECT imaging for psychiatry, a free brain healthy audit, and much, much more.

mybrainfitlife.com

Based on Dr. Amen's thirty years as a clinical psychiatrist he has developed a sophisticated online community to hold your hand to get thinner, smarter and happier, and younger. It includes:

- Detailed questionnaires, to help you know your BRAIN TYPE and personalize program to your own needs
- Interactive daily journal to track your numbers, calories, and brain-healthy habits
- Hundreds of brain-healthy recipes, tips, shopping lists, and menu plans
- Exclusive, award-winning 24/7 BRAIN GYM MEMBERSHIP
- Daily tips, even text messages to remember your supplements and stay on track
- Relaxation room to help you eliminate stress and overcome negative thinking patterns
- Plus much, much more. (mybrainfitlife.com)